Australia and the Wider World: Selected Essays of Neville Meaney

Edited by James Curran and Stuart Ward

SYDNEY UNIVERSITY PRESS

Published 2013 by SYDNEY UNIVERSITY PRESS
sydney.edu.au/sup

Sydney University Press, Fisher Library F03
University of Sydney NSW 2006 AUSTRALIA
Email: sup.info@sydney.edu.au

National Library of Australia Cataloguing-in-Publication entry
Author: Meaney, N. K. (Neville Kingsley), author
Title: Australia and the wider world: selected essays of Neville Meaney
                 edited by James Curran and Stuart Ward
ISBN: 9781743320259 (paperback)
Notes: Includes bibliographical references
Subjects: International relations
                 Australia--Foreign relations
                 Australia--Foreign economic relations
                 Australia--History
Other Authors/Contributors:
                 Curran, James, editor
                 Ward, Stuart, editor
Dewey Number: 327.994

Cover design by Miguel Yamin.

Cover image 'Chart of the world on Mercators projection', pub. London. ca 1907, reproduced with permission from Mitchell Library, State Library of NSW – M4 100/1907/1.

Contents

Introduction

James Curran & Stuart Ward

The essays in this work bring together a lifetime of scholarship and a lasting contribution to the story of Australia and the history of ideas in this country. Since the 1960s Neville Meaney has been asking new and probing questions about Australia's self-image and its engagement with the world. As the essays in this volume show, his efforts to try and unravel what he once memorably called 'the riddle of Australian nationalism' has raised important and often unsettling challenges for Australians as they try to make sense of their past and how it connects to their present and future. Bringing together the political, cultural, intellectual and diplomatic dimensions of the national experience, his work has been dominated by one overarching question: how have Australians attempted to reconcile their British heritage with their Asian moorings?

Neville Meaney's career as a historian began in earnest at a critical time in Australian history—the 1960s—when the certainties and orthodoxies of the British past were starting to crumble under the weight of changing domestic and international circumstances. The collapse of empire in Australia caused uneasiness and uncertainty about the nation's orientation on the world stage, a time when, according to one observer, historians didn't have the maps to make sense of a more fluid and multipolar world. Influenced by the modernist critique of nationalism pioneered by Hans Kohn, Neville Meaney took aim at a series of myths he felt were hindering an understanding of the nation's role in the world. In 1976, writing the preface to the first volume of his history of Australian defence and foreign policy, *The Search for Security in the Pacific, 1901–14*, he dedicated the book to his fellow Australians during what he called 'a spuriously dubbed period of new nationalism'. Here was a period when the 'ministers for nationalism', as he dubbed them, were ransacking the back catalogue of Australian history to discern a serviceable past. But Meaney would have none of it, suggesting that too many historians were becoming entangled in their own myths and 'slavishly' imitating European rites and rituals. He searched instead for the complexities and contradictions that rendered Australia's experience of nationalism different from elsewhere, and looked to discern the tectonic forces of history that moved beneath the surface of political events.

His second volume in this history, *Australia in World Crisis, 1914–23*, appeared at a similarly auspicious time—2009—when the country was seemingly in thrall to a new kind of sentimental nationalism. According to this reading, Australians were putting aside their characteristic reticence in overt expressions of national pride; flaunting the flag, bellowing the anthem with a new gusto at sporting events and crowding wartime commemorative sites abroad. A key aspect of this nationalist resurgence came in the form of the Anzac revival, and the torrent of works on Australia at war that have saturated the book market since the early 1990s—unit histories, soldier diaries, and the view from the trenches. Yet few paused to consider the response of the Australian political community, as a whole, to this world crisis. This second volume, as journalist Paul Kelly pointed out, 'threw a brick' at the mythology surrounding Australia's great war experience. As Meaney demonstrated, Australians fought that war on two fronts: a 'hot war' in Europe against Germany and its allies, and a 'cold war' against a rising Japan in the Pacific.

Those two volumes remain the signature works of his professional career. But the essays gathered here display the reach and breadth of his historical range and interests. It is appropriate that in the opening essay, Meaney is again giving consideration to how history can help to inform the public debate. In this 2011 lecture, presented first to the Australian Strategic Policy Institute and then to the Australian Institute of International Affairs, he asks whether a study of the rise of nationalism and modernisation in the West and Japan might help us better understand, and perhaps even anticipate, current geopolitical pressures in East Asia. At a time when so much of the debate over the United States and China is mired within an already tired 'zero-sum' paradigm, Meaney's lecture challenges current strategists and policymakers to look again at the underlying patterns that give shape to human affairs.

In section two, Meaney's three essays on Britishness and Australian nationalism are unified for the first time. Taken together they demonstrate the evolution of his ideas about Australia's response to the era of mass nationalism. He shows that there is every reason to suggest that Australians professed their Britishness in a more extreme, more intense form than in Britain itself. Far from being a cause for embarrassment for today's Australians, he argues that this phenomenon points to one of the central problems for Australian historical scholarship: how the country's European heritage has been 'adapted to environment and experience'.

The third section illustrates another key dimension of Meaney's intellectual life: the attempt to understand the nation's evolving response to Asia and how a historically Western nation has sought to come to terms with its geopolitical and geocultural environment. A challenging comparative study of Australia and Japan's post-war trajectory considers how both countries have been engaged in the task of becoming 'normal' nations: Japan by shedding its imperial past and Australia by gradually coming to terms with a world without Britain.

Throughout these essays several themes stand out—the evolution of Australia's Pacific policy, the coming of the Cold War, doubts about the American alliance, the Communist threat, relations with Asia and the end of racial discrimination in immigration policy. His interest lies chiefly with the intellectual origins of Australian ideas about the world and the problems faced by politicians and policymakers in giving them expression. It is fitting, then, that the final two chapters in the collection bring this forensic eye to the world-views and careers of Frederic Eggleston and H.V. Evatt, two of the most influential thinkers and actors in the history of Australian foreign policy.

Our primary purpose here, however, has been to combine these essays into one volume so that they might continue to stimulate the debate and discussion that Neville himself unfailingly encouraged amongst his students. These articles, then, represent only the public dimension of his contribution to scholarship in Australia. The time given to his students, of which we were great beneficiaries, perhaps symbolises his enduring contribution to the profession and to Australian intellectual life.

We first encountered Neville in the 1990s—a decade where Australian political history was in abatement and a new cultural history was making rapid headway. Neville was untroubled by the demise of the old diplomatic history, recognising that international relations needed anchoring in the broader political culture of the nation, and required more than a faithful account of meetings, cables and policy briefs from the archival coal face. Its value and potential were diminished if treated as a limited sub-specialization. But he was sufficiently old-fashioned to believe that the past held out themes of defining significance; that not everything was 'contested' or 'unstable', and that the study of politics and ideas remained a valuable point of entry into the national psyche. More to the point, he saw politics and international relations, not as a cul-de-sac of elite mannerisms, but as an extension of wider social, intellectual and cultural trends, particularly in democratic societies where political leaders are obliged to seek a popular mandate.

His postgraduate students will of course recall the many soirees at his waterfront home in Balmain. On these occasions one student would present a paper to his peers. These periods of intense questioning and argument were always preceded by a convivial meal—usually Neville's version of Irish stew, or flat steaks done (often charred!) under the oven grill—and a bottle or two from his seemingly cavernous wine cellar. In this environment of casual and easy congeniality, mixed with unrelenting rigour, was created a mutually supportive community of research students. Of course, the steep incline of his driveway provided a challenge when the evening came to a close—when each of us, particularly the presenter, was burdened neither by the food nor the wine but by the troubling yet invigorating cargo of new issues and new problems raised by the evening's reflections. It is to be hoped that the essays in this volume demonstrate once again Neville Meaney's passion for ideas and his unrelenting quest for new questions and new possibilities.

James Curran and Stuart Ward
University College Dublin and University of Copenhagen

1

Understanding the Asian Century

1

Modernisation and Nationalism: A Historical Perspective on East Asian Geo-Politics[1]

This is a version of a paper which I prepared for a 2011 Forum sponsored by the Australian Strategic Policy Institute and which I subsequently delivered at the Sydney Branch of the the Australian Institute of International Affairs. For the Forum I was asked to think creatively about the subject, to place the topic in a broad historical context and, if need be, to speculate imaginatively. It was a challenging and unusual request.

I started by reading a wide range of scholarly journals on international relations and international politics and, in doing so, I was struck by how much attention was being given to issues of economic and social change in East Asia and how little, relatively speaking, to the effects of modernisation on the countries undergoing this seismic transformation, and this was especially true for nationalism. As a result it seemed to me that it might be a useful exercise to go back to where modernisation and nationalism began, and to look at the rise of modernisation and nationalism in the Western world and Japan to see whether there were any insights to be learnt from such an exercise which might help us understand more fully the future pattern and possibilities for geo-politics in the East Asian region.

I approached the task with some trepidation. I am aware that history is full of surprises and that prophecy is the business of charlatans. Nevertheless as rational beings we have no choice in planning for the future but to draw upon the knowledge of the past in our decision-making, no matter how imperfect that knowledge may be. And it is with a keen sense of its shortcomings that I have put together this paper

The paper has three parts. The first deals with the relation of modernisation to nationalism, the second with the Western and Japanese experience of nationalism and the third with the relevance of that experience to understanding East Asia's modernisation and Australia's future strategic planning.

Modernisation and Nationalism

Modernisation is the general term used to sum up the great forces which, reaching a critical mass in Europe in the 19th century, first remade the Western world and now are in the process of remaking the rest of the world. With the application of science and technology to agriculture and manufacture, transport and communications, finance and administration, the pattern of self-sufficient face to face village communities which defined traditional Europe and which from generation to generation had reproduced itself, rapidly disappeared. The old economic and social order could not resist the dynamic energy of these

---

[1] This chapter was originally given as a lecture titled 'Modernisation and Nationalism: A New Perspective on East Asian Geo-Politics' at the Australian Strategy Policy Institute Conference on 11 August 2011 and at the Sydney Branch of the Australian Institute of International Affairs on 6 September 2011.

interlocking and mutually reinforcing developments. As peasant farmers and local artisans were drawn into and overwhelmed by modernisation's impersonal sectional, national and international economic systems they were confronted by a crisis of social identity.

Modernisation brought with it a need for new ideas of self and society. It challenged deeply engrained assumptions that the past prescribed the future and that a person's birth and family status predetermined their role and place in society. Contrariwise it encouraged people to seek self-fulfilment and self-realisation, a view sometimes expressed in that very modern, if misleading, catch cry, 'you can be what you want to be'. Yet while these changes might seem normal and natural for those, like ourselves, who take these modes of living and thinking for granted, this was not the case for those who had grown up in a world bounded by the cycle of the seasons and a fixed social order which gave them a settled sense of belonging.

For those uprooted from traditional life modernisation was a profoundly traumatic experience. They increasingly found themselves in great metropolises, alone in a mass society and at the mercy of economic and social conditions that were in a constant state of flux. In these circumstances they were at a loss to know how to connect to this disturbing and strange world and looked for ideas of social identity which would give meaning to their new mobile lives. And various ideas appeared to fill this need. Karl Marx who understood modernisation as exploitative capitalism called on its greatest victims, 'the workers of the world', to unite. But this international identity, while it had some influence in socialist movements and labour organizations could never overcome the appeal of nationalism. In this struggle for the modern mind the idea of culture nearly always trumped that of class and the idea of the people nearly always triumphed over that of the proletariat.

Nationalism's myths linked the past that had been lost with the disturbing present and the promise of a golden future. The major Western historians of the 19th century in their multi-volume works gave a scholarly authority and romantic aura to this new idea of belonging. These historians traced out a teleological narrative of their respective peoples who each had from their origins in forests or on frontiers shared common 'blood', language and customs and had over time been engaged in a noble struggle against hereditary overlords and foreign masters. Through state sponsored mass education, mass media and mass literacy these ideas were rapidly spread, and they were readily embraced. Nationalism had a powerful attraction for the modern imagination. It offered an intense social identity as a salve for the trauma of modernisation's isolation and anomie. In the nation the new moderns found the community that would make them whole and give them fulfilment, even if this should require self-sacrifice. Nationalism was a quasi religion with its hymns and rituals, saints and martyrs, sacred sites and holy days. Its prophets and high priests spoke of the national 'soul'. People achieved immortality by being prepared to give their lives for the preservation of their nation or what they often called their 'race'.

In the nationalised states it was the sovereign people not the hereditary princes who were the source of authority and, as Alexis De Tocqueville pointed out after visiting America in the 1830s, the sovereign people could be more tyrannical than any crowned head of Europe. On the one hand in a caste based society the monarch and his subjects were divided by station and status and consequently there was always a gap between the two which qualified the subject's duty to his superior and could even justify rebellion. On the other, each citizen in the nation was in principle an equal member of the people and to oppose the people was to be unfaithful to one's best self, to the very community through which one realised one's true self. George Bancroft, the great historian of American nationalism, declared that 'the voice of the people was the voice of God', and so to betray the people was to commit the ultimate treachery for which there was no forgiveness. It was because of this assumption, inherent in nationalism, that denouncing fellow citizens, for example as being 'un-American', came to carry so much moral force. As nationalism came to inform modern societies each people, with some exceptions, could only feel complete in a state composed of only and all those who shared the same cultural and racial myth, and as a result outsiders were often expelled or persecuted and wars fought in order to bring irredentist minorities into the 'Fatherland' or 'Motherland'.

With the coming of nationalism war too underwent a revolution. The *Sydney Morning Herald* spoke presciently when it declared in 1870 that 'the Franco-Prussian war has opened an epoch in which the war of races has clearly begun, and unless Divine Providence shall interfere, instead of contending dynasties, the races will have to fight for existence.'

Modernisation not only provided the means for inventing and improving technically advanced weapon systems but also produced a new attitude towards war. Wars were no longer struggles between dynastic houses and princely states but between peoples. Nationalism roused popular feeling over issues of ethnicity and territory. Questions of national pride stirred up competition among the great powers as they vied for pre-eminence. National security and sentiment was a major cause of World War I and World War II. In this new era wars became total as nation was pitted against nation in a battle for survival and supremacy.

Australia too was not immune to nationalism's siren song. Indeed quite the opposite. For Billy Hughes, the country's prime minister during the greater part of the First World War, nationalism was an 'inherent gift' of the race. It was defined by blood and encompassed all the other human qualities. It embodied 'the supreme reasoning of mankind.' In defending his War Precautions bill which would enable the government to treat as enemy aliens not only naturalised Germans but even Australians of German descent who were born in the country, he did so in these terms.

> If I were in Germany for 100 years…, I should still be British or Australian, and I would not think it wrong to do what I could for Great Britain or Australia. I put a German on exactly the same footing. His sympathy is for Germany in this struggle. Is it not a question of life and death with him as with us?

It was his view that people could not escape their biologically determined national loyalties and thus he put the blame for the war not merely on the Kaiser but also on the whole German race.

> The Kaiser may have led Germany, but she followed not only willingly but eagerly. Upon the shoulders of all classes and all sections lies the guilt. They were drunk with bestial passion, with the hope of world conquest –Junker, merchant, and workman alike.

The strength of national feeling often overpowered the instinct of self-preservation, both for the individual and the family. About four in ten of all eligible Australians volunteered to fight for their British Empire. It was a remarkable social phenomenon for which at bottom there is no other explanation than the depth of the Australians' commitment to a British national identity. Even if it were suggested that Australians involvement in the war was motivated by a desire to secure British protection it would still have to be asked, 'Why did they think that Britain should protect them?' And the answer to that question brings one back to the first explanation, namely that Australians thought of themselves as British and therefore success in the war was integral to their security as part of Greater Britain.

The Western and Japanese Experience of Nationalism

The end of the Great War ushered in the high period of European, American and Japanese nationalism. This conflict brought about the dissolution of the continental-based dynastic empires. The Paris Peace Conference, in contrast to the Congress of Vienna, adopted the principle of national self-determination in drawing up new frontiers, a decision which in many respects only confirmed what many ethnic groups in the midst of the war had already achieved for themselves. National self-determination did not, however, bring peace. On the continent most peoples, coming late to modernisation, felt intensely the insecurity and anxiety of social change and were exposed to the disturbing processes of ethnic cleansing as the break up of the dynastic empires led to confusions about allegiance and order. Many embraced authoritarian or totalitarian forms of government and accepted the rule of leaders who emerged out of the people and gave the alienated and disoriented a sense of order and purpose. This tendency to look for a strong answer to modernisation's socio-psychological problem was compounded by contingent factors such as irredentist movements and the Great Depression. In Germany's case the Weimar republic was associated with humiliating defeat and, as a result, when the crisis moment arrived its parliamentary democracy, lacking deep roots, was unable to resist the allure of a tyrannical nationalism.

World War II was a fully-fledged nationalist war. In this war all the great powers were nationalised states—even the Soviet Union described the conflict with Germany as 'The Great Patriotic War'—and the effects of the modernising process on these societies were everywhere present. The most extreme example of nationalism's influence over people's minds was to be found, however, not in Nazi Germany but in Imperial Japan, the only Asian country that, following the Western model, had become a modern state. Japan, like Germany, had come late to modernisation. Determined to avoid the fate of other Asian peoples it had set out in the late 19th century to build up its economic and military power on Western lines. Though at the end of World War I Japan had adopted a form of parliamentary government it did not last. Ultra nationalists, supported by the armed forces, denounced it as corrupt, divisive and foreign. With the coming of the Great Depression this brief democratic experiment was replaced by a fascist-type regime which focused loyalty on the divine emperor as the personal embodiment of the spirit of Japan. It instilled into the Japanese people through compulsory public education and military training the myth that they were a unique race superior to all others.

As in the case of other national myths, the Japanese drew on earlier traditions for the purpose of defining their new society. Thus they remade the feudal Bushido honour code of the *samurai* warrior and placed it at the centre of the story of their people. Bushido, in its origin, set out the rules governing the relations between a *samurai* and his liege lord and made disloyalty towards his master, in particular surrender to his master's enemies, the most heinous offence which could only be atoned for by committing *seppuku,* that is by self-immolation. In its modern guise this code was no longer limited to a privileged warrior caste but applied to all the people and it prescribed the duty of the people to their only liege lord, the Emperor who was the symbol of the nation.

The conscripted Japanese soldiers were drilled in this *Tennosei* or emperor-centred creed. They carried with them as part of their equipment a booklet, the *Senjinkun* or *Field Service Code,* which exhorted the men never to forget that for a Japanese death was preferable to surrender. And in the Pacific War the very small number of Japanese who became prisoners of war—most of whom were wounded or injured and unable to resist capture—bears witness to the potency of these beliefs. For those who ended up in the enemy's hands the shame was intolerable. Most gave false names so that their families would not know that they had betrayed the Emperor and thus during their imprisonment they wrote no letters home and received no letters from home. Their sole aim was to court death and so make peace with themselves. As a result, in POW camps some attempted suicide and yet others, with the same end in view, engaged in provocative acts which sought a showdown with their captors.

It was at a POW camp in Cowra, New South Wales where these nationalist beliefs were carried to their logical, if horrific, conclusion. In 1944 there were 1104 Japanese non-commissioned officers and other ranks held in this camp. They were of one mind that, as true Japanese, they had no other course open to them but to die. And so on 4 August, learning that the Australian authorities were preparing to separate the NCOs from the other ranks, the great majority agreed that the time had come to launch their long-planned breakout which had as its only aim collective self-immolation. One internee who had initially wavered set out in a farewell poem how he had remained loyal to the *Tennosei* and so had restored his sense of self-worth.

> If it is my lot to face death to serve the higher purpose of the Emperor I shall not cling to life…
>
> At last I am again true to myself. If fate decrees, 'Thou shall die', broken reed as I am, yet I shall not falter.

Of the 234 who died 183 were killed by gunfire and the rest committed suicide, some with the help of comrades. Two threw themselves under a Sydney bound train. Others when captured pleaded with their Australian guards to shoot them. Kanazawa Ryo, their leader, in trying after the event to explain the POWs behaviour, declared that 'It was the Japanese spirit which we always have in us which was the reason for the breakout.' These Japanese POWs were willing to submit themselves to the most extreme demands of nationalism and to redeem their honour by committing a form of *seppuku.* No other nation's soldiers behaved in this way. They surrendered when they knew that all was lost and only attempted a breakout of their camps when they had a plan of escape which might enable them to return home to join their comrades.

By the end of World War II the victorious English-speaking countries had come to believe that their liberal nationalism was the norm and that the form which the defeated Europeans and Japanese had adopted was a perversion, arising from adventitious factors.

And they were strengthened in this conviction by observing that all the defeated countries outside the Soviet bloc had, at the end of the war, embraced liberal democracy and even neutrals such as Spain and Portugal within a generation had followed suit.

On this assumption the British in granting independence to their Asian and African colonies had left them with model constitutions based on the Westminster system of parliamentary government. The Americans, for their part, gave the newly independent states very generous economic assistance to hasten on modernisation or what was called 'nation-building'. Despite the example of Germany, which at the point of the Nazi's coming to power was the most highly educated country in Europe, the Americans held that with the creation of an educated urban middle class the Third World countries would quickly become liberal democracies and side with the West in the Cold War. Yet in the event nearly all the constitutions were ignored or subverted and military regimes, one party states and ethnic and tribal conflicts became the dominant pattern, and most of these new states opted to stay neutral in the struggle between the Anglo-American-led 'Free World' and the Communist world.

When looked at dispassionately, there was a case to be made that the European continental countries and Japan expressed more fully the homogeneous imperative of nationalism than the English-speaking liberal democracies. If this were so then the British and American response to the socio-psychological trauma of modernisation would be the exception and not the rule. And it is true that there were particular conditions which acting together tended to restrain the nationalist dynamic in these countries and to make the Anglo-American response to modernisation the exception and not the rule. In the international arena the Anglo-Americans were for the most part isolated from the other great powers and their contending alliance systems. Coming very early to modernisation, they also had had more time to absorb the shock waves which followed in its wake. As a result they were able to carry pre-modern elements such as liberty under law, separation of the judiciary and the executive, parliamentary government, loyal opposition and peaceful transfer of power into the new era, and in different ways they incorporated these institutions and values into their national myths.

At the very time that British and the Americans were attempting to transform the newly independent Asian and African states into liberal nations modelled on their own political systems the West was entering into a post-nationalist stage. The Western Europeans were coming to terms with the psychological anxieties brought on by modernisation and were learning to accept the permanence of change. Spurred on by World War II's great costs in lives and treasure and the need to revive their economies, the French and Germans, formerly the chief antagonists in the wars of nationalism, founded a European Economic Community which grew by stages into a European Union.

The EU is the only new political entity in the modern era which has been formed without the support of an overarching national myth. Though it has come to possess the institutions of a state and many of its functions, it defines itself in terms of civic values. New members are required not only to have some geographical affinity with the continent but more importantly democratic constitutions and respect for human rights. This new political community is not based on a European myth of race and culture but on a liberal ideology of tolerance and openness. Even though individual members still retain power over key areas of policy such as defence, taxation, budgets and education they eschew the exclusiveness of the past and see themselves as multi-cultural societies working towards a more complete federation. The old nationalist histories which had been the source of inspiration and legitimation for these states as they underwent modernisation now gather dust on bookshelves or are treated as documents for scholarly research. Nationalism in Europe, with some marginal exceptions, has ceased to be the dominant narrative defining state and society.

The United States was, however, in an important way quite different. In the same period and for much the same reasons it began to reject racial elements in its modernising tradition and instead to foster diversity and inclusiveness. Multi-culturalism came to be looked upon with favour and hyphenate communities proliferated. Members of minorities were elected to and appointed to high offices. History books were rewritten to include the contributions of the formerly oppressed and excluded. But unlike the European nations who regarded their embrace of civic values as a renunciation of an ethnically defined nationalism, the Americans perceived these same developments not as a rejection of their past but rather as a vindication of their peculiar ideological myth. That is, while the Europeans used their liberal inclusive ideals as a means of ridding themselves of an arrogant and aggressive nationalism, the Americans saw the adoption of these ideas in Europe and the expansion of them at home as the fulfilling of their national story of a people born in liberty and democracy with a providential mission to redeem the world. Thus after the collapse of the Soviet Union President George H.W. Bush in his State of the Union Address celebrated the defeat of Communism in these terms, proclaiming that 'By the grace of God America won the Cold War ... A world once divided into two camps now recognises one sole and pre-eminent power, the United States of America ... We are still and ever the freest nation on earth ... the once and future miracle, that is still the hope of the world.'

Thus in the last fifty years the United States, acting as the avatar of freedom, used its overwhelming military power in major crusades. The first in Indo-China was directed towards halting the spread of Communist tyranny and the more recent in the Middle East was aimed at destroying radical Islamic enemies and ousting despotic regimes which gave refuge to these terrorists or were supposedly associated with them. The Americans sought neither territorial expansion nor economic hegemony. Rather they were bent on fulfilling their national destiny by, if need be, forcing people to be free. In accordance with their national myth they expected to be welcomed as liberators by the Vietnamese, the Iraqis and the Afghanis who would under guidance from Washington draw up Western type constitutions and embrace liberal democracy. The Americans would then be able to withdraw promptly from these countries leaving behind friendly governments who would be allies of the United States. In each of these countries, however, though the Americans established elected governments and trained and armed very large military and police forces they, after ten years of military occupation and democratic education, had no choice but to accept failure.

At the time of making their decisions to go to war the Americans acted on the assumptions of their national myth. There is no evidence that they took into account the history and culture of the countries they were invading or of the consequences of rapid modernisation on their ideas of social identity and loyalty. Chastened by these unhappy outcomes it seems unlikely that American leaders will be inclined to engage in further wars of liberation. Certainly President Barak Obama, who opposed the Iraq war from the outset, will not embark on such adventures. He has made this clear in his hastening on of the repatriation of American troops from Afghanistan and his resistance to all suggestions that American forces should become involved in the Arab Spring revolutions. When questioned by an American journalist on the central orthodoxy of American nationalism, that is whether he believed America to be a 'special nation', he replied very cleverly that, yes, he did, but then, after a brief pause, he added quietly that he also believed all other countries to be 'special'. It may be that the cumulative result of the wars against Vietnam, Iraq and Afghanistan may help to bring the Americans to revise their national myth so as to free them from the ideological imperialism which has led to their unilateral universalism and their egoistic altruism. Only then will the United States be able to achieve its proper stature as a world leader.

Modernisation and East Asia: China and Indonesia

I wish now to turn to East Asia which is in the early to middle stages of modernisation and, drawing on the experience of the West, to make some suggestions about the role that nationalism might play in the geo-politics of the Asian Century. For this purpose I propose to look briefly at China and Indonesia, the nations that are most important for Australia's economic and strategic security.

To Take China First

There is a large body of opinion which holds that the twenty–first century is to be the Asian or Asia Pacific century and that China will be the prime driving force in creating a new regional order. In the eyes of many, Napoleon's famous prediction that when the sleeping giant China awoke it would shake the world seems to be about to come true. It is widely held that if China's GDP continues to grow at the rate achieved in the last three decades it will by 2030, if not earlier, overtake that of the United States. This has led to many commentators forecasting that China like all rising great powers would in due course demand its place in the sun.

This conclusion, based on a simple linear projection of China's economic development under a stable government and on a similarly simple assumption that China could parlay its economic power into political influence, ignores internal social and political dynamics. The Chinese communist capitalists have not yet experienced the normal busts which follow the booms of the free market system . They have not experienced a major economic recession let alone a great depression, though some argue that the protests leading up to the Tiananmen Square massacre were precipitated by an economic downturn. When such a major nationwide economic crisis does take place it is likely that all the tensions inherent in modernisation will come to the fore and the Communist party's right to govern will be tested to the full.

It is questionable whether the Communist Party will be able to retain its 'Mandate of Heaven.' As we have seen, modernising peoples need myths to connect them to society and to legitimise their allegiance to the state. But these myths have to be credible and while the

Marxist philosophy of the Chinese revolution still informs the rites and symbols of the state this definition of China has to a very large extent lost its virtue. In schools and universities the required courses on Marxism are no more than empty formalities. In the country at large the practice of capitalism has made a mockery of the promise of communism.

The Communist leaders, recognising this, have already taken steps to strengthen their claims to be nationalists. They suppress ethnic Tibetan, Uighur and Mongolian secessionists in their western outlying provinces, defy Western critics who make heroes of Chinese intellectual dissenters and denounce Japan's school readers that downplay its imperial past, especially its responsibility for the Nanjing massacre. Indeed the latest Chinese history textbooks in Shanghai make gestures towards a new nationalist sensibility. The controlling narrative is no longer set in terms of class warfare, of the Marxist dialectic of slavery, feudalism, capitalism and socialism but rather takes the evolution of Chinese civilisation, of the Han people's 5000 years of continuous history, as the central unifying principle. They have to a large extent expunged the peasant revolts from the story and instead heap praise on those who have fought for national unity and harmony.

What will proceed from this discarding of the post-1950 revolutionary myth is unclear. Some Western scholars, especially Americans, are inclined to see liberal economics leading to liberal politics and the Chinese moving step by step towards something approaching a Western type of democracy. If these optimists prove to be correct then Francis Fukuyama's claim that the fall of the Soviet Union marked 'the end of history' might seem more plausible. But lacking any experience of multi-party democracy, peaceful transfers of power, loyal oppositions, separation of the executive and the judiciary and a free press this self-flattering Western vision does not seem to offer a feasible prospect. Even a movement towards such a reformation which releases the hold of the Communist party over the reins of power is more likely to create chaos and war-lordism than an effective liberal state.

The more likely outcome is that the Communist party will, by attempting to exploit a widely shared folk memory of a 200 year history of humiliation at the hands of Western and Japanese imperialists, remake itself as an anti-Western nationalist party, struggling against Western encirclement. But whether this transition would be achieved without stirring up internal divisions is an open question. There is considerable hostility towards the so-called 'princelings', namely the highly privileged children of the Communist party heroes who endured the 'Long March and fought to create the People's Republic. Much will depend on the People's Liberation Army. If the ideological revolution, by whatever means, were carried through peacefully then the new rulers might create an authoritarian or totalitarian nationalist regime not unlike those that spread through Europe in the first half of the last century. If this were to be the case then it would in all likelihood suppress even more rigorously the non-Han ethnic communities in the western provinces, annex Taiwan, push more forcefully for control over the disputed rocky outcrops and the surrounding seabed resources in the South and East China seas and demand respect for the Chinese diaspora in Southeast Asia.

The first is fully within its power. The second, analogous to Hitler's march into Austria, might well be accomplished without American intervention; the West has already conceded in principle that Taiwan is a province of China. The third would be riskier in that it would stir up anti–Chinese feeling along the whole western Pacific and would produce a much greater possibility of American intervention. The last, though responding to strong domestic national feelings, would, if the Chinese were to attempt to use force or threats of force, face them with logistical difficulties and would have the effect of uniting Southeast Asia against the Chinese, and cause the Americans to take counter measures. This alternative though it might seem to have some similarities to Nazi Germany's claims on Sudetenland is not for a number of reasons comparable. Would the hubris of super power nationalism tempt China to take great risks? Would it replicate the irrationality and fanaticism of the Japanese in the era of the Pacific War? The greatest deterrent to such aggressive actions would be the recognition that any military confrontation between China and America, even if begun with conventional weapons. would contain within it the possibility of escalation to some form of a nuclear war.

Indonesia and Australia's 'Arc of Instability'

However nationalism might work its way out in China any major tensions or conflicts arising from an expansionist state would be settled in the North Pacific between Beijing and Washington. For obvious geographical reasons the same could not be said for Indonesia. Whatever happens in Indonesia touches Australia nearly and Australia alone would probably have to carry, at the least, the greater share of the burden of any troubles or confrontations that materialise from that quarter.

Since the end of the Pacific war Australia's national security planning has been focussed first and foremost on its archipelagic frontier which stretches from Indonesia in the west to Fiji in the east. It is this immediate neighbourhood for which Australia must take prime responsibility and it is for this reason that it should be properly the prime concern of policymakers. All these island states in the post-independence era have had much difficulty in establishing fixed and efficient forms of governance. Indeed around the turn of the 21st century they were subject to so many disturbances—the Asian financial crisis, the overthrow of the Suharto military regime in Indonesia, the East Timorese independence movement, the break down of law and order in Papua New Guinea, the violence and anarchy in the Solomons and the military coup in Fiji—that some reporters and politicians referred to the whole region as an 'arc of instability.' Though with the seeming settlement of the major problems this rather patronising phrase has now disappeared from the lexicon of defence and diplomacy nevertheless it does sum up an unhappy truth about these states. The people of these former Western colonies are suffering from the trauma arising out of a rapidly compressed modernising process, including rural-urban dislocation, political instability and socio-psychological anxiety. It is important for Australian policymakers to realise that these troubles are not just passing problems but structural ones.

To illustrate the nature of this peculiar Australian strategic challenge it is fitting to take the case of Indonesia. Indonesia overshadows all the other island states. It has well over ten times the population of Australia and is the fourth most populous country in the world. At the present rate of growth it will within a generation equal that of the United States. Its GDP has, from a very low base in 1949, grown to equal Australia's. It contains extensive reserves of energy and mineral resources and has a substantial and diversified industrial sector and has a seat at the G-20 meetings of the world's foremost economies. It is the dominant power in ASEAN, possessing a 300,000 strong armed force and apart from Papua New Guinea is Australia's nearest neighbour.

From the time that Indonesia gained its independence Australia has seen its near neighbour as its most critical national security problem. Dangerous differences have arisen over many issues, including the fate of Netherlands New Guinea, the Konfrontasi of Malaysia, the Indonesian annexation of Portuguese Timor, the infringement of PNG's borders and the East Timorese struggle for independence. Australia since the initial clash over West New Guinea has managed its Indonesian relationship with considerable skill. Even at the time of the Konfrontasi when Australian soldiers were fighting against Indonesians in the jungles of Borneo, Canberra did not break off diplomatic relations with Jakarta, did not halt its aid programs nor force Colombo Plan students in Australia to return home. It was also very hesitant in committing its troops knowing that when the British departed it would be left to deal with the legacy of Indonesian ill-will. Moreover at these tense moments successive Australian governments have used their influence to discourage the press from embarking on anti-Indonesian crusades. As a result, these sharp differences that carried with them the possibilities of major conflicts were resolved without lasting damage to the relationship.

Since America's defeat in Vietnam and Britain's withdrawal from East of Suez Australia has taken every opportunity to improve the relationship with Indonesia. Australia's 2009 Defence White Paper repeats in substance the principles of post 1975 defence reports. It asserts that Australia's defence should be based on 'the principle of self-reliance', that its immediate neighbours are not a source of threat to Australia and that Southeast Asia, including Indonesia, is of great strategic importance because any attack on Australia must come from the north, that is north of Indonesia. In addition it has a very positive view of Indonesia's development over the last decade, especially its multi-party democracy, economic reforms and co-operation in fighting terrorism. The White Paper envisaged that Indonesia is likely to be a secure and cohesive partner in the region.

There remain, however, three difficult problems, all of them connected to the problem of nationalism.

First, there is the problem of Indonesia's political stability. There is reason to doubt whether Indonesia's present democracy will survive the testing times that lie ahead. Since independence it has experienced four distinct political forms of government, a federal Western style democracy, a 'guided democracy', a New Order military dictatorship and finally a liberal-tending form of democracy. The belief that once a liberal democracy is established it will necessarily endure is too easy an assumption and does not conform to Western experience during the onset of modernisation. East Asian nations have had even more difficulties to cope with than the Europeans and the Japanese. The Burmese, Thai, Cambodian, Filipino, Sri Lankan and Pakistani as well as the Indonesian experiments with liberal democracy have not given these states political stability. Liberal democracies need more than written constitutions and elections in order to become settled forms of government. They require popular acceptance of quite complex institutions, conventions and values. The reason for India's relatively successful democracy was that the Congress Party's founding elite were educated in British universities where they were introduced to the Westminster tradition of parliamentary government, a tradition which after independence they embodied in their nation's constitution and passed on to subsequent generations of their compatriots. Indonesian leaders had no similar background to draw upon.

Second, there is the secessionist issue. While Indonesia has little reason to fear external threats it is highly probable that it will continue to be disturbed by secessionist movements. The two most dangerous are in Aceh in northern Sumatra and in Papua. Jakarta in order to make peace with the Aceh Islamic and cultural rebels has granted that province a very large measure of autonomy. As a result of the bargain Indonesian troops have been withdrawn from the province, a former rebel has been elected governor and elements of Islamic Sharia law forbidding gambling, drinking alcohol and any relations between men and women who are not married or of the same family have come into force. The local authorities have also closed 35 Christian churches. Whether this degree of independence will satisfy the culturally distinct Acehnese people is a moot point. Whatever the outcome, the peace terms do challenge the integrity of the country and weaken the authority of the central government.

Papua at the other extreme of the island nation also has a separatist movement though it is not as well organised. From the 1970s some indigenous Papuans unhappy with being under Jakarta's rule have been engaged through OPM (Organisasi Papua Merdeka or Free Papua Organisation) in a struggle for independence. President Yudhoyono has granted Papua the status of an autonomous province and the right to elect their own government but since Javanese migrants, it is said, now outnumber the native people these concessions will not appease the insurgents. It is possible to imagine that OPM will in the future attract more sympathy from their fellow Melanesian animists and Christians across the border in Papua New Guinea. Such a development, however, would carry grave danger for Port Moresby. If the Indonesians responded aggressively, it would also pose a serious problem for Australian decision-makers. The core of the 2006 Lombok agreement for the Indonesians was to obtain Australia's commitment to 'respect and support' Indonesian 'territorial integrity, national unity and political independence' and to refuse to support any persons who were engaged in separatist activities. The Indonesians fear that Australia will, following the East Timor precedent, provide a refuge for fleeing rebels and thereby become a support base for the independence movement.

Third, there is the problem of Indonesia's nationalism. Unlike China Indonesia does not have ready to hand the ingredients for a unique narrative about a historic 'people' of common blood, common culture and common history from which to create a national myth. At the establishment of the Republic there was a search for a philosophy to give meaning to the nation. Almost from the outset the *Pancasila* five principles—belief in God, a just and humane world, unity of the nation, consensus democracy and social welfare— were adopted for the purpose and incorporated in the first constitution. But the *Pancasila* derived from a Western liberal tradition. It did not give the Indonesian people a mythic past of their own which defined them as a unique nation and legitimised their territorial boundaries.

By the time that President Suharto came to power the era of the founding fathers was over and the appeal of anti-colonial nationalism was fading. Faced with separatist insurgencies in Aceh, East Timor and Irian Jaya Suharto recognised that *Pancasila* could not in its then form provide the social cement which could keep the nation together, and he set up a

Culture and Education Department to 'indigenise' the *Pancasila*. The Department 'found' long established native sources, mostly in Java, for all five principles, and so claimed that these values were derived from Indonesian tradition. This version of *Pancasila* has been spread through the universities and the military training schools and widely welcomed.

But this version of a secular nationalism may, as is the case in some other predominantly Islamic countries, have to contend with a religious alternative. Since the fall of the Suharto regime Islamic parties have entered politics and attempted to amend the Constitution to oblige all Muslims to abide by Sharia law. But even though the country is almost ninety per cent Muslim the national parliament rejected the proposal. Even if the Islamic parties at some future time did have a majority in parliament and attempted to pass a sharia law it is unlikely that the army would accept a theocracy. Indonesia is undergoing a massive modernising process and is suffering from uncontrolled internal migration, and mega-urban sprawl. What Jakarta will do under pressure from the ensuing socio-psychological anxiety remains an open question the answer to which will have important repercussions for Australia and its relations with Indonesia. Indeed it might turn out to be the key strategic problem which Australia will have to face in the coming decades.

Concluding, I have to admit that in carrying out this analysis of contemporary China and Indonesia in the light of the history of Western nationalism I have not taken into account the great difference in the international framework between that time and this. Unlike the League of Nations, the United Nations has a near universal membership and has a very active role not only in humanitarian, social welfare, health and cultural affairs but also in peacekeeping and peace enforcing, even if in the latter respect this has only been accepted for very small failed states. Today there are also other international institutions such as the IMF and the WTO which regulate financial relations and world trade. Moreover in every region of the world there are other inter-government organisations which aim at fostering co-operation and mediating local disputes. In the Asia Pacific Australia belongs to, among others, APEC and the East Asia Summit. Further, as a result of the globalisation of the world's economies and the widespread systems of digital communication, many people are connected across national frontiers and are linked by an extensive range of professional and other non-government bodies. There is also a growing awareness that nations have a common interest in working together to solve problems that affect the survival of the planet, such as global warming, environmental destruction, pandemics and the spread of weapons of mass destruction.

But even after making allowance for these significant steps towards global peace and justice, it is important to recognise that the process of modernisation in East Asia, as in other parts of the world, is still proceeding, and it seems not impossible, looking back at the Western and Japanese experience, that newly rising great powers like China and Indonesia might still adopt an aggressive nationalism that would menace the region and even bring about military conflict. It might therefore seem wise for Australia when making geo-political assessments and deciding on strategic policy to bear this in mind.

2

Britishness and Australian Nationalism

2

Britishness and Australian Identity: The Problem of Nationalism in Australian History and Historiography[1]

This article explores the conceptual problems and contextual assumptions found in the treatment of Britishness in Australian history, especially as they have affected the understanding of Australia's relations with the world. It examines firstly the problem of the teleology of nationalism and its uses in Australian history, secondly the notion of Britishness in Australian identity, thirdly the Australian view of Britain and the Empire/Commonwealth in the twentieth century and lastly the implications of this for tensions between the community of culture and the community of interest in Australia.

Since the breaking of ties with Britain in the 1970s, much has been written on and around the subject of Australian identity and Australia's relations with the world, but there has been little attempt to stop and reflect upon the paradigms which give meaning to these studies. This article attempts to begin that process.

The most fundamental difficulty surrounding this subject arises from the failure to think carefully about the phenomenon of nationalism. There has been some very understandable confusion about when Australia became a nation and what the proper tests of national independence are. The Justices of the High Court have recently exercised themselves on this question without reaching any conclusion before pronouncing Britain to be a 'foreign' country.[2] But among a significant number of scholars, especially those concerned with the central questions of national history such as civic community, cultural identity, federation, republic, war and foreign relations, there has been a tendency to assume that European Australians have been engaged from early in their history in an inexorable struggle for national independence.

The story of this teleological movement is told in various ways. Most of those who subscribe to it incorporate either explicitly or implicitly a number of the following elements in their accounts: that this impulse towards independence was latent from the time of the arrival of the first European settlers; that it was evident in the fight against transportation and for colonial self-government, and in the ethos created by the diggers on the goldfields, most notably in the Eureka Stockade incident; that the 1890s gave it a literary form and inspiration; that Federation was an expression of an Australian cultural identity; that the Anzac experience produced a sense of Australian distinctiveness; that Billy Hughes' fight for separate representation at the Paris Peace conference and in the League of Nations was a blow struck for Australian nationhood; that Curtin's denunciation of the British betrayal

[1] This essay is based on a paper delivered at the Australian Historical Association conference at Hobart in September 1999. It was subsequently published as 'Britishness and Australian Identity: The Problem of Nationalism in Australian History and Historiography', *Australian Historical Studies*, 32 (April, 2001), pp. 76–90.

[2] *Sue v. Hill* (1999) 163 Australian Law Reports (ALR) 648 at 649.

at Singapore and the Labor government's assertive foreign policy during and after World War II marked or should have marked a break with subservience to Britain and Empire.

It should also be noted that a strong strand in this Whiggish interpretation of Australian history has been the so-called 'Radical National' school. These historians have regarded the labour movement and the Labor party as the chief agents in defining and prosecuting Australian nationalism, and some have seen in the Labor party since World War II the standard bearer of assertive nationalism combined—it might be thought oddly—with liberal internationalism.[3]

For all its protagonists, however, this version of Australian history has been presented as the story of 'thwarted' nationalism.[4] It was 'thwarted' because unfortunate circumstances, the need for British protection, cultural hegemonic practices or British manipulations aided and abetted by local 'Anglo-Australians' had frustrated again and again the achievement of the national destiny. Hence when after the 1970s the links with Britain were finally severed, it was natural from this perspective that histories and historical exhibitions should appear entitled 'A Nation at Last'.

But there are problems with this interpretation of Australian history—and not least with the explanations for why it was consistently thwarted.

The writing of this nationalist history has often proved to be quite troublesome. David Day, for example, who had started out wanting to tell the story of World War II as the *Great Betrayal* which led to national emancipation, had at the end to concede, despite himself, that Australia was the *Reluctant Nation*: that Australians, in the face of the greatest provocation, were unwilling still to cut the British ties, affirm their own separate identity and embrace what he called a 'possible independent destiny'.[5] For him there were no

---

[3] For some explicit examples, see Stephen Alomes, *A Nation at Last? The Changing Character of Australian Nationalism, 1880–1988* (Sydney: Allen & Unwin, 1988); Robert Birrell, *A Nation of our Own: Citizenship and Nation-Building in Federation Australia* (Melbourne: Longman Cheshire, 1995); David Day, *The Great Betrayal* (Melbourne: Oxford University Press, 1988) and *The Reluctant Nation* (Melbourne: Oxford University Press, 1992); Bill Gammage, *The Broken Years* (Canberra: Australian National University Press, 1974); Helen Irving, *To Constitute a Nation: A Cultural History of Australia's Constitution* (Melbourne: Cambridge University Press, 1997); W.F. Mandie, 'Cricket and Australian Nationalism in the Nineteenth Century', *Journal of the Royal Australian Historical Society*, 59 (1973), pp. 225–26, and *Going it Alone: Australia's National Identity in the 20th Century* (Melbourne: Penguin, 1978), chapters 1 and 2; Christopher Waters, *The Empire Fractures: Anglo-Australian Conflict in the 1940s* (Melbourne: Australian Scholarly Publishing, 1995); C.H.M. Clark, *A History of Australia*, vols 4, 5, 6 (Melbourne: Melbourne University Press, 1978, 1981, 1987). The frontispiece to volume 4, 'The Earth Abideth for Ever, 1851–1888', juxtaposes Henry Parkes, 'England's Name the Magic Still' and Henry Lawson, 'The Land Belongs to You', and sets the tone for these final three volumes, the best and worst examples of the radical national myth, the very myth which Clark had declared at the outset of the great work that he was going to transcend.

[4] For a precise use of this term see Gareth Evans and Bruce Grant, *Australia's Foreign Relations in the World of the 1990s* (Melbourne: Melbourne University Press, 1991), p. 17: 'The origins of Australia's thwarted nationalism in the twentieth century can thus be seen at the end of the nineteenth century.'

[5] Day, *Reluctant Nation*, p. 311.

sufficient explanations for this behaviour: it seemed inexplicable that the people just were 'reluctant'. It was a puzzle. And indeed it is this puzzle which is at the core of the problem.

The starting point for attempting to unravel this puzzle is the recognition that this use of nationalism in Australian history accepts uncritically nationalism's own teleological view of history, namely that all history is a struggle by 'peoples' towards achieving self-realisation, most commonly and completely in independent sovereign states. This treatment of nationalism in Australian history ignores the broadly agreed conclusions of contemporary scholars of nationalism, who have rejected nationalism's own claims that it is an innate or given dynamic in human societies and contrariwise have argued that nationalism is a historically contingent, socially constructed idea or myth about a 'people'.[6] If these scholars' findings are accepted, and there are good reasons for doing so, then it should be possible to throw off the tyranny of nationalism's own assumptions and so open the path to new interpretations of the Australian language and experience of identity. Historians will have to ask new questions about the past. If nationalism is historically contingent, when then did social change in Australia produce the modernising circumstances which created the need for a nationalist myth as the primary form of collective self-definition or social identity? And when the national era arrived, what form or forms did this myth or idea take? How, for example, did the 'Bush Legend' fare in comparison with the 'British race' idea? In addressing these questions it is also important to bear in mind that nationalism is a jealous god and that national myths are absolute in their exclusions as well as their inclusions, that a nationalism by definition is about a unique people; it is only in the post-nationalist Western era that dual nationality has come to be tolerated. Therefore the Australian puzzle cannot be resolved by a glib assertion that Australians shared two equal and complementary myths. If in Australia the nationalist era threw up two distinct myths about the same people then they had to be engaged in a violent struggle for supremacy, nothing less than a civil war—and clearly that was not the case.

In dealing with nationalism what has to be remembered is the nature of the phenomenon. The tests of nationalism for Australians are not how partisan Australian spectators are at Test matches, whether Australians have different accents from the English or whether Australians dislike inherited class distinctions or warm beer. Inside Britain, among the constituent countries and counties there are many different provincial and local loyalties, accents, customs and social attitudes. In employing nationalism as an analytical term, what has to be examined is the idea that Australians, like the Cornish for that matter, had of themselves as 'a people'. It should not be assumed that because one talks of 'Australians' as a social group or a political community, Australians have a distinct national myth which has set them apart from other peoples and driven them towards achieving sovereign independence. The nature of the dominant idea which gives national character to a people,

---

[6] Hans Kohn, *The Idea of Nationalism: A Study in its Origin and Background* (New York: Macmillan, 1945); Eric Hobsbawn and Terence Ranger, eds, *The Invention of Tradition* (Cambridge: Cambridge University Press, 1983); Ernest Gellner, *Nations and Nationalism* (Oxford: Oxford University Press,1983); Benedict Anderson, *Imagined Communities: Reflections on the Origin and Spread of Nationalism* (London: Verso, 1983); Walker Connor, *Ethnonationalism: The Quest for Understanding* (Princeton: Princeton University Press, 1994).

especially in a democratic political culture like Australia's, is revealed most authoritatively in the rhetoric of leaders of representative institutions, in the content of history and literature curricula, in oaths of loyalty and public rituals and in the popular enthusiasm for symbols, anthems and ceremonial days.

If ideas of nationalism are not expressions of the essence of a people's being but historically conditioned imaginings, then it will not today derogate from Australian dignity or self-worth to contemplate the possibility that in the nationalist era[7] Britishness was the dominant cultural myth in Australia, the dominant social idea giving meaning to 'the people'. It might even be possible to suggest that Britishness was more pervasive in Australia than in Britain itself.

The evidence that Australians in this nationalist era thought of themselves primarily as a British people is overwhelming. Though the full picture cannot be shown here it is worth bearing in mind some of the more outstanding elements. The oaths of loyalty in public schools were British: for example, 'I love my country the British Empire, I salute her flag the Union Jack'. In South Australia this form of oath was adopted by a Labor government during the First World War and endured until the 1950s. As for history curricula, whether in school or university, Australian history when it was taught was most often taught as a footnote to the grand story of the British peoples' great Empire which covered a sixth of the globe. The maps of the world on every schoolroom wall showed in vivid red the Empire on which the sun never set. Empire Day for most was celebrated as a sacred occasion; Australia Day by contrast was a secular picnic. Wattle Day could never compare with Empire Day in its symbols of nationhood and identity.[8] Australia introduced Empire Day a decade before Britain did, and it was always celebrated more widely and more devoutly in Australia than in Britain.

Anzac Day was commemorated as Australian Britons' contribution to the Empire's cause. The Union Flag led the march, sometimes in conjunction with Australia's own Union Jack flag and sometimes alone. Of all Australian institutions, the Returned Sailors', Soldiers' and Airmen's Imperial League of Australia and its successor the Returned Servicemen's League, which assumed the custodianship of the Anzac myth, were unwavering in their loyalty to the British Crown. And certainly until the 1970s the RSL was not at odds with popular opinion. C.E.W. Bean who wrote in praise of the distinctive qualities which the Australian soldiers had displayed during the First World War, saw these qualities as belonging not to a unique Australian people but rather to those he thought of as better Britons. As late as 1947, that is after the 'Great Betrayal' at Singapore, 65 percent of Australians when asked in a public opinion poll whether they wished to have British or Australian nationality opted for being

---

[7] It cannot be gainsaid that Australia like most Western European countries has passed through a nationalist era in roughly the same time frame, the 1870s to the 1960s.

[8] Stewart Firth and Jeanette Hoorn, 'From Empire Day to Cracker Night' in *Australian Popular Culture*, eds Peter Spearritt and David Walker (Sydney: Allen & Unwin, 1979). Though the essay shows that in New South Wales Catholic schools did not generally observe Empire Day, and in the decades immediately following the conscription referenda conflict of World War I militant labour also rejected it, nevertheless in the public schools and Protestant independent schools down to the 1950s the occasion was a focal point for expressions of identity and loyalty. Likewise the public celebrations, involving local, state and federal dignitaries, had great support in the community.

British.[9] In Australia, unlike Britain, at the beginning or end of most public occasions, concerts, plays, films, dances, even sporting finals the 'national Anthem', namely 'God Save the King' or 'God save the Queen', was played and everyone stood to show respect for the crowned symbol of the British peoples. The first visit of a reigning monarch to Australia in 1954 was an unparalleled quasi-religious national event which brought huge crowds of people into the streets to pay homage to the one whom the *Sydney Morning Herald* declared was the symbol of 'the supreme achievement of the British race'.[10]

Seen without the distorting effects of teleological spectacles, the heroes of 'nationalist' history appear to have identified with this myth of Britishness. Peter McCormick's 'Advance Australia Fair' was written to honour Australians as a British people. One stanza, subsequently excised from the sanitised version of the post-British era, proclaimed that

Britannia then shall surely know

Beyond wide oceans' rolls

Her sons in fair Australia's land

Still keep a British soul.

William Lane the 'republican' socialist,[11] Henry Lawson[12] and A.B. 'Banjo' Paterson[13] the Bush Legend balladeers, Rex Ingamells and the Jindyworobak literary nationalists,[14] Billy Hughes, John Curtin and Ben Chifley, the political leaders who stood up to the British authorities in defence of Australia, all had feet of British clay.

The Chifley case is on this point most instructive. In July 1948 the British Government, troubled by Chifley's seeming lack of understanding of the need for Britain to seek a Western Union against the Soviet threat in Europe, invited the Australian Prime Minister to London where it was hoped he would be led to see reason. After Chifley had had a meeting with Attlee and his chief ministers, the Cabinet Secretary in some alarm wrote to the British Prime Minister suggesting that he should speak to Chifley to try to change his mind. The subject was not, however, Communism and Europe—it was Chifley's Britishness. Chifley had told the British ministers as they were facing up to the question of uniting the Commonwealth against Soviet expansionism that 'the United Kingdom, Australia and New Zealand were the only parts of the Commonwealth which fully represent the British tradition'. But since Britain wished to have the cooperation of the new South Asian members of the Commonwealth in its Middle East strategy, this Australian view of Britishness was

---

[9] *Australian Gallup Polls*, no. 470–77 (November–December 1947).

[10] *Sydney Morning Herald*, 3 February 1954.

[11] Neville Meaney, '"The Yellow Peril": Invasion Scare Novels and Australian Political Culture', in Ken Stewart, ed., *The 1890s: Australian Literature and Literary Culture* (St Lucia: University of Queensland Press, 1996), pp. 231–41.

[12] For an example, see Lawson's 1917 poem, 'England Yet' in Leonard Cronin, ed., *A Fantasy of Man: Henry Lawson, Complete Works, 1901–1922* (Sydney: Lansdowne Press, 1984), p. 704.

[13] See (A.B. Paterson) 'With French to Kimberley', *Sydney Morning Herald*, 29 September 1900 for Paterson's identification with the British 'race'.

[14] Rex Ingamells, *Royalty and Australia* (Melbourne: Halcraft Publishing Co., 1954), with an introduction by R.G. Menzies.

embarrassing. 'In short', the Cabinet Secretary wrote to Attlee, Chifley had to be persuaded to see that Australia could not, anymore than Britain, 'afford … to see the Commonwealth reduced to those countries which he regards as [and he quoted Chifley's words from the previous day's meeting] "fully representing the British tradition and outlook" '.[15] Britishness meant more to the Australian prime minister than to the British themselves. Though it is true that the Labor and conservative parties differed somewhat in the way they expressed their Britishness—Labor was less inclined to be deferential—nevertheless these differences were of degree, not kind. After the bitterness of the conscription crises of 1916–17 the new anti-conscription Labor party adopted as a party objective the socialisation of the means of production, distribution and exchange, a most radical economic objective, but they never placed separation from the Empire or the attainment of a republic on their platform. That had to wait until the 1990s.

Before proceeding further a word or two should be said to justify the earlier suggestion that Britishness may have been a more powerful national idea in Australia than Britain. Firstly it should be noted that Australia's late nineteenth century political culture provided more fertile soil for the growth of nationalism as a social ideal. British-settled Australia had little in the way of pre-modern traditions to limit its acceptance. In Britain, by contrast, nationalism had to vie with long-established and deeply-rooted local loyalties and hierarchical allegiances. The late nineteenth century colonists, disturbed by the insecurities of an urban-centred and modernising democracy, responded wholeheartedly to this new form of collective identity. The sense of having but a fragile hold on a vast land set in an Asian sea intensified further the emotional trauma and made the colonists even more receptive to the atavistic idea of community.[16] In Australia much more than Britain the monarch became the symbol of the historic British race or people, rather than the head of a hereditary class system. In Britain liberalism as well as conservatism provided barriers to the full embrace of nationalism. 'My country, right or wrong' never had the same resonance in Britain as Australia.[17]

Even if Australians responded more completely to the siren song of nationalism, why did this take on the character of Britishness? The Australian colonists, unlike the American colonists, had not rebelled against the Mother Country—the colonies were proud to be members of the British Empire—and thus they found it easy to accept their racial and cultural heritage as the basis for their idea of nationalism. Moreover the British myth made more sense in Australia than Britain. Among the myths of the Western nations that

---

[15] *Minute*, Sir Norman Brook to Attlee, 9 July 1948, CAB 21/1793, Public Record Office (hereafter PRO).

[16] For a perceptive contemporary discussion of this historical and sociological process, see Charles Henry Pearson, *National Life and Character: A Forecast* (London: Macmillan, 1893).

[17] Edmund Barton, the leader of the Federation movement, speaking of the Boer War in the New South Wales parliament, said that 'when our empire is at war with any other power whatever, it becomes our turn to declare the motto, "The Empire right or wrong" ', New South Wales, *Parliamentary Debates*, 19 October 1899, pp. 1495–96. G. Elmslie, leader of the Victorian Labor Party, addressing a patriotic meeting in the Melbourne Town Hall Meeting at the outbreak of World War I, stated that 'His cry was everyone's cry: "My country, right or wrong" '. And by 'country' Elmslie meant the British Empire. See *Age*, 7 August 1914.

of 'Britishness' or the 'British race' was one of the most artificial and, on the face of it, implausible, especially in the British Isles.[18] It incorporated the English, Welsh, Scots and the Irish, each of whom had their own homeland, language, traditions and ways of life. This British experience was not of one people but of peoples in conflict. To a greater or lesser extent the Welsh, Scots and Irish bore a grudge against or felt animosity towards the English who had forced them into the Union. As a gesture towards this reality the myth sometimes appeared under the title of the 'Anglo-Celtic' race, thereby almost admitting that the 'British' were not one people. In Australia on the other hand the transplanted migrants from the British Isles mixed together in their new homeland and in many respects homogenised their traditions, the English tending to prevail and the Irish Catholic to be the most resistant. Consequently Britishness as an idea had more relevance for Australia than the United Kingdom. Taking then the superior predisposition of the Australians to embrace nationalism and the more natural appeal of Britishness for Australians, it is understandable that at the outbreak of the First World War, whereas the people of Britain were divided over the question of entering the European conflict,[19] the Australian politicians, parties and people were as one in their support for the British Empire's cause.

Yet another piece of the puzzle which needs some attention is the way in which Australians depict their relationship to the British Empire/Commonwealth. The exponents of an Australian 'national' myth identify the heroes of the story through their attacks on British presumptions or betrayals. That is, Australia is defined not by a myth celebrating its own unique values but rather as against Britain. True Australians will not suffer the British to treat them as colonials. They will speak up defiantly and demand respect. They will openly criticise British governments and refuse to follow them blindly. This use of Anglo-Australian differences and quarrels as signs of an Australian nationalism is, however, misleading. Australians had two views of Britain and the Empire, which while they overlapped were quite distinct. One treated Britain as the metropolitan superior, the heart of the Empire, and Australia as the colonial subordinate, a peripheral adjunct. The other saw the Empire as a multi-polar structure, an alliance of British peoples in which all the white constituent elements were entitled to consideration and dignity, Australia equally with Britain. The teleological 'nationalists' consider the first view to belong to un-Australian or Anglo-Australian imperialists—Bob Menzies being the arch-villain—and interpret the assertions of equality under the second as evidence of an independent Australianness. Yet both are manifestations of an identification with Britishness—they only differ on how it should be expressed. The criticisms of Britain and British policy, no matter how extreme their form, were arguments about the empire from inside the empire. Whenever the empire was challenged from without nearly all the critics closed ranks with their fellow Britons at home and abroad in defence of Britain and the British peoples.

---

[18] This may explain why there are so very few studies of British nationalism, especially compared with the wealth of works dealing with English, Scottish, Irish and Welsh nationalism.

[19] There were resignations from the Liberal cabinet over the issue and opposition in the House of Commons from both Liberal and Labour members. See Cameron Hazlehurst, *Politicians at War, July 1914 to May 1915: A Prologue to the Triumph of Lloyd George* (London: Jonathan Cape, 1971), pp. 33–39.

The only serious attempt to articulate an authentic Australian myth, that is a myth which could support an exclusive Australian nationalism, was Russel Ward's *Australian Legend*. In this work, taking his cue from Frederick Jackson Turner's American Frontier thesis, Ward developed a coherent myth about the formation of specific Australian qualities out of the experience of a nomadic tribe of bush workers or 'noble Bushmen' in the outback. Since the values embodied in this Legend, such as mateship and suspicion of authority, derived from interaction with a peculiarly Australian landscape, they could be seen to be uniquely Australian. From the convict era to federation he traced the development of these characteristics and drew on bush ballads and short stories to illustrate their origin and nature. They seemingly owed nothing to a British heritage.[20] But setting aside the question of the accuracy of the legend—that is not relevant to the nationalist issue—it would have to be said that this typology was never invoked by Australian leaders in their quarrels with Britain or for the purpose of establishing a separate national identity. Australians very rarely appealed to the Bush Legend or celebrated the bush songs and heroes on great national days or at times of great national crises. On those occasions the oratory, rituals and symbols were overwhelmingly British in character. It is a tribute to the lingering power of the radical nationalist myth that Prime Minister John Howard, often said by his critics to be a man of the 1950s, wanted 'mateship' as a traditional Australian quality to be included in the Preamble to the Constitution which was put to the people together with the referendum on the Republic in November 1999. In the post-nationalist era, however, popular feeling was against it and the word had to be withdrawn. 'Mateship' as a familiar, folksy term for mutual loyalty and responsibility was not as such rejected, but there was little support for incorporating it in a publicly proclaimed statement of values which gave a formal identity to the people and celebrated Australia as a multicultural society.

To argue that the Australians' Britishness was the result of imperial cultural hegemony and colonial dependence on British protection has many problems. Even if it could be shown that imperial agents and influences were able to shape the definition of loyalty in Australian public life, it still has to be asked how it was that the Australian democracy accepted these ideas.[21] Such hegemonic or dependency theory tends arrogantly to assume to know what the people if they were allowed to be true to themselves would have believed. It will not concede to the people of the time their own autonomy and bases its argument on a social psychology which sees people as the mindless products of cultural manipulation or security imperatives. Australians did often attribute to themselves many

---

[20] Russel Ward, *The Australian Legend* (Melbourne: Melbourne University Press, 1958).

[21] John M. Mckenzie's *Propaganda and Empire: The Manipulation of British Public Opinion, 1880–1960* (Manchester: Manchester University Press, 1984) shows how a wide range of British voluntary and educational institutions and cultural and literary forms were used to inculcate the idea of loyalty in the empire. He does not, however, offer any explanation as to how the imperial enthusiasts became addicted to empire in the first place, and why the British people should have responded as strongly as they did to this propaganda. There is the assertion of 'manipulation' but no examination of what this might imply and entail. It is clear also from this study that Britishness in the British Isles was much more associated with pride in the dependent colonial empire in Asia and Africa than it was in Australia, where Britishness meant first of all belonging to the Commonwealth of the white self-governing British peoples.

of the characteristics of the Bush Legend and as is so often the case with such legends, these values did help shape the life of the community, even if in praising themselves for these qualities they generally ignored their negative side. But these values were not national. They were more accurately to be viewed as provincial distinctions, comparable to those of Cornwall or Yorkshire. Despite the claims of the *Australian Legend* to be considered as a proper national myth, it would appear that Russel Ward himself tacitly conceded that it could not aspire to that status. Though Ward maintained that the aim of his book was 'to trace the origins and development of the Australian legend or national mystique' and that the values embodied in this myth influenced even the choice of the title 'Commonwealth' for the federal union and the character of the AIF celebrated by C.E.W. Bean, nevertheless he admitted, almost in passing, that 'Since World War I … it has become more and more clear to everyone that Australian patriotic sentiment does not usually or necessarily involve weakening in attachment to Britain, but rather the reverse'.[22]

Australia has some special difficulties in finding its own place in the established discourse concerning nation and nationalism. Extrapolating from the experience of their own countries nearly all European scholars have stressed the centrality of a cultural myth—that is one centred on ideas of common stock, language, history, folklore, customs, religion as the basis for nationalism—and they have further contended that nationalism in seeking to unite politically all those who share the common culture also provides through the formation of the nation state protection for the common interests of the people. They assume that the community of culture and the community of interest are naturally one. In Europe where the new nations built around a distinct cultural myth were created out of contiguous territories this might generally be true. But in Australia's case this was not so, as the great geo-political divide between Australia and Britain created a gulf between the community of culture and the community of interest. As David Potter pointed out some time ago in a perspicacious article on the problem of nationalism, there are in fact two bases for modern nationalism, for the ways in which peoples think of themselves as belonging to a distinct community. One is a sense of sharing a common culture and the other a sense of sharing common interests. Potter suggested that while for European peoples the two had merged easily there were other examples of modern nationalism, as in the South in the American Civil War or post-imperial Africa, where this was not so.[23] And he might well have added Australia. When these two ideas of community clashed Australians, despite themselves, opted for the community of interest over the community of culture.

By the end of the nineteenth century the Australian colonists had already found that they shared a set of common interests which were in many respects different from and even sometimes in conflict with those of the Mother Country. This set of common interests

---

[22] Ward, pp. v, 52, 212–13. See also Ward's explanation for Australia's almost unanimous support for the British cause at the outbreak of World War I in *Australia Since the Coming of Man* (Melbourne: Macmillan, 1987), p. 165: 'Fourteen years of national independence and advancement within the Empire seemed to have liquidated the small but vociferous minority of the "nineties"' for '[a]lmost everyone seemed to feel their Britishness as the extension and guarantee of their Australianness rather than as any kind of limitation on it'.

[23] David Potter, 'The Historians' Use of Nationalism and Vice Versa', *American Historical Review*, 67 (July, 1962), pp. 924–50.

included all the major policies which brought Australia in contact with the wider world, namely trade, immigration, defence and Pacific policy. Certainly Britain was the major market for Australian exports and the major source of capital for its development, and Australians looked to Britain for a sustained supply of new migrants and hoped that the British navy would be able to defend them against foreign foes. But experience had taught Australians that there was no natural coincidence of interests, or at the least that such a coincidence could not be relied upon. Britain's commitment to free trade stood in the way of colonial economic development; Britain's need for Asian allies and its sensitivity to the feelings of its dependent Empire in India made it unsympathetic to Australia's 'Whites Only' immigration policy; Britain's preoccupation with the balance of power in Europe caused it to give a low priority or to be indifferent to Pacific defence and foreign problems. As a result there was a lack of harmony between Australia's community of culture and community of interest, and when these ideas of community clashed the Australians, even if they found it uncomfortable to do so, chose the nation of interest over the nation of culture.

Thus at the very high point of British race nationalism the Australians rejected British proposals for an Imperial federation and instead created their own federal union. In principle the Australian federation was almost as novel and untried an experiment as an Imperial federation would have been. The Australians were unwilling to subordinate their interests to British interests, that is to allow their economic and defence resources to be disposed of by a British dominated Imperial parliament. But their sense of sharing a community of interests propelled them into joining together in a federal union which was granted the fundamental powers of a state, namely to dispose of their lives and treasure for the common good.[24] Australian leaders frequently, and it must be added unthinkingly, used the term 'nation' to refer to both collectivities. Prime Minister Hughes, for example, during his visit to Britain in 1918, in speaking to the British Empire League referred to the Empire as 'a nation such as ours, with traditions such as ours' but in addressing the British Empire Parliamentary Association he praised the Empire as a 'league of free nations'.[25] In the first instance he was alluding to the cultural nation and in the second to the political nation.

From the foundation of the Commonwealth Australian governments pursued policies which were at odds with and sometimes in defiance of British wishes. Much to the diplomatic embarrassment of the British government they insisted on having a White Australia immigration policy, ironically a policy which was aimed at maintaining the British character of the country. From the outset they rejected British arguments that Europe posed the only or the greatest threat to the Empire's security and they resisted all British pressure to take part in Imperial defence planning based on that assumption. They would not permit Australian forces to be part of an Imperial military reserve. Against British wishes the 1904 (Australian) *Defence Act*, while providing for conscription for the defence of Australia, would permit only volunteers to be enlisted to fight overseas for the Empire. Australians would identify themselves with the Empire's cause when Britain was at war but would not beforehand agree to a common policy or agree about how its forces or resources

---

[24] Neville Meaney, *The Search for Security in the Pacific, 1901–1914* (Sydney: Sydney University Press, 1976), ch. 1.

[25] *Times* (London), 20 June 1918; *Sydney Morning Herald*, 24 June 1918.

might be deployed. And this policy remained intact, apart from a limited amendment to cover Australia's immediate defence perimeter during the Pacific War, until 1964. Likewise from its first decade the Commonwealth took foreign policy positions and initiatives on Pacific questions which were unpalatable to the British. Despite or even possibly because of the British 'betrayal' at Singapore it was the Chifley government immediately after World War II which came closest to agreeing to participate in imperial defence planning. Though after World War II Australia's independent activity on the international stage was more pronounced and institutionalised, nevertheless the rationale for it was essentially the same as that which had informed Australian behaviour from the early years of the century.

At the 1946 Commonwealth Prime Ministers' Conference the Chifley government agreed to co-operate with Britain and New Zealand in defence planning. Because of the difficulty in determining whence a threat might arise and what other support might be available Chifley, like his predecessors, remained cautious about committing his government to a prearranged plan for British Commonwealth defence. At a Council of Defence meeting in March 1947 he observed that

> The United Kingdom has not the capacity and strength she formerly possessed.
>
> Our strategic position in the Middle East has been greatly weakened. India appears to be on the way out.
>
> Canada and South Africa are non-co-operative.
>
> Britain, Australia and New Zealand alone are prepared to take measures and co-operate in a plan.

Australia had to accept that 'the strength of a system of Empire Co-operation is now greatly weakened', and that 'the British Commonwealth could not fight a major war without United States cooperation'.[26] This did not mean that Australia should abandon the goal of imperial cooperation in defence—Chifley had already committed Australia to cooperation in the Guided Missile Project at Woomera and in its Joint Intelligence Machinery. But it did imply that such cooperation was secondary to achieving a regional arrangement with the United States for the protection of the Southwest Pacific and South-East Asia.

In October 1948 the British Government at a Commonwealth Prime Ministers' Conference sought to obtain the Dominions' cooperation to work in harmony with the United States and Western European countries in a common front against Soviet global expansionism. The Australians with the New Zealanders were the most affirmative in their response, though they made any practical action dependent on assurances about Pacific security. External Affairs Minister Dr H.V. Evatt declared that the Australian Government was 'in general agreement' with the British proposals and confirmed that 'If war came it would not be a regional war; and consultation on defence should take place on the Commonwealth as well as a regional basis'.[27] In response, however, to subsequent British

---

[26] *Minute*, Council of Defence, 12 March 1947, *Documents on Australian Foreign Policy, 1937–1949*, 14 vols (hereafter *DAFP*) (Canberra: Australian Publishing Service, 1975–1998), vol. 12 (1947), pp. 302–06; see also Chifley to Attlee, 16 September 1947, PREM8/743, PRO; and *DAFP, 1947*, vol.12, pp. 358–59.

[27] Minutes of the third, ninth and eleventh meetings of the Commonwealth Prime Ministers

requests that Australia join with them in regional and global defence planning—they particularly wanted Australian military assistance in the Middle East—Chifley informed Attlee that though Australia had an interest in pursuing regional planning it would require '[s]omething more concrete than the statement of the United Kingdom Chiefs of Staff ... that "we consider the threat in the Pacific can be adequately matched by American naval and air strength"' before it would consent to participate in global arrangements which might involve Australian forces being used outside its immediate neighbourhood.[28]

From Federation all Australian governments refused to join in imperial defence schemes which did not provide adequately for their security in the Pacific. While Chifley was perhaps more predisposed to collaborate with the British in Imperial defence planning, he would not participate in any global arrangement until he had some assurance that Australia's own territory was properly safeguarded, which in the circumstances meant an American guarantee. The Menzies Government which came to office in December 1949 was of the same mind; it was not until after the signing of the ANZUS Pact that it agreed to British requests to send Australian forces to the Middle East.

Yet this pattern of independence in policymaking neither derived from Australian national sentiment nor helped in any substantial way to foster it. Australian leaders' Britishness led them, as cultural nationalism requires, to persist in looking for common policies which could unite all British peoples. But such schemes tended to founder upon the need to defend Australian interests against competing interests within the Empire. Thus Alfred Deakin, one of the strongest opponents of the British Government's proposals for Imperial Federation at the end of the nineteenth century, saw no contradiction in becoming President of the Victorian Imperial Federation League. As a British race patriot he fervently desired British Imperial unity but, as a strong critic of British indifference to Australia's Pacific concerns, he was adamant that it could only be accomplished by giving Australia and the other Dominions an equal say in the framing of Imperial policy. He feared, he said, that the British government's lack of sympathy for Australia's security was driving the Australians, 'despite themselves'—that is against their deepest instincts—to have a Pacific policy of their own. But he never gave up the struggle.

Similarly when the British government during the First World War established an Imperial War Cabinet made up of the British and Dominion Prime Ministers for the purpose of determining a common defence and foreign policy, Billy Hughes was wary of how it might work in practice. On the surface, as the British Prime Minister Lloyd George had described it, it appeared to meet Australian requirements. That is, there would be one imperial policy but it would be arrived at through unanimous agreement. No policy therefore could be adopted without Australia's consent. Hughes endorsed the idea but was sceptical of Lloyd George's commitment to the principle and he demanded 'a formal but

Conference, 12, 19 and 20 October 1948, including Confidential Annex and British Memorandum, 'The World Situation and its Defence Aspects', P.M.M. (48) I, attached to minutes of eleventh meeting, 20 October 1948, CAB 133/88, PRO.

[28] Chifley to Attlee, 7 February 1949, *DAFP, 1948–1949*, vol. 14, p. 204. For a more extended account of this episode, see Neville Meaney, *'Primary Risks and Primary Responsibilities' in the Pacific: The Problem of Japan and the Changing Role of Australia in the British Commonwealth, 1945–1952* (London: Suntory Centre London School of Economics and Political Science, 2000).

real recognition' that '[t]he Dominions were participants in the councils of the Empire on a footing of equality'.[29] Only such an assurance would justify Australian acceptance of this machinery for resolving the tension between the community of culture and the community of interest.

All subsequent Australian leaders down to the 1960s remained true to their cultural faith, hoping to find in imperial cabinets or conferences or in continuous consultation or better information the way forward. Time and time again the British failed the Australians, showing little or no understanding of their Pacific preoccupations, reneging on promises to consult about policymaking or 'betraying' them at Singapore. But the Australians, after venting their high indignation, never lost hope. It was as though they said to themselves that next time it would work, next time it would be different. But it didn't and it wasn't. From a contemporary perspective what surprises is the strength with which Australians clung to this dream of the unity of the British peoples. The power of the British myth in Australian consciousness made it almost impossible for Australians to accept that they had no alternative but to be themselves. It was events outside Australia's control, the transformation of the British Commonwealth and Britain's decision to find its future in Europe, which forced Australians finally to see that their British dream was an illusion, to acknowledge that Britain was a 'foreign country' and to try to find their own place in the world.[30] From all this it would not then be unfair to draw the conclusion that the history of nationalism in Australia was not one of thwarted Australianness but rather of thwarted Britishness.

And what has happened in recent times to the imperatives of nationalism?

If nationalism has arisen out of a social crisis created by a particular set of historical circumstances then one might expect that when that crisis passes the need for nationalism in its classic form might also be expected to decline or disappear. So as Britishness has lost its appeal as a central defining idea—partly of course as a result of British actions—it is understandable that an alternative, exclusively Australian, myth has failed to replace it. In the 1970s, after the collapse of Britishness, a radical national myth was put forward for a brief moment by culture-makers to fill the void. The rash of films dealing with the Boer War and the First World War which appeared at that time were infused with the themes of *The Australian Legend*. In Peter Weir's film *Gallipoli*, for which David Williamson wrote the script, the Mel Gibson hero is endowed with the prime characteristics of Russel Ward's Bushman. He is of Irish Catholic descent, a nomadic working class lad who cares little for authority or pomposity. He enlists in the AIF out of a desire to join his mate in the great adventure. He mocks the English officers' class-based pretensions, plays hard in Cairo and then when he has to face up to war at the Dardanelles is repelled by the British mismanagement which results in the senseless slaughter of the Anzacs.

But this nationalist attempt to fill the gap left by the dissolution of Britishness has been short-lived. The new Australian symbols of nationhood have not attracted fervour comparable to that invested in their British predecessors. It seems that the intense social

---

[29] Shorthand Notes of Imperial War Cabinet Meetings (26), 23 July 1918, CAB 23/43, PRO.

[30] On this question, see Stuart Ward, 'Discordant Communities: Australia, Britain and the European Community, 1950–1963', PhD thesis. University of Sydney, 1999.

identity of nationalism is no longer needed. Indeed contemporary Australians can give positive support to multi-racialism and multiculturalism, ideas which are the very antithesis of an all-encompassing, conformist nationalism. What holds the post-nationalist society together remains obscure. The question poses an emotional dilemma. It touches sensitive nerves. It is as though even to consider the subject means for some admitting to the disturbing loss of a cultural identity, for others the raising again of the spectre of an oppressive white monolithic Britishness. And not a few struggle simultaneously with both responses. The present confusion on the subject, the lack of enthusiasm for this nationalist opportunity, should not be construed as a sign of Australians' moral failure to celebrate that they are 'a nation at last'. Rather it indicates that they are adapting to a period of social change which as in Western Europe, is bringing forth new civic ideas. And part of this process of adaptation to the new times must require a proper reassessment of the role of Britishness in Australian history.

3

Britishness and Australia: Some Reflections[1]

Do you realize that, if you go in England from one county to another, men speak with a different accent … ? Yet you can go from Perth to Sydney, and from Hobart to Cape York, and find men speaking the same tongue with the same accent … We are all of the same race, and speak the same tongue in the same way. That cannot be said of any other Dominion in the Empire, except New Zealand, where, after all, it can be said only with reservations, because that country has a large population of Maoris. We are more British than the people of Great Britain, we hold firmly to the great principle of the White Australia, because we know what we know.[2]

William Morris Hughes, Prime Minister of Australia, 1919

Recent scholarship has suggested that Australian nationalist historiography based on the Bush and Anzac Legends and radical Labor mythology has distorted our understanding of Australian identity and that British race patriotism was dominant until the 1970s. Australian nationalism was not 'thwarted'; rather, it was based on a local patriotism which saw itself as part of a pan-Britishness. This Britishness was probably stronger in Australia than in Britain itself: Australians had, in the words of the original 'Advance Australia Fair', a 'British soul'. Anglo-Australian differences—and these were often profound ones over foreign, defence, immigration and trade policies—were merely conflicts over interest. They neither derived from cultural difference nor led Australians to create a separate myth of themselves as a unique people.[3] In order to understand this argument it is important to discuss three issues. The first is conceptual, namely the problem of nationalism in history. The second is contextual, namely Britishness in British historiography. And the third, and more specific, is the 1941–49 period in Australian history, which is seen by the great majority of nationalist historians, especially the 'radical nationalists', as either marking Australia's break with Britishness or setting the pattern for the subsequent achievement of independence.

---

[1] This essay was originally published as 'Britishness and Australia: Some Reflections', *Journal of Imperial and Commonwealth History*, 31 (May 2003), pp. 121–35.

[2] Commonwealth of Australia, *Parliamentary Debates*, 10 September 1919, p. 12175.

[3] Neville Meaney, 'Britishness and Australian Identity: The Problem of Nationalism in Australian History and Historiography', *Australian Historical Studies*, 32 (2001), pp. 76–90; and Stuart Ward, *Australia and the British Embrace: The Demise of the Imperial Ideal* (Melbourne, 2001). See also Stuart Ward, 'Sentiment and Self-interest: The Imperial Ideal and Anglo-Australian Commercial Culture'; Richard White, 'Cooees cross the Strand: Australian Travellers in London and the Performance of National Identity'; John Rickard, 'Imagining the Unimaginable?'; and Jane Connors, 'Identity and History', *Australian Historical Studies*, 32 (2001), pp. 91–108, 109–27, 128–31 and 132–36 respectively.

I

To begin, then, with the problem of nationalism. The idea of Britishness is first and foremost about nationalism. Yet while those scholars who have addressed the British question implicitly accept this, very few have given thought to the conceptual phenomenon which defines their subject and informs their conclusions. As a result historians, or at least those historians concerned with ideas of political community and culture, still tend to interpret their subject within the parameters set by nationalism's own teleological view of the past, namely that all history has been directed towards fulfilling the destinies of unique peoples, of achieving their self-realisation, most commonly in sovereign states.

This approach, however, ignores the relatively recent findings of Western political theorists who have in different ways rejected nationalism's own essentialist claims and therefore its view of history. They have argued, by contrast, that nationalism was socially constructed and historically contingent, that it was a product of a particular set of social conditions and a particular time in history. These scholars have maintained that the stories which served nationalism's purpose and gave meaning to each people's belief in its separate and exclusive identity were myths about 'imagined communities', to use Benedict Anderson's rather well-worn phrase.[4]

It may well be that this critique of nationalism is itself a response to new times and a new social psychology. Benedetto Croce's maxim that 'All history is contemporary history' contains more than a grain of truth. It is only when new times and new circumstances undermine established orthodoxies that they become historical problems. It would seem that this is what is happening to nationalism in the Western world. Nationalism, which arose first in the West, has now almost run its course there. The great nations that from the late nineteenth century fought at great cost 'total wars' of peoples against peoples have for the last 40 years been engaged in building a European Union. It is a new political structure which, unlike all its nineteenth- and early twentieth-century forebears, is held together not by a national myth but by a shared commitment to liberal civic values and what might be called a modern way of life. The great historians of the nineteenth century who created national myths for their respective countries, such as George Bancroft in America, Jules Michelet in France, J.A. Froude in Britain, and Helmut von Treitschke in Germany, are now read, if at all, as documents revealing the ideological character of their time.[5]

---

[4] Benedict Anderson, *Imagined Communities: Reflections on the Origin and Spread of Nationalism* (London, 1983); Eric Hobsbawm and Terence Ranger, eds, *The Invention of Tradition: A Study in its Origin and Background* (Cambridge, 1983); Ernest Gellner, *Nations and Nationalism* (Oxford, 1983); and Walter Connor, *Ethnonationalism: The Quest for Understanding* (Princeton, 1994). It is rarely recognised that Hans Kohn in his work, *The Idea of Nationalism: A Study in its Origins and Background* (New York, 1945), that is almost 40 years earlier, had already anticipated this relativist view of the origin and nature of nationalism, declaring it to be 'a state of mind' which had arisen in the nineteenth century out of a peculiar set of social forces. But Kohn's astute intellectual insight had no impact on either the scholarly or political world of his day. The times were not propitious for such a challenge to nationalism.

[5] Stefan Berger, Mark Donovan and Kevin Passmore, eds, *Writing National Histories: Western Europe since 1800* (London, 1999).

Nationalism has become a major problem for the social sciences.[6] Western historians have not only removed nationalism from its proud position at the centre of the discipline but also are beginning, even if tentatively, to respond to the new insights into the nature of nationalism. Some from the older generation bemoan the fact that national identity is under challenge, while younger members of the profession seek a way of coming to terms with the end of nationalism.[7] In the aptly-titled work *Imagined Histories: American Historians Interpret the Past*, which shows the influence of Anderson, its editors, Anthony Molho and Gordon S. Wood, admit that it was 'Only at this moment [1999]—when the identity of the United States and the discipline of history are shifting in profound ways—are we able to perceive clearly the peculiar ways Americans have written about the past.' Here in this book Wood, a previously committed nationalist historian, begins, even if uncertainly, the process of unpacking nationalism's assumptions and opening up new ways of understanding America's mythology.[8] Britishness has not escaped this process.

II

Although there can be no question but that this interrogating of Britishness is connected to the broader examination of nationalism in the Western world, its immediate origins can be traced to Britain joining the European Economic Community. J.G.A. Pocock's clarion call for a new subject called 'British History', which began the whole enterprise, was issued from Christchurch, New Zealand in 1973.[9] He, as a New Zealander, has subsequently confessed that the lecture

> was composed and delivered after the great divorce which occurred when you [the British] told us that you were now Europeans, which we as New Zealanders were not … What you did, of course, was irrevocably and unilaterally to disrupt a concept of Britishness which we had supposed that we share with you … In effect, you threw your identity, as well as ours, into a condition of contingency, in which you have to decide whether it is possible to be both British and European … , while we have to decide in what sense if any we continue to be British or have a British history.[10]

---

[6] Anthony D. Smith, *Nationalism and Modernism: A Critical Survey of Recent Theories of Nations and Nationalism* (London, 1998), gives an overview of the extraordinary extent of the debate which has emerged since the 1970s.

[7] Even United States historians have been affected by this critical approach to nationalism. While veteran scholars whose *weltanschauung* was formed in the high era of nationalism could protest against the failure of their American vision (see Arthur Schlesinger Jr., *Disuniting of America*), many more, such as Joyce Appleby in her presidential address to the Society of American Historians in 1995, celebrated the collapse of the hegemonic myth.

[8] Anthony Molho and Gordon S. Wood, eds, *Imagined Histories: American Historians Interpret the Past* (Princeton, 1998), p. 3.

[9] J.G.A. Pocock, 'British History: A Plea for a New Subject', *New Zealand Historical Journal*, 8 (1974), pp. 3–21.

[10] J. G. A. Pocock, 'Conclusion: Contingency, Identity, Sovereignty', in Alexander Grant and Keith J. Stringer, eds, *Uniting the Kingdom? The Making of British History* (London, 1995), p. 297. For the impact of Britain joining the EEC on Australia, see Ward, *Australia and the British Embrace*.

British scholars, in reacting to Pocock's plea and the problems of identity raised by Britain's entry into the European Community have, however, confined their research and writing to the history of the United Kingdom and Ireland and to its connection to British North America. In the last 20 years there has been a plethora of works dealing with the origin and nature of English or British nationalism and the relation of the Celtic peoples to England. By contrast there has been hardly any work on Greater Britain or, for that matter, on the classical era of British race patriotism at the end of the nineteenth century which shaped the British-settled colonies' sense of identity.[11] Indeed, the indifference to this period highlights the failure of the historians engaged in the 'New History' to reflect on the concept of nationalism and, more to the point here, to take seriously the problem of Britishness for the latter-day, that is nineteenth- and twentieth-century, British diaspora. It is noteworthy that Pocock himself has not shown any desire to fill this gap: his scholarly endeavours have been devoted almost entirely to civic humanism and republicanism in the seventeenth- and eighteenth-century Anglo-American world.

The burden of Pocock's complaint is that Britain by going into Europe had cut itself free from a global sense of Britishness which had given New Zealanders their identity. In his article he expressed New Zealanders' resentment at British indifference to their cultural fate—'we were to learn that you cared as little for our past as for our future'—sentiments which had their echoes, even if in more subdued tones, in Australia and Canada. In a 1999 *American Historical Review* forum on 'The New British History in Atlantic Perspective', Pocock, returning to the initial impulse that had started this hare running, could not forbear from repeating the old refrain:

> One of the origins of the 'New British History' lies in the perceived need they (the colonies of settlement—the former dominions or neo-British) are under to rewrite British history, in order both to enhance their own understanding of their own and to point out to the United Kingdom British that there is a history of common substance, which Europeanisation must not be allowed to write out of existence.

---

[11] For surveys of works on Britishness which have been published since 1973, see Grant and Stringer, eds, *Uniting the Kingdom?*; and Tony Claydon and Ian McBride, eds, *Protestantism and National Identity: Britain and Ireland, c.1650–1850* (Cambridge, 1998). David Cannadine in his chapter on 'British History as a "new subject": Politics, Perspectives and Prospects', in Alexander and Stringer, eds, *Uniting the Kingdom?*, 24, commenting on the dearth of studies on Britishness in the nineteenth and twentieth century, has remarked, 'How odd it is that "British history" as a subject should be at its weakest for the very period when British history itself in many ways reached its zenith.' Norman Davies, in his iconoclastic attack on the careless use of the word 'British' in *The Isles* (London, 1999), has a chapter on 'The British Imperial Isles, 1707–1922', but its treatment of the British settled colonies and Dominions is perfunctory and superficial. Pocock's ambition to have a British history which would incorporate the British settled colonies has to overcome the United Kingdom historians' predisposition to see these colonies as part also of the dependent Empire and therefore, given their relative insignificance, especially when compared to India, to pay them little attention. Douglas Cole's pre-Pocock article, 'The Problem of "Nationalism" and "Imperialism" in British Settlement Colonies', *Journal of British Studies*, 10 (1971), pp. 160–82, remains the only serious attempt to deal with the conceptual questions, but his work still does not show how these ideas of British race nationalism were generated in England and the degree of their acceptance in the United Kingdom.

For Pocock this wider British history should not be limited to eighteenth-century North America. Australia, New Zealand and South Africa, even if the latter was an unsuccessful venture, needed to write 'their own histories and their own British history'. And he concluded defiantly, 'There was a British world, both European and oceanic, in the nineteenth and twentieth centuries: it had a history, which will have successors.'[12]

Pocock's call for such a new British history has fallen mostly on deaf ears in the antipodes as well as the United Kingdom. Australian and New Zealand historians, no less than their British counterparts, have evinced little or no inclination to take up this cause.[13] For Australians and New Zealanders their British past has become something of an embarrassment. On the one hand, a new breed of social historians responding to the decline in nationalism's appeal has focused on its victims, that is those who had been marginalised by nationalist history, and developed in its place a pluralist alternative. On the other, those still captive to nationalism's claims have recognised that, after the United Kingdom had abandoned its fellow Britons across the sea, they could no longer define themselves through a history the core of which had rejected them. In the case of Australia these historians have sought to create a new exclusive nationalist history written against Britain and its supposed betrayals. The new teleological history, frequently given a radical slant, has seen Australia's past as a story of 'thwarted' nationalism, a thwarting which was the result of British manipulation, Anglo-Australians' subversion and security dependence.

III

The decade of the 1940s is seen by most Australian nationalists as the crucial period in which Australia, under the greatest provocation, moved to cut the British ties and affirm its own identity. It was, according to this quasi-nationalist view, the decade in which Australians realised or ought to have realised—there is a confusion here which betrays the scholarly difficulties of the argument—themselves as a distinct people. Under the leadership of the Curtin and Chifley Labor governments—and for the radical historians the Labor Party and the labour movement are the heroes of the teleological story—it is claimed that Australia was or ought to have become a nation at last. The titles of David Day's two major works on Australia in the Second World War, namely *The Great Betrayal* and *Reluctant Nation*,[14] reveal this approach. Down to the fall of Singapore Britain showed no interest in Australia's fate and exploited Australia's loyalty for its own ends. Subsequently, however, despite Australia's resentment of British behaviour and its insistence that Australia's forces should be used in the south-west Pacific to defend it against Japanese aggression, Day had to recognise reluctantly that somehow these events did not produce a popular demand for a separate Australian nationalism and the severing of the links that bound Australia to Britain. The curious title, *Reluctant Nation*, expressed Day's disappointment that the

---

[12] 'The New British History in Atlantic Perspective: An Antipodean Commentary', *American Historical Review*, 104 (1999), pp. 499–500.

[13] James Belich, *Making Peoples: A History of the New Zealanders. From Polynesian Settlement to the End of the Nineteenth Century* (Auckland, 1996); and *idem, Paradise Reforged: A History of the New Zealanders. From the 1880s to the Year 2000* (Auckland, 2001), are perhaps exceptions.

[14] David Day, *The Great Betrayal: Britain, Australia and the Onset of the Pacific War*, pp. 1939–42

salutary lessons of wartime had not been translated into a crusade for independence which he seems to have believed was the natural culmination of this history.

Why then were Australians so unwilling to claim their independence from Britain and its Empire? The answer is clear. They, even under the testing circumstances of the Second World War, could not think of themselves as other than a British people. The idea of Britishness which Australians had embraced at the end of the nineteenth century, at the outset of the modern nationalist era, was so deeply embedded in the society that no alternative was seriously contemplated. John Curtin, the Labor Prime Minister, who has been seen as the putative symbol of this national emancipation, cannot fulfil the role. Australian nationalists have often cited his New Year message at the end of 1941, in which he famously called on Australia to turn to the United States 'free of any pangs as to our traditional links or kinship with the United Kingdom', as a cry for independence. It cannot serve the purpose. In his early years while on the periphery of politics Curtin had espoused socialist and pacifist causes and shown little interest in nationalism of any kind. But, propelled into the centre of the country's political life, he could not, as wartime prime minister, avoid the issue and he responded with the language of the heroes of Federation and all their successors. He, like them, believed in a white British Australia. Following the Japanese attack on Pearl Harbor and Australia's declaration of war on Japan Curtin in a radio broadcast asserted that 'We Australians ... shall hold this territory and keep it as a citadel for the British-speaking race.'[15]

'British-speaking' may sound odd but, though a malapropism, it did say something about Australia's idea of itself.[16] Australia's myth was not English but British, as William Morris Hughes proudly proclaimed in 1919. Australians, as the British myth would have it, believed in some incongruous way that those of English, Scottish, Irish and Welsh descent shared one culture and one history, and in Australia where they were all mixed together this was the 'race' to which they belonged. Thus since nationalism required that each 'race' of people had to have its own distinct culture and language Australia as a British people must have a British language. This phrase was not a slip of the tongue. Curtin repeated it many times, even in England, and his successor as Prime Minister, Ben Chifley, followed Curtin's usage. In Britain, where Britishness never had the same resonance, this curious effort to nationalise language for British nationalist purposes never appeared. Churchill's history was a history of the English-speaking peoples. In the United Kingdom, English dominance meant that England could be used for the whole. Since the need for a modern nationalism was never felt there in the same degree as in Australia, there was no great demand that the distinct country, county and local loyalties give way absolutely to a British one.

Australia's Britishness was a white Britishness and Curtin wholeheartedly endorsed this full version of national identity. In an Australia Day address in January 1942, at the time when the fear of a Japanese invasion seemed imminent, Curtin declared that 'We

---

[15] *Sydney Morning Herald*, 9 Dec. 1941.

[16] 'British-speaking race' is unknown to the Oxford Dictionary and those working on its revision. The Macquarie Dictionary editors also have no references to the phrase. The Macquarie editors have only one related reference, namely to 'British-speaking man', which appeared in an obscure work, *Australia Limited*, by A.J. Marshall, which was published in 1942 in Australia.

carry on the purpose of Captain James Cook: we maintain the tradition of Captain Arthur Phillip. This Australia is for the Australians: it is a White Australia, with God's blessing we shall keep it so.'[17] Here, by looking back to a British explorer hero and the first British governor, the teleological story of Australia gained its legitimacy. Curtin admitted that he 'felt intensely the horror of a Japanese invasion because of the incompatibility of race and blood'. But his desire to continue the work of making Australia 'a second Britannia in the Antipodes' was imperilled not only by the immediate Japanese danger but more generally by the 'teeming millions of coloured races to the north of Australia'. To meet this future it was imperative to hold fast to Australia's racially exclusive immigration policy and at the end of the war to encourage substantial numbers of white British to settle in the country.[18]

In harmony with these assumptions about Australia Curtin also looked forward to closer ties with Britain and the other Dominions. His answer to Britain's so-called 'betrayal' was not independence and separation but more effective arrangements for Dominion participation in the making of a united empire's defence and foreign policy. For this purpose he wanted at the end of the war a reformed British Empire with permanent machinery for consultation and information. And he took these proposals with him to the Prime Ministers' conference which was held in London in May 1944.[19] Arriving in London he again and again expressed in fulsome language Australia's British race ideal. To the Empire Parliamentary Association he stated that:

> Numerically—because Australians are over 90 per cent British stock—and in every other aspect, the Australian people are a replica of Britain and the way of life in Britain. In the southern hemisphere 7,000,000 Australians carry on a British community as trustees for the British way of life in a part of the world where it is of the utmost significance to the British-speaking race that such a vast continent should have as its population a people and a form of government corresponding in outlook and in purpose to Britain.[20]

In this rendering of the 'New Britannia' the newness was not in its adaptation to its peculiar history and geography but in its latter day founding. It was a 'replica' of the old country. Its destiny was to be a trustee of British civilisation in the South Pacific. Yet, despite Curtin's rather naive hopes, the Commonwealth Prime Ministers poured cold water on his plans. For Churchill his proposals were embarrassing. The British leader had no desire to give the Dominions a greater share in imperial policymaking. He also knew that the Canadian, South African and Irish Prime Ministers, who in the previous two decades had

---

[17] *Digest of Decisions and Announcements and Important Speeches by the Prime Minister* [hereafter DDS] (Canberra, 1942), 24 Jan. 1942, cited in James Curran, ' "More than Empty Words?": Prime Ministerial Rhetoric and Australian Nationalism, 1972–1996', PhD thesis, University of Sydney, 2001, p. 46.

[18] David Day, *John Curtin* (Sydney, 1999), p. 518; and *Reluctant Nation*, p. 179.

[19] *DAFP, 1937–1949* (Canberra, 1988), vol. 7 1944, p. 263. At the meeting of the Prime Ministers on 3 May 1944, Curtin explained that while he made no apology for asking for American assistance when Australia was 'seriously threatened', the result of American support had been that 'a continent which was an integral part of the British empire, and was occupied and defended by British people, had been held through a period of grave peril'. He maintained that 'The acceptance of American help had in no way affected the Australians' deep sense of "oneness" with the United Kingdom.'

[20] Cited in Curran, ' "More than Empty Words?" ', p. 47.

carried through a constitutional revolution which had been designed to obtain autonomy, would have none of it. As a result Curtin's proposals for a more closely integrated empire failed at the first hurdle. Returning home, even though he had not achieved the cooperation of Britain and the other Dominions, he maintained that Australia's future role in the world would be as an 'integral part of the British Commonwealth'.[21]

The Labor Prime Minister's conception of Australia and its relation to Britain was consonant with that which had held sway since the end of the nineteenth century. The imagery invoked by Curtin of a 'New Britannia' menaced by 'teeming millions to the north' drew on the orthodox language depicting Australia in the world. Similarly, Curtin's attempt to deal with British slights or failures by seeking better means of influencing the British government's decisions and so ensuring that the unity of the British race would not again be fractured was in accord with earlier leaders' practice in meeting similar problems.[22] Curtin's oratory and behaviour cannot be explained away by opportunist arguments, whether political or strategic. Suggestions that Curtin adopted the language of British race patriotism merely to win elections will not stand up to the most superficial scrutiny. Given that Curtin spoke and acted in this way it has to be asked: 'why might he think it would be useful?' And the answer must be that he believed that Australians generally identified themselves with this British race tradition, that is, that Britishness was indeed Australians' national myth. Furthermore, if this is so, then it must also be asked, 'how did they come to accept the myth?' And if the answer is that they were acculturated into accepting it, then since Curtin was himself part of the same society, he could not have easily escaped the process, and there is no evidence that he did. Curtin did not select the language of Britishness for certain audiences, whether in Australia or the United Kingdom. He had no choice. There was no alternative Australian myth he could offer the people in rallying them against the foreign foe.

In the post-war era Australia had to deal with a set of interconnected policy questions which tested Australia's Britishness. These included European immigration, citizenship and naturalisation, the Irish Free State's withdrawal from the British Commonwealth, India's joining the renamed 'Commonwealth' as a republic, and Anglo-Australian cooperation in regional and global defence. To all the Chifley government gave answers that followed from the assumptions with which Curtin and all his predecessors had approached the world. Chifley as well as senior members of his cabinet such as Dr H.V. Evatt, Minister for External Affairs, and Arthur Calwell, Minister for Immigration, all spoke the same language of British race nationalism. Chifley, though less hyperbolic than Curtin, nevertheless expressed the same sentiments as his former leader. In the 1946 election campaign he described the Australia which he hoped to lead as 'the great bastion of the British-speaking race south of the equator'.[23]

It was this British self-definition which underpinned the Chifley government's treatment of those topics which touched on Australia's relations with Britain, the British

---

[21] *Current Notes on International Affairs*, 15 (1944), p. 153.

[22] Neville Meaney, ed., *Under New Heavens* (Port Melbourne, Heinemann Educational Australia: 1989), pp. 393–425.

[23] Curran, ' "More than Empty Words?" ', p. 50.

Commonwealth and the world. In introducing the government's post-war immigration policy, which extended a welcoming hand to non-British as well as British Europeans, Calwell maintained that he hoped that 'for every foreign migrant there will be 10 people from the United Kingdom', and that these foreign migrants would quickly assimilate themselves into a British Australia.[24] When Canada passed legislation providing for a distinct Canadian citizenship and thereby nationality, Australia in the light of the changing nature of the Commonwealth was prompted to address the question. From the time of federation no Commonwealth parliament had thought it necessary to provide for an Australian citizenship. The concept had no standing in law. Indeed in 1906 the High Court had stated that, 'We are not disposed to give any countenance to the novel doctrine that there is an Australian nationality as distinguished from a British nationality.'[25] In the late 1940s the Australian people showed no interest in exchanging their status as British subjects for that of Australian citizens. At the end of 1947, 65 per cent of Australians in a Gallup opinion poll said that they would prefer to keep a British nationality rather than have a separate Australian nationality.[26] When in 1948 the Chifley government introduced its *Nationality and Citizenship Act*, Calwell, as the responsible minister, assured parliament that it was not designed in any way 'to make an Australian any less a British subject'.[27] The Act was pre-eminently intended to lay down the conditions for naturalising the large number of non-British Europeans who were to enter the country under the new migration programme. British migrants continued to enjoy all the privileges of citizenship without becoming naturalised.

The negotiations accompanying the admission of India to what became the Commonwealth of Nations and the withdrawal of Eire from the British Commonwealth compelled the Australian government to reflect upon the meaning it gave to Britishness. Both these new developments disturbed the foundations of Australia's faith in the British Commonwealth. Although the Irish question was the more straightforward, Australia desperately wanted to avoid the breach. It exerted its influence to prevent Britain taking a hostile position and treating Ireland as a foreign country. Eire's severance of ties with the Commonwealth was both politically and culturally dangerous. It challenged Australians' idea of Britishness. Those of Irish Catholic descent would no longer be able so easily to fit under this cultural umbrella. It was the view of both Evatt and Chifley that, even after separation, if that could not be averted, Irish citizens should continue to be treated as though they were British subjects.[28] And this was provided for in the *Nationality and Citizenship Act*.

---

[24] The Coalition government which came to power in December 1949 fully endorsed this aim. The Minister for Immigration, Harold Holt, in addressing a Citizenship Convention declared that: 'Australia, in accepting a balanced intake of other European people as well as British, can still build a truly British nation on this side of the world.' See James Jupp, ed., *The Australian People* (Sydney, 1988), p. 858.

[25] *Attorney-General for Commonwealth v. Ah Sheung* (1906), 4 *Commonwealth Law Reports*, p. 951.

[26] *Australian Gallup Polls*, pp. 470–77 (November–December 1947). Only 28 per cent opted for a separate Australian nationality.

[27] Commonwealth of Australia, *Parliamentary Debates*, September 1948, p. 1060.

[28] Cables, Evatt to Chifley, 14 and 17 October and 23 November 1948, and Heydon to Burton, 17 November 1948, *DAFP, 1948–1949*, vol. 14, pp. 129–35.

Likewise they were to be entitled to all the privileges enjoyed by white European British under the nation's migration policy. It was the Chifley government's hope that Eire at some future time would want to rejoin the Commonwealth and they wished to ensure that the measures accompanying separation would place as few obstacles as possible in the way of achieving that end.

India's case was more taxing. The newly independent India, which was not British, either ethnically or culturally, would accept membership only if it were admitted as a 'Republic' and the word 'British' was omitted from the title of the body. These conditions, if conceded, would represent a fundamental change in the character of the Commonwealth. Nevertheless both Britain and Australia, for economic and strategic reasons, desired that India should be associated with the Commonwealth in some form, if that proved to be practicable. Australia, more than Britain, still found the Indian terms difficult to swallow. Evatt, along with the New Zealand Prime Minister, Peter Fraser, resisted almost to the end of the negotiations. Evatt urged that everything possible be done to convince India to become a member of the Commonwealth on the existing basis. He wanted 'British' retained in the title and India to acknowledge the position of the Crown as the focus of loyalty and unity.[29] Cabling Chifley from London on 18 December 1948, after representatives of the 'Old Commonwealth' governments had discussed among themselves India's proposal, Evatt put forward a compromise:

> What is developing is an idea I have long entertained and you have frequently expressed, namely, that there is a group of British Commonwealth nations with intimate associations such as the United Kingdom, Australia and New Zealand, and that equally there are other Nations with associations which are not so intimate. This may lead to two classes of membership of the Commonwealth— full membership and what might be called associate membership.[30]

This idea of a two-tier Commonwealth did not find favour with the other governments. At the April 1949 Prime Ministers' Conference Chifley, under pressure from the United Kingdom, finally accepted India's terms. Nevertheless he made it clear to the Indian Prime Minister, Pandit Nehru, that 'there would be no weakening of the links now joining Australia to the Crown'. In explaining Australia's position he stated that, 'There were sentimental, historic, economic, defence and other reasons which ensured effective assistance to the United Kingdom if required of it, perhaps even in some cases irrespective of rights and wrongs of the case.'[31] Chifley was echoing Edmund Barton's words at the time of the Boer War when the leader of the Federation movement had declared for the empire,

---

[29] Raj and Janis Darbari, *Commonwealth and Nehru* (New Delhi, 1983), p. 53.

[30] *DAFP, 1948–1949*, vol.14, p. 115. On 7 November Chifley, in an address to the nation about the changing Commonwealth, had spoken of 'the willingness of purely British units like Britain, Australia and New Zealand; units like Canada and South Africa which have large French or Dutch sections; and units like India, Pakistan and Ceylon, proud of old civilizations long predating any British links, to work closely and effectively for common ideals and concrete objectives.' See *DDS*, no. 140, 12 October–21 November 1948, p. 17. See also Frank Bongiorno, 'Commonwealthmen and Republicans: Dr H.V. Evatt, the Monarchy and India', *Australian Journal of Politics and History*, 46(2000), pp. 33–50.

[31] Cable, Australian High Commission, London, to E.J. Holloway, 22 April 1949, *DAFP, 1948–1949*, vol.14, p. 119.

'right or wrong'. After the event the Labor ministers continued to speak of the 'British Commonwealth' as though to their mind no change had occurred.

The Chifley government also desired to give effect to Australia's Britishness in policymaking, most notably in defence. As nationalism itself prescribed, Chifley, like all his predecessors, wished to be united with the other British peoples in facing the world. Indeed the post-war Labor government showed a greater willingness to collaborate with Britain on defence in peacetime than any previous administration. It readily agreed to cooperate in the Guided Missile Project at Woomera and in its Joint Military Intelligence machinery. At the 1946 Commonwealth Prime Ministers' conference Chifley accepted that Australia should join with the United Kingdom and New Zealand in defence planning. He regretted that the British Commonwealth was losing its unity and therefore its position in the world. At a Council of Defence meeting in March 1947 he observed that 'the United Kingdom has not the capacity and strength she formerly possessed', that 'India appears to be on the way out', and 'Canada and South Africa are non-cooperative'. As a result it was only Britain, Australia and New Zealand that were 'prepared to take measures and cooperate in a plan'.[32] Although discouraged, especially by the attitude of the Canadians and the South Africans, he still remained convinced that Australia and New Zealand, those Dominions which were wholly British, should continue to work with the United Kingdom in seeking a joint policy for both regional and global defence.

Yet, as in the case of Curtin, the British government, while seeing some advantages in fostering such ideas, was disturbed by the Australian insistence that such cooperation should be restricted to Australia and New Zealand. In London in July 1948 when the British ministers were endeavouring to persuade Chifley that the Commonwealth countries should work together to resist Soviet expansionism, they were much troubled by Chifley's view that: 'The United Kingdom, Australia and New Zealand were the only parts of the Commonwealth which fully represent the British tradition', and by implication that they were the only members who could therefore be relied upon to work together in meeting an external threat. The British were not only looking towards a close association with the Canadians in an Atlantic security arrangement but also hoped that the new South Asian members of the Commonwealth could be induced to assist with the defence of the Middle East. Thus the British Cabinet Secretary, after learning of Chifley's attitude, wrote to Clement Attlee, the British Prime Minister, suggesting that he should try to convince Chifley that Australia, no more than Britain, could 'afford to see the Commonwealth reduced to those countries which he regards as [and he quoted Chifley's words from the previous day's meeting] "fully representing the British tradition and outlook"'.[33] Britishness meant more to the Australians than to the British themselves.

At the Commonwealth Prime Ministers' meeting later that year when the British government appealed to the assembled leaders to join together, in association with the United States and Western Europe, to combat Soviet aggression, Evatt acting on Chifley's authority was of all the Commonwealth representatives the most supportive. Evatt declared

---

[32] Minute, Council of Defence, 12 March 1947, *DAFP, 1947*, vol.12, pp. 302–06.

[33] Minute, Sir Norman Brook to Attlee, 9 July 1948, Cabinet Office papers [hereafter CAB], CAB 21/1793, Public Record Office, London.

that Australia was 'in general agreement' with the British proposals and confirmed that: 'If war came it would not be a regional war: and consultation on defence should take place on the Commonwealth as well as a regional basis.'[34] Unlike the Canadians, South Africans and the Indians, who responded rather coolly or negatively, the Australians for sentimental reasons wanted to be united with the United Kingdom in facing up to the world crisis.

In the era of the Cold War, as in every preceding era since Federation, however, this sentimentally driven desire for making common cause with Britain was frustrated by the fact that Australia and Britain held two different views of the empire. Whereas Britain tended to treat the British-settled countries as subordinate colonies and to see them as expendable resources available for the protection of the heart of the empire, Australia thought of the empire as being made up of separate and equal British peoples all of whose interests were entitled to the same degree of security. Curtin had when reaffirming Australia's British identity and loyalty underscored the point by insisting that Australia was 'a Dominion not a colony'. Consequently Chifley, in responding to Britain's post-conference requests to begin regional and global defence planning—it particularly wanted Australian assistance in the Middle East—followed this tradition, and informed Attlee that though Australia had an interest in regional planning the Australian government would require '[s]omething more than the statement of the United Kingdom's Chiefs of Staff ... that "we consider the threat in the Pacific can be adequately matched by American naval and air strength" before it would consent to participate in global arrangements which might involve Australian forces being used outside its immediate neighbourhood.'[35] Since Britain itself lacked the power to guarantee Australia's security in the Pacific, only an American commitment similar to that which the United States was negotiating for Western Europe would serve. Without such an assurance the Chifley Labor government, like all its predecessors in peacetime, would not ahead of time give the British any promise of assistance. It is worth noting that the succeeding Menzies government similarly rejected British overtures to have Australian forces stationed in the Middle East until after the ANZUS pact was signed in September 1951.

IV

To conclude. First, since nationalism is a product of particular times and circumstances, of a particular stage in history, it does not establish the 'essence' of a state or a society. It was preceded by and will be replaced by different dominant loyalties and identities. Indeed in the Western world, including Australia, this latter process may now be well under way. Second, following from this, it is not impossible to believe—and it would not

---

[34] Minutes of the third, ninth, and eleventh meetings of the Commonwealth Prime Ministers Conference, 12, 19, and 20 October 1948, including confidential Annex and British Memorandum, 'The World Situation and its Defence Aspects', PMM (48)1, attached to the minutes of the eleventh meeting, 20 Oct. 1948, Public Record Office, Lndon, CAB 133/88.

[35] Cable, Chifley to Attlee, 7 Feb. 1949, *DAFP, 1948–1949*, vol. 14, p. 204. For a more detailed account of the episode, see Neville Meaney, *'Primary Risks and Responsibilities' in the Pacific: The Problem of Japan and the Changing Role of Australia in the British Commonwealth, 1945–1952* (London, 2000)

demean Australians to accept—that Britishness was more important in Australia than in Britain. And finally, Australians cannot hope to come to terms with Britishness in their past unless they face up to its importance in what might be called the nationalist period of their history, and so free themselves from the trammels of British race and culture orthodoxies, the legacy of which still haunts the present in many different and obfuscating ways. Until then Australians will be unable to deal properly with their British inheritance, which is not the same as Britishness. It may be, as Pocock has asserted for New Zealand, that Australia needs a new British history which incorporates the Oceanic Greater Britain into its tale. Thirty years after Pocock's appeal, however, there is no sign that British historians are likely to heed this plea. Perhaps Australians and New Zealanders have to do this for themselves.

4

'In History's Page': Myth and Identity[1]

'Britishness' resonates throughout Australian culture and has been incorporated, either directly or indirectly, into every major representation of Australia's modern history. Following the United Kingdom's entry into the European Economic Community in 1973, which signalled Britain's intention to seek its future in Europe and its abandonment of 'Greater Britain', Australians had no choice but to give up their British identity and with it their British rites and symbols. Searching for substitutes they chose in a 1977 national poll 'Advance Australia Fair' as their new anthem. It convincingly defeated the bush ballad, 'Waltzing Matilda' and 'The Song of Australia' both of which, in contrast to 'Advance Australia Fair', had a distinctly Australian flavour.'

Indeed it might be said that Australians were comfortable with 'Advance Australia Fair' because it was more central to their idea of themselves, or at least a remembered idea of themselves. A hundred years earlier when Peter McCormick was moved to write the words for 'Advance Australia Fair' he penned a hymn celebrating Australia's Britishness. His invocation that 'history's page' should 'at every stage advance Australia fair' was informed by the only history Australians in the race patriot era could imagine, namely a history that would show them to be worthy members of the British race and Empire. As a stanza, excised from the latter-day sanitized version of the anthem, put it,

> Britannia then shall surely know
>
> Beyond wide oceans' rolls
>
> Her sons in fair Australia's land
>
> Still keep a British soul.

That the Australian people should have preferred 'Advance Australia Fair', even while drawing a veil over its origins, is emblematic of the continuing, if now almost unacknowledged, influence of the British past upon the present and of Australians' difficulties in coming to terms in the post-nationalist era with that past.

Australia's representations of the British Empire and of Britishness have been central to the stories giving meaning to the country, and it is the purpose here to offer an overview of the changes that have taken place in the character of these representations and their meaning for Australia's relations with Britain and the Empire from the beginnings of self-government. The chapter identifies three distinct periods; first the era of liberal republicanism, covering the initial period of colonial self-government, 1840s to 1860s; secondly, the British national or race patriot era, which lasted from the 1870s to the 1950s; and thirdly, the post-national or what is sometimes called the 'multicultural' era which, after a brief gestation in the 1960s, came into its own in the 1970s.[2]

---

[1] This essay was originally published as 'In History's Page: Myth and Identity', in Deryck Schreuder and Stuart Ward, eds, *Australia's Empire* (London, Oxford University Press: 2008).

[2] In this chapter I am developing a theory-based sketch of 'Britishness' in Australia which

In the first period it was political leaders and newspaper editors who, often also filling the role as cultural leaders, gave voice to colonial self consciousness and defined the relationship to Britain and the Empire. The colonists constructed their new political system in the classical period of British liberalism. After the struggle to stop transportation of convicts and end despotic military rule they took as their ideal for this 'new Britannia in another World' a British-derived view of ordered liberty and an Enlightenment belief in universal human progress.[3] Identifying with the Whig history of the English Civil War and the 'Glorious Revolution' they turned to the most advanced reform movements in Britain, especially the Chartists and Utilitarians, to find the inspiration for their Antipodean commonwealth. As the People's Advocate, the most radical newspaper in New South Wales, put it, 'If we wished to look for a "Model" it is to the Constitution of England we should look modified so as to suit the wants and requirements of the present age.' In its opinion England 'enjoyed a larger store of personal liberty and rational freedom than is perhaps enjoyed by any other country in the world, not excepting even America.'[4] Upon the basis of these ideas they drew up their constitutions and proceeded to extend the boundaries of self-government, giving the suffrage almost immediately to all men and by the end of the nineteenth century also to women.

Freed from the prescriptive privileges of the Old World the Australian colonists undertook to carry forward and develop further this inheritance of liberty. They were intent on producing a most advanced form of the British polity in which the people's will would prevail. Public meetings were held to protest against the conservatives who, led by William Charles Wentworth, wished to establish a hereditary upper house in the New South Wales constitution. Newspaper editorials denounced these attempts to incorporate this aristocratic principle in the new political order. Henry Parkes, who more than any other colonial politician embodied the radical liberal fervour of the era, saw this dispute as a continuation of the struggle for parliamentary democracy which had brought about the English Civil war. Writing in his newspaper *The Empire*, he used the words of the English Whig historian T.B. Macaulay to chastise Wentworth for betraying the colonial cause. He cited Macaulay's scathing attack on an earlier Wentworth, Sir Thomas Wentworth, a renegade parliamentarian who had taken the side of King Charles I: 'His earlier prepossessions were on the side of popular right. He knew the whole beauty and the value of the system which he attempted to deface. He was the first of the Rats, the first of those statesmen [in Australia (sic)] whose patriotism has been only the coquetry of political prostitution.'[5]

---

was published as 'Britishness and Australia: Some Reflections' in the *Journal of Imperial and Commonwealth History*, 31 (May 2003): 121–35. This article was a sequel to another published as 'Britishness and Australian Identity: The Problem of Nationalism in Australian History and Historiography', *Australian Historical Studies*, 32 (April 2001): 76–90.

[3] For the background to Enlightenment influences in the Australian colonies, see John Gascoigne, *The Enlightenment and the Origins of European Australia* (Cambridge, Cambridge University Press: 2002). The phrase 'a new Britannia in another world' is taken from William Charles Wentworth's 1823 poem *Australasia*.

[4] *People Advocate*, 21 April 1849 and 13 November 1852.

[5] *Empire*, 22 April 1851.

Likewise the colonists, in so far as they interested themselves in the distant conflicts agitating the western world in the mid-nineteenth century, saw Britain as the standard-bearer for the historical process by which peoples everywhere were freeing themselves from tyranny. Commenting on the failure of the 1848 revolutions in Europe, *The Empire* asserted that the British people 'remained the representative of that mighty progress which, in spite of such impudent pretenders as Louis Napoleon and such impassioned sots as the Parisian citizens, is still safe from the assaults of tyranny'—and will still increase in light and power, and finally triumph in the happiness of our race'.[6] Accordingly dominant opinion in the press, the public, and the Parliament depicted the Crimean War as an Anglo-French crusade on behalf of liberty against Tsarist Russia, the most reactionary power in Europe. At a demonstration of loyalty in Sydney, Henry Parkes, echoing the sentiments of many others, maintained that the war was 'so far as England and France were concerned ... a most righteous one, and merited the co-operation of every lover of liberty'. The Victorian Legislative Council in adopting a resolution of support for the British cause similarly declared the war to be one 'of freedom against despotism'.[7]

In this early period, although the colonies were creating their 'new Britannia in another world', a world in which the Indigenous people were being supplanted and Asian peoples were pressing upon their borders, they did not for the most part define their Britishness in exclusive race terms. During the Crimean War the political leaders could speak of the British as 'their brave fellow countrymen' who had the same blood, the same feelings and the same interest as Englishmen',[8] while still holding to the Enlightenment view of the unity of humankind and the British liberal doctrine of the equal rights of all under the Crown. The greatly respected historian of early Tasmania, John West, writing as editor of the *Sydney Morning Herald*, repeatedly expressed the view that 'humanity is broader than nationality and substantial progress is not to be sacrificed to what, after all, is a sentiment.'[9]

When, in the 1850s and early 1860s, European miners, angered by Chinese competition on the Victorian and New South Wales goldfields, forcibly expelled the 'Celestials' from the diggings and called for restrictions to be placed on them, the colonial legislators were very reluctant to enact discriminatory measures. The Parliaments in adopting such laws encountered spirited objections from those who regarded the poll taxes and limits on free entry into the colonies as contrary to Enlightenment ideas of liberty and British ideas of justice. Butler Aspinall, who represented a goldfields electorate in Victoria's Legislative Assembly, declared the colony's proposed actions against the Chinese to be 'unEnglish [sic] and discreditable'. Furthermore these Acts, which only applied to Chinese, were defended more frequently as unhappy expedients intended to meet a particular problem of law and order than as a means to protect a White or Anglo-Saxon race. And so, after the gold-rush fever subsided, the colonies rescinded their anti-Chinese legislation. The Reverend John Dunmore Lang, a fiery advocate of republican independence, who had voted for the New South Wales legislation, took the lead in 1867 in seeking its repeal, arguing that the Chinese

6 *Empire*, 24 March 1852.
7 *Sydney Morning Herald*, 23 May 1854; *The Age*, 12 January 1856.
8 *Argus*, 19 December 1855 and 12 January 1856.
9 *Sydney Morning Herald*, 5 July 1860.

were as moral, able and civilized as their British neighbours and that therefore there were no grounds for continuing to make these insidious racial distinctions.[10]

The colonists also accepted the British liberal idea of Empire, namely that the settler colonies would eventually seek and obtain their independence from the Mother Country. Though there were differences of opinion over whether separation and a republic should be sought immediately, it was generally agreed that complete self-government, probably accompanied by a federation of the colonies, was their destiny and that this would be accomplished with British goodwill and leave a legacy of mutual sympathy and a shared heritage.[11] The Melbourne *Argus* predicted that 'The day will assuredly come when Victoria will become a nation, and when her citizens will transfer to her this allegiance.' Likewise *The Empire* editorialized that there was 'nothing unseemly in entertaining the idea of separation'—nay, it is rather a truly English piece of wisdom to look at the event as a prospective certainty'. And the *Hobart Courier* expected that 'bye and bye, in the progress of the years, and it may be at no distant period, the political ties may be gently and kindly unloosed.' Australians would then be willing 'to accept our own responsibilities to make ourselves as a federation of Australian states'.[12] This independence was not to come about through violent revolution. The Australians were not to follow the American example. Indeed it was claimed that achieving control over their own destiny would make Australians more inclined to be Britain's close friend and ally.

By the 1870s, however, Australia was undergoing rapid modernization and, in response to this, the colonists, like other western peoples caught up in this same social maelstrom, were seeking psychological security by redefining community in more intense, exclusive terms. It was a process which equated nation with race, thus defining each people by fusing the cultural with the biological. At the end of the century Charles H. Pearson, an English liberal intellectual who had for the sake of his health migrated to Victoria, concluded that Australia was in the vanguard of this movement towards a collectivist identity. Summing up his experience in *National Life and Character: A Forecast*, he pointed out that the colonies' newness, egalitarian democracy, and proximity to Asia, had produced the most intense reaction to the trauma of modernization.[13] National sentiment, which the West had so lightly dismissed, became the all-encompassing social cement of the new order. Peter McCormick's anthem in praise of Australia's own Britishness might well be seen as an early expression of this new sensibility, an expression of a White British identity which considered the Aborigines a dying race,[14] banned 'coloured' people from migrating

---

[10] *Proceedings of the Legislative Council and Assembly of Victoria* (first session, 1856–57), p. 269; D.W.A. Baker, *Days of Wrath: A Life of John Dunmore Lang* (Melbourne, Melbourne University Press: 1985), pp. 487–88.

[11] Mark McKenna, *The Captive Republic: A History of Republicanism in Australia, 1788–1996* (Cambridge, Cambridge University Press: 1996), chs 3 and 4.

[12] *Argus*, 13 July 1854; *Empire*, 13 February 1851 and 5 February 1856; *Courier*, 25 February 1854.

[13] Charles H. Pearson, *National Life and Character: A Forecast* (London, Macmillan and Co.: 1893), pp. 17–26, 98–111, 187–92, 220–26.

[14] Henry Reynolds, *Dispossession: Black Australians and White Invaders* (Sydney, Allen & Unwin: 1989), ch. 4; Richard Broome, *Aboriginal Australians: Black Response to White Dominance* (Sydney, George Allen & Unwin: 1982), pp. 90–94.

to the country, and denied those already within its borders basic civil rights, including naturalization, the franchise, and employment in some occupations.[15]

At this time a school of English historians, including Sir John Seeley, E. A. Freeman, J. R. Green, and J. A. Froude, influenced by the spirit of the age, took for their central theme the unique character of the Anglo-Saxon, Anglo-Celtic, or British people and their peculiar tradition of parliamentary government. This new nationalism celebrated the trinity of race identity, imperial power and individual liberty. Seeley's *Expansion of England*, published in 1883, was particularly important in giving these works an imperial dimension, and creating an image of a global Greater Britain in which all those of British race and culture were united as one people.[16] Popularized through a thick texture of cultural practices, through newspapers, school readers, adventure stories, and public rites and ceremonies, this history gave the colonists a vivid and pervasive representation of these new ideas of social belonging.[17] The Australian settlers proudly thought of themselves as bonded with all those who shared the same 'crimson thread of kinship'. Talk of independence and a republic was banished to the fringes of political debate.

In this process Henry Parkes, the leading nineteenth-century colonial statesman, was the bellwether. By the 1880s he had turned his back on ideas of separation and embraced Seeley's vision. Celebrating the centenary of the arrival of the First Fleet, Parkes, the then Premier of New South Wales, announced that he sought 'no separation' from Britain but rather hoped 'that the red line of kinship' would unite the colonies to Britain 'for generations to come'. As he rallied his fellow Australians to support new and more absolute laws aimed at keeping out all Chinese, he did not argue the necessity of civic order but the imperative of race. These alien Asians were a threat to the 'British character' of the colonies. Explaining the new discriminatory policy to London, Parkes said that 'blood' was all, that there could never be any sympathy or peace between the two races. The Australian colonists were determined 'to preserve the British type in the population'.[18] By the mid-1890s the colonies had agreed to legislate to prevent the migration of natives of Asia, Africa, and the Pacific islands. When the Commonwealth Parliament in its first major piece of legislation adopted the so-called White Australia policy, leaders of all parties defended their actions on these same grounds.

Even as they adopted this British race identity, many colonists still had what Parkes described as a 'local patriotism' or 'the feeling of a warm Australian patriotism'.[19] That is, there had grown up, especially among the native-born, an affection for the bush and

---

[15] Matthew Jordan, 'Rewriting Australia's Racist Past: How Historians (Mis)Interpret the "White Australia" Policy', *History Compass*, 3 (July 2005).

[16] J.W. Burrow, *A Liberal Descent: Victorian Historians and the English Past* (Cambridge, Cambridge University Press: 1981), especially pp. 2–4, 34–35, 102–06, 124–25, 172–73, 188–92, 200–05, 248–49, 281–85, 290–96; Deborah Wormell, *Sir John Seeley and the Uses of History* (Cambridge, Cambridge University Press: 1980), pp. 154–55.

[17] D.E. Roberts, 'The Role of State Education in the Development of National Identity, 1872–1918', PhD thesis, Monash University, 1999.

[18] New South Wales, *Parliamentary Debates*, Legislative Assembly (1887–1888 session), vol. XXXII, 3 April 1888.

[19] 'Our Growing Australian Empire', *The Nineteenth Century*, January 1884, p. 141.

the land. There was a sense, derived from experience, of belonging to a country which possessed its own distinctive fauna and flora, its own seasons and character. The Reverend W. H. Fitchett, the author of *Deeds that Won the Empire*'—a very popular work dedicated to 'the Imperial race'—was critical of those who, looking back nostalgically at the 'Old Country', failed to appreciate the different beauty of their new home. Though Australians were 'of purely British stock', their country had its own natural appeal. It was his view that 'for resonant, far-running and thrilling sweetness, an Australian magpie, heard in the keen air of a spring morning is equal' to 'Shelley's Lark' or 'Tennyson's brook'.[20] Imbued with this spirit, education departments began to include Australian geography, literature, and history in school curricula and the New South Wales government instituted an annual 'Wattle Day'.

Yet this love of the land did not replace the pride in race. As Parkes noted, Australia's folk songs and folk culture were comparable to those which had appeared in other colonies of settlement or were to be found in the different parts of the British Isles, including the counties of England. Despite such differences, generated by place of birth or land of adoption, all were united by 'blood' as one people, and it was this national myth above all else which made them British. For Australians indeed the superior virtues of the land they had occupied often led them to proclaim that they were better Britons. Australia was, in Fitchett's words, 'the very happiest example of the colonising genius of the British race'.[21] For Australians indeed the superior virtues of the land they had occupied often led them to proclaim that they were better Britons.

There were among the English, Scottish, Welsh, and Irish Australians different degrees of support for the Empire and Britishness, those of English and Ulster Irish Protestant descent being generally the most enthusiastic and those of Irish Catholic origin the most reserved. Indeed just as Seeley in his *Expansion of England* used English as synonymous with British so many English migrants like Parkes, much to the chagrin of the Celts, especially the Irish, persisted with the practice in Australia.

The Irish Catholics could not easily forget English oppression. Irish Catholics were in the forefront of the colonies' few and limited instances of armed resistance to British authority, whether Vinegar Hill in 1804, Eureka Stockade in 1854, or among the bushrangers, most notably Ned Kelly. Yet even though historic grievances against the English did play a part, to a greater or lesser extent, in these acts of defiance, they could not be considered to represent Irish Australians' attitudes to the Empire. While Peter Lalor, the leader of the miners at the Eureka Stockade, grew up in an Irish patriotic family, neither he nor other major figures among the multi-national body of diggers who took up arms urged Australian independence in their camp meetings or their list of complaints. It is true that the bush ranger, Ned Kelly, in justifying himself did make much of the wrongs done by the English to the Irish peasantry, but it is equally true that Irish Catholics were well represented in the Crown's constabulary which hunted him down and captured him.

---

[20] W. H. Fitchett, *Deeds that Won the Empire: Historic Battle Scenes* (London, George Bell & Sons: 1903), p. v; and *The New World of the South: Australia in the Making* (London, Smith, Elder: 1913), pp. x–xi.

[21] W. H. Fitchett, *The New World of the South*, p. xii.

In the latter part of the nineteenth century all the colonies when introducing compulsory education made their own contribution to the Irish Catholics' persecution mentality. Following the example set by Victoria in its 1872 *Education Act* the colonial governments, at the same time as they established public schools to cater for all pupils, withdrew state funding from Church schools.[22] Since the Catholic bishops believed the state system to be a Protestant or, even worse, an irreligious institution, they regarded this denial of state aid as a great injustice and called on their Irish flock to pay for separate parish schools. Indeed the clergy linked the education question to the Irish national cause, and the teaching orders, monks and nuns primarily drawn from Ireland, attempted to give this substance by balancing British history with Irish history and imperial loyalty with Australian loyalty. If the public schools' readers gave children history of the British race centred on England and its military, imperial and parliamentary heroes, the Catholic readers gave prominence to Irish patriots and martyrs who had fought against their English overlords.[23]

There is doubt, however, about the strength of Irish Catholic antagonism towards the idea of being British. The Irish, even more than Australians of Scottish and Welsh descent, may have carried with them memories of England's past wrongs and resented English pretensions to superiority, but they for the most part had little trouble in identifying with the British or Anglo-Celtic race and the British Empire. William Bede Dalley, a son of Irish convicts and a devout Roman Catholic, was the first colonial leader to commit Australian troops to fight in an Imperial cause. As acting Premier of New South Wales in 1885 he sent a military contingent to assist Britain in the war against the Mahdi in the Sudan, arguing that 'British blood-Australian blood', the two being identical, had been shed in defence of the Empire.[24] Cardinal Patrick Francis Moran, the Archbishop of Sydney, approved of Dalley's action and sentiment, and in 1888 he set out what became the orthodox Irish Catholic position declaring that 'whilst the Australians are then one in heart and in hand with their brothers of the dear mother country, we are not less loyal to the empire of which we are proud to form part ... The freedom which we enjoy is the mainstay of the empire's strength, and we desire that Ireland should, to the fullest extent, enjoy the same freedom without which the Empire cannot stand.' On this latter point Moran was speaking not only for his flock but also for the majority of Australians who favoured self-government or 'home rule' as the solution for the Irish problem.[25]

Irish Catholics were roughly a quarter of the population and were spread fairly evenly within and across all the colonies. They had little choice but to accept their minority status

---

[22] A.G. Austin, *Australian Education 1788–1900: Church, State, and Public Education in Colonial Australia* (Melbourne, Pitman: 1961); Dennis Grundy, *Secular, Compulsory and Free, The Education Act of 1872* (Melbourne, Melbourne University Press:1972).

[23] Brother Ronald Fogarty, *Catholic Education in Australia 1806-1950* (Melbourne, Melbourne University Press: 1959); Roberts, 'The Role of State Education', pp. 47–100; S.G. Firth, 'Social Values in the New South Wales Primary School, 1880–1914: An Analysis of School Texts', in A.G. Austin, ed., *Melbourne Studies in Education* (Melbourne, Melbourne University Press: 1970), pp. 123–59.

[24] New South Wales, *Parliamentary Debates*, Legislative Council (1884–1885 session), vol. XVI, pp. 5–9, 17 March 1885.

[25] Patrick O'Farrell, *The Irish in Australia, 1788 to the Present* (Sydney, University of New South Wales Press: 1993), p. 163.

and to come to terms with the ethos of the dominant society. Moreover, under democratic self-government, convict and free settlers from Ireland, as from other parts of the British Isles, were able to aspire to the highest political offices in the land. It is Patrick O'Farrell's judgement that, despite everything, 'the Irish in Australia identified proudly with the power and prestige of the Empire' and looked forward to Ireland being 'as free as they were in Australia'.[26]

However, with the rise of mass nationalism and the Australian adoption of the British race myth, the meaning of freedom under self-government came under question. In the nationalist era each distinct western people accepted that its destiny could not be fulfilled and that it could not be culturally or morally whole until those who shared the myth were united within a common polity. Seeley himself looked forward to the creation of an Imperial Federation, and to this end was a foundation member of, and leading figure in, an English-based Imperial Federation League. Though the precise form that this Federation might take was never very clear, the impulse which had brought the subject to the centre of imperial thought and argument remained powerful. At its core was the conviction that somehow or other the British race should be able to develop common policies which would enable its scattered branches to face the world as one.

From the outset, Australian leaders, even many of those who had imbibed most deeply of the British race sentiment, had difficulties in accepting the Imperial Federationists' proposal for a political union. Parkes, enmeshed in the fabric of Australian public life, felt the dilemma most keenly and tried to find language and institutions by which to solve the national problem. Swept along by a vision of Greater Britain, he was convinced that if 'the English people' —and here he slipped into Seeley's confusing nomenclature—'held together in one world-embracing-Empire' they would be 'destined for a historic mission beyond that of all previous nations'. Writing in an English journal he said that should this come to pass the people of the British Isles would have to adopt a different attitude towards the colonies of settlement. Australians were 'more purely British than any other [people] outside the shores of Britain'. To counter the English perception that the Australians were but colonial dependencies of the Mother Country and therefore not entitled to be treated as equals, he claimed that they were in some key respects better Britons showing the way to the future regeneration of the race. Referring especially to the Australasians' democratic constitutions and equal liberty he asserted that this 'Young England' was 'in all the best characteristics of the race, more English than Old England itself'. If Australians were to participate in the common destiny then, as Seeley had argued, the English people had to accept the overseas British as belonging to Britain as 'one part of the nation belongs to all other parts in the United Kingdom'. Australians had to be treated not as subordinate colonials but as equal partners sharing 'in all the glory of the British Empire'.

For this purpose, Parkes contended, as the passions of nationalism required, that the Empire had to find the means of binding the British peoples together 'in one great self-sustaining, consanguineous political organism'. Yet this could not be achieved through colonial representation in either the British Parliament or the British Cabinet. Not only were there constitutional objections but, even more, it was clear that, since the colonists

---

[26] Patrick O'Farrell, *The Irish in Australia*, p. 163.

would always be in a minority, these schemes could not be relied upon to protect their peculiar interests, such as their claim to annex eastern New Guinea or more broadly their assertion of an 'Australasian Monroe Doctrine for the South Pacific'.[27]

Parkes' only suggestion was that after the colonies federated as 'The British States of Australia'—the name presumably adapted by analogy from the United States of America'— the new body should establish a Council of Australia in London which would have responsibility for dealing with the British government. At different times he asserted, without understanding the distinction, that the ultimate solution should be, on the one hand, an organic union or, on the other, a 'great alliance' of powers meeting on 'equal ground'.[28] Race culture and state interests were not easily reconciled, and so the centripetal attractions of mythic history could never overcome the centrifugal pressures of divergent geography.

Australian Federation did nothing in itself to resolve the issue. It neither rejected a possible imperial union nor endorsed such a future. Nevertheless it was meant to embody the most advanced form of the Anglo-Saxon tradition of parliamentary government. Parkes, in giving the new structure the title of Commonwealth, showed his reverence for this tradition which the Australians had done so much to advance. From the sixteenth century this distinctively English word had been used to describe the ideal polity, that is, a form of government responsible to the people and committed to the common weal or common good. Very well read in the Whig history of the English Civil War he saw it as a noble struggle by the people and parliament in defence of liberty. The Australian colonists had inherited a form of government which had been 'fought for, died for, by our ancestors'. Parkes' fellow Australians in creating the Federation were admonished 'to honour the heroic Englishmen of the seventeenth century who must ever command the homage of the students of our constitutional history ... The magnificent fabric of freedom ... which the Stuart kings had labored so strenuously to destroy, rose from their ashes with renewed splendour; and every age since has produced wise and enlightened men to enlarge its foundations'.[29]

Until the 1960s, Australian politicians, intellectuals, and historians continued to wrestle with the problem of racial unity and imperial consolidation. They continued to puzzle over how their Commonwealth could be connected in a lasting and equal union with the other British peoples. Alfred Deakin who during the movement for Australian Federation had opposed all British initiatives for Imperial Federation, saw no contradiction in subsequently accepting the Presidency of the Victorian Imperial Federation League. In his Presidential Address he reiterated Parkes' theme that 'The same ties of blood, sympathy, and tradition

---

[27] Roger C. Thompson, *Australian Imperialism in the Pacific: The Expansionist Era 1820–1920* (Melbourne, Melbourne University Press: 1980), pp. 84–86 and 104–06.

[28] 'Our Growing Australian Empire' and 'Australia and the Imperial Connection', *The Nineteenth Century* (January 1884), pp. 132–49 and (May 1884), pp. 867–72; New South Wales, *Parliamentary Debates*, Legislative Assembly (1890 session), vol. XLIV, p. 57. See also Bruce Mansfield, *Australian Democrat: The Career of Edward William O'Sullivan, 1846–1910* (Sydney, Sydney University Press, 1966), pp. 257–65.

[29] Sir Henry Parkes, *Fifty Years in the Making of Australian History*, vol. 2 (London, Longmans, Green and Co.: 1892), pp. 400–04.

which make us one Commonwealth here make the British of today one people everywhere.' In the Address, Deakin referred six times to the British Empire as 'nation' and only once to Australia.[30]

Indeed it was in the two decades immediately following Federation that the most serious efforts were made to find some agreed form of Empire-wide cooperation which, while protecting the distinct geopolitical interests of the diaspora, would unify the British race in the face of foreign threats. Against the background of a growing competition of the great western nations for survival or supremacy a group of British intellectuals, infused with a missionary zeal, established the Round Table as a secret organization to study how the organic unity of the Empire should be accomplished. These apostles of the new imperialism understood that if they were to succeed they would need to win over the self-governing Dominions, and so they formed branches throughout Greater Britain.

For the members of the Australian branches, who, like those of all other branches, were recruited mainly from the ranks of academics, lawyers, and senior government officials,[31] the approach of the Round Table came at a most propitious time. It was the high era of British race patriotism. In 1905 the Australians instituted an Empire Day for celebrating what Prime Minster George Reid called 'the grandest and greatest Empire that was ever formed'.[32] Labor and Liberal leaders vied with one another to prove their loyalty to the British race and Empire. With the British government's enactment of the Irish Home Rule bill, Irish Catholics also felt able to give their wholehearted loyalty to the Empire. Accordingly when the First World War broke out all classes and communities were united in their support for the Mother Country. At a great meeting in the Melbourne Town Hall the Liberal Premier of Victoria, addressing the overflow audience as 'my fellow Britishers', called on them to be ready to make sacrifices for the Empire. The leader of the Labor Party declared that if they 'faltered or hesitated they would be less than Britishers'. And John Gavan Duffy, speaking as 'an Irish Catholic Nationalist', urged the Irish Australians to 'stand shoulder to shoulder, knee to knee' to fight 'the battle for an empire whose flag flew over all the world, from East to West, the greatest empire the world had ever seen'.[33]

In this atmosphere the Round Table branches or 'moots'—an old Anglo-Saxon word with connotations of free men meeting in a common assembly—applied themselves with great enthusiasm to the task. Indeed Australia probably made a greater and more thoughtful contribution to this search for organic unity than any of the other Dominions. Under the patronage of Alfred Deakin, the Melbourne 'moot' was the most active and reflective, and the powerful intellect of its secretary, Frederic Eggleston, did not allow members to indulge themselves in emotional fantasies. Eggleston cautioned that 'Imperial Union is not an end

---

[30] Cited by James Curran in his John Curtin Ministerial Library Visiting Scholar Public Lecture on 19 April 2004 at the Curtin University of Technology, Perth, Western Australia. Available online at john.curtin.edu.au/events/speeches/curran.html.

[31] Leonie Foster, *High Hopes: The Men and Motives of the Australian Round Table* (Melbourne, Melbourne University Press in association with The Australian Institute of International Affairs: 1986), Appendix A, 'Members of the Australian Round Table', pp. 189–243.

[32] *Sydney Morning Herald*, 25 May 1905.

[33] *Age*, 7 August 1914.

in itself. It may be the means to an end. That end is the realization of the unity of the British race and its mission of civilization to the world.[34] As British race patriots they had high hopes, but like Parkes before them they were compelled to face the difficulties that had condemned all previous schemes.[35]

The First World War brought to the fore the problem with which Parkes, his political successors, and the Round Table had wrestled. Australia's Prime Minister, Billy Hughes, more than any other political leader, felt profoundly and articulated repeatedly the British race vision. He declared that as a result of the war, the British people had been saved from degeneracy and decay and 'had found its soul'. The war had 'drawn all parts of the Empire and all classes closer together'. It had 'welded together, by bonds that time will not dissolve … the loose federation known as the British Empire into one homogeneous nation'. Therefore he hoped that the word 'Empire' could be given greater meaning and that the experience of the war would cause the British people scattered around the globe to 'cement for ever a Federation'—Empire'—call it what you might'—which will ensure the peace of the world'.[36] When the British Prime Minister David Lloyd George, influenced by leading Round Table members, created an Imperial War Cabinet composed of himself and the Prime Ministers of the Dominions, Hughes welcomed it. Charged with responsibility for framing the trade, defence, and foreign policy of the Empire it seemed the long-sought solution for the problem of reconciling the autonomy of the Dominions with the desire to achieve British unity in the wider world.

While the war gave the movement for British race consolidation a greater urgency it also highlighted the difficulties of the idea. The Imperial War Cabinet was not a cabinet but rather a council of prime ministers responsible to different parliaments. Imperial policy therefore required the consent of all the governments of the Empire. In practice Lloyd George was not willing to be hamstrung in making Britain's world policy. He would not allow Britain's freedom of action to be limited by what in effect was a Dominion right of veto. As the end of the war drew near and the question of peace terms moved to centre stage Hughes saw Lloyd George's unilateral decision-making as a betrayal of the imperial idea, and he complained to his colleagues in Melbourne that there was 'no imperial Government in this great crisis, although there may be an Imperial War Cabinet'.[37] When Lloyd George failed to consult him about the armistice terms which contained the basis for peace and involved specific Australian concerns, Hughes recognized the inadequacy of the Imperial War Cabinet. Having learnt his lesson he followed the Canadian lead and insisted that Australia at the Paris Peace Conference should be represented not only on the British

[34] 'Imperial Union', *United Empire*, 4 (January 1913), pp. 91–93.

[35] Warren Osmond, *Frederic Eggleston: An Intellectual in Australian Politics* (Sydney, George Allen & Unwin: 1985); Neville Meaney, 'Frederic Eggleston and Australia's Role in International Affairs', *Australian Journal of Politics and History*, 51(3) (September 2005); Neville Meaney, *The Search for Security in the Pacific 1901–1914* (Sydney, Sydney University Press: 1976), pp. 258–60.

[36] W.H. Hughes, *'The Day'—and after: War Speeches*, arranged by Keith Murdoch and introduced by the Rt. Hon. Lloyd George (London, Cassell: 1916), pp. 12, 16, and 61.

[37] Cable, Hughes to Watt, 23 October 1918, W.H. Hughes Papers, National Library of Australia (hereafter NLA), MS 1538/23/233.

Empire Delegation—the symbol of race solidarity—but also in its own right on the same terms as other small allied nations—an expression of its own separate interests.

The war had cast a shadow over Australian expectations about imperial union. Three of the most able members of the Melbourne Round Table moot, John Latham, Robert Garran, and Frederic Eggleston, who were in Britain at the time of the dispute over the armistice, saw great danger in Lloyd George's behaviour. John Latham spoke for them all when he wrote to the British Round Table:

> The consultative principle embodied in the Imperial War Cabinet is supported by no legal or even conventional sanctions. It depends upon an assumed basis of common loyalty and good faith … The neglect to consult the Dominions at this critical juncture, whether due to design or indifference, causes me the most grave apprehension as to the future of the Empire.[38]

The Australian Round Table never quite recovered from this blow, but its members still could not face abandoning a goal the achievement of which would alone make them whole.

Australians' difficulties in coming to terms with these developments showed up in the universities' treatment of the history of Britain and the British Empire. From early in the twentieth century the teaching of history had come under the control of the universities, and thus the modern intellectual discipline began at this point to play a formal role in the making of Australia's 'history page'. Professors of history not only designed the university syllabi and educated the teachers of the subject but also often presided over school syllabi and wrote the textbooks. Though the academy offered history as a science concerned with the systematic collection and analysis of documentary evidence, most of its practitioners, like their counterparts in other western universities, could not escape the romantic impulse to place the national story at the centre of their teaching and writing. And for Australian historians, many of whom were members of the Round Table, this meant primarily the story of the British peoples and their Empire with Australia as a modest appendix to the grand narrative.

These historians, like the Round Table and the country as a whole, expressed different though overlapping views of Britishness and the Empire. The overwhelming majority would have accepted Keith Hancock's much cited description of Australians as 'independent Australian Britons' in which, while all the words were important, 'most stress' was laid upon the last.[39] Beyond this, however, they could be said to divide into four schools, each of which addressed one of the main elements in the Australian conception of Britishness and the British Empire. For convenience these schools might be labelled conservative imperialism, liberal imperialism, liberal humanism, and radical nationalism.

The most important conservative imperialists were Ernest Scott, Professor of History at Melbourne University (1913–36) and John M. Ward, Professor of History at Sydney University (1939–79). Both Scott and Ward were sympathetic to the Round Table's aims but were able to adapt to the changes which during the periods in which they held their chairs

---

[38] Copy of letter, Latham to Philip Kerr, 9 November 1919, Latham Papers, NLA, MS 1009/19/23-25.

[39] Keith Hancock, *Australia* (London, Ernest Benn: 1930), p. 66.

saw first the transformation of the British Empire into the British Commonwealth and then the latter's transformation into the Commonwealth of Nations.

In his *A Short History of Australia*, Scott, commenting on Germans' expectations that at the outbreak of the First World War Australia would seize the opportunity to separate from the Mother Country and set up a republic, wrote that the Germans might have as 'truthfully prophesied that Yorkshire would declare its independence or that Manchester would become a republic'. He went on to add that Australians were 'proud of their race' and that British history, which was their history, was the source of the 'racial genius' which had enabled them to conquer and develop their new land.[40] During the First World War the challenge to the British race was so great that he even urged the establishment of an Imperial Federation through the mechanism of an Imperial Parliament,[41] an institutional answer to the problem of imperial union which nearly all Australians had long since rejected.

When, however, with the coming of peace, that objective proved chimerical he accommodated himself to the Canadian—and South African—led demand for autonomy which was given formal expression in the Balfour Declaration and the Statute of Westminster. An epilogue to the 1936 edition of the *Short History* revealed his acceptance of this reality. The language of race disappeared and he explained that the Dominions were now 'freely associated' with Britain and each other, and that the British government had given up all claims to legislate for the Dominions unless at their request. Nevertheless these innovations were the final stage in the search for a resolution of the problem of the self-governing Dominions' relations to the Mother Country. They had 'brought to a conclusion a process of historical development within the British Empire'. And the effect of autonomy, especially in the case of a foreign war, was played down. The creation of the British Commonwealth did not separate the Dominions from the Empire. It merely indicated that they occupied 'a distinctive position within it'. The British Commonwealth was 'a great confederacy of nations', and even though the Dominions were 'independent within their own spheres ... the whole is not only mightier than its parts, but grander'.[42]

Ward, though of a later generation, was in many respects still made in the same mould. He idealized the British Empire, believing that it 'had brought civilisation and order to the world'. He respected the role of power in international relations and had no pressing desire to seek reform of the Empire. On the other hand his adherence to the Burkean tradition of English liberty allowed him, like Scott, to adjust to necessary changes and their incorporation into the evolving British and British Imperial constitutions. The inevitability of the Asian and African dependencies achieving self-government had to be faced, and the conversion of the British Commonwealth into the Commonwealth of Nations managed so as to cause the least friction. For him, British liberty was formed from the accretion of precedents arising out of the interplay of historical and cultural forces. Australia might

---

[40] Ernest Scott, *A Short History of Australia*, 6th edn., (Melbourne, Oxford University Press: 1936), p. 363.

[41] Stuart Macintyre, *A History for a Nation: Ernest Scott and the Making of Australian History* (Melbourne, 1994), p. 85.

[42] Scott, *Short History*, pp. 374–75.

have its own interests and character but Australians from their colonial foundations were British 'in social origin, culture and political inheritance as much as in status, law and institutions.'[43]

Foremost among the liberal imperialists were George Arnold Wood, Professor of History at Sydney University (1891–1928), and Sir Keith Hancock, Professor of History at Adelaide University (1926–34), at Birmingham University (1934–44), and at the Australian National University (1957–61). These historians, while sentimentally attached to Britain, nevertheless understood British liberty as a principle for critiquing Empire and bringing about progressive reform. Wood, born into an English Dissenting family, admired the British Liberal Prime Minister W.E. Gladstone for keeping Britain out of European power politics and opposing imperial expansion. Like many Liberals in England, Wood spoke out against Britain's role in the South African War and came close to being dismissed by the University for taking this stand. Since Britain in the First World War was fighting German militarism and autocracy in defence of small countries, Wood had no hesitation in supporting the Empire, briefly endorsing conscription and even Imperial Federation. In an article for the *Australian Worker* he suggested that such a union of the British peoples would be the best way both to defend White Australia and 'increase the power of British workers in all parts of the world to fight for justice and peace'. Like most liberals, he was, however, disillusioned by the peace terms imposed on Germany, and quickly lost interest in the question of Empire.[44]

Much affected by the great human suffering of the First World War, Hancock was suspicious of the arrogance of nationalism, especially when it appeared in the guise of imperialism. Unlike Australian Prime Minister S. M. Bruce, who feared that the 1926 Balfour Declaration would lead to the disintegration of the wider 'British nation', Hancock saw the principle of autonomy as a wise application of the British liberal tradition to Empire. It seemed natural to him that, though devised to meet the problem of the White Dominions, it should eventually be extended without regard to race or culture to India and the dependent colonies.

In the introduction to his *Survey of British Commonwealth Affairs 1918–1939*, Hancock argued that free association in a Commonwealth was the British answer to the conundrum of Empire. It did not loosen the ties between its members; rather, since the nations of the Commonwealth cooperated voluntarily out of respect for shared ideals, it would make for a greater harmony and unity than any attempt to impose an imperial sovereign, whether the British government itself or some form of imperial Federation.[45] Hancock's biography

---

[43] J.M. Ward, *Empire in the Antipodes: The British in Australasia, 1840—1860* (London, Edward Arnold: 1966), p. 1, and *Changes in Britain, 1919—1957* (Melbourne, Edward Arnold: 1968), pp. 264–66.

[44] 'Should We Have Imperial Federation?', *Australian Worker*, 18 January 1917; Max Crawford, '*A Bit of a Rebel': The Life and Work of George Arnold Wood* (Sydney, Sydney University Press: 1975), Prologue and chs X–XIV.

[45] Commonwealth of Australia, *Parliamentary Debates* (1926 session), vol. CXIV, pp. 4772–76, 3 August 1926; W.K. Hancock, *Survey of British Commonwealth Affairs*, vol. 1 (Oxford, Oxford University Press: 1937), ch. 1.

of Jan Smuts was intended, by showing how this had worked for the Afrikaners in South Africa, to illustrate that this answer was equally valid for all the colonies whether European settled or Asian and African dependencies.

The liberal humanist school was primarily the creation of Max Crawford during his long tenure as Professor of History at Melbourne University (1937–70). Crawford had little interest in either the hegemonic or fraternal Empire. As a student of Wood's he had been exposed to the liberal tradition in British history, especially the great moral and political issues involved in the 'Puritan Revolution'. At Oxford these interests had been expanded to include the European Renaissance and the problems of freedom and necessity. Nevertheless, he placed at the core of Melbourne's course structure the English Civil War.

A rich source for debates on fundamental questions about liberty and authority, power and morality, religion and truth, free will and determinism, the study of the English Civil War offered an insightful perspective on the ideological conflicts of the 1930s, 1940s, and 1950s. If it did not directly convey an intellectual and historical justification for British and therefore Australian social democracy—any imposed orthodoxy was anathema to the liberal spirit of enquiry—the spirit of the Department tended by its very openness to support that end. While it gave full scope to Marxist analyses of the inequality and injustice of capitalism, it, like one of its heroes, R. H. Tawney, looked to an English parliamentary answer; that is, as Tawney himself put it, after a public discussion and debate all issues would be brought to the House of Commons for resolution.[46]

The 'radical nationalists', led by Brian Fitzpatrick, Russel Ward (Professor of History, University of New England, 1967–79), and Robin Gollan (Professor of Australian History, Australian National University, 1976–89)—the latter two for relatively brief periods being members of the Australian Communist Party—derived from a resentment of both the British ruling classes' treatment of Australia as a subordinate colony and the London-centred Empire's supposed exploitation of its resources and people.[47]

Russel Ward's classic work, *The Australian Legend*, argued that the rise of an authentic Australian nationalism with its roots in the nomadic working class of the bush had been thwarted by the imperial authorities acting in collusion with a local Anglophile bourgeoisie. When, however, the radical nationalists are examined more closely it would appear that they did not deny Australians' sense of loyalty to Britain and the Empire or the pervasiveness of Britishness in Australian culture.[48] The focus for their work was an internal quarrel inside Australia about class and social justice and inside the Empire about the relations of the Dominions to the Mother Country. Their prime concern was that Britain should treat

---

[46] R.H. Tawney, *The British Labor Movement* (New Haven, Conn., Yale University Press: 1925), p. 147.

[47] Brian FitzPatrick, *British Imperialism and Australia, 1788–1833* (London, George Allen & Unwin: 1939) and *The British Empire in Australia* (Melbourne, Melbourne University Press: 1941); Robin Gollan, *Radical and Working Class Politics: A Study of Eastern Australia, 1850–1910* (Melbourne, Melbourne University Press: 1960); Russel Ward, *The Australian Legend* (Melbourne, Oxford University Press: 1958).

[48] Russel Ward, *The Australian Legend*, pp. v, 52, 212–13 and also *Australia Since the Coming of Man* (Melbourne, Macmillan :1987), p. 165.

Australia as an equal partner and recognize Australia's distinctive values and interests. They were particularly hostile to conservative Australians' 'cultural cringe' or 'groveldom'.[49]

It was Irish Catholics and trade unionists, with their legacy of bitterness from the conscription controversies, who were most attracted to radical nationalism. Yet when the Empire was threatened by an external enemy most radical nationalists rallied to the common cause. They too were captive to Australia's Britishness. During the Second World War and the immediate post-war years, Labor Prime Ministers John Curtin and J. B. Chifley, who were of Irish Catholic descent and had been deeply involved in the First World War anti-conscription movement, proclaimed again and again that Australians belonged to the 'British-speaking race' and were guardians of British civilization in the South Pacific. In 1954 at the time of Queen Elizabeth's first visit to Australia the Age marvelled that:

> Labor premiers with Irish names, who could not for the sake of their careers be seen even holding a top hat, behaved as correctly and spoke as warmly, if not as elegantly, as the chancellors of ancient universities.

The Irish Catholic Labor Premier of New South Wales Joseph Cahill, in welcoming the Queen to Sydney compared her landing at Farm Cove to Captain Arthur Phillip's arrival on the same spot in 1788. 'It was', he said 'from that very point that our British Civilization fanned out to encompass a continent'. And he continued, reciting what might be thought of as Australia's then national creed, 'our origin is British, our soul is British. We think British, we act British.'[50]

In more recent times, however, Peter McCormick's 'British soul' has withered on the vine. Neither Prime Ministers nor Premiers make this kind of speech any more. Courses on the British Empire or Commonwealth of Nations have disappeared from the history syllabi. British history itself has been absorbed into European history. The histories of Asia, Africa, and America are no longer treated as subordinate parts of British imperial expansion but rather as subjects in their own right.

Since the 1950s, historical circumstances have conspired with social changes to undermine Australians' desire and ability to keep their British identity. Like other peoples who were in the vanguard of modernization, Australians, as they became inured to the permanence of change, no longer felt the extreme psychic trauma which had caused them to embrace race nationalism. Moreover, following the defeat of Nazi Germany and the rebellion of African and Asian peoples against European imperialism, the West's race nationalism was widely condemned and became a source of great embarrassment in the international arena.

Against this background Australia's White British self-definition began to lose its virtue. This process was given a specific impetus as a result of the remaking of the British Empire and the sundering of ties with Britain. The British Commonwealth after being

---

[49] Interview with Russel Ward for National Library of Australia Oral History Project, 8 November 1986; C.M.H. Clark, *A History of Australia*, vol. IV: *The Earth Abideth For Ever, 1851–1888* (Melbourne, Melbourne University Press: 1978), p. 406.

[50] *Age*, 2 April 1954 and 'State Dinner Speech by the Premier of New South Wales',4 February 1954, National Archives of Australia, A9708 RV/AK Part 3. I am indebted to Oliver Jones for these quotations.

transmuted into a multicultural, multi racial Commonwealth could no longer serve, even nominally, Australia's national purposes. As British power waned so did its role as a great power protector and a market for exports. Perhaps the final blow was the United Kingdom's decision in the 1960s to turn its back on 'Greater Britain' and to seek its future in Europe.[51] Australia's British myth had come undone and as a result the Australian people were confronted with a crisis of identity.

This was recognized at the time. It was probably Donald Horne who was the first to discern what these changes portended. In 1968 the editor of *The Bulletin* wrote: 'There is a commendable emptiness in Australians about their place in the world, the need for a new rhetoric, a new approach, as if Australia were beginning again.'[52] Politicians, pundits, journalists, and scholars all remarked on this emptiness. The Australian historians' response was as awkward as the question. Those still seeking a nationalist answer hoped to fill the void by writing an exclusive Australian history page and so offer the people an 'Australian soul'.[53] Others urged Australians to define themselves anew by developing close ties with East Asia, opening their doors to migrants from all countries, and creating a multicultural society.[54] More frequently scholars, repelled by nationalism's record of exclusion and oppression, turned their backs on the question of national community and sought instead to uncover the sufferings of the victims of that social idea. Their aim was to restore the outsiders to their proper place in the story of the making of Australia.

None of these different paths have, however, produced a viable myth for the contemporary community. The nationalists have failed to strike a responsive chord in the public imagination. Australians, like western Europeans, have lost the appetite for atavism. 'Advance Australia Fair' may have echoes of an older British nationalism but even in its new guise it cannot evoke the quasi-religious emotions of 'God Save the Queen' or 'Rule Britannia'. Indeed the difficulties that the authorities encountered in trying to find an anthem to replace 'God Save the Queen' showed how nationalism had lost much of its appeal. The public competition launched by the Whitlam government in 1973 was a fiasco. Though over 2500 entries were received none were found to be plausible. A number of eminent literary and musical figures grasped, even if only intuitively, the reason for the failure. Australia's leading composer, Peter Sculthorpe, commented that what was being sought was 'a national anthem that's stirring and heroic—and I don't think things are like that any more'. In his opinion, 'the thought of that kind of anthem being written is laughable—society's changed too much.' Similarly Judith Wright, one of the country's most

[51] Stuart Ward, *Australia and the British Embrace: The Demise of the Imperial Ideal* (Melbourne, Melbourne University Press: 2001), ch. 10.

[52] *The Bulletin*, 20 January 1968.

[53] Most notably C.M.H. Clark in the last three volumes of his *A History of Australia*, vol. IV, *The Earth Abideth For Ever, 1851–1888* (Melbourne, Melbourne University Press: 1978); vol. V, *The People Make Laws, 1888–1915* (Melbourne, Melbourne University Press: 1981); and vol. VI *'The Old Dead Tree and the Young Tree Green', 1916–1935* (Melbourne, Melbourne University Press: 1987).

[54] Stephen Fitzgerald, *Is Australia an Asian Country? Can Australia Survive in an East Asian Future?* (Sydney, Allen & Unwin: 1997), especially pp. 14–15 and 176–79; S. Castles, M. Kalantzis, B. Cope, and N. Morrisey, *Mistaken Identity: Multiculturalism and the Demise of Nationalism in Australia* (Sydney, Pluto Press: 1992).

distinguished poets, explained that it was 'an impossible task to write a national anthem in the twentieth century when we are starting to believe that nationalism has its limitations'.[55]

The most general term now used to describe Australia is multiculturalism. The professed pride in cultural diversity is as much a reaction against nationalism itself as against Australia's former White British race identity. But, whatever other role they may play, neither Eurasianization nor multiculturalism can, by its very nature, offer a myth for an Australian community. In avoiding this question it is as though the culture makers and perhaps even the public at large have been fearful that if any attempt should be made to look for a unifying social idea the only answer would be some form of nationalism with all its potential for reviving the evils that multiculturalism has endeavoured to eradicate.

The problem of a unifying social idea will, however, not go away. Communities cannot exist without them. Lacking any other alternative the legacy of Britishness has kept surfacing, and sometimes in surprising places. Indeed founders of feminist and Aboriginal historical studies, whose early works have tended either directly or by inference to dismiss past national orthodoxies as the cause of intolerance and oppression, are in different ways beginning to express concern about this lack of attention to what Miriam Dixson has called the Anglo-Celt 'core culture'.

In *The Imaginary Australian: Anglo-Celts and Indentity'—1788 to the Present* Dixson, one of the pioneers of the 'new wave' feminist movement, makes a heartfelt plea for an explicit reaffirmation of British culture as a necessary barrier against social and political disintegration. While admitting that this 'core culture' has in the past legitimized prejudice and caused injustice, she also sees it as the source of the ideas which have empowered those who have fought for equal rights for all citizens and all cultures. In her view the preservation of this national heritage is a precondition for modern democracy and its renewal in Australia.[56]

Likewise Henry Reynolds, in a series of path-breaking works on Australia's autochthonous people, has over time moved the focus of his work from the Aborigines themselves to British colonial policy. In *The Other Side of the Frontier* he has dealt with Aboriginal resistance to the European invasion, in *Frontier* with the settlers' racial attitudes towards the dispossessed, and then in *The Law of the Land* and *This Whispering in Our Hearts* with the legal and moral principles which underpinned British authorities' attempts in the first half of the nineteenth century to safeguard the rights of the Aborigines to their traditional lands.[57] These latter two works were inspired by the unspoken assumption that a re-examination of Australian colonial experience as part of the British Empire might offer the only historical basis for reconciliation. They convey the message that though the British

---

[55] *Age*, 14 April 1974 and *Sydney Morning Herald*, 4 July 1973.

[56] Miriam Dixson, *The Imaginary Australian: Anglo-Celts and Identity, 1788 to the Present* (Sydney, University of New South Wales Press: 1999), especially pp. 162–65. See also Miriam Dixson's *The Real Matilda: Women and Identity in Australia, 1788 to the Present* (Ringwood, Vic., Pneguin: 1976).

[57] H. Reynolds, *The Other Side of the Frontier* (Melbourne, Penguin: 1982); *Frontier* (Sydney, Allen & Unwin: 1987); *The Law of the Land* (Ringwood, Vic., Penguin: 1988); *This Whispering in Our Hearts* (Sydney, Allen & Unwin: 1998).

reformers of the 1830s and 1840s failed in their efforts to protect Aboriginal land rights the principles upon which they acted might well provide the Australian heirs to that British heritage with a new starting point for settling this vexed question.

Whether the specific arguments of Dixson and Reynolds are valid is beside the point. What they do suggest, however, is that the major issues preoccupying contemporary historians seem inescapably, even if often unwittingly, to lead back to a study of Australia's British past and to a reconsideration of that past in the light of Australia's changing circumstances. None of the new directions have in themselves been able to give meaning to the post-nationalist community to which all belong and which in many ways all share. None have met the need of connecting the present to the past, of dealing with the problem of continuity and discontinuity, or of constructing a history of Britishness in Australia which would help to make sense of the new era.

'Postmodern' playfulness—the last refuge of the desiccated intellectual which sometimes appears in the scholarly treatment of this subject, is a ludicrous response to the problem of understanding human society. In his *Quarterly Essay*, 'Made in England: Australia's British Inheritance', David Malouf has by contrast recently offered a measured reassessment of the British inheritance and by so doing has underscored its importance for any future discussion of Australian culture.[58] At the least the essay is a reminder that this is a subject which Australians can only ignore at their peril. With out a study of Australia's Britishness, conducted free from the emotional trammels of the past, Australians will not be able to escape fully from McCormick's history page and find a more certain way of legitimizing the values and institutions which in practice hold the commonwealth together. Only such a study can provide an intellectual grounding for treating and evaluating Australia's present problem of social identity.

---

[58] David Malouf, 'Made in England: Australia's British Inheritance', *Quarterly Essay*, 12 (2003).

3

Asia and White Australia

5

'The Yellow Peril': Invasion Scare Novels and Australian Political Culture[1]

Yearly the condition of affairs became more serious and the hatred of the white masses for the yellow enemies more bitter. When our story opens in the winter of 1908, it only needed a leader to light the flames of racial war.

> Sketcher' (William Lane), 'White or Yellow? A Story of the Race War of A.D. 1908', *Boomerang*, 18 February 1888.

The Mongols after a sleep of centuries, had awoke at last. Still brave as lions, enduring as dogs, and rapacious as wolves they had shaken off their death-like stupor and again taken up their glorious tradition of the past ... Strong as ever in their belief in their absolute superiority to all mankind, and armed with the very weapons which in the past had brought about their humiliations, they were coming under the old banner of blood and fire to avenge past insults and win new possessions.

> Kenneth Mackay, *The Yellow Wave*, London: Richard Bentley & Sons, 1895, p. 214.

But it is the problem which in initial importance overshadows all others. For the alienated extreme Northern corner—Australia irridenta—is flourishing with a hostile civilization. Under lenient British rule a new Japanese empire is in the making ... A truce has been called until 1940 A.D. Till then the Commonwealth must get ready for its relentless march to the North to save the purity of the race by sweeping the brown invaders back over the coral sea.

> C.H.Kirmess, *The Australian Crisis*, (Melbourne: George Robertson, 1909), p. 335.

From the 1880s to the first World War, the fear of an Asian invasion, whether migratory or military, was a major theme in Australian literature as it was in Australian politics. It excited the imagination of utopian socialists, bush balladeers and radical reformers, and was a central, if misunderstood, motif in the 'Legend of the Nineties' which strove to define a 'National Culture.'[2]

---

[1] This essay was originally published as ' "The Yellow Peril", Invasion Scare Novels and Australian Political Culture' in Ken Stewart, ed., *The 1890s: Australian Literature and Literary Culture* (St. Lucia: University of Queensland Press, 1996).

[2] Vance Palmer's *The Legend of the Nineties* (Melbourne: Melbourne University Press, 1954) remains the classical analysis of the legend. In many ways it was a damning critique of the legend as a basis for Australian political culture. Yet while recognising its illusions and limitations he nevertheless at the end of the appraisal identified with this national vision. There was no quibbling about Australian fears of alien evils, especially Asian ones, but he explained this xenophobia in

This literary preoccupation, which amounted almost to an obsession, expressed itself through cartoons, short stories,[3] plays,[4] films,[5] and most substantially of all, novels. Of the latter the three most important were 'White or Yellow? A Story of the Race War of A.D. 1908', written by William Lane under the pseudonym of 'The Sketcher', which appeared in the Brisbane weekly the *Boomerang* from 18 February to 5 May 1888; *The Yellow Wave: A Romance of the Asiatic Invasion of Australia* by Kenneth Mackay, which was published in 1895; and *The Australian Crisis* by C.H. Kirmess (Frank Fox?), which came out first as a serial entitled 'The Commonwealth Crisis' in the Sydney journal the *Lone Hand* between October 1908 and August 1909, and was turned into a book in 1909 under the more nationalistic title.[6] These three novels responded to three successive phases in the Australian saga of 'The

---

terms of the utopian myth itself. The European settler 'wanted to think of Australia as a new world, having as few links as possible with the Europe he had left behind. None at all with the near-by continent of Asia' (pp. 15–16).

[3] For example, 'A Hero of Babylon' by C.A. Jeffries, *Lone Hand*, 1 (May, 1907): 61–65.

[4] For example, Randolph Bedford's *White Australia*, which was first staged in Melbourne in 1909.

[5] For example, Raymond Longford's *Australia Calls*, which was written by C.A. Jeffries and John Barr and shown for the first time on 19 July 1913 at Spencer's Lyceum Theatre in Sydney.

[6] In earlier studies I had concluded that C.H. Kirmess was probably a pseudonym for Frank Fox, who was at the time of the publication of 'The Commonwealth Crisis' editor of the *Lone Hand* (see *Search for Security in the Pacific, 1901–1914* (Sydney: Sydney University Press, 1976), pp. 159–161 and *Australia and the World* (Melbourne: Longman Cheshire, 1985), pp. 176–180).

The evidence for such a view was quite substantial, even if circumstantial. On the one hand the only record that someone called C.H. Kirmess had existed was this one novel. Extensive research failed to uncover any other publications by Kirmess. Not one letter to or from Kirmess could be located in the manuscript collections of the National Library and the Mitchell Library, and his name did not appear on the New South Wales electoral rolls for 1908–1910 or in the *Sands Sydney and New South Wales Directory* for 1908. On the other hand Fox shared Kirmess's apprehensions and pursued an editorial policy aimed at alerting the Australian public to the Japanese menace. He had made contributions to the *Lone Hand*, both fictional and analytical, which in a more limited way aired the same alarmist issues. Moreover Fox specifically used the 'Commonwealth Crisis' to buttress his arguments about Australia's strategic vulnerability to the menace of Japan in *Problems of the Pacific* (London: Williams and Norgate, 1912), pp. 251–57. The summary of the plot came trippingly off the pen and it was the only literary source which he referred to in the whole work. Furthermore Fox in 1923 published under his own name a novel, *Beneath an Ardent Sun*, which had a theme and style very similar to that of *The Australian Crisis*. Finally the adoption of a pseudonym seemed reasonable. Writers of invasion novels quite often hid behind noms de plume. Fox himself had already employed a pseudonym, 'Frank Renar', for his first book *Bushman and Buccaneer*. I had even wondered whether Fox might have taken a pseudonym for *The Australian Crisis* from the memoirs of J.F. Archibald which appeared in the first issue of the *Lone Hand*. In his autobiography Archibald, who was Fox's mentor and patron, had reported that he was taught at the Warrnambool grammar school by a fine old scholar, 'Mr Henry Kemmiss'. Both 'Kemmiss' and 'Kirmess' were unusual names in 19th century colonial Australia. As a result, however, of information received from Noel McLachlan of Melbourne University and Stuart Sayers, the historian of Lothian publishers (*The Company of Books: A Short History of the Lothian Book Companies 1888–1988*, Melbourne: Lothian, 1988, p. 39) I am now convinced that someone who called himself Charles H. Kirmess was the author of *The Australian Crisis*. Kirmess had entered

Yellow Peril', firstly Chinese immigration, secondly Chinese invasion and thirdly Japanese invasion. And each had something to say not only about Australian perceptions of Asia but also about the consequences of a perceived Asian threat to Australian political culture. In all the novels it is possible to detect a search for a vision of community in a newly-established, modernising society.

The invasion scare novel was a relatively new fiction genre which took off following the Franco-Prussian war. In an era of technological progress, mass nationalism and collectivist idealism, such cautionary tales had widespread appeal. The newly self-conscious 'nation' or 'race'—and the terms were often used interchangeably as colour and culture were compounded—saw itself engaged in a struggle with other nations or races for survival or supremacy, and the language of Social Darwinism lent a pseudo-scientific authority to this view of international politics. The prospect of technological marvels being harnessed to the chariots of war added a frightening and fascinating dimension to this scenario; indeed science fiction appeared simultaneously with the war novel and was often merged with it. The romance of peoples striving to triumph over rivals and to fulfil their historic destinies stirred deep emotions.

The invasion scare novel was in origin an English creation, and it was in England that the genre was most successful. From George Chesney's *The Battle of Dorking* (1871) to

---

into a contract with John H. Lothian and Son of Melbourne to publish the book, and in the Lothian papers in the Victorian State Library (Ms. 6026) there is a collection of letters between C.H. Kirmess and Lothian publishers (including twenty-one letters from Kirmess, nineteen of which are in his own hand) covering the period 22 August 1908 to 23 April 1910. The handwriting is certainly not that of Fox, and the content and character of the letters attest to their authenticity. The letters reveal that Thomas Lothian met Kirmess in Sydney and established a good working relationship with him, and Kirmess had business dealings with Fox and Arthur Henry Adams, who succeeded Fox as editor of the *Lone Hand*. Kirmess even spoke of having collaborated regularly with 'several well-known Sydney University men', though to what end remains obscure.

Kirmess gave his address as 168 Cathedral Avenue, Sydney. This was the residence of a Mrs. Charlotte Emma Brown who it appears kept a boarding house. One James Allen, a miner, was along with Charlotte, David, and James Brown, recorded on the NSW electoral rolls as living at this address. Why Kirmess was not on the electoral roll is unclear. He was certainly interested in the politics of the time. John Holroyd, a Melbourne bibliophile, has stated that about 1970 Thomas Lothian told him that Kirmess was of German nationality and that he returned to his homeland just before the outbreak of the First World War (Kirmess in his last letter to Lothian, dated 23 April 1910, said that he was returning 'to' Europe the following month.) If Kirmess had German nationality then this would explain his absence from the electoral rolls. On the other hand Kirmess wrote fluent, idiomatic English and was very much at home in an English-speaking culture.

McLachlan has even speculated that Kirmess might have been attached to the German Consulate in Sydney and that *The Australian Crisis* might have been intended to stir up Australian distrust of the Mother Country. It is difficult to comment on such suggestions, but it should be pointed out that suspicions that Britain would not help Australia at a time of a crisis with an Asian power had a long history among Anglo-Australians. Kirmess' contribution to this fear was merely to apply it in the most thoroughgoing manner to the prospect of a Japanese invasion. From the novel and the letters, there is every reason to believe that Kirmess seriously believed in the 'White Race' and wished both Britain and Australia to build up their naval and military presence to meet the 'Yellow Peril' in the Pacific.

William Le Queux's *The Invasion of 1910* (1906), most of these stories told of French or German invasions of the British Isles. They had a clear purpose, namely to alert the nation to its defenceless position, to turn the people from their feckless, indolent ways, and to convince the country of the necessity of increased defence expenditure and disciplined military training. It was a popular, even populist literature. In this first age of mass literacy, writers were using novels to influence public opinion on the questions of the hour, whether social reform or foreign danger. The invasion novel aroused hostility to the national enemy. Inside Britain they uncovered nests of spies, generally foreigners, who were bent on sabotage and subversion. While the consequences for the political life of the nation were not always drawn out, it was frequently the case, as in *The Invasion of 1910*, that parliamentary institutions were found wanting, and a strong new leader, embodying the true spirit of the nation, emerged out of the old ruling class to rally the people and save the day.

Though the small European countries, unlike the great powers, did not follow the English example and produce their own invasion scare fiction—perhaps reflecting their sense of helplessness[7]—Australia produced a number of creative works which spoke to the nation's peculiar geo-political circumstances and racial anxieties.[8] Australians, as proud Britons, avidly read English novels such as *The Invasion of 1910*, and performed English invasion scare plays such as Guy Du Maurier's *An Englishman's Home*. Yet, despite their attachment to Britain and the British Empire, no Australian author wrote an invasion novel, or for that matter a play or film script, in simple imitation of the English model. None of the plots of the Australian novels were set in Britain. Nearly all—including the most significant and influential—took for their story line what was a distinctively Australian concern, namely an Asian threat to white Australia. Australian novels, like the English ones, reflected their nation's strategic vulnerability and political culture. Indeed a common sub-theme running through the Australian novels was Britain's indifference to Australia's plight, and its inability or unwillingness to help Australia resist the Asian menace.

The Australians also drew very different political lessons from the national crisis created by the threat of invasion. Whereas English authors, such as Chesney in *The Battle of Dorking*, attributed Britain's failure to rise to the challenge of foreign threats to 'power ... passing away from the class which had been used to rule, and to face political danger ... into the hands of lower classes ... untrained to the use of political rights and swayed by demagogues',[9] the Australians found that fault lay not only with the unsympathetic British who left the colonies to fend for themselves, but also with the local ruling class who toadied to the imperial authorities and lacked the virtue, will and energy of the common people. The heroes of white Australia in these stories were depicted in the nationalistic guise of 'The Legend of the Nineties'. They either rallied under the Southern Cross banner of the

---

[7] I.F. Clarke, *Voices Prophesying War, 1763–1984* (London: Oxford University Press, 1966), pp. 44–9.

[8] Neville Meaney, *Search for Security in the Pacific, 1901–1914* (Sydney: Sydney University Press, 1976); Myra Willard, *History of the White Australia Policy to 1920* (Melbourne: Melbourne University Press, 1923), ch. 2–3; A.T. Yarwood and M.J. Knowling, *Race Relations in Australia: A History* (Melbourne: Methuen, 1982), ch. 8, 10.

[9] Clarke, *Voices Prophesying War*, p. 57.

Eureka goldfield rebels of 1854, or were the true sons of the Bush and therefore best fitted and able to devote themselves to Australia's welfare.

If it is true, as Vance Palmer has asserted in *The Legend of the Nineties*, that William Lane's 'New Australia' experiment in Paraguay 'covered the substance of the Australian dream itself, the idea of a closed continent, of building up a free community apart from the world',[10] then this dream was concocted not out of an Australian bush experience but from English and American radical ideas, and in this ideal society racial purity was at least as important as the democratic equality. In 'White or Yellow?' as much as in 'New Australia', race was the principal and necessary basis of community.

It is difficult to trace the intellectual origins of Lane's racial idea of the good society. Unlike Mackay and Fox, Lane was not Australian born and bred. He had grown up in Bristol and did not arrive in Australia until 1885. He had spent some time in North America and while a journalist in Detroit had acquired radical sympathies. He was much influenced by Henry George's *Progress and Poverty*, Edward Bellamy's *Looking Backward* and Laurence Gronlund's *Cooperative Commonwealth*. But it is difficult to see how these American writers could have shaped his racial views. Most commentators have tended to dismiss the question by claiming that Lane was merely reflecting the prejudices of the Australian labour movement, which when organised as the Australian Labor Party adopted as its first objective 'the cultivation of an Australian sentiment based on racial purity'. However the religious intensity with which he held his racial beliefs would seem to belie such an easy explanation.

Perhaps Michael Wilding's suggestion that Lane was an heir to the Ranter-Leveller tradition of the English Civil War and the fact that that tradition contained elements, especially in the late nineteenth century, which lent themselves to the development of racial notions of community, might be helpful here. The English revolutionaries had justified their right to rebel on the basis of the historical myth that the Norman Conquest had replaced an egalitarian, self-governing, Anglo-Saxon society with a monarchical and aristocratic despotism. Lane at times invoked such arguments to justify resistance to the ruling class: 'Our parliamentary system is ... only a degenerated survival of the assembly at which in primitive times our Teutonic forefathers gathered, free and equal, to make for themselves laws for their governance'. The good society which had been subverted by a foreign invader was an Anglo-Saxon Teutonic one and by inference, the good society was to be attained by restoring this lost world.[11] Lane's 'Race War of A.D. 1908' would seem to have had such a goal in view.

The story begins with a flashback to 1888 when 'imperialist traitors' undermined the independence of the Australian colonies. By agreeing to the 1887 naval defence scheme, under which the colonies subsidised the local British squadron rather than build their own, they took a first step towards crushing Australia's spirit. Shortly afterwards 'British troops garrisoned her ports, British ships watched her coasts, British interests dominated her parliaments and British diplomacy fanned the local jealousies that kept the colonies apart'.

---

[10] Palmer, *The Legend of the Nineties*, pp. 158–9.

[11] Michael Wilding, introduction to 'John Miller' (William Lane), *The Workingman's Paradise* (Sydney: Sydney University Press, 1980), pp. 29–32, 35.

In 1889 the British government had quashed the colonies' anti-Chinese legislation, and as a result 'the gates of Australia had been thrown open to the yellow men'. Through a generous distribution of titles and honours, the local elite was suborned, and the scattered resistance easily crushed. In the subsequent twenty years the number of Chinese in the colonies grew to twelve million, or over a quarter of the total population. Chinese competition reduced the great majority of whites to a status inferior to that of the European masses. The 'Plutocracy and Landocracy', whose white members fraternised freely with their yellow counterparts, imposed their will on the common people. By 1908 the racial tension arising out of dispossession and alienation had reached a critical point.

Against this background the narrative recounts how the Queensland premier, Lord Stibbins, a native born son of a mining speculator, sought, by marrying his daughter Stella to Sir Wong Hung Foo, 'the head and fount' of the Chinese community, to establish an imperial dynasty to rule over Australia. At his palatial mansion, Taringa Park, in Brisbane's best suburb, Stibbins laid out his plans before Wong. Using the well organised, docile Chinese and the officials who depended on government patronage, he intended to carry out a coup against the ' "white trash", this braggart mob which is at once unreasoning and uncontrollable'. Wong, enthusiastically entering into the conspiracy, believed that they could hoodwink the British until the Chinese government could send cruisers to protect their new regime from outside interference. At first Stibbins would act as viceroy for China, but once they had consolidated their position they would announce their independence and proclaim 'a dynasty that in the future will rule the world'.

Stibbins' daughter was both repelled and attracted by Wong. As she watched him 'within her leapt up the instinct of race … involuntarily she felt repelled by the tawny skin, rounded forehead and flattened nose, even while the glittering eyes and brutal mouth possessed for her a strange fascination'. But seduced by the promise of imperial pomp and power, she fell in with her father's wishes.

On the very day of the wedding, however, Wong ravished and murdered the daughter of a white farmer, John Saxby, who was adventitiously the leader of the Anti-Chinese League. This fiendish act became the signal for a rising against the Chinese usurpers and their white collaborators. 'War to the Yellow devils! War to the bitter end', cried Bob Flynn, the girl's fiancé and Saxby's right-hand man. The League's pre-arranged signal was given, the alarm bell was rung and the great majority of the whites rallied to the cause. This latest outrage 'had awoken the Anti-Chinese instinct, had driven to madness every man who was crushed down and injured by the competition of the aliens, and had filled the land with a fanatical indignation'. In Brisbane alone ten thousand men sprang to arms, and it was expected that the whole of white Australia would follow their example.

The white vigilantes attacked the Chinese quarters, Taringa Park and ultimately Parliament House. In the heat of the battle it became evident that race, not class, was the critical issue at stake. At Taringa Park, Stibbins' wife and daughter, after learning of Wong's infamous crime, repented their race folly. Lady Stibbins herself shot down Wong, and when the Chinese tried to retaliate, the white officers and men in the government forces turned on their erstwhile 'Turanian' allies and threw in their lot with the Anti-Chinese League. The cry of 'law and order' could not suppress the imperatives of blood and race. Similarly in the Queensland senate, the conservative white politicians rejected Stibbins' appeal for support in putting down the rebellion. He had 'misjudged the intensity of the white instinct which existed among his own caste'. Isolated he had to face alone the wrath of the Chinese, who hacked him to pieces.

With White Australia united, the Anti-Chinese League carried all before them. The victory bells 'told of a successful revolution and of the race battle well begun'. The vanquished Chinese were sent north 'like great droves of cattle', and expelled from the country 'as fast as fear could drive and ships could carry'. Australia declared its independence, and the United States, which had excluded the Chinese in the 1880s, sent a fleet to prevent Britain from attempting to restore its rule. The concluding message was that 'when the race-fight came and when the whites shook off the trammelling of the traitors who … cared only for gold and greed, and nought for the white race, Australia was true to her destiny. In spite of white Chinamen, she stayed white'.

The story was inspired by the contemporary controversy over Chinese immigration in Brisbane, Queensland and Australia. From the opening of the northern goldfields in the mid-1870s, revived fears about the Chinese presence in the colonies gathered strength. The mining, maritime, market gardening and cabinet-making industries evinced a pronounced dislike of their 'celestial' competitors. By the mid-1880s this hostility to the Chinese, though still based primarily on the union movement, was acquiring a cultural and intellectual character. At a time when the idea of the modern organic people was at the centre of political discourse, the racial challenge was felt acutely. Many European settlers were asking themselves whether it was possible to achieve a new social order when aliens, who did not share the same common assumptions about life, labour and leisure, about morality, mores and manners, permanently resided in their midst. As Lane's *Boomerang* editorialised on 27 April 1888, while the instalments of 'White or Yellow?' were still being published, 'It is more than a social or national movement that is upheaving around us … it is a true racial struggle'.[12]

Soon after Lane arrived in Queensland, anti-Chinese agitation gained a new lease of life. Troubles on the northern goldfields in 1886, the influx of large numbers of Chinese into Darwin, including the entry of one thousand in December 1887 alone and the tour of Imperial Chinese Commissioners in the winter of 1887 for the purpose of investigating the treatment of their fellow countrymen, combined to create a network of Anti-Chinese Leagues, firstly in Queensland and then in the other eastern colonies. These associations were obviously the model for the Anti-Chinese Leagues which in 'White or Yellow' fomented the race war. Lane had a rich experience to draw on. In August 1887 the Brisbane League had organised an anti-Chinese conference with representatives coming from ten Queensland groups and from Sydney. By January 1888, the anti-Chinese bodies had agreed on a common programme which aimed, through punitive poll and residential taxes, not only at discouraging new Chinese emigrants, but also at encouraging those Chinese already resident in the colonies to return home. Taking advantage of an inter-colonial trade union Congress in their city, the Brisbane Anti-Chinese League in March 1888—as the

---

[12] Kathryn Cronin, 'The Yellow Agony', in Raymond Evans, Kay Saunders, Kathryn Cronin, *Exclusion, Exploitation and Extermination: Race Relations in Colonial Queensland* (Sydney: ANZ Book Co., 1975), p. 290.

Boomerang serial was reaching its climax—held a packed meeting at which the president of the Melbourne Trades Hall Council, who was also president of the Melbourne Anti-Chinese League, the Vice-President of the Sydney Anti-Chinese League, and representatives from South Australia and Tasmania, supported a resolution which demanded that 'in the moral, social, political and commercial' interests of the colonies, measures should be taken 'to bring about the entire prohibition of Chinese immigration'.[13]

In Queensland first and then in the other colonies, the anti-Chinese movement and the Anti-Chinese Leagues were winning greater respectability. Though the Brisbane League had been set up by European cabinet-makers who were hard pressed by competition from Chinese craftsmen, its leadership, by mid-1887 had passed into the hands of a contractor and the owner of a large tailoring establishment. The anti-Chinese cause was becoming increasingly a populist one.[14]

Lane gave a similar social character to his Brisbane Anti-Chinese movement. Though he had made John Saxby, the president of the Farmers' Union, secretary of the Anti-Chinese League, he put 'a big shopkeeper' at the head of the Committee of Public Safety which had responsibility for controlling the rebellion. The composition of Lane's League, while not identical with the Brisbane League of 1887–88, nevertheless had a similar mixture of unionists and non-unionists, employees and employers, propertied and propertyless. In its ranks were on the one hand miners, seamen and building labourers, and on the other, landowning farmers like Saxby and shopkeepers. The anti-Chinese agitation was supported by an even wider social spectrum. After the League's call to arms, manufacturers and merchants threw in their lot with the white rebels. Even some squatters, mine owners and planters, who were the backbone of Stibbins' party, immediately joined the white forces. Lane hailed this evidence of racial solidarity: 'It was gladdening to see that here and there blood proved stronger than self-interest'. Moreover at the height of the crisis, the military officers and troops deserted the government and went over to the whites, and the conservative politicians who represented planter and pastoral interests refused to cooperate with Stibbins and his Chinese allies. Though Lane, in his authorial voice, rejoiced at the overthrow of the 'white Chinamen' who 'cared only for gold and greed and naught for the white race', only Stibbins, at the end of the story, was left in this category. All other whites, even if for some it was a reluctant decision, had accepted that race was more important than caste or class.

By positing that Britain had rejected the colonists' anti-Chinese legislation in 1888, and thereby allowed the Chinese to become so numerous by 1908 in Australian society, Lane was echoing well-established fears about British attitudes to the colonies. The British Government's decision to disallow the Queensland *Goldfields Amendment Act* of 1876 because it violated the Anglo-Chinese Convention of 1860 had left a bitter memory. Indeed in 1887 and early 1888 many of the anti-Chinese zealots believed that Britain would not renegotiate the Anglo-Chinese treaty to remove the legal obstacles to exclusion, and that Britain would use the treaty as an excuse to nullify further colonial attempts to oust the

---

[13] *Courier* (Brisbane), 7 March 1888.

[14] Andrew Markus, *Fear and Hatred: Purifying Australia and California, 1850–1901* (Sydney: Hale and Iremonger, 1979), pp. 133–38.

Chinese. Lane claimed that if the colonies had had such men as Saxby and his anti-Chinese supporters in 1888, 'the white man's Australia of 1888 could have held her own against a banded world'. It was a declaration to Lane's fellow colonists that, if the Anti-Chinese Leagues acted with sufficient determination, the British could be compelled to bow to their demands that the 'Chinese must go'.

At the end of 'White or Yellow?' it was clear that, given Britain's betrayal of its colonies, Australia had to become a republic. Lane gave colour to this point by having his rebels fight under the Eureka emblem, the 1854 symbol of colonial resistance to British tyranny and of Australia's first attempt to become an independent republic. 'Since we have no hope in England and because her aid will be given to the Chinese against the whites', Saxby asked his followers to swear that 'Australia shall be free and that the Chinese shall go'. With the hoisting of the Eureka flag, 'Men grasped each other's hands and turned aside to hide their moistened eyes'. A venerable survivor of the Eureka Stockade incident was present to add his blessing to the undertaking.

But what was to be the character of this White Australian republic? The novel in fact pays little attention to this question. It was as though once the Anti-Chinese Leagues, all 'good men and true', had gained their victory, a pure, selfless and just new order would emerge naturally. Lane had little use for parliamentary government. By 1908, in his telling of it, parliamentary politics was about privilege and plunder. While Stibbins' constitutional party stood for British supremacy and Chinese equality, the opposition consisted merely of the dissatisfied who were waiting for their turn to exploit the fruits of office. Admittedly Lane explained that the British had corrupted parliament and concentrated power in the upper house which was dominated by property holders at the expense of the people's assembly. Nevertheless there was no hint that a reformed parliament might be installed under the new republic. During the rising, the white rebels had established a Committee of Public Safety to control the revolution, and the body was clothed with complete powers: 'Absolutism sprang up, an absolutism to which men yield an unhesitating obedience'. As a result of the insurrection, 'the people were at last the government ... and the whites of Northern Australia had now no rulers but themselves alone'. This was all the reader was vouchsafed. The republic appeared to be a self-fulfilling ideal. The 'good men and true' who were entrusted with its governance could not but bring about a new and better world.

It must be wondered whether Lane was not gratified to learn that on Saturday, 5 May 1888, as he was bringing his story to a triumphal conclusion, Brisbane's anti-Chinese enthusiasts were, as it almost seemed, taking the 'Sketcher's' advice and resorting to direct action to secure a racially pure society. On that day Brisbane's whites launched their own modest campaign in the real race war. Crying 'Down with the Chinese' and 'the Chinese must go', a one-thousand strong mob attacked the shops, factories and houses of the race enemy in every part of the city. It was the largest anti-Chinese riot ever to take place in Brisbane. The *Courier* commented that 'The real reason of the demonstration is hard to tell, but it is generally believed to have been at least encouraged by persons whose social position should have placed them above such behaviour'.[15]

Race was the key condition for Lane's good society. For him the selflessness of purity was all: purity in sexual relations (he was unequivocally opposed not only to sexual intercourse

---

15 *Courier* (Brisbane), 7 May 1888.

between the races but also to any form of sexual relations outside marriage), purity in physical health (he was, in addition to being a teetotaller, a severe critic of Chinese opium smoking and their supposed racial diseases such as leprosy and plague), purity in political and economic life (he was a stern enemy of the monopolist, speculator and influence peddler). Above all, he stood passionately, even pathologically, for racial purity.

Through his whole career as communitarian and journalist he was loyal to the racial ideal of 'White or Yellow?'. In drawing up the plans for 'New Australia' in Paraguay, he made it one of the founding principles that no coloured person should be admitted to membership of the utopian society. It has been alleged that one of the reasons why he left 'New Australia' and established Cosme in 1894 was the fear that many of the original settlers would not be able to resist 'the admixture of the native'.[16] At Cosme, the toasts on Foundation Day were set out in the order of importance of the principles underpinning the grand adventure, first 'The Race We Spring From', second 'Cosme and Communism', and last 'Sweethearts and Wives.'

After becoming disillusioned with the Paraguayan experiment, and accepting a post as leader writer and then as editor in 1914 of the New Zealand *Herald*, Lane became a prophet of British race patriotism. Selfish interests were still abhorrent to him. He showed, at this time, no more sympathy for the rights of individuals or the materialism of capitalism than he had when he wrote 'White or Yellow?' In his editorial at the outbreak of World War I he saw 'the red blood in war' as the British people's 'redemption from the canker of selfish and unwholesome peace. Today the British are brothers. Wealth counts for less than it has done for a hundred years, and clan counts more. All that is noblest and best in us rises to the challenge of circumstances. We know that we are the custodians of a sacred trust, the guardians of the national life of the British'.

Looking back to the era of 'White or Yellow?', he contended that 'It was the dread of Asiatic invasion that brought the Australians into line, that tamed the growing class—hatred of the Commonwealth by the knowledge that the poorest and richest in Australia had much to lose and much to defend … War with all its evils and horrors teaches the great lesson of nationality'. Still conscious of the issues which had separated the colonies from the mother country in the 1880s, he reproved 'the British at home' who 'forgot that the British should be brothers, that they should help one another to better things and stand by one another against the world'.

The ambition to achieve the good community remained, even if it was now defined somewhat differently. He remained a social visionary to the end. The war would bring about a new community for the British race: 'We shall root out the slum conditions. We shall see that no child lacks in a civilization bursting with riches. We shall teach them to be in peace as in war, helpful brothers to one another, loyal and loving children of a world-wide Britain that can only live while for her they are glad to die'.[17] In giving up his republicanism Lane had not renounced the ideals of his earlier years. The essentially racial view of the good society which informed 'White or Yellow?' was fulfilled, not denied, in his latter-day crusade for a visionary British Empire of white, Anglo-Saxon brothers.

---

[16] Wilding, introduction to 'John Miller' (William Lane), *The Workingman's Paradise*, p. 35.

[17] William Lane, writing under the pseudonym 'Tohunga' (Maori for prophet) in *Herald* (New Zealand), 8 August 1914.

Kenneth Mackay, author of *The Yellow Wave*, was also an archetypal representative of the 'Legend of the Nineties'. Unlike Lane, Mackay was born in Australia and brought up on rural properties. He was a bushman and balladeer, a celebrator of the values of the outback. He had an affinity with both the land and those who worked it. His first book of poetry, *Stirrup Jingles from the Bush and the Turf*, which was dedicated to Adam Lindsay Gordon, received the *Bulletin*'s proudest encomium, as showing 'quite enough talent to go a lone hand'. Thus, in contrast to Lane, he was inspired more directly by bush mythology than social ideology.

Mackay's invasion scare novel, which centred on a Chinese military invasion of Northern Australia, was set against a quite complex picture of international politics. The salient features of this threatening world, however, were taken from the foreign policy issues of his time, from the perceived threat of China to Australia, and of Russia to the British Empire. By the end of the 1880s the fear of a Chinese military invasion in support of a migratory invasion had become a major concern of colonial Sinophobes. Rumours that the Chinese Commissioners who visited the colonies in 1887 were spying out the land preparatory to founding a colony fed this anxiety. Moreover, the great number of Chinese pouring into the Northern Territory at the end of the year was taken as palpable evidence of these more ambitious intentions.[18]

Sir Henry Parkes, the Premier of New South Wales, gave respectability to such opinions, and became the major purveyor of the Chinese imperialism thesis. In 1888 he declared that Chinese settlement in Australia was assuming 'a form entirely new'. He adjudged that 'the Chinese Government was privy to what was taking place in the Northern Territory' and thought that there might be 'design of a considerable number of Chinese to form a settlement in some remote part of the Australian territory ... where they might become strong enough to form, in the course of time, a kind of Chinese colony'.[19] Parkes subsequently made this prospect of a Chinese invasion the cornerstone of his appeal for federal union. Taking an even stronger line on the possibility of a Chinese invasion in his Presidential Address to the first federal convention in 1891, he repeated his warning: 'I think,' he said, 'it is more than likely that forms of aggression will appear in these seas which are entirely new to the world. We have evidence abundant on all hands that the Chinese nation ... are awakening to all the power which immense population gives them in the art of war, in the art of acquisition, and all the other arts known to a European civilisation ... and it seems to me ... that if we suffer in this direction at any time ... it will be by stealthily ... effecting a lodgement in some thinly-peopled portion of the country, where it will take immense loss of life and immense loss of wealth to dislodge the invader'.[20] The Australian federation movement was formed in the shadow of the fear of Asia, and Parkes, 'the father of federation', was also in the same sense 'the father of the Yellow Peril'. Mackay's concept of 'The Yellow Peril' might well in broad outline owe something to Parkes' portrayal of the Chinese menace.

---

[18] Cited by Willard from the *Herald* (New Zealand), pp. 71–75; Markus, *Fear and Hatred*, pp. 136–142.

[19] New South Wales, *Parliamentary Debates*, vol. XXX, pp. 3788–89, 5 April 1888.

[20] *Official Report of the National Australasian Convention Debates, 2 March to 9 April, 1891* (Sydney, G.S. Chapman: 1891), p. 3160, 13 March 1891.

Mackay's fears of a Chinese invasion were associated with Russian threats to the British Empire and set against a changing balance of power in Europe and the Far East. During the 1880s and early 1890s Russia was challenging the British Empire in Afghanistan and the Balkans. Its ultimate aim was to seize Constantinople from Turkey and so gain direct access to the Mediterranean and the Near East. Thus from Pendjeh in 1884–5, to Bulgaria in 1887 and Pamir in 1894, British relations with Russia were troubled by one crisis after another, each of which raised the spectre of war. During these war scares some Australians expressed alarm that a Russian squadron might raid their ports and commerce.

In *The Yellow Wave*, Mackay projected these circumstances forward to 1954 and gave them an eccentric twist. According to Mackay, the strategy of the Czarist Empire was to launch attacks simultaneously against India and Australia. By tying up British military and naval resources in these conflicts, the Russians would be able to capture Constantinople almost unopposed. For the purpose of carrying through the Australian side of the scheme, the Russians entered into an alliance with China, and Philip Orloff, an Australian-educated son of a Russian merchant, who was masquerading as an American adventurer, had the responsibility for turning the Chinese army into a modern fighting machine. When the day came, the Russian fleet, in cooperation with the fleet of its French ally, drew off the British Far Eastern squadron. In Australia the invaders linked up with Russian agents, who, while pretending to be railway builders and merchants, had gained control of much of North Queensland and were preparing the way for Chinese domination of the interior of the continent. Though the Russian interest in Australia was merely a function of their European strategy, the Chinese, having been blocked by the Russians and Japanese in Asia, sought an outlet for their growing population in a southward advance. It was their intent, once the Australians had been routed, to rid themselves of their Russian commanders and advisors and to take possession of the conquered territory.

For Mackay, the dangers which Britain and Australia faced in the international arena were not just a sensational setting for the romantic drama of a star-crossed love match between Orloff, the Australian traitor, and Heather Cameron, the daughter of a 'dauntless bushman'. Rather they were real and enduring, and through his novel the Australian people were to be shown the seriousness of their situation. In his own public life he demonstrated his belief in Australia's peril. As a member of the New South Wales Legislative Assembly and as a volunteer military officer, he spoke again and again of the lowering cloud descending on Australia. Addressing the house on the Coloured Race Restriction Bill in 1896, he warned that the time was coming when 'we shall have to defend our position against some of these Asiatic nations … I believe that unless some step is taken, racial troubles will take place in Northern Queensland. Unless some step is taken to prevent an invasion of coolies and aliens into that territory, it will be a very poor buffer to put against an invasion of Asiatics in the future'.[21]

At the end of 1897 during his campaign to raise a five hundred strong volunteer cavalry regiment from the ranks of the bushmen—the first such light horse regiment in Australia—he gave interviews to a number of Sydney newspapers in which he enjoined their readers to heed the lessons of *The Yellow Wave*. He told them that it was 'only from the East that I have

---

[21] New South Wales, *Parliamentary Debates*, Legislative Assembly, 13 October 1896, p. 3963.

ever anticipated danger'. The increasing influence of Russia—itself an Asian power—over China would 'Russianise China' and enable Russian officers to create a modem Chinese army. Australians should not be misled into judging the Chinese fighting ability from 'the poor specimens of coolies' who had migrated to the colonies. Drawing perhaps on the knowledge of his father, who before coming to Australia had been engaged in the Chinese tea trade, he pointed out rather inexactly that the Chinese had a military tradition dating back to Tamerlane. 'Chinese' Gordon had shown conclusively that Chinese soldiers, if properly led, were as brave as any others. The Japanese victory over China in 1895 had encouraged the Australian public to think that the Chinese were impotent, but their defeat was the result of poor leadership not of shoddy material. With Russians in command, the Chinese would be a very different proposition.[22]

In terms very similar to those used in his novel, Mackay asserted that, while the Russians themselves were not interested in the permanent conquest of Australia, the same could not be said of the Chinese. The Chinese considered 'that they owe a debt of vengeance to Australia'. Mackay believed that the Chinese Commissioners at the end of the 1887 tour of Australia had vowed that 'China would yet find a way to repay Queensland for the indignities heaped upon her countrymen'.[23]

When, as *The Yellow Wave* described it, a Russian-led Chinese army landed at Port Parker [Burketown] in North West Queensland, they at first carried all before them. The ground had been well prepared. Chasing imperial honours and deferring to foreign investors, Sir Peter McLoskie, the colonial premier, the 'high priest of land-grant railways and cheap alien labour',[24] had permitted British and foreign capitalists to buy up most stations in the Northern Territory and North Queensland, and to replace white workers with cheap coolie labour, and, as a result, the invaders encountered little resistance. Indeed the local Chinese turned on their white masters and joined the invaders. Mustering their forces at Charleville, they stood poised to launch themselves against Brisbane and the southern colonies.

The conservative colonial politicians were ill-prepared to meet the emergency. Heedless of the Asian menace, they had placed their faith in the British fleet and neglected Australian defence. When the blow fell, they were aghast to find that the British Admiral in command of the Sydney station refused to help. Russia had simultaneously moved against India and Turkey, and so the Admiral explained that since 'Interests affecting England's very existence were at stake … the colony must rely for defence solely on themselves'.[25]

In the event it was left to the bushmen in the outback to mount the only serious resistance to the 'Yellow Wave'. The bushman hero of the story who led the resistance, Dick Hatton, was a man after Mackay's own heart. Like Mackay he was skilled in bushcraft and horsemanship, as well as in sketching and balladeering.[26] Driven off his small Northern

---

[22] *Sunday Times*, 26 December 1897.

[23] *Sunday Times*, 26 December 1897; *Daily Telegraph*, 29 December 1897; *The Catholic Press*, 1 January 1898.

[24] *The Yellow Wave*, Mackay, p. 212; both Stibbins and McLoskie were probably based on Sir Thomas McIlwraith.

[25] Ibid., p. 350.

[26] Ibid, p. 37.

Territory station, he found it difficult to stick to any one line of work. Before any other, he had suspected the Chinese and Russian designs on Australia, and he used his popularity with young bushmen to form 'Hatton's Rangers', a volunteer body of light horse. After news of the enemy landing reached Hatton and his men, they concentrated at Fort Mallarraway, the only property run and worked by white men, which stood in the path of the oncoming alien hosts. Outnumbered, Hatton's men retreated towards Brisbane. There they linked up with volunteers flooding in from all the other colonies. In the ensuing battle, the whites' lines, despite the valiant efforts of Hatton's cavalry, were broken by Orloff's disciplined Chinese soldiers. At this point Orloff, who had taken Heather Cameron captive, began to feel some remorse for the part he had played in the subjugation of his native land. At Heather's insistence he abandoned the leadership of the invading force, hoping to escape with his love to start a new life. Such race infamy, however, could not be permitted to enjoy a happy ending and so when a vessel, possibly of a British fleet coming to the rescue of Australia—this is left strangely unclear—rammed the boat in which the lovers were fleeing, they were sent to a watery grave. The future of Australia was left unresolved.

Mackay, like Lane, was a public figure caught up in the political life of his times. He was elected to the New South Wales Legislative Assembly in 1895 as the member for Boorowa, a rural constituency, and from 1899–1933 he was a member of the Legislative Council. During these years he was a minister of the Crown and held numerous other official positions.

In many respects Mackay agreed with Lane about the ills that beset colonial society. They were at one in identifying the villains who had corrupted the good community. Mackay's Sir Peter McLoskie, like Lane's Lord Stibbins, was the villain responsible for fostering and protecting the interests of absentee capitalists who had bought up large tracts of land and brought in coloured labour to work their investments. Such actions had forced Australian squatters and farmers off their properties and denied white men their proper place in the economy and society. These colonial leaders had no sympathy with the producing classes in the colony. They tacitly conspired with the plutocrats to sell out white Australia's inheritance. As a result of their activities Mackay complained that the intent of the Land Acts of 1861 to divide up the great leaseholds had been defeated: 'shadowy syndicates sprang into life among the festering garbage of broken oaths and shameless trickery. Stations grew larger and fewer; millions of improved acres became as complete a blank in respect to human existence and national wellbeing as a mangrove swamp or a worked out mine. All signs both of family life and local wealth disappeared'.[27]

But there were also differences of emphasis in the two authors' social analyses. For Mackay, aspiring labour no more than ascendant capitalism offered the answer to national problems: 'Neither alone possessed the right of shaping the nation's destiny'. Rather he believed that the country's surest hope resided in the 'vast number of people who, in the popular sense, were neither capitalist nor yet labourer', but who nevertheless comprised 'the real intellectual and creating power of Australasia'.[28] It was these people who possessed the capacity to regenerate colonial society and to restore the wealth of white Australia.

---

[27] Ibid., p. 157.

[28] Ibid., pp. 112–13.

Mackay, perhaps influenced by Lane's 'New Australia' experiment, established in *The Yellow Wave* a small-scale cooperative which was organised in accordance with his visionary ideals. Fort Mallarraway, planted in the midst of the vast territories dominated by overseas proprietors, stood as an exemplary rebuke to those outsiders and their colonial collaborators. Fort Mallarraway was founded as a 'cooperative settlement' in reaction to a political culture rent by the conflicts between capital and labour. As a result of their disquiet with the tendency of colonial society, '100 men belonging to that class who stand between capital and labour, and who set more store by brains than either money or muscle', purchased a property which they could run as a community according to their own lights. Under the constitution the station was governed by a committee of three elected by members every twelve months. All shared the manual tasks. No one was paid a salary or a fee. Each man as a producer held an equal share in the increasing value of the property. The cooperative was a great success. In raising sheep and breeding cattle it proved itself superior to the syndicate-owned properties that were worked by cheap coloured labour. Fort Mallarraway remained, in good times and bad, independent of the government, the banks and the labour unions. Despite its antipathy to unions, it is nevertheless difficult to see how Mackay's cooperative differed in substance from Lane's 'socialist' utopia.

Mackay's ideal Australia was, however, unlike Lane's, based avowedly on the bush legend. Fort Mallarraway was not only set in the bush, but the men who worked it were of the bush and the principles which regulated it came out of the bush experience. Like Hatton's Rangers, these men were resourceful, self-reliant and held together by bonds of mateship, which meant that each was willing to sacrifice himself for the other. They represented the values celebrated in Mackay's bush ballads. In Mackay's novel it was the men of the outback, not the urban-based Anti-Chinese League, who formed the core of the resistance to the Asian invasion.

On the other hand Mackay's view of the role of parliament in colonial political life was quite similar to Lane's. In *The Yellow Wave* parliament had nothing to offer the country. The leaders of government and the opposition parties were equally responsible for selling out Australian interests to overseas speculators. Politicians were depicted as stupid and self-serving, their sole aim being to plunder the government's coffers and to bedeck themselves with imperial honours. Even after they were faced with the crisis of the invasion they continued to scrabble among themselves.[29] The New South Wales parliament was unable to take prompt action in support of its neighbour because the politicians insisted on debating at length the question of whether they had constitutional authority to send troops across the colonial border. The troops, not the parliament, broke the impasse when they volunteered to a man to go to Queensland's aid.

The people were the heroes of the story. They refused to tolerate the ineptitude of their political leaders. Capital and labour put aside their differences in order to combat the 'supreme racial peril'.[30] As in Lane's 'White or Yellow?', social classes were united in a racial community for the purpose of defending white civilisation. When news of the invasion had reached Brisbane, angry crowds had stormed parliament and even threatened to lynch the

---

[29] Ibid., p. 845.

[30] Ibid., p. 351.

premier. They demanded action from their leaders or their replacement. Hatton's Rangers was the supreme embodiment of the spirit of the people. Created in the backblocks it formed the nucleus of a new organic community. Hatton's leadership, which gave unity and harmony to the whole, was not derived from his class origins, his official appointments or formal qualifications, but from the respect in which he was held by his men: 'Beloved by the men he had gathered around him, he in return treated them as comrades, who having tacitly acknowledged him as their leader, were prepared, while calling him friend, to obey him with unquestioning promptness'.[31]

The Yellow Wave, like the other two novels, was also a tract in favour of Australian federation and independence. From a number of aspects, Mackay attacked the British connection. Britain failed to protect Australian interests. It drew off Australia's best men to help fight the Empire's battles in India—implied here is a criticism of the New South Wales contingent which was sent to the Sudan in 1885.[32] While the ties remained, Australian political leaders would sacrifice Australian interests in order to please British authorities and financiers. Many of them had forsworn their earlier republican ideals in order to win favours and titles from the Mother Country.[33] Finally the novel claimed that it was the British absentee landlords and investors who had destroyed the settler society and brought in Asian labour in place of the independent white man. Mackay, as a politician, was somewhat more diplomatic in dealing with the British relationship, but, even so, when the issue of race was at stake he indicated he was willing to countenance the consequences. It was, he said, 'our first duty to keep our race pure, let the consequences be what they may'.[34] Mackay had come to the conclusion that Australia had to rely on its own resources for its defence. He was himself a keen advocate of military and political federation. His own cavalry regiment of bushmen was intended to show the way. 'Among its ulterior objects' he said, 'it aims at fostering a national spirit among men in the country districts'.[35]

Mackay, like Lane, was certain that race was the foundation of community. But he, again like Lane, was never clear about the limits of that community. Despite the republican tone of *The Yellow Wave*, Mackay in late nineteenth-century Australia found it difficult to unscramble the loyalties to Australia, Britain and the British Empire. All three shared in different ways the same notion of race. And Mackay, like Lane, found that when it was tested not against the local challenge of a 'Yellow Peril' to Australia but against a foreign challenge to the Mother Country, it could embrace the whole white British Empire. At the time of the Boer War he led the New South Wales Imperial Bushmen's Contingent to fight in South Africa. The bushmen's cavalry, which had been raised to defend Australia against a Chinese invasion, saw its first action in a British Imperial War in a distant continent.

Charles Kirmess, the author of *The Australian Crisis*, also came under the spell of the 'Legend of the Nineties,' and his invasion story was informed by the same romantic vision. Unlike Lane and Mackay, he was not a public figure. Indeed very little is known about

---

[31] Ibid., p. 378.

[32] Ibid., p. 344.

[33] Ibid., p. 114.

[34] New South Wales, *Parliamentary Debates,* Legislative Assembly, 13 October 1896, p. 3963.

[35] *Sydney Morning Herald*, 11 December 1897.

his background, education and occupation, or about what caused him to write the novel. *The Australian Crisis* may owe something of a debt to Mackay's *The Yellow Wave*. Looking at them in a broad perspective there are a number of similarities in the plots of the two novels. In both novels the 'Yellow Peril' manifested itself through a clandestine Asian landing in the Gulf of Carpentaria; the coloured invaders had planned the enterprise very carefully and executed it most efficiently; the British failed to come to the colony's aid; and a force of mounted bushmen, who had spontaneously responded to the call, offered the only resistance to the violation of White Australia. Kirmess' work was, however, the most powerful and complete of all the Australian invasion scare stories, and its exploration of the crisis of political community was more comprehensive and penetrating than that offered by either Lane or Mackay.

Kirmess' tale, written twelve years after Mackay's, addressed what was, by general consent, a much more dangerous and immediate foreign threat. Kirmess, in making Japan the enemy at the gate, spoke directly to the anxieties of the time. Following Japan's victory over the Russians in 1905, the first Asian victory over a European nation in the modern era, it became the dominant power in the Western Pacific. At the same time Britain, answering Germany's challenge in the North Sea, withdrew its capital ships from the Far East, and Australians came to fear for their safety. They had no faith in the Anglo–Japanese alliance, since it was not based on a mutual exchange of benefits. Moreover it was known that Japan bitterly resented the 'White Australia' immigration policy. Australia seemed vulnerable to a downward thrust of Japan into the South Pacific.

Between 1905 and 1909, the year in which *The Australian Crisis* appeared in the bookstores, Australian political leaders reached a consensus about the Japanese 'Yellow Peril'. Alfred Deakin, who was Prime Minister for most of this period, recognised clearly the meaning of Japan's victory over Russia for Australia. It opened up 'wider possibilities for all Asian nations', but most of all for Japan. As a result of the Battle of Tsushima, 'Instead of two fleets in the China Sea belonging to separate—even opposing powers—we shall now have one fleet, only it will be as strong as the two former fleets, and will operate under one flag'. Allan McLean, who was deputy prime minister in the Reid Government, made the point even more sharply: 'The stupendous struggle in the East must awake the people of Australia to the fact that we have been living in a fool's paradise … Japan has astonished the world … We now find one of the great naval and military powers within a very short distance of our shores'.[36] A Labor spokesman on defence, Senator George F. Pearce, was equally apprehensive; 'Japan has shown she is an aggressive nation. She has shown that she is desirous of pushing out all round … Is there any other country that offers such a temptation to Japan as Australia does?'[37]

The Australians were not reassured by the British renewal of the Anglo–Japanese alliance in 1905. It was in their view no substitute for a British Pacific fleet. The Liberal prime minister Joseph Cook told the Colonial Office that Australia 'should not be left to

---

[36] *The Herald* (Melbourne), 12 and 13 June 1905.

[37] Commonwealth of Australia, *Parliamentary Debates* (1905 session), vol. XXIX, p. 5346, 22 November 1905.

depend upon the continuance of such a delicate security as an alliance'.[38] So great was the Japanese threat, surpassing as it did all other previous invasion scares, that the political leaders pressed for the introduction of compulsory military training and for the creation of an Australian navy. A National Defence League was formed in November 1905 to persuade the public of the necessity of adopting these measures, and Frank Fox, the editor of the *Lone Hand* who was responsible for serialising 'The Commonwealth Crisis', became the co-editor of the League's journal, the *Call*. Kirmess's work, by rendering a fictional dramatisation of the Japanese menace, made a major contribution to this campaign.

As Kirmess put it in the preface to the book, the novel was meant to rouse the Commonwealth 'to a sense of its danger'. In contrast to Lane and Mackay, he placed his invasion scare not in the distant future but in 1912: 'I know what is possible under the known circumstances of the hour almost, today or tomorrow. And I think if that has no power to compel the citizens of the Commonwealth to seriously consider their position, no dreadful vision of a distant future will'.[39] The prospect of a Japanese invasion was in the air. Japanese merchants, fishermen, tourists and circus performers were reported by the press to be engaged in mapping the country and spying on Australian defences. In early 1907 a rumour was even circulated that Japanese settlers had illegally landed in the Northern Territory and established a little colony.[40]

Though the reviews were overwhelmingly favourable—the Sydney *Bulletin*, *Sydney Morning Herald* and the *Sydney Star* being particularly positive[41]—the influence of the book is hard to gauge. Kirmess, in drawing up a circular to promote his book noted that since its publication, the Commonwealth government had 'hurried forward some vital safety measures', namely legislation to acquire the Northern Territory from South Australia, to introduce compulsory military training and to establish an Australian navy.[42] Yet while ministers and members supporting these bills employed arguments which could have been taken from *The Australian Crisis*, no mention was made of the novel in these debates.[43] Similarly following a tour of Northern Australia in 1913, three senior naval and military officers submitted reports to the Commonwealth Government in which they maintained that Japan posed a major threat to Australia's northern perimeter and that all defence planning should be directed at once and exclusively to counter this grave possibility. If not prevented from gaining a foothold, Japan would use its occupation of northern lands to extort concessions from the Australian and Imperial governments.[44] It was as though

---

[38] Letter, Cook to Governor-General, Lord Denman, enclosed in despatch, Lord Denman to Lewis Harcourt. British Colonial Secretary, 3 March 1914, PRO, C.O. 532/66.

[39] Kirmess, p. 6.

[40] *The Call*, May, 1907).

[41] *Age*, 10 July 1909; *Bulletin*, 17 June 1909; *The Leader*, 5 June 1909; *Star*, 12 July 1909; *Sydney Mail*, 14 July 1909; *Sydney Morning Herald*, 29 May 1909.

[42] Letter, Kirmess to Lothian, 12 October 1909, V.S.L., Ms. 6026.

[43] For example see Commonwealth of Australia, *Parliamentary Debates* (1909 session), vol. LI, pp. 3613–19, 21 September 1909.

[44] 'Secret Report on the Naval Defence of Australia' by Commander W.H. Thring, 5 July 1913, AA MP 1049/13, file 15/854; 'Secret Memorandum by the Chief of the general Staff on the Northern

they had written their reports after reading and digesting the lessons of *The Australian Crisis*. Rather than influencing the politicians or the professional officers Kirmess probably provided no more than a fictional account of what in official circles was becoming the conventional wisdom.

In his novel, Kirmess related how the Japanese Government had secretly despatched a convoy containing soldier settlers to establish a colony on the uninhabited coast of the Northern Territory—just west of Burketown. When eventually the Australian people learnt of this alien occupation, 'there arose the cry from the slopes of the Pacific to Cape Leeuwin, that the Japanese must go'. The Commonwealth Government appealed to London to intercede with the Japanese on their behalf. But the British, preoccupied with combating the German naval challenge, did not wish to offend their ally, and they tacitly accepted Tokyo's explanation that the colony was the work of a private philanthropic organisation which sought to help poor Japanese who were victims of famine. While the Japanese government indicated that it would release these citizens from their allegiance so that they could swear an oath of loyalty to the British Crown, it gave no indication that it would tolerate their forcible expulsion.

The British authorities were in a quandary. They desired to support their Dominion but could not afford to incur Japan's hostility. Since vanquishing Russia, Japan had begun to construct a navy which would 'overawe even the Mistress of the Seas', and by this means it hoped to force the British to accept its position in the Northern Territory.'[45] Though the Royal Navy was still superior to Japan's at the time of the invasion, the Admiralty could not risk sending a significant proportion of its Home Fleet to the Pacific for fear that the remaining elements 'would not be strong enough to guarantee the safety of the Heart of the Empire against the ambitions of European rivals.' Moreover Britain depended on Japan for the protection of its extensive economic and political interests in the Far East.

Australians at first could not but believe that Britain would insist on the Japanese evacuation of the occupied territory: 'There was too much at stake for Great Britain, for Anglo-Saxondom and for White Humanity, to allow of any lukewarmness'.[46] When, however, the British imposed a blockade preventing both parties from having access to the disputed lands, and then arbitrarily proclaimed a protectorate over a greater part of the Northern Territory—and so used the Pax Britannica against British Australia—the Commonwealth recognised that they would have to rely on their own resources to safeguard their national sovereignty. Even their sister dominions, which had initially protested against Britain's failure to support Australia, were induced by financial pressure to turn a blind eye to Australia's predicament.

The British betrayal angered the Australian people. Looking for scapegoats, they found it easy to vent their frustrations on the coloured residents in their midst. In the riots that followed many Asians were lynched. Anticipating the action of the street mobs at the outbreak of World War I, the Chinese quarters of Melbourne were attacked and property

---

Territory of Australia, and its Effects on Local, Naval and Military Preparations' by Brigadier General J.M. Gordon, 16 June 1913, AA B197, file 1855/1/6.

[45] Kirmess, p. 71.

[46] Ibid., pp. 87–88.

destroyed. In the feverish atmosphere, new elections were called. During the campaign Moderates who urged caution were not only silenced but often physically assaulted. The national fabric was unravelling. The Japanese had planted a colony in the Northern Territory, the Commonwealth and State Parliaments had lost their authority, the financial system was in trouble and, after the victory of the extremists in the Eastern States, Western Australia, which did not wish to sever ties with the Mother Country, seceded from the Federation.

Yet while urban Australia was wracked by internal dissension and social disorder, the bushmen, who, living closer to nature, understood better that 'force, brutal force' was in the circumstances the only path to salvation, determined to act. The bushmen 'bore an undying hatred against an enemy who contested the white supremacy and who was doubly loathed because of his inferiority of race, environment and ideal'.[47] They spontaneously formed themselves into an irregular mounted corps—called aptly the White Guard—for the purpose of engaging the intruders. The White Guard relished the elemental nature of their task. The extinction of the invaders was their aim: 'That was after all was said, the only way to punish and to end the intrusion of the alien race on Commonwealth soil.' No quarter would be given or expected in the fight for racial supremacy. Regretfully the Japanese women, like their menfolk, were to be slaughtered. Yet, despite their gallant efforts, the White Guard was defeated by superior Japanese numbers and organisation. Only a handful out of the original 1200 escaped to Darwin to tell the tale.

By the end of 1912 the Commonwealth was left with little choice. The British had no sympathy for the Australian cause; liberal humanitarians were revolted by the ruthless treatment of the Asian residents and conservatives were 'resigned to the thought that Communism—as they termed it—must run its full course in Australia'. They were convinced that 'the helpless and demoralised Commonwealth was now less than ever worth the risk of exposing the Heart of the Empire to danger'. In order to put a stop to Australian provocations, the British government, after consulting the Japanese, demanded that the Northern Territory be handed over to them: to force the issue the British blockaded Australia's main ports and posed a complete boycott on trade, causing depression and riots. The Commonwealth government succumbed to the pressure and accepted the British ultimatum. Under the terms of the agreement the Commonwealth handed over the Northern Territory to Great Britain and received an assurance in return that the Japanese colony would not be granted independence before 1940. As a result, the narrator concluded grandiloquently, 'A truce has been made until 1940 A.D. Until that time White Australia has to prepare itself for a final struggle to determine whether the White or Yellow Race shall gain final supremacy'.[48]

Kirmess's treatment of the consequences of an Asian invasion for political culture was more probing and perceptive than either Lane's or Mackay's. For him, as for the others, the challenge to national survival and integrity created a political crisis and called into question the nature of political community. Parliament, which continued to dispute technical points, to play to party interests and to obstruct necessary action, made itself irrelevant. In the author's view the Long Parliament, by acting in this manner, had brought about the English

---

[47] Ibid., p. 144.

[48] Ibid., pp. 334–36.

Civil War. The United States Congress similarly had allowed Fort Sumter to spark off the American Civil War, and in the French Revolution, the National Convention had made possible the rise of Robespierre's reign of terror.

At one level, Kirmess pursued his analysis as though he was a detached sociological observer, but at another, more fundamental level he was a partisan in the story he unfolded. In the latter role his sympathies were with the triumphant 'Extremist Party' which emerged out of the popular protests against the orthodox parties' timidity and indecision. The Extremists had a pronounced radical bias. They absorbed the Labor Party, which had gained in popularity during the crisis, because it had, from its inception, been unqualifiedly for a White Australia, and had taken a stronger stand than its moderate rival against British domination. Moreover, Labor's policy of paying for national works from income tax and graduated land tax, rather than from British loans, was now seen to be for the common welfare. 'Behind the Government the Labour Party is fighting. None of their responsible leaders would think of taking mean party advantage now. The people outside regard them with friendly eyes. They have always stood for White Australia.'

Caught up in the hysterical urgency of his own story, Kirmess exclaimed 'But, why restate these things? It takes time even to tell the truth and time is precious'. It was as if the author's political reflections, like the politicians' shillyshallying, were an obstacle to the people taking action to save themselves.

Kirmess despaired of parliament, for parliamentarians could not help themselves. It was 'with the best of intentions ... settling down to raise points', and as a result, a whole week was lost. The people, who knew that their existence was at stake, became impatient: 'Outside the people cry with one voice: Dissolution! New elections! The Sovereign of Australia wants to take his fate into his own hands'.[49] At the polls, the Extremists swept away the old party system and achieved a great victory. The Extremists were not properly a new party. They arose at the demand of the people. They incorporated many from the old parties into their ranks. They were elected to represent the whole nation.

In accordance with the 'Legend of the Nineties', Kirmess had envisaged Australia as an idealised community, as Bernard O'Dowd's 'Delos of a coming sun god's race'. But the alien invasion blasted these hopes. Before Australia's

> congenial blue skies a new Greece was arising, a more perfect Athens, scorning slavery and conferring the sacred rights of citizenship upon its entire manhood and womanhood, and which, even as in Athens of old, those deserving citizens had been ostracized who monopolized political favour, would dare to ostracize Old-World monopoly and injustice.

Australia's vision had faltered because Australians had neglected to look to their own defence and relied on others to protect them. Only by assuming this prime responsibility of community would Australia once again be able to recapture the dream, to be 'in the vanguard of humanitarian progress'. For this purpose 'Everyone of thy sons shall be a warrior, everyone of thy daughters a warrior's helpmate ... Then, only then, thou mayst safely continue thy triumphant march. Then thou will enter into thy proud Twentieth Century Nationhood, which will be a joy, not an oppression'.[50]

---

[49] Ibid., pp. 93–97.

[50] Ibid., pp. 312–13.

Yet, even if Kirmess's dream had descended into a nightmare, nevertheless the experience of the Australian crisis clarified much about his good society. Even if some of the consequences of the people assuming their sovereign powers, such as the lynching of Chinese and the destruction of their property and the intimidation and harassment of Moderate Whites, did not altogether merit his approval, they were condoned as a necessary price to be paid for the survival of the good society. The dissolution of the parliament of parties at the behest of street crowds and the creation of a one-party populist state was part of a natural purging and purifying process in the interests of the ideal racial community.

The racial character of the good society can be seen most strikingly in the White Guard. It was the bushmen who, after parliament and politics had failed, epitomised the idealised will of the people and took direct action to save the people. Those who responded to the call were 'the typical Australian: the hardy pioneer who wrestled with and conquered hostile nature and the heart of the Continent, the selectors, stockmen, miners, drovers, carriers and other bushworkers'. Kirmess commented that 'A finer body of men never took the field to do battle for Aryan ideals'. In this portrayal of the White Guard one comes closest to his vision of society. At its core it was neither socialist nor radical. It was first and foremost racial.

Though Kirmess did not acquire either intellectual or political recognition through his writing, nevertheless *The Australian Crisis* did make a profound impact on Frank Fox, the editor of the *Lone Hand*, who was also a leading member of the National Defence League. And it is through Fox that the broader significance of Kirmess's novel can be best understood.

Like Lane, Mackay and Kirmess, Fox embraced the 'Legend of the Nineties'. Born in South Australia in 1874 he had learnt his journalist craft on the *Bulletin*. He was also a friend of Mackay's and shared the latter's idealisation of the bushman as the Australian type.[51] Fox's first book, *Bushman and Buccaneer*, was a defence of or at least an apology for Harry 'The Breaker' Morant, who personified the authentic Australian of Fox's imaginings.

For Fox *The Australian Crisis* was a tract for the times. It addressed some of the most persistent themes running through the *Lone Hand*: the lack of a white population in Northern Australia; the fear of Asia, especially Japan; the suspicion that Britain might not assist Australia to repel a Japanese invasion; and the need for Australia to look to its own defences. Fox had turned the *Lone Hand*, which originally was intended to be a literary adjunct to the *Bulletin*, into a vehicle for his political preoccupations. The first issue contained a story, 'The Secrets of a Prime Minister', presumably written by Fox, the plot of which revolved around the problem of how to deport a 'colony of Asiatics' from the Northern Territory. In August 1908 Fox used the occasion of the visit of the American Fleet to write a homily about Japan, 'the not altogether trusted champion of the Yellow Race', which pursued 'a policy of aggressive Asiatic Imperialism' and challenged 'the long accepted principle of the hegemony of the 'White Race'. If war came, Australia would be 'quite unable' to strike any blow to justify our position as the garrison, the lonely outpost of the White Race in these seas'. In his monthly column he regularly expatiated on the Northern Territory, 'Our Unguarded Gate' which was 'far nearer to the naval bases of Asia

---

[51] See Australian War Memorial Library, Kenneth Mackay papers, PR 87/207.

than to Sydney and Melbourne'. It was 'Australia's fate to be pushed into the van of the certain conflict' since Australia was territorially 'the southern part of Asia, the natural outflow for surplus population'. With British leaders convinced that a war with Germany was inevitable, he wondered whether Britain, in order to keep Japan's goodwill, might put Australia 'into the bidding as a disposable pawn'.[52]

Given Fox's view of Australia's strategic predicament, it was natural that he should have a high opinion of Kirmess' work. In an editorial footnote to the first instalment of Kirmess's 'Commonwealth Crisis', he declared that this 'forecast romance' was 'something more than a novel'. In order to bring it more quickly before the reading public, he had not included illustrations. Fox desired to use the novel to further the cause of national defence. Fox, who had numerous political friends in the ranks of the Labor party and among the radical protectionists (most notably Alfred Deakin), had intended, according to Kirmess, to use his contacts to have the message of 'The Commonwealth Crisis' discussed in the federal parliament at the end of 1908, but the Deakin government had fallen before this could be effected.[53] In March 1909 Fox travelled to London for the purpose of founding a newspaper which would awaken Britain to its responsibilities for the British-settled empire overseas. As part of this campaign he published *Problems of the Pacific*, in which he argued the case that 'The Continent [Australia] must be held by the British race', and that it was 'almost as certain that it must be attacked one day by an Asiatic race'. To bring home the point he summarised the plot of 'The Commonwealth Crisis', commenting that the idea of a 'colonising invasion' of Australia by Japan was quite possible.[54] No other literary work was cited for this purpose.

Though Fox, shortly after his arrival in England, had written to Deakin that 'I look on life here as exile', such provincial nostalgia did not survive the experience of living at the centre of the Empire. He quickly made himself at home in Britain, and with the passage of time his Australian mission withered on the bough. Following the outbreak of the First World War he joined the British army. In the post-war period he became a leading figure in the Imperial Press Association, devoted himself to Imperial causes, and was knighted for services to the Empire. It was as though he had betrayed the land of his birth and the aspirations of the 'Legend of the Nineties'. Indeed it might be considered that when in 1923 he published the novel *Beneath an Ardent Sun*, which was also centred on an Asian invasion of Australia, he was rewriting *The Australia Crisis* to suit his new loyalties and the Empire's new circumstances. In the later work, the Asian invaders were more tactfully 'Cambodians' rather than 'Japanese'. The 'Feverish Party'—the counterpart to the Extremists—stirred up public opinion in favour of the interlopers' forcible eviction. The hero of the story, however—now a Moderate—spoke up for soundness and sense in solving the Australian crisis. Henry Trent 'pricked the government of the day and let out the rank gases of the bombast'. With the support of the bushmen—'for at bottom the Australian has a good fund of sober earnestness'—Trent became Prime Minister. When Britain urged caution

---

[52] *The Lone Hand*, June 1907, p. 179; August 1908, p. 352; November 1908, p. 97; February 1909, p. 470; March 1909, p. 589.

[53] Letter, Kirmess to Lothian, 2 June 1909, Victoria State Library, Ms. 6026.

[54] Frank Fox, *Problems of the Pacific* (London: Williams and Norgate, 1912), pp. 107–99, 252–57.

out of concern for Germany's ambitions in Europe, and a minister denounced Australian jingoism, the cry went up that Britain was ready to betray Australia and sacrifice the White Australia policy.[55] Trent, however, stood fast and refused to be pushed into a confrontation with the Mother Country. Instead he set out on a compromise path which would 'secure all that is necessary for the safety and racial purity of Australia … without being offensive to a chivalrous, friendly nation'.[56] His quiet diplomacy was very successful. The 'Cambodians' were cooperative and the Commonwealth helped finance their repatriation.[57] The crisis faded away almost as quickly as it had appeared. Statesmanlike leadership had reconciled British and Australian interests, and the British Empire emerged from the ordeal stronger than ever.

Lane, Mackay and Fox seemed over their lifetime to have moved from a belief in Australian nationalism to a commitment to British race patriotism and the British Empire. In explaining this transformation it would be easy to say either that they simply became conservative with age, or that they were seduced by the hope of imperial recognition and distinction. But such a reading misses what was most important about the 'Legend of the Nineties'. Lane, Mackay and Fox did not betray an exclusive Australian national dream. The assertion of Australian independence in these novels derived not so much from a search for an autonomous nation based on a bush idyll or a utopian ideal, as from resentment at Britain's rejection of the British Australians. Even the most reluctant of the three, Kenneth Mackay, was firm that Australia must declare it independence if Britain vetoed the colonies' immigration laws, and so threatened the British character of their society. As they worked through these problems in changing personal and international circumstances, they all came to equate the good community with the British 'race', though in this respect it is worth noting that the most conservative, Mackay, was the least passionate about his Britishness. The upshot was not so much a recantation of an earlier vision embodied in the 'Legend of the Nineties' as the realisation of its more fundamental meaning, that of race.

For Australians at the end of the nineteenth century and in the early twentieth century the great social and political question was the defining of the good community. The novelists were unwittingly engaged in working out through their invasion scare stories the issues surrounding this question. They employed their imagination to explore the consequences flowing from a crisis brought on by the prospect of Asian invasion. At the end of it all it was clear that the religion of race as culture was more important than respect for traditional institutions or the rights of man. In the hour of national peril there was no room for diversity or dissent. The Anti-Chinese League, and even more Hatton's Rangers and the White Guard—the forerunners in a sense of C.E.W. Bean's Anzacs, Jack Lang's Labor movement and Eric Campbell's New Guard—personified the heroic values of the 'Legend of the Nineties'. Frank Fox in 1926, after the social disorders of the Great Strike in England, took up the old questions in a book entitled *Parliamentary Government: A Failure*.[58] Once

---

[55] Frank Fox, *Beneath an Ardent Sun* (London : Hodder and Stoughton: 1923), pp. 119–24.

[56] Ibid., p. 166.

[57] Ibid., pp. 285–6.

[58] Frank Fox, *Parliamentary Government: A Failure* (London: Stanley, Paul & Co, 1928). See especially chapters III and VII.

again, in a crisis, parliament had failed the people. Parliament was inherently corrupt, and unless there was reform the British Empire, like the Roman Empire before it, would die of 'bread and circus' politics. He looked to the example of Italian Fascism adapted to the British tradition to find the answer. The new Fascist principle which he wished Britain to accept was that 'the governance of a self-respecting community can be organised on the basis of setting up as the primary assumption the duty of the individual to serve the community not the right of the people to share in the community'. The attraction of Fascism for Fox was not so much a product of his conversion to British Imperialism as an adaptation to new circumstances of the Australian 'Legend of the Nineties'.

D.H. Lawrence, in bringing fresh eyes to bear on Australia at the end of World War I, perceived that the central problem of the country and its political culture was community. In a new society it could not be taken for granted. As British settlers built new cities and farms and civilised the land, so they felt a need to find community. In his novel *Kangaroo*, Lawrence's two protagonists, Willie Struthers, the socialist leader, and *Kangaroo*, the nationalist leader, were locked in battle over different conceptions of community. Both sought, in Lawrentian language, 'the new ties between men, in the new democracy ... the new passional bond in the new society'. *Kangaroo* offered the continuation of the A.I.F. camaraderie; for Lawrence's Diggers 'the war was the only time they felt properly alive'. Struthers on the other hand offered a class community, a socialist community based on the solidarity of labour. But even when united with the world's workers in spirit, Struthers assured his followers that this would not mean they would 'take the hearts out of our chests to give it to Brown Brother to eat. No, Brown Brother and Brother Yellow had on the whole best stop at home and sweep their own streets rather than come and sweep ours'.[59]

What then these novels have suggested is that race, viewed as culture as well as colour, was the common denominator informing the Australian vision of the good society contained in the 'Legend of the Nineties', and that 'race' in this same sense was its most important and enduring legacy.

---

[59] D.H. Lawrence, *Kangaroo* (London, W. Heinemann: 1923), pp. 218–9, 341–54.

6

The End of 'White Australia' and Australia's Changing Perceptions of Asia, 1945–1990[1]

This paper attempts to explore a central, if strangely neglected, question in Australian history, namely, how the Federation's ideal of 'White Australia' and its perception of Asia as the alien other have in the last two decades come to be discarded and replaced by the notion of the 'multicultural' society and Australia as integrally part of Asia and prospectively a 'Eurasian' nation.

Though this change represents the transformation of what for three generations had been the absolute orthodoxy of national existence, historians have made little effort to account for this transmogrification. Perhaps most contemporary scholars feel so antipathetic to 'White Australia' that the abolition of racial discrimination and Asia-phobia is seen as natural, inevitable and long overdue. Perhaps at this level many share the view of one of my students who, when asked about the question, declared that by abandoning 'White Australia' Australians had at last been able to purge themselves of their guilty consciences. But such an ahistorical approach to the subject will not do, for those who eagerly espoused 'White Australia' did so on racial principles which, they believed, were also moral principles. The major treatments of the subject, whether approving or disapproving, have demonstrated that the authors of Australia's racially-discriminating policy advanced moral arguments, among others, to justify their position.[2] Indeed, it should be borne in mind that the same kinds of public figures, namely academics, clergymen, creative artists and social reformers who, acting as the conscience of the nation, have since 1945 been in the forefront of the struggle to overturn 'White Australia', were at the time of its adoption to be found defending the moral character of 'White Australia'. There can be no plausible Whig history of progress which can link that past with this present. There are no heroes who from the beginning of 'White Australia' fought against great odds and so brought us to this point, unless possibly they are members of the International Workers of the World (IWW) or the Australian Communist Party, and it would be a brave soul indeed who argued that case. The common clues to a historical question are missing. Without any great disturbance to the social and cultural fabric, and within a relatively short period of time, Australian ideas

---

[1] This essay was given as a paper at the Conference on 'Australia and the End of Overseas Empires 1945–75', at the Sir Robert Menzies Centre for Australian Studies (London, 29–30 April 1994). It was originally published as 'The End of "White Australia" and Australia's Changing Perceptions of Asia, 1945-1990', *Australian Journal of International Affairs*, 49 (November, 1995), pp. 171–90.

[2] Myra Willard, *History of the While Australia Policy* (Melbourne: Melbourne University Press, 1923); Humphrey McQueen, *A New Britannia* (Harmondswarth: Penguin, 1970); A.T. Yarwood, *Asian Migration to Australia: The Background to Exclusion, 1896–1923* (Melbourne: Melbourne University Press, 1964); Charles Price, *The Great White Walls are Built: Restrictive Immigration to North America and Australasia, 1836–1888* (Canberra: Australian Institute of International Affairs in association with Australian National University Press, 1974); Andrew Markus, *Fear and Hatred: Purifying Australia and California, 1850–1907* (Sydney: Hale and lremonger, 1979).

of Asia and of race and, as a consequence, of Australia itself, have undergone a remarkable metamorphosis.

Charles Henry Pearson, the End of Empire and 'White Australia'

The departure point for this study is Charles Henry Pearson's *National Life and Character: A Forecast* which was published one hundred years ago just as the cause of 'White Australia' was gaining momentum and which both anticipated the end of European empires and provided an insight into the new forces bringing about a racially exclusive view of society and the 'White Australia' policy. In 1871 Pearson, an Anglo-Australian intellectual, resigned his Chair in Modern History at King's College in the University of London and migrated to Australia where he became a leading figure in the political and cultural life of the colony of Victoria. *National Life and Character,* which he wrote at the end of his public career, was a wide ranging investigation of tendencies in modern social thought based on his colonial experience. The work, in both the kind of issues canvassed and the level of analysis achieved, was not unlike Alexis de Tocqueville's *Democracy in America*, and it made an impact in English-speaking countries, eliciting responses from such eminent personages as W.E. Gladstone, Theodore Roosevelt and Henry Adams.[3] His most notable prediction, which for the time was almost unthinkable and attracted most attention, was that Asian, African and South American people would in due time free themselves from European domination and compel their former imperial masters to accept them as powers to be reckoned with in the international community. As he put it:

> The day will come, and perhaps is not far distant, when the European observer will look round to see the globe girdled with a continuous zone of the black and yellow races, no longer too weak for aggression or under tutelage, but independent, or practically so, in government, monopolising the trade of their own regions, and circumscribing the industry of the European; when Chinamen and the nations of Hindostan, the States of Central and South America, by that time predominantly Indian, and it may be African nations of the Congo and the Zambesi ... are represented by fleets in the European seas, invited to international conferences, and welcomed as allies in the quarrels of the civilised world ... We were struggling among ourselves for supremacy in a world which we thought of as destined to belong to the Aryan races and to the Christian faith ... We shall wake to find ourselves elbowed and hustled, and perhaps even thrust aside by peoples whom we looked down upon as servile, and thought of as bound always to administer to our needs.[4]

Pearson was, like de Tocqueville, a European intellectual aristocrat reflecting on the future from the vantage point of lessons learnt in the New World but, unlike his French precursor, Pearson had become part of that world and did to a large extent identify himself with its democratic homogeneity, state socialism and race patriotism. He had come to see

---

[3] John Tregenza, *Professor of Democracy: The Life of Charles Henry Pearson, 1830–1894, Oxford Don and Australian Radical* (Melbourne: Melbourne University Press, 1968), pp. 231–32.

[4] Charles Henry Pearson, *National Life and Character: A Forecast* (London: Macmillan, 1894), 2nd edn, pp. 89–90.

the Australian colonies as the pioneers of the modern and the embodiment of the future. 'Nevertheless, it is', he wrote, 'surely safe to say, that political experiments which half a dozen self-governing British communities are instinctively adopting, deserve attention as an indication of what we may expect in the future'.[5] While this product of mid-nineteenth century English liberalism could, like de Tocqueville, ponder the coming order of things with a certain detachment, it is clear also that he had in Victoria surrendered much of his elitist, cosmopolitan and individualist beliefs and associated himself with the new movements and sensibilities appearing in Australian political culture. Thus after predicting the rise of the 'coloured' races he had to admit that, 'Yet in some of us the feeling of caste is so strong that we are not sorry to think that we shall have passed away before that day arrives'.[6]

Pearson gave little attention to the implications of the emergence of independent Asian, African and South American states for Australia and its immigration policy. His view would seem to have been that these states would be restricted to their natural habitat, the tropical regions spreading north and south from the equator, and that the Europeans would retain their position in the temperate zone. Since climate would determine the geopolitical division of the races, Australia was a marginal case. For him the Australians were 'guarding the last part of the world, in which the higher races can live and increase freely, for the higher Civilisation'. And in this context, 'The fear of Chinese immigration which the Australian democracy cherishes, and which Englishmen at home find it hard to understand, is, in fact, the instinct of self-preservation, quickened by experience'.[7] Pearson, as a product of a classical not a national education, considered that the failure of the Australians to so guard national existence would be a loss to 'the whole civilised world'. The cause of British Australia was the cause of what A.J. Toynbee was later to call 'the West'. It was therefore his conclusion that 'whatever extends the influence of those races that have taken their faith from Palestine, their laws of beauty from Greece, and their civil law from Rome, ought to be a matter of rejoicing to Russian, German, Anglo-Saxon, and Frenchman alike'.[8]

Yet at the same time Pearson was justifying the Australian actions against the Chinese as a defence of 'the White Race' and Western values, he was also describing the growth of an intense social bonding which was stirring powerful feelings of 'patriotism' or nationalism. Though he did not himself make the connection, this new 'race patriotism' might, more than any other factor, explain why the British Australians had become so greatly sensitive towards and irrationally fearful of the Chinese, and why within three years of the publication of *National Life and Character*, the colonial premiers agreed to enact legislation barring the entry of all 'coloured' people into the country. Pearson claimed that, in contrast to earlier times when people had a first loyalty to a city or tribe or liege lord or dynastic family, 'Patriotism' was

> now the feeling that binds together people who are of the same race [in this usage, common at the time, meaning 'nation'], or who at least inhabit the same country, so that they shall try to preserve the body politic ... It enjoins the sacrifice of

---

[5] *National Life and Character*, p. 19.

[6] *National Life and Character*, p. 90.

[7] *National Life and Character*, p. 17.

[8] *National Life and Character*, pp. 14–15, 17.

property, liberty, or life for the attainment of these objects. It favours the existence of whatever is peculiar and local; of a distinctive literature, manners, dress, and character. When it conceives the common country to be weak, it tries to discard every foreign element as dangerous.

Furthermore, he added that 'it is essential to the perpetuity of this sentiment that the nation should be homogeneous'.[9] In qualifying 'of the same race' with 'or who at least inhabit the same country', it is probable that Pearson was attempting to account for the phenomenon of the Australian colonists who, though part of the British 'race', also shared a peculiar sense of social solidarity and identity. Because of their proximity to Asia, this led them in defence of a White British Australia to oppose all 'coloured' migration and even to threaten a break with the Mother Country should the Imperial authorities attempt to block these aspirations.

The Establishing of 'White Australia' and the Fear of Japan

'White Australia', as Pearson had forecast, became a foundation policy of the Federal union, a fundamental principle of national life. The social trauma created by rapid modernisation at the end of the nineteenth century caused the mass democracy to seek security in a homogeneous community of interchangeable and indistinguishable individuals. And race became the badge of all that was familiar and the barrier against all that was foreign. When an individual Chinese was able to assimilate himself completely into British Australia, he could be accepted, even popular. Mei Quong Tart, a wealthy Sydney merchant, had grown up in a European family and become a Christian. He was naturalised in 1871 and in 1899 volunteered to fight for Queen and Empire in the Boer War. He was much in demand on festive occasions to sing Scottish airs and he was, according to the native-born Scotsman George Reid, 'the only man living who has got the true original Gaelic accent'. On his death in 1903 the Mayor of Ashfield had the flag on the Town Hall lowered to half-mast and forty of his fellow Masons and many other notables attended the funeral.[10] Tart was being honoured for having rid himself, or so it seemed to White Australians, of all marks of his Chinese culture and taken on a persona which made him one with the British colonists. But Tart's case was highly unusual. In general skin colour difference was an absolute impediment to inclusion.

Those colonists who were most disturbed by the modernising of society and looked to a collectivist spirit to make them whole were the most fervent advocates of 'White Australia'. The Labor party which came into being simultaneously with the movement for racial exclusion made 'The Maintenance of White Australia' the first plank on its 'fighting' and 'General Platform'.[11] William Lane, the socialist visionary, declared that the colonists'

---

[9] *National Life and Character*, pp. 197–99 and 200.

[10] Mrs Quong Tart, comp. and ed., *The Life of Quong Tart, or, How a Foreigner Succeeded in a British Community* (Sydney: W.M. Maclardy, 1911), especially pp. 5–17, 25–45 and 84–91.

[11] This was also the case on the West Coast of the United States. Alexander P. Saxton in *The Indispensable Enemy: Labor and the Anti-Chinese Movement in California* (Berkeley: University of California Press, 1971), especially chapters 6 and 7, shows that it was opposition to the Chinese which brought into being the Workingmen's Party, its prime objective being the halting of all

effort to oust the Chinese was 'more than a social or national movement ... it is a true racial struggle'. Lane envisaged Australia being engaged in a conflict which was at once racial and moral. The Chinese were grossly sensual and given to unspeakable vices. To protect the purity of the White race it was necessary not only to prevent more Chinese from entering the colonies but also to evict those who were already polluting Australia. In the conclusion to his novel 'White or Yellow? A Story of the Race War of A.D. 1908', after the Europeans in Queensland had vanquished the race enemy in a bitter civil war, they sent the surviving Chinese north 'like great droves of cattle' and expelled them from the country 'as fast as fear could drive and ships could carry'.[12]

In the debate, however, over the 1901 Immigration Restriction Bill which became the basis for the enforcement of the 'White Australia' policy, all sides of the Parliament defended the principle in racial terms. J.C. Watson, the first national leader of the Labor party, declared that 'the objection I have to the mixing of these coloured people with the white people of Australia ... lies in the main in the possibility and probability of racial contamination'. The Protectionist Prime Minister, Edmund Barton, and his Attorney-General, Alfred Deakin, put essentially the same view. Citing Pearson's *National Life and Character*, Barton warned that unless the Commonwealth kept out all 'coloured' people, Australia would eventually be overwhelmed by immigrants 'of an inferior race', and he did not think that 'the doctrine of the equality of man was really ever intended to include racial equality'. Deakin, a former colleague of Pearson, also addressed the issues in the language of his friend's thesis: 'We here find ourselves touching the profoundest instinct of individual or nation—the instinct of self-preservation—for it is nothing less than the national manhood, the national character, and the national future that are at stake'.[13] Asia became the spectre haunting the Australian imagination. In 1908 Deakin, then prime minister, drawing once again on Pearson highlighted national anxieties about Asia and the menace of the 'Yellow Peril' to 'White Australia'. Replying to Richard Jebb who had sent him a paper on Asian immigration, Deakin declared that there was 'nothing worthy of recollection prior to it except Pearson's splendid volume on National Character when the first note of alarm was sounded'. And he informed Jebb that Australians were looking forward to welcoming the visit of America's 'Great White Fleet' to their shores first and foremost 'because of our distrust of the Yellow races in the North Pacific and our recognition of the *entente cordiale* spreading among all white men who realise the Yellow Peril to Caucasian civilization, creeds and politics'.[14]

By the time of the inauguration of the Commonwealth the heightened awareness of Asia had produced a settled consensus that Australia should be a homogeneous white British nation and that the strictest measures should be taken to protect society against the

Chinese immigration.

[12] *Boomerang*, 27 April and 5 May 1888.

[13] Commonwealth of Australia, *Parliamentary Debates* (1901–1902 session), vol. IV, p. 4633, 6 September 1901 andvol. IV, p. 5233, 26 September 1901; vol. III, p. 3503, 7 August 1901; and vol. IV, p. 4804, 12 September 1901.

[14] Letter, Deakin to Jebb, 4 June 1908, Deakin–Jebb Correspondence, National Library of Australia 339/1/19A–B.

inter-mixture of 'coloured' peoples. The policy of 'White Australia' was, as W.K. Hancock expressed it in *Australia*, 'the indispensable condition of every other Australian policy',[15] and so it remained until the end of the 1960s.

Until World War II, Australians perceived Japan as the chief and almost only source of Asian threat to the national ideal. The Western empires in the region, the United States in the Philippines, the French in Indochina, the British in Malaya, the Dutch in the East Indies, and the Portuguese in Timor, secured the immediate near North. China was in a chronic state of internal disorder, subject to Western influence and humiliated by Japan. Though Australians mentioned frequently and with some apprehension the prospect of 'the awakening of China' it was not regarded as a threat. On the other hand Japan's modernisation and its military domination of the Western Pacific made it a power to be reckoned with. Japan was the first non-European state to achieve what Pearson had predicted. It was the first such state to be 'invited to international conferences, and welcomed as allies in the quarrels of the civilised world'. Following Japan's defeat of Russia, the first victory of an Asian nation over a European one, all Australians' fears about Asia and the 'Yellow Peril' came to be focused on that country. Australian leaders felt that Japan might take advantage of its new status and capability in a time of European division to demand concessions over 'White Australia'. Deakin in writing of Australia's 'distrust of the Yellow races in the North Pacific' had Japan specifically in mind.

During World War I there was great concern about how Japan, even as Britain's ally, would act and there were good grounds for Australian suspicion. The frequent visits of Japanese naval squadrons were a vivid reminder of the reality of the 'Yellow Peril'. Commenting on one such visit to Sydney in 1916, W.E. Boote, the editor of the *Australian Worker*, wrote his brother: 'Great feting of visiting Japanese in town. Crowds of them are in the streets. Australians will never mix with them. One look at these Japanese ... is enough to spoil the blend', and he confessed that he would 'sooner have the Kaiser here than the Mikado'.[16] At the Paris Peace Conference in 1919 the Australian Prime Minister, Billy Hughes, in opposing Japan's wish to include a racial equality clause in the League no Nations Covenant was acknowledging these fears which he fully shared.

Japan's success during World War II in seizing the West's colonial possessions nevertheless came as a great shock. The British Empire's victory in World War I had helped to repair Australia's confidence in the ability of Britain and the other Western powers to act as a *cordon sanitaire* between Japan and Australia and to provide a guarantee against 'the swarming hordes of Asia'. Australia happily accepted British assurances that the Singapore base was impregnable. Thus when the Japanese rapidly overran the Philippines, French Indochina, the Dutch East Indies, Portuguese Timor and, most of all, British Malaya, and Japanese naval and military forces arrived on the Commonwealth's own frontiers, it was clear to the Curtin Labor government that Australia had been mistaken in placing their trust in the European empires.

Yet this shock did not cause them to undertake a thorough reappraisal of the given assumptions. They did not read the signs of the times aright. They did not grasp that the

---

[15] W.K. Hancock, *Australia* (London: E. Benn, 1930), p. 66.

[16] M.E. Lloyd, ed., *Sidelights on Two Referendums, 1916–1917* (Sydney: William Brooks, 1952), p. 43.

Japanese routing of the Europeans would have radical consequences for the future of Asia. Rather, they expected that after Japan's surrender the old regional order would be restored and, accordingly, Dr H.V. Evatt, Australia's masterful External Affairs Minister, sought to counteract the evident weakness of the European colonies by establishing Australian bases in the archipelagoes to its North and Northeast, in the Dutch East Indies, Portuguese Timor and French New Caledonia. Through such a strategy Australia would be able more directly to use the European possessions against a resurgent Japan. To meet the problem Evatt proposed 'the formation of a great Southwest Pacific zone of security against aggression' in which Australia 'would act with such colonial powers as Holland, France and Portugal, as well as with the United States and Great Britain'.[17]

When, however, following the end of the war it became clear that anti-colonial movements stimulated by the Japanese were bent on shaking off imperial shackles and that the European powers would not be able to suppress them, the Australian government pursued policies aimed at producing pro-Western regimes in the newly-independent Asian nations and at keeping the former European metropolitans associated with their former colonies. The Chifley Labor government recognised that the anti-colonial movement, immediately evident in the Indonesian struggle against the Dutch, presaged a new and unpredictable regional environment 'South East Asia is so full of explosive possibilities', John Burton, an official of the External Affairs Department, wrote Evatt in October 1945,

> that only fairly drastic remedies applied will now have any hope of successfully resolving the situation by meeting the legitimate demands of the native peoples whilst at the same time preserving some order and stability by permitting the return of the previous administration, experienced and skilled in handling these peoples.[18]

Evatt speaking on the independence movement in the East Indies in November 1946 likewise declared that '[o]ur idea is that Dutch sovereignty should not be terminated, but that the people of Indonesia should obtain a substantial measure of self-government'.[19] Australia approved wholeheartedly the Dutch-Indonesian Linggadjati Agreement of March 1947 which embodied these principles, and which provided for an Indonesian federation within a Netherlands-Indonesian union that controlled foreign, defence and even some aspects of economic policy. It was only the Dutch attempt to impose their will on the Indonesians in violation of the spirit of the Linggadjati Treaty that caused the Australians to begin espousing the Indonesian cause in the United Nations. The Australians realised that the Indonesians could not be coerced into submission, that that was no way to achieve a stable Southeast Asia. Even so their efforts were directed to obtaining a peace along the lines of the March 1947 agreement and one which would keep the Dutch associated with the Indonesians. Indeed Australia, even as it was pressing for Indonesian self-government,

---

[17] *Daily Telegraph*, 18 August 1943.

[18] Cable, Burton to Evan, 14 October 1945 in Department of Foreign Affairs and Trade, *Documents on Australian Foreign Policy, 1917–49* (Canberra: Australian Government Publishing Service, 1989), vol. VIII, p. 500.

[19] Commonwealth of Australia, *Parliamentary Debates*, House of Representatives, vol. 189, p. 339, 15 November 1946.

was seeking Dutch cooperation in fulfilling its post-war plans for forward defence against a dangerous Asia. On the eve of the signing of the Linggadjati Agreement, Burton had asked the Netherlands government to allow Australia to establish a military base in Dutch New Guinea and to administer Dutch Timor.[20] In the aftermath of World War II, Evatt spoke of Australia's sense of loneliness as the trustee for British civilisation in the South Pacific, and the Chifley government endeavoured to persuade the United States to join with Britain and Australia in a mutual defence scheme for the region. But through the late 1940s all the Labor government's efforts in this direction were in vain.

Australia's conditional support for Asian independence movements did not, however, herald a softening of the 'White Australia' policy. Indeed, in the immediate uncertainties of the post-war era Australia's attitude towards Asian immigration tended to harden. Arthur Calwell, the Minister for Immigration, looked towards boosting the nation's population in order to ensure 'Australia's security, economic stability and destiny as a major Pacific power'. In justifying his ambitious aim of attracting 70,000 new migrants annually, he spoke the language of 'Populate or Perish' which had been the rhetoric of the 'Yellow Peril' doctrine since the 1890s. The Japanese downward thrust into the South Pacific 'when Australia faced its gravest peril' was held up as a warning. 'Armies recruited from the teeming millions of Japanese threatened to overrun our cities and broad hinterland. They were so many. We were so few.' It was Australia's duty, he said, employing Pearson's word, to 'guard' against new armed conflicts.[21] This new program, because of the urgency of the task, proposed to offer assistance to migrants from Continental Europe as well as the United Kingdom, though it was hoped that there would be only one 'foreigner' for every ten Britons, and that the 'foreigners' would be quickly assimilated into a White British Australia. At the same time Calwell applied the 'White Australia' policy more rigorously and inhumanely than ever before, denying Filipinos, Indonesians and Japanese the right to live with their Australian spouses in Australia.

Calwell proudly announced that 'so long as the Labor party remains in power, there will be no watering down of the White Australia policy'.[22] At the San Francisco Conference which drew up the Charter for the United Nations, Evatt was as assiduous as Hughes had been in 1919 in striving to prevent the international organisation from being able to interfere with matters of domestic jurisdiction, especially a state's control over immigration policy. This was essential for without such a specific exclusion he feared that

> it would be possible for an Asiatic Power to object to our migration Policy and if it could be shown that a threat to peace had arisen the Security Council could proceed to recommend a settlement involving change in our Migration Policy as a condition necessary to remove the threat to peace.[23]

---

[20] Margaret George, *Australia and the Indonesian Revolution* (Melbourne: Melbourne University Press in association with the Australian Institute of International Affairs, 1980), p. 74.

[21] Commonwealth of Australia, *Parliamentary Debates*, House of Representatives, vol. 189, pp. 502–03, 22 November 1946.

[22] *Sydney Morning Herald*, 24 March 1949.

[23] Cable, Frank Forde and Evatt to Chifley, 18 May 1945, *Documents on Australian Foreign Policy, 1945*, vol. 8, p. 169.

The Western Presence in Cold War Asia and the Maintenance of a Homogeneous British Australia

During the 1950s and 1960s these concerns about external interference in Australia's immigration policy took palpable form as a movement against racism, inspired by international revulsion against Nazi Germany and Third World resentment against European arrogance, gathered pace. Australians, as never before, were exposed to world opinion, and politicians, diplomats, academics, business people and trade unionists at meetings of the United Nations, the International Labour Organisation and the Commonwealth of Nations and in many other international forums encountered the hostility of the emerging nations, most notably the Asian nations, to the 'White Australia' policy. Indeed, even at home some public figures, mainly academics and church leaders, in various degrees influenced by the international critique of racism, began to agitate for a modification of Australia's colour bar, and at the end of the 1950s an Immigration Reform Group was formed with the modest aim of persuading the Commonwealth to admit 1,500 non-European immigrants annually.[24] And the authorities did make some concession to these pressures. R.G. Menzies' Liberal-Country Party government administered the restrictive policy somewhat more humanely and flexibly than their predecessors, especially in the categories of family reunion and political refugees. They also allowed non-Europeans who had been resident in Australia for fifteen years to apply for naturalisation, and admitted some 'distinguished and highly qualified non-Europeans for indefinite stay'. Furthermore in 1958, the government revised the 1901 Act, removing the dictation test, which as a method of exclusion had proved to be an embarrassment, and left the decision over entry solely to the discretion of the minister.

But despite these modifications, the fundamentals of the 1901 policy remained in place and both sides of parliament, supported by a substantial national consensus, still openly avowed their allegiance to the established view. The parliamentary debate over the new Act was notable for its lack of interest in the issue of Asian migration. The Labor opposition's criticism of the government was not directed towards their policy on Asian migration but rather at their failure to preserve the British character of the country. It attacked the government for allowing too many non-British Europeans into the migration program. Evatt told Menzies that Australia 'will be and must be primarily a British community'. Clyde Cameron, who was to become minister for immigration in Whitlam's second Labor government, similarly affirmed Labor's belief 'in keeping Australia British', true to 'the British tradition of freedom and equality under the law'.[25] A British White Australia was necessary to preserve the core of Australia's political culture, which was a British inheritance.

During the early years of the next decade, as a result of the growing influence of the newly-independent Asian and African nations, the campaign against racism gathered added momentum. South Africa, because of its apartheid policy, was forced to resign from

---

[24] Kenneth Rivett (ed.) for Immigration Reform Group, *Immigration: Control or Colour Bar? The Background to White Australia and a Proposal for Change* (Melbourne: Melbourne University Press, 1962).

[25] Commonwealth of Australia, *Parliamentary Debates,* House of Representatives, vol. 18, p. 115, 27 February 1958; and House of Representatives, vol. 21, pp. 1256–57, 16 September 1958.

the Commonwealth of Nations, and the UN adopted a 'Declaration on the Elimination of All Forms of Racial Discrimination'. While Australia joined in denouncing South Africa's racial laws and gave its unqualified approval to the UN Declaration it was nevertheless unable to silence the critics of its 'restrictive' immigration policy. The American and Canadian governments' decisions to remove race bias from their immigration laws placed further pressure upon Australia.[26] Moreover, Australia's increased involvement in Asia—its dependence on Japan as a market for its primary exports and its military commitments in Southeast Asia—heightened its sensitivity to the issue.

Consequently, after Harold Holt succeeded Menzies as Prime Minister in early 1966, the Australian government initiated a substantial review of immigration policy and introduced two major reforms in the administration of existing policy. First, they put non-European residents on the same basis as Europeans for the purpose of the qualifying period for citizenship and secondly, and more importantly, applications from non-Europeans were to be considered on the grounds of 'their ability to integrate readily' and their possession of attributes and skills 'positively useful to Australia'. Hubert Opperman, the Minister for Immigration, conceded that as a result of the reforms 'the number of non-Europeans settling in Australia would be somewhat greater than previously'. The parliamentary debate which ensued—though it was not strictly a debate since both sides agreed on the reforms—had a rather different tone from that of the 1950s. On this occasion the chief speakers for all parties either made no mention of 'White Australia' or disavowed the phrase as a proper description of Australia's immigration policy. The Labor and Country party members were proud to say that the term had been expunged from their respective organisations' platforms. Furthermore, while there were very few references to British Australia nearly every speech touched on Australia's relations with Asia.[27] Holt summed up the matter when he declared in introducing his new government's policy that it was

> Australia's increasing involvement in Asian developments, the rapid growth of our trade with Asian countries, our participation on a larger scale in an increasing number of aid projects in the area, the considerable number of Asian students … receiving education in Australia, the expansion of our military effort, the scale of diplomatic contact, and the growth of tourism to and from the countries of Asia which made it desirable for Australia to review its immigration procedures.[28]

---

[26] In 1964 the Democratic Party platform promised 'to eliminate discrimination based upon race and place of origin' from America's immigration law, and in the following year, after the Democrats' victory in the election, Congress passed an act which abolished the existing national and racial quotas and went far towards fulfilling the party's pledge. See Lawrence Fuchs, *The American Kaleidoscope: Race, Ethnicity and the Civic Culture* (Hanover, New Hampshire: Wesleyan University Press, 1990), p. 233.

[27] It should, however, be noted that all the measures favouring British migrants were not affected by the changes, and the Department of Immigration in a briefing document for the minister in 1965 laid it down that British migration 'has been and will remain a cornerstone of Australia's rapid population building', that 'the British connection has the first interest of the government'. Cited by R.T. Appleyard, 'Post-War British Immigration' in James Jupp, ed., *The Australian People: An Encyclopedia of the Nation, Its People and Their Origins* (North Ryde, NSW: Angus and Robertson, 1988), p. 100.

[28] Commonwealth of Australia, *Parliamentary Debates*, House of Representatives, vol. 50, p. 34, 8

Yet both government and opposition stressed that these reforms were not a deviation from or a rejection of past policy. As the prime minister expressed it Australia's 'basic policy has been firmly established since the beginning of our Federation'. It had community support, and all that the government had in mind was to administer the policy 'with a spirit of humanity and with good sense'.[29] The minister for immigration assured the house that 'the basic aim of preserving a homogeneous population will be maintained'.[30] The foundation policy was not now defined overtly in racial terms but in those for which, in a sense, race had served as a crude shorthand, namely a homogeneous society. In the 1966 debate nearly all speakers emphasised this point—some alluding to the need to avoid 'Little Rocks' in Australia. Settlers had to be assimilated. They had to 'fit in'. They had to be absorbable. Since this objective assumed an essentially mono-cultural, if not an absolutely monochrome, society, it meant that Australians still viewed their nation as a community, sharing one heritage of language, law, religion and mores, that is, a predominantly White British Australia. Insofar as there was change and colour was separated from culture they were, figuratively speaking, contemplating the possibility of having more Quong Tarts in their midst. Bill Snedden, Minister for Immigration in 1968, anticipating an alternative that was beginning to creep up on the country, asserted that the new immigration policy was 'certainly not a policy which is directed towards the creation of a multi-racial society'.[31] *Plus ça change, plus c'est la même chose.* Australia even down to the end of the 1960s held to Pearson's view that the arrival of the Asian, African and South American states on the international stage need have no deleterious consequences for Australia's national ideal.

Why was this so? Why did Australians believe that they could with a few cosmetic measures avert the international community's critical gaze from their immigration policy and escape being treated, like South Africa, as a pariah nation? Why did they not understand the necessity of a more radical change if they wished to avoid giving offence to the newly emerging nations? In answer it has to be allowed that this racially conditioned Australian policy was deeply rooted in the Federation's history and that the very generation which was being challenged from outside had been brought up in that tradition knowing no alternative. Thus the forces for change had to overcome powerful domestic resistance. Similarly, Australians could with some plausibility believe that they would not have to face the fate of South Africa since the major criticisms were directed not at a pattern of discrimination against Asians and Africans within the country but at the rules governing the admission of settlers into the country. These arguments, however, do not in themselves seem adequate to account for why Australians in the 1950s and 1960s did not take more seriously the hostility to the 'White Australia' policy, especially from Asia.

Another factor which would appear to be more important in explaining why Australia felt able to resist the pressures for change was the protection afforded Australia by a formidable

---

March 1966.

[29] Ibid.

[30] Ibid., p. 69, 9 March 1966.

[31] Cited in Kenneth Rivett, ed., *Australia and the Non-White Migrant* (Melbourne: Melbourne University Press, 1975), p. 31.

Western presence in the region. In these two decades the contraction of European empires was more than matched by the expansion of Western influence in Asia and the Pacific as the 'Free World' sought to contain communism and the Sino-Soviet bloc. Consequently, Australia as a partner of the United States and United Kingdom and, to a lesser extent, France was more secure than at any time in its history. Australians could implicitly believe that this partnership, institutionalised through ANZUS, ANZAM and SEATO, provided them with a stronger defence against alien Asia and gave them a more certain guarantee for their British tradition than in any previous period.

R.G. Casey, External Affairs Minister for most of the 1950s, in reflecting on Australian foreign policy towards the end of his stint in office, warned of how World War II had 'demonstrated our new weakness', the threat from Asia to Australian survival. He noted that Australia could not have held out for long 'as a lone outpost of democracy in the Pacific if Britain and then America had been defeated'. Through its history Australia had not been able to rely on its own strength, 'but principally on combined efforts with our friends'. In the post-war years, 'Even without the threat of Communist expansion from the north, our position as a lightly populated country on the edge of Asia and possessing a high standard of living and a selective immigration policy, would create problems enough'. The only answer was for Australians to take 'our place in a team'. And this Western team in Asia would enable Australia to keep its homogeneous society and British character.[32] So secure was Australia in these years that while mouthing all the standard slogans of the Western alliance about the threat of Communist imperialism and the danger of 'falling dominoes', it spent two or three times less per capita than its great power protectors, the United States and the United Kingdom, on defence.

Indonesia remained the only unpredictable element in the immediate environment, unpredictable both as to where it stood in the East-West conflict and as to how the Western allies would behave should Australia find itself on unfriendly terms with its nearest neighbour. This did arouse a certain degree of concern over whether Indonesia might be a regional problem that Australia might have to contend with alone. Accordingly, just as in World War I, the Commonwealth government, fearing it might be left to fend for itself against Japan, had arranged for the appointment of a lecturer in Japanese at the University of Sydney in order to have an expert available to train military officers in Japanese language, to translate intercepted Japanese cables and advise the authorities generally on Japan,[33] so in the 1950s with the possibility of conflict with Indonesia in view, the Commonwealth offered funds for the establishment of Departments of Indonesian Studies in Melbourne, Sydney and Canberra which could be used not only to teach undergraduates but also 'the Services and persons needing limited courses'.[34] As in the case of Japan, the support for the

---

[32] R.G. Casey, *Friends and Neighbours: Australia and the World* (Melbourne: F.W. Cheshire, 1954), pp. 3, 10, 20.

[33] Minute, G.F. Pearce, Minister of Defence to Brigadier-General Hubert Foster, 24 April 1916, Australian Archives (hereafter AA), A3688, file 488/R1/55; letter, T. Trumble, Acting Secretary of Defence to Warden and Registrar, University of Sydney, 7 May 1917, University of Sydney Archives, G3/13.

[34] Letter, confidential, Ronald Mendelsohn, Prime Minister's Department to William J. Weeden, Director of Commonwealth Office of Education, 26 January 1955, AA, A1361/1 file 49/5/4 Part 1. I

study of Indonesian language and culture followed from the perception of Asia as a threat. Nevertheless, the Indonesia problem was always manageable. Indonesia, unlike Japan, was no match militarily for Australia, and while the United States and Britain could not be depended upon to prevent Indonesia from acquiring West New Guinea, it was reasonable to expect that they would help Australia resist any attack on its home territory. As long as Britain and, even more pertinently, America were committed to protecting Western interests in Southeast Asia, Australia could comfortably assume that its status as a Western nation and its immigration policy which confirmed this status were not in jeopardy.

The 'Multicultural' Society and Australia as a Part of Asia

By the end of the 1960s, however, the commitment of Australia's 'Great and Powerful Friends' to the region was in the process of rapid dissolution. Britain, giving up its imperial pretensions, withdrew from East of Suez and sought a new future for itself in the European Community. America, after failing in Vietnam, retreated from Asia. The Nixon Doctrine stipulated that the United States would never again become militarily involved in a land war in Asia and would expect its Asian/Pacific allies to take upon themselves the main burden of their defence. Asia was being left alone to be itself with all its diversity and complexity, cooperation and conflict. As America pulled out of Indochina and Britain retired from Malaysia it became very quickly apparent that Australia had only one path to the future and that was to be found in accommodation to Asia.

For those conservatives who had identified themselves completely with the Western allies and Western cause in the region, there were at first some recriminations and regrets. A number of cabinet ministers talked in language which suggested Australia had been betrayed. The Minister for Air, Peter Howson, after learning of President Johnson's post-Tet decision in April 1968 to scale down the war in Vietnam and to open unconditional negotiations with the enemy, recognised that the United States was admitting defeat and would inevitably retreat from Asia. And he confided to his diary, 'To my mind, it's the first step of the Americans moving out of South-east Asia and that within a few years—three or four possibly—there'll be no white faces on the Asian mainland … from now on, and to a much greater extent, we shall be isolated and on our own'.[35] Australian disillusionment with its putative Western patrons had a long history dating back to before World War I. But in contrast to the expectations of Deakin, Fisher, Hughes, Curtin and Evatt, Australian leaders in the 1970s had no hope that what had happened could be reversed, that at some future time Britain and America would return. This time the Western retreat from Asia was final. Australia's loneliness as a Western power in the region was permanent. Australians had only one possible 'home' now and that was Australia, Australia in Asia.

Accepting this geopolitical reality Australian leaders wasted little time lamenting the loss of the past as they began to face up to the future. It was widely recognised as Malcolm

---

am indebted to Peter Phelps for this latter reference.

[35] Peter Howson, *The Howson Diaries: The Life of Politics* (Ringwood, Victoria: Viking Press, 1984), p. 415, entry for 2 April 1968.

Fraser, the Minister for Defence, declared that Australia was 'entering a new era'.[36] All the growing ties to Asia which Holt had listed were seen in a new light and given a new meaning. And with this new perception of Australia's singular relationship with Asia there came a new willingness to rethink Australia's definition of itself and to remake its immigration policy. Speaking in Singapore in January 1971 Prime Minister John Gorton affirmed what three years earlier his Minister for Immigration had denied. Gorton told his fellow Asians

> I think if we build up gradually inside Australia a proportion of people who are not of white skin, then as that is gradually done, so there will be a complete lack of consciousness of difference between the races. And if this can be done as I think it can, then that may provide the world with the first truly multi-racial society with no tensions of any kind possible between any of the races within it At any rate, this is our ideal.[37]

This was the first occasion on which a prime minister or, for that matter, any cabinet minister, had named 'multi-racialism' as the Australian ideal. Even so it would appear that Gorton's idea of a 'multi-racial society' was one in which the migrants, selected regardless of race, integrated into the existing European culture or remained a minority culture inside a predominantly British Australia. In the same speech he praised Singapore for its achievement in creating a 'multi-racial society' and he said

> you are 90 per cent Chinese or 85 per cent Chinese and therefore Singapore is homogeneous as we will keep Australia homogeneous, that nevertheless enables you to say you are a multi-racial society. Well, we are moving a little bit that way.[38]

Both the Whitlam Labor government which came to office in December 1972 and the succeeding Fraser Liberal-Country party government set aside the orthodoxies of the past and accepted the finality of Australia's new geopolitical circumstances. Both governments recognised that Australia's future lay with an Asia freed from Western control, that Australia could no longer treat its Asian neighbours as the front line for defending 'White Australia'. They understood that they had to deal with Asia on its own terms. Whitlam, for example, at the Institute of Political Affairs Summer School in 1973 made the keynote of his address the need to foster 'new forms of regional cooperation', and by this he meant not the development of ANZUS or SEATO but the cultivation of direct relations with Asian nations, both individually and collectively.[39]

Surprisingly, despite all the earlier predictions that a Vietcong triumph in Vietnam and a Western retreat from Asia would bring China and communism to Australia's doorstep and that as a result Asia would become an ever present danger to Australia's survival, when these feared events failed to come to pass Australian leaders surveyed the new picture with equanimity rather than anxiety. Even Fraser's apprehensions were more directed towards Russian interference in the region than to possible troubles generated from within Asia

---

[36] Commonwealth of Australia, *Parliamentary Debates*, House of Representatives, vol. 66, p. 232, 10 March 1970.

[37] Cited in Rivett, *Australia and the Non-White Migrant*, p. 32.

[38] Cited in Rivett, *Australia and the Non-White Migrant*. p. 31.

[39] *Australian Foreign Affairs Record*, 44 (January 1973), pp. 33–34

itself. It is true that the balance of power in the region at the end of the Vietnam war favoured Australia's benign view of its new position. The coming to power of an anti-communist military regime in Indonesia preoccupied with domestic stability and development, the formation of ASEAN which was fearful of China and hostile to Vietnam, the antagonisms between Russia and China and between Vietnam and China, all these elements combined to create an Asia which was so divided in itself that Australia on the southern rim could not feel menaced. Nevertheless, given Australia's earlier perception of Asia it is remarkable that Australia moved so speedily and positively—and without any reference to the balance of power—to seek 'enmeshment' with its neighbourhood. It was perhaps symbolic of this revolutionary change that Fraser, who had been a senior minister in the Liberal-Country party governments which had made ANZUS and SEATO the basis of their foreign policy and had gone 'all the way with L.B.J.' in Vietnam, should have made his first overseas trip as Prime Minister not to London or Washington but to Beijing and Tokyo, the capitals of Australia's old enemies, where he sought new allies and new alliances.

Accepting the imperative of having to live with this new Asia, the Whitlam and Fraser governments embraced without reservation the notion of Australia as a 'multicultural' and 'multiracial' society and pursued an immigration policy committed to the 'avoidance of discrimination on any grounds of race, colour of skin or nationality'.[40] Whitlam publicly repudiated the 'White Australia' policy, and the government was as good as its word. In all immigrant categories, covering occupational needs, family reunions and humanitarian asylum, the government applied a colour-blind approach. The criteria against which would-be migrants were judged became much more open. Preference for British or European settlers was abolished, and assisted passages became available to all on an equal basis. Al Grassby, Whitlam's first minister for immigration, could claim with some justification that 'every relic of past ethnic or racial discrimination' had been eliminated. And the Fraser government accepted the new policy without demur. Indeed, since the Whitlam government had reduced the overall target it was not until the Fraser government came to office that the full effects of these changes in principle were evident. From 1975 to 1984 Australia took in 90,000 Indochinese refugees and something like 100,000 other Asians and Pacific Islanders, and as a result the percentage of the non-European born in the population increased from 0.5 in 1947 to 2.5 in 1984. Under the Hawke government in the 1980s Asian migrants came to represent more than a third of the total intake. If Asian migration were to continue at that rate the Department of Immigration, Local Government and Ethnic Affairs estimated that Asians or, at least, those of Asian descent would by the year 2030 become approximately 10–15 per cent of the Australian population.[41]

---

[40] Cited by W.O. Borrie, 'Changes in Immigration Since 1972' in Jupp, ed., *The Australian People*, p. 111; it is worth noting that already by 1968 community leaders, on behalf of the non-British Europeans who had migrated to Australia since the end of World War II, were articulating the concept of 'multiculturalism' and urging its adoption, but that it was not until after the disappearance of the Western presence in the region and the opening of the doors to Asian migration on a non-discriminatory basis that the Commonwealth government took up the notion and made it the key distinguishing definition of contemporary Australia.

[41] Cited in Nancy Viviani, 'Australia's Future in Asia: People, Politics and Culture', *Australian Cultural History* (July 1992), p. 107.

During the 1980s Australia made what Foreign Affairs Minister Gareth Evans called 'constructive engagement with Asia' the centrepiece of its foreign policy. The Commonwealth government for the first time in the nation's history commissioned a series of reports into relations with Asia and by implication into Australia's future. The reports covered nearly every aspect of the relationship, the Dibb report on defence, the Garnaut report on trade and investment, the Ingleson report on Asian language and culture in higher education and the Fitzgerald report on immigration. They all stressed the importance of Asia in Australia's future and the need to develop a cooperative spirit in dealing with the region. There were, however, some differences between the first three reports and the Fitzgerald report on the meaning of this new relationship with Asia for Australia's own identity.

The Dibb report, carrying through the general spirit of the 1976 strategic review, argued that 'independence and self-reliance' should be the basis of defence planning. It considered that Australia faced no foreseeable threat from the region—the more distant Asian powers being preoccupied with their own problems and the more immediate neighbours in Southeast Asia and the South Pacific having neither capacity nor motive. As an essential part of the new approach it recommended that Australia should 'thus seek to cooperate with South-east Asian and South Pacific friends in the development of their defence capability, and in particular with Indonesia 'the most important neighbour' by 'promoting a sense of community'. Defence was not to be thought of as being constructed against Asia but in association with immediate neighbours for the purpose of collective security.[42]

The Garnaut report focused primarily on what it called the Northeast Asian ascendancy, Japan, China, South Korea and Taiwan, the engines driving the economic growth in the whole region. For Garnaut, Australia's future prosperity and independence depended on seizing the opportunities afforded by the rapid rate of development in these four economies. These countries were 'more deeply complementary to Australia in their resource endowments and in the commodity composition of their trade than any other economies on earth', and this complementarity extended beyond trade to include people and capital for Australia's own development needs. Moreover, just as the Dibb report urged openness and mutuality in Australia's defence relations with Southeast Asia so too the Garnaut report favoured a liberal, non-discriminating trade policy and training in Asian languages and cultures for fostering the economic ties.[43]

The report of 'Asia in Australian Higher Education', which was sponsored by the Asian Studies Council and of which John Ingleson was the research director, advanced the most dramatic claims for the changes which had overtaken Australia since the 1970s. Australia was linked to Asia through geopolitics, trade, investment and migration 'in a way profoundly different from any other country'. Because of this if Australians were 'to manage their future as part of the Asian region' knowledge of Asian languages and culture had to be widespread through the country. And in the grandest claim of all leading up to

---

[42] Paul Dibb, *Review of Australia's Defence Capabilities,* March 1986 (Canberra: Australian Government Publishing Service, 1986), pp. 33–7, 44, 48, 58.

[43] Ross Garnaut, *Australia and the Northeast Asian Ascendancy* (Canberra: Australian Government Publishing Service, 1989), especially pp. 1–6.

its proposal for radical changes in the course structures of the universities' humanities and social science faculties, the report asserted that the teaching about Asia was 'part of the Australianisation of curricula in higher education … Asian studies is the obverse of the coin to Australian studies'. It seemed to be saying that Chinese and Japanese languages as opposed to French and German were natural parts of an Australian education and suggesting that to be Australian one had also to be Asian.[44]

Only the Fitzgerald report on immigration entered a cautious note into the general chorus of enthusiasm celebrating Australia's new future with Asia. It approved whole-heartedly the end of 'White Australia' and the adoption of a non-discriminatory immigration policy. Furthermore, because the 1958 legislation was still imbued with 'the mood and flavour of the 1901 Act', the report recommended the adoption of a model Bill which would symbolise the break with the past and reflect 'a more positive and forward-looking approach to immigration policy and administration'. It found no justification for the fears of those who believed that the rising percentage of Asians in the immigration program would have disruptive social consequences, and it happily accepted that the Australia of the twenty-first century would be very different from the Australia of the1940s. There was in the report nothing but praise for the new immigration policy which was creating 'a racially diverse but harmonious community, a cosmopolitan Australia'.

Nevertheless, in discussing what Australia should expect of its migrants the report emphasised the harmonious community, not the cosmopolitan diversity. The abandonment of forced assimilation did not necessarily entail the abandonment of a 'Commitment to Australia', a phrase used as the sub-title for the report. Its comments on 'multiculturalism' were ambivalent or critical. 'Multiculturalism' was 'one part of what Australia is about and therefore only one part of what immigration is about'. And again, 'the sad irony is that this first real effort in recent times to bring immigration into the mainstream without forced assimilation has tended to assist in keeping it out'. The conclusion was that it was 'the Australian identity that matters most in Australia. And if the Government will affirm that strongly, multiculturalism might seem less divisive or threatening'. What then was the national identity which should be offered to incoming settlers? On this question the report disowned any attempt to suggest 'a prescription of core values'. They were 'too disputed' and 'too much in flux'. But almost simultaneously, indeed on the very same page, the report provided such a prescription: 'The commitment to Western liberal values is fundamental. So also are ideas about equality, about the individual in relation to society and about the right to challenge authority'.[45]

Fitzgerald's reservations about 'multiculturalism' as a response to the question about Australia's future addressed a fundamental ambiguity in the meaning and use of the term. From 1973, when Grassby gave the first unqualified endorsement to the 'multicultural'

[44] 'Asia in Australian Higher Education', submitted to the Asian Studies Council (January 1989), pp. 13, 33–7.

[45] Stephen Fitzgerald, *Immigration: A Commitment to Australia* (Canberra: Australian Government Publishing Service, 1988), especially pp. 4–12, 111–12.

society,[46] there was much confusion about how it was to be understood, whether on the one hand, in reaction to a past of British Australian arrogance and ignorance, it was intended to represent a positive tolerance of the diverse minority cultures, or whether on the other it stood for an Australia in which all cultures, including the British, were in every respect equal and therefore, following the demise of 'White Australia', was being put forward as a new idea of the nation. Grassby's main point seemed to be that 'old Australians', especially in the light of the changed relations with Asia, should learn to accept and appreciate the cultures which the non-British migrant groups, those commonly referred to as ethnic minorities, had brought to Australia and made a part of Australia. Under the Fraser government the term was broadened to include Australians of all cultural backgrounds, whether, as the government's Council on Population and Ethnic Affairs stated, 'they are Aboriginals, or trace their roots to the British Isles, continental Europe, Asia, Africa, the Pacific nations or the Americas or regard themselves simply as Australian'.[47] It was as though the Council was suggesting that this was the essence of 'Our Developing Nationhood'. The Minister for Immigration, Michael McKellar, appeared to give some official recognition to this view when he stated that 'the concept of multiculturalism does embrace all cultures in a nation' and 'the Aboriginal people are an integral part of the Australian multicultural society'.[48] If this were the new defining national idea then all that held Australians together was mutual tolerance of their differences and the goodwill of each culture towards all others.

Though the movement for 'multiculturalism' predated the end of 'White Australia' its success in the 1970s and 1980s was accompanied by the arrival of significant numbers of Asian migrants which gave rise to the Blainey and Howard questioning of the implications for social cohesion.[49] All governments, however, rejected the notion that Asian migrants represented such a problem and insisted that 'multiculturalism' was not at odds with national unity. Grassby had said that all migrants who came to Australia would, in accordance with the Labor party's platform, have to be able 'to integrate here successfully'. Likewise the Fraser government, even as it took unity in diversity as its watchword and pursued the goal of 'a cohesive, united, multicultural nation', also claimed to be 'cognizant of the sentiments, the common values and the aspects of life in Australia that, irrespective of our ethnic backgrounds, we treasure and want to preserve'.[50] The language was as awkward as the problem itself. What it was into which all 'ethnic' groups should integrate or what 'the

[46] A.J. Grassby, 'A Multi-Cultural Society for the Future' (Canberra: Department of Immigration Reference Paper, 1973).

[47] Cited from *Australian Council on Population and Ethnic Affairs, Multiculturalism for all Australians: Our Developing Nationhood* (Canberra: Australian Government Publishing Service, 1982), in Jupp, ed., *The Australian People*, p. 130.

[48] Commonwealth of Australia, *Parliamentary Debates*, House of Representatives, vol. 115, p. 1105, 13 September 1979.

[49] For similar, though better considered, American concerns, see Arthur M. Schlesinger Jr., *The Disuniting of America: Reflections on a Multicultural Society* (New York: Norton, 1992).

[50] Commonwealth of Australia, *Parliamentary Debates*, House of Representatives, vol. 88, p. 638, 20 March 1974; Commonwealth of Australia, *Parliamentary Debates*, House of Representatives, vol. 109, pp. 2727–32, 30 May 1978.

common values' were with which all Australians should identify remained unclear and elusive.

Succeeding governments made different and sometimes conflicting stabs at an answer. Whitlam and Grassby did at one brief moment, during the celebration of the 119th anniversary of the Eureka Stockade 'little rebellion',[51] seem to hint that a unifying Australian myth, 'a new nationalism' to replace that of British Australia, might be found in the 'Legend of the Nineties', the Bush legend most graphically depicted in Russel Ward's *Australian Legend*. [52] But except for Peter Weir's films of 'Breaker Morant' and 'Gallipoli', such a suggestion gained little support and made little impression. The old radical national tradition evaporated almost as quickly as that of 'British race patriotism' of which it was a derivative, if dissident, element. The Fraser government for its part did vaguely put forward 'democracy' and 'democratic principles' as the core values holding the nation together. But somehow this too was unsatisfactory. It was not specifically Australian and was so general as to be meaningless.

In 1989 the Hawke government, perhaps responding to the concerns of both the ethnic communities and the Fitzgerald report, produced a *National Agenda for a Multicultural Australia: Sharing Our Future* which at one and the same time attempted to define 'multiculturalism' and, by also setting its limits, to lay down the essentials of national unity-those structures, principles and values which hold the nation together. 'Multiculturalism' as a policy, that is, as an idea to which the nation was dedicated, meant the right of all Australians, 'within carefully defined limits', to express and share their individual cultural heritages and to enjoy equal rights to social justice and economic opportunity. The limits which were given equal importance required that all Australians should have an 'overriding and unifying commitment to Australia'. And this commitment involved the acceptance of 'the Constitution and the rule of law, tolerance and equality, Parliamentary democracy, freedom of speech and religion, English as the national language and equality of the sexes'. Here was the most specific statement yet which related the diversity of 'multiculturalism' to the unity of the nation. And it is noteworthy that this official pronouncement followed the Fitzgerald report and subordinated 'multicultural' rights to the commitment to the nation.

The 'multicultural' agenda paper, however, unlike the Fitzgerald report, did not equivocate either about the national norms or their source. Indeed, in this paper the source was not a general Western tradition but more precisely a British heritage. In the prime minister's foreword he asserted that the migrants from 140 countries who comprised the 'multicultural' society were drawn to Australia by its 'British heritage and institutions'. The concluding section on a 'Better Australia' amplified this point when it claimed that, 'The customs and institutions which we recognise as Australian today are largely British and Irish in origin'. While it allowed that 'the institutional structure transplanted to Australia was often modified, sometimes dramatically, to reflect our own history and circumstances'— this presumably is what was meant by an earlier reference in the paper to Australia's

---

[51] 'Speeches by Prime Minister the Hon. E.G. Whitlam, Q.C., M.P., and the Hon. A.J. Grassby, M.H.R., at Ballarat, 3 December 1973' (Canberra: Department of Immigration, 1973).

[52] Russel Ward, *Australian Legend* (Melbourne: Oxford University Press, 1958).

distinctive 'culture'—nevertheless 'our British heritage' remained 'extremely important to us' as 'a potent source of unity and loyalty'.[53] Such a formulation of social cohesion would seem to mean that since British culture was the foundation of the national culture it was privileged and therefore all other cultures had to accept its primacy.

Gareth Evans and Bruce Grant in their authoritative survey of *Australia's Foreign Relations In the World of the 1990s*,[54] which faced up to the implications of enmeshment with Asia, embodied more fully the contradictory tendencies inherent in the debate over national identity. On the one hand in dealing with Australia's Asian future they declared that 'it is simply no longer an option for Australia to see itself first and foremost as a transplanted European nation'. Australians, in struggling for 200 years against the reality of their geography, had considered themselves to be an 'Anglophone and Anglophile outpost'. The 1987 Beazley Defence White Paper, which gave effect to the Dibb report, marked 'a conceptual watershed in Australian foreign policy' which liberated Australian foreign policy and, by extension, it might be thought, Australia itself from dependence on the British connection. On the other hand, however, when they dealt directly with Australia's relations with Britain, they accepted that the British inheritance affected every aspect of Australian life and culture: 'Britain's influence on Australia has been so extensive ... the ties of history, kinship and culture ... so pervasive that the relationship seems to exist independent of governments and their policies'. Furthermore, when they treated the issue of human rights as part of Australia's diplomacy in Asia they maintained that Australia must be true to itself and represent these values abroad. Yet in trying to establish the origin of these Australian values they at one point were represented as deriving from universal principles inscribed in the United Nations Declaration of Human Rights, at another they were a legacy from Australia's Western tradition and again at another they were attributed to a purely Australian experience of the persecuted, the convicts at Botany Bay and diggers at Eureka, strengthened by the influx of new migrants. Apart from this latter reference 'multiculturalism' hardly entered into their discussion of the new Australia.[55]

It is clear that while new national and international circumstances, especially the end of 'White Australia' and the changing perceptions of Asia, have led to the abandonment of the ideal of a homogeneous British 'White Australia', all attempts to redefine the contemporary nation have been ad hoc and confused and have failed to produce a satisfactory substitute. One alternative would seem to suggest that Australia is a 'multicultural' society, a nation of nations. A second, which can be seen as a particular application of the first, employing a geopolitical determinism, exhorts Australia to reject the notion of a transplanted European or British outpost and to embrace a bi-racial or Eurasian future. And a third urges that the essence of the nation is to be found in a modified British heritage. The first two stress the discontinuity between the past and the present. They either take for granted the commonalities which enable people of diverse cultural backgrounds to cooperate in a

[53] *National Agenda for a Multicultural Australia: Sharing our Future* (Canberra: Australian Government Publishing Service, 1989), pp.v, vii, 1–2,50–2.

[54] Gareth Evans and Bruce Grant, *Australia's Foreign Relations In the World of the 1990s* (Melbourne: Melbourne University Press, 1991).

[55] Evans and Grant, pp. 16–20, 29–30, 33–5, 42, 285 and 327–30.

relatively peaceful manner or they attribute them to supposed universal principles, such as democracy. The third, by contrast, maintains that the common core of national life, represented by parliamentary government, a common law legal system and the English language—which all communities, aboriginal, old and new settlers alike, accept—derives from a particular tradition, a monolithic and timeless British tradition modified to suit Australian conditions. Neither approach, however, convinces. The former refuses to recognise what is patently evident, namely that the shared language, institutions and value are a British legacy: indeed 'multiculturalism' insofar as it ignores the special status of the British tradition runs the risk of becoming a policy of 'repressive tolerance', to use a phrase coined by Herbert Marcuse for other purposes in the 1960s, namely, a policy which persuades migrants from non-British cultures to give their allegiance freely to their country on the basis of a false assurance that all cultures are equal. The latter, on the other hand, while acknowledging the importance of a British tradition, mistakenly explains its influence in a simple, linear fashion. That is, it assumes that there was a unified, unchanging British culture which was brought in one colonial fell swoop to Australia and which was subsequently and systematically transformed by Australian experience. Similarly, it overlooks the fact that present-day Australia is the product not only of the modification of a British heritage but also of Australia's own distinct ideals, most notably 'White Australia'.

This debate over national identity requires a better sense of history. While there has been an adaptive continuity of language, legal system and political structures, the ideas giving meaning to the British legacy have undergone considerable change. In the era of mass nationalism which gave rise to 'White Australia', a relatively liberal and open definition of the British subject and British Empire was replaced by a racially closed one. In this new era which lasted into the 1960s Australians for the most part thought of themselves as British race patriots. Indeed, Australians forming a democratic settler society on the fringe of alien Asia were more affected by this new nationalism than the British themselves. Race and culture were one, and language, law, and parliamentary government were seen as the fruit of British genius, as belonging exclusively those of British stock. Even the monarchy became more than the head of a honorific, hierarchical and constitutional order and was reinvented as the symbol of the British people and their world-wide Empire. In the post-imperial age, however, when most developed countries have come to accept the permanence of change and no longer feel the same need for an intense social identity, Australians also have abandoned nationalism's myths and have become more relaxed about diversity and difference both at home and abroad. The view of the British inheritance, as found in the *National Agenda for a Multicultural Australia*, stresses not culture or race but institutions and principles. These latter, even though they require, along with the English language, some understanding of a British constitutional and political tradition for their full exercise, can be shared by citizens of all ethnic origins. The harmony of the commonwealth is no longer dependent upon racial uniformity and cultural conformity; the essentials of community while demanding a first loyalty are not all encompassing. The end of 'White Australia' and the changed perceptions of Asia, the most dramatic marks of the new Australia, can only be understood properly in the context of a new history, perhaps one which allows a republic to mean more than the absence of monarchy and sees the core values of the contemporary nation as a modernised version of the Western philosophical tradition of civic republicanism[56] filtered through Anglo-Australian experience.

---

[56] For some recent works exploring the historical uses of this concept see Gisela Bock et al., eds, *Machiavelli and Republicanism* (Cambridge: Cambridge University Press. 1990); Paul Rahe, *Republics Ancient and Modern* (Chapel Hill, North Carolina: University of North Carolina Press, 1992); Peter Riesenberg. *Citizenship in the Western Tradition* (Chapel Hill, North Carolina: University of North Carolina Press, 1992); and Daniel T. Rodgers, 'Republicanism: The Career of a Concept', *American Historical Review*, 79 (June 1992), pp. 11–38.

7

Australia and Japan: A Comparative History[1]

This is the story of Australia's relationship with Japan. It is a curious story, a story that is intimate, intense and of long standing. In addition to revealing much about Australia's and Japan's interwoven destinies it has also something to say more generally about Australia's evolving response to Asia, about Australia as a historically Western nation coming to terms with its geopolitical and geocultural environment.

All that most Australians or Japanese know about their shared history is the dramatic and the obvious. From the distant past they tend to remember the bad things. Australians, even those of a new generation, know of the Pacific War, when Japan threatened invasion and treated prisoners of war cruelly. For their part, the Japanese carry with them the memory of White Australia and the hurt that this racially discriminating policy caused. In recent times more positive, if no less simple, images have come to be superimposed upon the old. Australians perceive contemporary Japan as a great market for Australia's mineral and fossil fuel resources and a major source of investment and tourists. The Japanese envisage Australia as either a vast, relatively unpopulated land of farms and mines or a leisured haven blessed with sunshine and beaches, koalas and other cute marsupials.[2]

It is the purpose of this book to place these images in their historical context and so provide a new picture of the Australian–Japanese experience.

The General Problem

The story of Australia and Japan is an episode in the West's engagement with the East and the East's response to the West's expansion. It is part of the great and troubled saga of European imperialism, of the projection overseas of the European nations' technological and military might, accompanied by their cultural and spiritual heritage. From the 16th century to the early years of the 20th century Europeans explored and mapped the globe and imposed themselves, directly or indirectly, upon every part of it.

Of all the extra-European world, East Asia was the region most remote and most mysterious. It was likewise the most resistant to penetration and domination. Here the West found civilisations that were highly developed and determined to keep the barbarians at arm's length. China, as the centre of the world, could not imagine that the Europeans sought anything other than to pay homage to the Middle Kingdom. The Ming and Qing dynastic rulers believed that their great empire would be able to overawe these interlopers and keep them in their place. On the other hand, Japan, an island state, felt vulnerable

---

[1] This essay was originally published as 'Australia and Japan: A Comparative History' in Neville Meaney, *Towards a New Vision: Australia and Japan across Time* (Kensington: University of New South Wales Press, 2007).

[2] Neville Meaney, Trevor Matthews and Sol Encel, *The Japanese Connection: A Survey of Australian Leaders' Attitudes Towards Japan and the Australia–Japan Relationship* (Melbourne: Longman Cheshire, 1988), pp. 64–92.

and exposed. After witnessing the disturbing results of Portuguese, Spanish and Dutch meddling in its affairs, it had in the mid-17th century closed its ports against the foreigners and shut itself off from the world. Not until two centuries later were Western powers able to force open the doors of these countries and incorporate East Asia into their international system. But even then, the West never subjugated China or Japan. Though the Chinese empire collapsed internally, it was never conquered. As for Japan, it rose to the challenge, assimilating the secrets of Western success, adapting itself to modernisation, and so evolving its own style of nationalism and emerging as an integral, if uneasy, part of the new world order.

Australia was the last creation of this age of European imperialism. Established at the nether end of the world, at the antipodean pole in the South Pacific, this British-settled colony was the ultimate and most fragile symbol of the West's global supremacy.

For the Europeans who settled Australia, Japan became central to their understanding of Asia as well as to the defining of themselves. The few Australians who, in the latter part of the 19th century, experienced Japan were fascinated by this oriental nation, which, instead of succumbing to the superior power of the European empires, preserved its independence by learning Western ways and converting itself into a modern state. With Japan's emergence as an imperial power in its own right, marked most dramatically by its defeat of Russia in 1905, this fascination turned to fear. In the age of race nationalism, Australia saw Japan as the embodiment of the Yellow Peril, of the Asia that threatened its continued existence as a lonely white British outpost. During World War II, when Japan advanced to Australia's doorstep, these fears were on the point of being realised.

Following the signing of the Peace Treaty for the Pacific Australian–Japanese relations entered a new era. Australia forged new ties with Japan, which, like Australia, was a dependent Cold War ally of the USA. It also, like Australia, was anxious to contain the Sino-Soviet bloc in an Asia that was escaping from the shackles of European imperialism. Through the US connection Australia accepted Japan as a friendly associate in the West's struggle against communism. Australia also found in Japan, as it rebuilt its economy, an expanding market for primary products. For three decades Japan became by far Australia's best customer and as such essential to its welfare. Simultaneously with the retreat of the European powers from the region, the defeat of the USA in Vietnam and the collapse of the Soviet Union, the two nations drew even closer to one another.

Australia has never been as important to Japan as Japan has been to Australia. Japan, in seeking to Westernise and to define itself against the West, looked directly to Europe and the USA. Australia was but a part of the British empire, a small, peripheral offshoot of the original culture. A few adventurous Australians did visit Japan and some even settled there, but by comparison with Europeans and Americans their numbers were insignificant. For good reasons, the Japanese often had trouble in distinguishing them from other English-speaking peoples. Japan, after opening itself to the world and encouraging emigration and trade, encountered Australia as part of the European-settled Pacific littoral. If Australia stood out in the Japanese mind, it was as the Western nation that, under its White Australia policy, inflicted the greatest humiliation upon Japan and Japan's aspirations to be accepted as an equal, civilised nation. Down to World War II Japan had never thought of Australia in any sense as belonging to Asia. It never included Australia in its Greater Asia Co-Prosperity

Sphere scheme. Thus Japan, in going to war in 1941, did not plan to conquer Australia; the air and sea attacks on Australian cities and ports were simply a by-product of specific strategic circumstances.

The onset of the Cold War in Asia in the 1950s caused Japan to take greater account of Australia. Assisted by its US guardians, Japan began to restore its economy, and in so doing discovered in Australia a reliable supplier of nearly all the major raw materials it needed. As a result Australia started to loom larger in Japanese thinking. In the Cold War years, however, Japan, while allied to the USA, still kept a low profile. Unlike Australia, it neither joined the Southeast Asian Treaty Organisation (SEATO) nor took part in the Vietnam War. Recovering from the humiliation of defeat and the legacy of imperialism it played a more passive or discreet role. It sought to find an acceptable Asian way of responding to the crises that rocked the region.

In the aftermath of the West's withdrawal from the region, Japan found it difficult to adjust to the new Asia. Though it achieved the status of a global economic power, second only to the USA, it still felt insecure. Situated in Northeast Asia it was confronted by nuclear powers with which it had differences and whose actions were unpredictable. Japan still wished to depend on US assurances, but recognised their contingent nature responded to the new uncertainties by fostering, even if tentatively, the development of an Asian consciousness that sought Asian solutions for Asian problems. Australia, acutely aware of the retreat of its Western friends from Asia and of its own inevitable involvement in Asia, turned its back on its white race self-definition and looked for ways to engage with the region.

As a result both Japan and Australia came to see each other as sharing a common vision, namely, a desire to retain America's security role in the region, to incorporate Asia economically into the wider Asia-Pacific Economic Co-operation (APEC) and to work for the acceptance of an Asian identity not hostile to the West, which would take in Australia as well as Japan. Its links to Britain being ever more attenuated, Australia welcomed its new partnership with Japan as a way of helping it to reconcile its European past to its Asian future. Similarly, Japan, with its ability to rely on the USA seeming more problematic and China emerging as a rival for regional leadership, sought to bond more fully with Australia. In the decades following the signing of the 1976 Basic Treaty of Friendship and Co-operation, Australian–Japanese relations have been marked by a great growth in the diversity and intensity of the ties that bind the two countries together.

More so than any other nations in East Asia or the West Pacific, modern Australia and modern Japan have been fashioned out of the era of Western hegemony. Because of this they have had comparable, if quite different, problems in making sense of their respective Westernness. Simply put, the question for Australia has been how to connect its Western heritage to Asia, and for Japan how to connect its Asian tradition to the West. And the central issue for this story is how, over more than 150 years, against the background of great changes in international circumstances, the Australian and Japanese answers to these questions have shaped their relationship.[3]

---

[3] For a discussion of the problems of comparing nations see Mattei Dogan and Dominique Pelassy, *How to Compare Nations: Strategies in Comparative Politics* (Chatham, New Jersey:

Liberal enlightenment and race nationalism

The initial encounters between Australians and Japanese took place in the latter half of the 19th century. At this time the Japanese were emerging from their long period of seclusion under the shogunate, the rule of the Tokugawa aristocratic dynasty, and the British colonists were putting down roots in their new land, assuming responsibility for governing themselves and beginning to take note of the wider world in which they found themselves. For both peoples it was a stirring time, a time of adventure and enterprise, a turning point in their respective histories that made them aware, and then wary, of each other.

In Japan, as the pressures to open its doors had mounted, the Tokugawa authorities, having observed how the European powers had forced China to submit, decided to accede peacefully to the West's demands rather than allow their country to be subjugated by the foreigners' superior arms. The issue was brought to a head with the arrival in the Bay of Edo (Tokyo) in 1853 of an American naval squadron under the command of Commodore Matthew C Perry. The US government had instructed Perry to persuade the Japanese to open their ports to commerce, coaling provisions and shipwrecked sailors. His 'Black Ships', two of which were steam-powered and belched out soot-stained clouds of smoke, were intimidating. One Japanese wrote apprehensively of an invasion of the land of *kami* (Japanese spirit) by 'Barbarians ... in floating volcanoes'.[4] The West's technological superiority could not be gainsaid.

When Perry returned the next year, the Japanese agreed under the Treaty of Kanagawa (Yokohama) to give refuge to stranded seamen, to allow trade in two ports and to permit Washington to appoint a consul. The United States, however, was not satisfied by these limited concessions, and four years later Japan signed a more general commercial treaty that provided for the exchange of diplomatic representatives, opened up many more ports for trade, set a fixed tariff for imports and gave the Americans the 'extraterritorial' right to be tried in their own consular courts according to their country's laws. Other Western nations, including the UK, immediately claimed the same privileges: Japan had no choice but to grant them similar terms.[5]

The collapse of Japan's isolation under threats from the West was deeply disturbing for the quasi-feudal society over which the shoguns presided. It was not easy for the Japanese to accept that the Westerners were the civilised peoples and that they themselves were the barbarians. Following a rebellion of clans opposed to the Tokugawa rule, a rebellion carried out under the slogan of 'Revere the emperor and expel the barbarian', the shogunate was overturned and the emperor vested with full authority. After the Meiji emperor's restoration

Chatham House Publishers, 1984) and for a model study of Japanese–American relations in this context, see Akira Iriye, *Power and Culture: The Japanese–American War, 1941–1945* (Cambridge, Mass.: Harvard University Press, 1981).

[4] Arthur Walworth, *Black Ships of Japan: The Story of Commodore Perry's Expedition by* (New York: Knopf, 1946), p. 71.

[5] W.G. Beasley, *Japan Encounters the Barbarians: Japanese Travellers in America and Europe* (New Haven, Yale University Press: 1995), pp. 37–38; Michael R Auslin, *Negotiating with Imperialism: The Unequal Treaties and the Culture of Japanese Diplomacy* (Harvard University Press: Cambridge, Mass., 2004), especially Conclusion.

in 1868 those who had led the uprising realised that the Westerners could not be thrown out and that the only way Japan could regain its autonomy would be by mastering the knowledge of the foreigners and making Japan into a modern nation. Yukichi Fukuzawa, speaking for a new generation of Japanese intellectuals, urged 'departure from Asia and entry into the West'.[6]

Thus the new regime reconstructed state and society along Western lines. The Charter Oath not only declared that individual Japanese should be free to pursue their own chosen occupations and that the national interest should transcend all others, but also that 'base customs of former times should be abandoned' and 'knowledge should be sought throughout the world'. To this end the government sent missions to all the Western countries to learn their secrets, especially those of science, technology and industry. Between 1860 and 1890 they despatched approximately 900 Japanese abroad to study every aspect of Western life, and hired over 3000 Western experts to help with the reform program. During these years the old caste system and clan loyalties were abolished, and the government introduced a modern industrial and financial system, modern means of transport and communication, a rationalised and centralised national administration, a universal compulsory education scheme and military conscription for all 21-year-old males. It was the reformers' intent to 'increase the prosperity of the state and to strengthen its military power'. By this they hoped to earn the respect of the West.

At first many of the Japanese politicians and intellectuals who initiated these changes had sought civilisation and enlightenment (bunmei-kaika) from the West, as well as technological know-how and material progress. They had considered their own customs, values and philosophies to be base and inferior. They had taken over Western ways holus-bolus, in their clothes, hairstyles, food, entertainment and architecture. They had tried to incorporate advanced Western social thought into their legal, political and educational institutions. Democracy, utilitarianism, liberalism and individualism were quite fashionable ideas in the early years of the Meiji Restoration. There was even a feeling among some reformers that the Japanese should complete the Westernising process by becoming Christians. In 1885 the Japanese foreign minister told the head of the French legation in Tokyo that 'Japan has borrowed everything from the West ... One step more remains to be taken – to borrow in the same way from the West the Christian religion.'[7]

Within a generation, however, the Japanese were reacting against this indiscriminate Westernisation. They had experienced the arrogance of Europeans and had witnessed their imperial domination and mutual hostility. Moreover, like Western peoples, the Japanese found the change from a traditional to a modern society very unsettling. The breakup of village life, with its established order, an order in which each person had an inherited and fixed position, created social and psychological insecurity. As Lafcadio Hearn, who had

---

[6]   Cited by Tetsuo Najita and H D Harootunian, in Richard Hall et al. (eds), *The Cambridge History of Japan*, 6 vols, Cambridge University Press: Cambridge, 1988–99), vol. 6 (1995); Peter Duus (ed.), 'The Twentieth Century', pp. 711–34.

[7]   Cited in Richard Sims, *French Policy Towards the Bakufu and Meiji Japan* (Japan Library: Richmond, Surrey, 1998), p. 96; for this Westernising process and the Japanese Enlightenment, see Marius B Jansen (ed.), *The Cambridge History of Japan*, vol. 5, 'The Nineteenth Century' (1989), chapter 7, 'Japan's Turn to the West', pp. 448–76 and chapter 11, 'Meiji Conservatism', pp. 674–79.

held the chair in English literature at Tokyo Imperial University until 1893, remarked of the new Japan, 'Nothing is more characteristic of [Japanese] life than its extreme fluidity.' But it was a fluidity that was looking for a fixed channel to give it a sure direction. As a consequence the Japanese, like the Western peoples who had suffered the same traumas of modernisation, created a national myth out of elements from their past traditions that gave meaning to the new social order and provided the individual with a new social identity.[8] And this Japanese myth was directed against the West.

Although by the end of the Tokugawa era Japan's leaders had freed themselves intellectually from subservience to a Sino-centred world and had come to think of Japan as an autonomous entity that was at least equal if not superior to China, it was not until after the social revolution of the late 19th century that these ideas were converted into a national myth.[9] This myth, which idealised a common racial heritage personified in the divine figure of the emperor, anchored the mobile, dynamic society in the certainties of a supposedly unchanging Japaneseness. Japan might borrow the means of achieving material and military power from the West, but it should not forsake the 'national essence'. What was learnt from the West was then to be used for Japan's own national purposes, to secure its own independence and possibly also that of the whole of East Asia.

Shigetaka Shiga, an influential figure in this reassessment of Japan's response to the West, was prompted to question the wisdom of uncritical imitation following a trip in 1886 on a Japanese naval vessel that cruised through the South Pacific. There he discovered, as he wrote in *Conditions in the South Seas* (*Nan'yo jiji*), that the 'white race' had conquered all the islands because the native peoples, seduced by the wonders of European culture, had not had the will to resist. The lesson he drew from this was that 'If the coloured races do not now exert themselves, then ultimately the world will become the private possession of the white race'. Japan had to be true to its destiny. As the first editor of the journal *Nihonjin* (*The Japanese*), which gave expression to this school of thought, Shiga stressed the importance for the Japanese people, even while they assimilated foreign influences, of preserving their national identity, the *kokusui hozon*. He regretted that his education had concentrated so exclusively on American and European history and philosophy. Japan should know more about China, Korea and the South Seas. Japan's geographical position dictated its future. Though himself an opponent of an aggressive nationalism and the Asia League's desire for Japan's imperial expansion he still believed that Japan had a role in the East comparable to that of Britain in the West.[10]

---

[8] For a brief but insightful discussion of the use of the terms 'Westernisation' and 'modernisation' for this period in Japanese history, see Albert M Craig (ed.). *Japan: A Comparative View* (Princeton: Princeton University Press, 1979). pp. 3–8.

[9] Ronald P Toby, *State and Diplomacy in Early Modern Japan: Asia in the Development of the Tokugawa Bakufu* (Princeton: Princeton University Press, 1984) , especially pp. 219–46; Susan L Burns, *Before the Nation: Kokugaku and the Imagining of Community* (Durham, NC: Duke University Press, 2003), chapter 7 and Conclusion; for an example of Japanese myth making, see Inazo Nitobe, 'Bushido – The Moral Ideas of Japan', in Alfred Stead, *Japan by the Japanese: A Survey by its Highest Authorities* (London: Kegan Paul, 1904), pp. 256–62, in which Nitobe identifies Bushido and Shintoism as representing 'the totality of the moral instincts of the Japanese race, and as such ... coeval with our blood'.

[10] Kenneth B Pyle, *The New Generation in Meiji Japan: Problems of Cultural Identity, 1885–1895*

From the end of the 1880s these ideas prevailed and Japan came to adopt a nationalist and imperialist policy. Under the 1889 constitution, which established a new system of government, the emperor was enshrined as an absolute, sacred monarch. The constitution itself was the gift of the emperor to his subjects. Though the constitution ostensibly followed the German model, the spirit animating it was Japanese. Though the forms of government were Western, including a prime minister, cabinet and diet (parliament) the manner of their operating was Japanese. The Imperial Rescript of 1890, which gave new direction to education, was an official expression of the national mythology. Elements from Japan's traditional religions – Shinto, Buddhism and Confucianism – were integrated to provide the mystical nationalism and moral precepts informing the document. Japan was the creation of the emperor's ancestors. Its founding principles were everlasting. They, in addition to extolling virtues such as duty to family and society, enjoined duty to the state, which would 'guard and maintain the prosperity of Our Imperial Throne coeval with heaven and earth'. In conclusion the rescript declared that these ancestral values, 'The Way', were 'infallible for all ages and true in all places'.[11] In contrast to the Charter Oath there was no reference to base customs that had to be discarded and no exhortation to youth to seek 'knowledge throughout the world'.

The upsurge of national feeling was fuelled by Japan's desire to have the Western powers accept it as an equal. The Japanese resented the unequal treaties (*fubyodo joyaku*) of the 1850s and 1860s that had derogated from their sovereignty and accorded them the status of an uncivilised people. Popular outrage at this indignity was very strong. Successive governments, hastening to embrace Western institutions and adopting Western legal and commercial codes, were motivated by their concern to prove themselves. They hoped thereby to induce the Americans and Europeans to surrender their special privileges. The new nationalism gave this objective a greater urgency.

The Japanese pursued the cause single-mindedly. In 1894 with the signing of the Anglo-Japanese commercial treaty they gained their first breakthrough. Under the treaty's terms Britain agreed to give up its extraterritorial rights and, shortly thereafter, the other powers agreed to follow its example.[12] Britain's decision was not simply a recognition of Japan's civilised progress. Rather more important was Japan's success in defeating China in the Sino-Japanese war. In doing so, it had bid defiance to Russia while gaining a colonial empire in Taiwan and the Pescadores and a predominant influence in Korea. As a result Britain began to conceive of Japan as a possible ally against Russia in Asia. Japan's new

---

(Stanford: Stanford University Press, 1969), especially the Introduction and pp. 19, 57–68 and 82–3, and *The Cambridge History of Japan*, val. 5, pp. 696–720; for the Japanese intellectuals' use of the notion of the Orient, or *toyo*, as the concept around which a national identity as developed against the West, see Stefan Tanaka, *Japan's Orient: Rendering Pasts into History* (Berkeley: University of California Press, 1993); for Shigetaka Shiga's conflicted view of Japanese imperialism, see Masako Gavin, *Shiga Shigetaka, 1863–1927: The Forgotten Enlightener* (London: Curzon, 2001), pp.117–37.

[11] Carol Gluck, *Japan's Modern Myths: Ideology in the Late Meiji Period* (Princeton: Princeton University Press, 1985), pp. 26 and 127–33; GB Sansom, *The Western World and Japan* (New York: Alfred A Knopf. 1970), pp. 362–66 and 464–55.

[12] Ian H Nish, 'Japan Reverses the Unequal Treaties: The Anglo–Japanese Commercial Treaty of 1894', *Journal of Oriental Studies*, 13 (July 1975), pp. 137–45.

international position was made evident when, in 1900, it joined the major Western nations in sending military forces to Beijing to help put down the Boxer rebellion. The Anglo-Japanese Commercial Treaty foreshadowed a new role for Japan in East Asia and the world. As one Japanese official summed it up at the time, 'We may congratulate ourselves on having at one blow swept away the disgrace of the last twenty years and with one struggle entered into the "Fellowship of Nations".'[13]

While the Australian colonists in this very period were undergoing a similar process, there were marked differences between the Australian and Japanese experiences. First, there was the matter of size. Australia by the time of federation in 1901 had a population of only 3 million compared to Japan's 49 million. It could not pretend to be a regional power, at least beyond the confines of the Southwest Pacific. Second, and more importantly, modern Australia, unlike Japan, did not regard Europe as an enemy of its independence. Australia was not of Asia. In establishing Western institutions in the new land the Australians, unlike their Japanese counterparts, did not see these forms and structures as alien. As a European-settled society, they were proud members of the British empire and continued, even after achieving self-government, to identify with Britain and to look to Britain for cultural values and national security. Australians' increasing awareness of their proximity to Asia, even as it led to rifts with the Mother Country over questions of immigration, defence and Pacific policy, intensified their British race patriotism. Australians for the most part never sought to 'cut the painter' or to turn their back on their European heritage. Their anxieties about Asia were focused on how, as Henry Parkes put it in 1888, 'to preserve the British character' of their country. Unlike Japan it was not a desire to protect a national essence that created tensions between Australia and the West. Rather, it was Australian Britons' fears that the Mother Country might in the case of European troubles think them expendable and abandon them to the teeming millions of Asia.

Founded in 1788 as a British convict gulag, modern Australia by the middle of the 19th century had attracted many free settlers who, lured to the great southern continent by the prospect of growing rich through wool or gold, set about creating a New Britannia in another world. From colonies placed at strategic points around the continent and Tasmania these migrants moved into the interior, pushing the Aboriginal inhabitants out of their path, taking possession of the land, and then clamouring for the right to manage their own affairs. Primarily of English, Scottish and Irish descent they brought with them not only British culture but also a British liberal philosophy, especially as this was embodied in the democratic Chartist movement.

The Australian colonies gained local autonomy in the 1850s at the high point of classical liberalism. The British authorities, sharing these liberal assumptions, agreed that colonies were a burden to the Mother Country. Whitehall had learnt the lessons of the American War of Independence. It accepted that distance produced conflicts of interest, that colonists would not for very long submit to the rule of London and that the colonies would inevitably fall like ripe fruit from the imperial tree. The colonists did not have to struggle for self-government: the British were only too happy to be rid of the expense and the responsibility.

[13] Ian H Nish, *The Anglo–Japanese Alliance: The Diplomacy of Two Island Empires, 1894–1907* (London: The Athlone Press, , 1966), p. 11.

The only question at issue with London was the form that the colonial constitutions would take and here the colonists had their way. The free and freed settlers opposed the convict system. It undermined the self-respecting character of their civil society. They rebelled against the autocratic rule of the military governors, the colonial shogunate, and claimed for themselves British traditions of constitutional liberty. Like their Japanese counterparts, the reformers, intellectuals, writers and artists who were in the vanguard of the liberal movement organised themselves in so-called Constitutional Associations. They sought to reproduce British-style political institutions and practices and to obtain parliamentary government shorn of the hereditary House of Lords and the prescriptive privileged franchise. Unlike their Japanese counterparts – and, for that matter, the British in the British isles – they were not burdened by a feudal past and so during the next two decades were able to give effect to their ideals. Among the first measures adopted under these constitutions were universal manhood suffrage, the separation of church and state and the opening up of the great pastoral leases for selection by yeoman farmers. In this liberal era the colonists believed that the state should play a very limited role. It should not interfere in people's consciences or livelihoods. Religion, education and the economy were not the business of government. Good citizens should be self-reliant and self-sufficient and contribute to their local community.[14]

Just as the colonists expected that Australia would in time grow to full independence, so the liberal reformers considered that separation would bring with it a republic. The colonists did not imagine this future as one achieved against or in defiance of Britain. Neither independence nor a republic were envisaged as a rejection of Britain. *The People's Advocate*, the great champion of the republican cause, declared that in proposing 'a Republican form of government for the colonies we must not be understood to express sentiments hostile to English institutions'. Rather, republican Australians would be Britain's 'strong ally ... zealous to show ourselves a worthy offspring of the bravest nation on earth ... a nation pre-eminent ... in enlightened government, in energy and progressiveness'. The British heritage was valued for its superior achievement in cherishing 'personal liberty and rational freedom'. Similarly, the colonists, again reflecting British liberal attitudes, did not regard the Crown as a sacred institution, the symbol of a mystical nation of 'one blood and one stock'. For Henry Parkes, a leading liberal reformer who was well read in the history of the 17th century English Civil War, the British monarch was 'an officer of the state and that is all'. It was the people who decided 'whether a certain person or a certain family shall occupy a royal position or not'.[15]

This New Britannia was being planted in another world, an Asian world, and from this time Asia began to appear as a darkening cloud on the horizon. Though the peoples of Asia were reeling before the incursions of the Western powers, the European settlers could not

---

[14] JB Hirst, *The Strange Birth of Colonial Democracy: New South Wales 1848–1884* (Sydney: Allen & Unwin, 1988), especially Preface, Introduction and chapter 14.

[15] *People's Advocate*, 21 April 1849, II May 1850, 13 November 1852 and 27 May 1854; *Empire*, 30 May 1854; Neville Meaney, 'Australia and the World', in Meaney (ed.), *Under New Heavens* (Melbourne: Heinemann, 1989), pp. 383–93; see also Mark McKenna, *The Captive Republic: A History of Republicanism in Australia, 1788–1996* (Cambridge: Cambridge University Press, 1996), chapters 2–4.

help but be troubled by their propinquity to this strange and alien continent. From these Australians' first experience of this other world, namely, through Chinese immigration, anxious voices were heard questioning what it might portend. As early as 1851 the *Sydney Morning Herald* was warning against this danger. Since the colonies were a 'community of British subjects' they should not welcome 'a large and continuous introduction amongst us of foreigners from any part of the world'. But the Chinese were especially to be discouraged. They differed from the British Australians in their 'complexion, language and customs', indeed, 'in almost everything but their human nature'. They were 'incapable of being brought into what Englishman understand and value as true civilisation'.[16] The colonists feared that Asia might overwhelm them as they themselves had overwhelmed the Aboriginal peoples.

With the influx of large numbers of Chinese following the discovery of gold in New South Wales and Victoria these apprehensions took on a palpable form. By the end of the 1850s there were some 42 000 Chinese in Victoria and 15 000 in New South Wales; that is, the Chinese comprised one in seven of the Victorian and one in fourteen of the New South Wales adult male population. The European miners, resentful at having to compete with 'the celestials', often resorted to violence to expel them from the diggings. But the diggers could not easily reconcile their Chartist belief that 'all men are born with free and equal rights' with their demand that the Chinese be excluded from the goldfields. At the hearings of an 1854 Victorian Royal Commission one of their leaders maintained that this principle did not apply to the Chinese because 'they were not civilised'. When it was pointed out that they regarded themselves as highly civilised and the question was asked as to who was to judge civilisation, the miners' representative could only offer the ethnocentric answer that 'the whole of European history and history of parts of Asia has shown us as to what is civilisation'.[17]

European Australians had difficulty in accepting this argument. Though the three most affected colonies, Victoria, New South Wales and South Australia, did pass discriminatory laws they did so only after fierce debate and with some reluctance. The legislation was neither general nor absolute and these measures applied to the Chinese and no other Asians. And they did not exclude Chinese. They limited the number who could be landed from any one ship and levied poll and residence taxes on those who did enter the country. Within a few years, as the Chinese population began to decline, all these discriminatory statutes were repealed. These Acts did not represent the acceptance of a racially based definition of society. They were a liberal era's pragmatic response to a particular problem of social order.

By the end of the 19th century, the Australians, like the Japanese, were undergoing a sociopsychological revolution that was transforming their ideas of monarchy, nation and race. As the Australian colonies, like Japan, experienced the full effects of modernisation on transport and communications, commerce and industry, education and ideology they became a predominantly urban mass society. The ideal of the self-sufficient family farm gave way before the demands of agribusiness and a commercial and industrialising economy. In Australia, as in Japan and other countries that came late to modernisation, the state played a large part in promoting this process, building railways, protecting manufacturers, regulating

[16] *Sydney Morning Herald*, 6 November 1851.

[17] C A Price, *The Great White Walls are Built* (Canberra: Australian National University Press, 1974), p. 10.

industrial relations, instituting universal education and providing for the conscription of a citizen militia. The Australians, following the pattern of other modernising nations, embraced nationalism as a new, intense identity that would enable them to cope with these deeply disturbing changes. Paralleling the Japanese, the Australians, because of the rapidity of their social renovation and the peculiarities of their geocultural circumstances, adopted a rather extreme version of nationalism.

Australians, for this purpose, responded to the call from a new generation of English intellectuals and politicians to define themselves first and foremost as members of the 'Anglo–Saxon' or 'Anglo–Saxon–Celtic' race. The new imperialists had denounced liberalism for abandoning the British diaspora, the Greater Britain scattered around the globe, and urged, in contradistinction to the liberals, a reintegration of the empire. They encouraged pride in the British race and blood. Parliamentary institutions were seen as an expression of the special genius of the British peoples. The Crown became more than the head of the constitution; the monarch was reinvented as the symbol of British history and heritage and, like the Japanese emperor, became the personal embodiment of the race.[18] Influenced by these sentiments the British government, in 1887, on the occasion of Queen Victoria's Golden Jubilee, brought to London representatives from all parts of the empire and held the first conference of the self-governing colonies.

In Australia this doctrine of British Race Patriotism was taken up with great enthusiasm. Like their Japanese counterparts the rising generation through universal, compulsory education was socialised into the nationalism of race and empire, symbolised by the monarch. The textbooks in the classroom, the ceremonies in the playground, all helped spread the quasi-religion of British imperialism. [19] The popular press, in reaching out to the newly literate masses, promoted the ideals of empire and celebrated Pax Britannica. Australian authors also contributed to the myth-making; *Deeds That Won the Empire*, written by the Reverend WH Fitchett, principal of Melbourne's Methodist Ladies College, sold over 100 000 copies. Queen Victoria acquired an exalted, almost sacred place in national life. She covered the country with the mantle of her name. In January 1888 the centenary of European settlement was heralded in with the unveiling in Queens Square, Sydney, of a statue of Victoria, *regina et imperatrix*.

The new spirit of British race loyalty was most evident in the colonists' support for the empire at war. In despatching a military contingent to help restore British prestige in the Sudan in 1885, the New South Wales premier declared that, 'We do not stop to question, we only know that British blood – Australian blood – has been shed ... and we respond accordingly'. Similarly, at the time of the Boer War, Edmund Barton, who was to become Australia's first prime minister, asserted that Australians were 'for their country right or

---

[18] D Cannadine, 'The Context, Performance and Meaning of Ritual: The British Monarchy and the Invention of Tradition', in E Hobsbawm and T Ranger (eds), *The Invention of Tradition* (Cambridge: Cambridge University Press, 1983), pp. 101–64.

[19] D E Roberts, 'The Role of State Education in the Development of National Identity, 1872–1918', PhD thesis, Monash University, Melbourne. 1999; for Japan, see Teruhisa Horio, *Educational Thought and Ideology in Modern Japan* (Tokyo: University of Tokyo Press, 1988).

wrong', and by country he meant the British empire.[20] More than 16 000 volunteered to fight for the imperial cause in South Africa. When the empire was at war, democratic and egalitarian Australia was less tolerant of dissent than was the tradition-bound, class-structured Mother Country. To honour the new secular faith, Australia instituted Empire Day in 1905, a decade before Britain. It could be said that the British race idea was more successful in reshaping social identity in Australia than in Britain itself.[21]

From Prussia's defeat of France in 1871, Australians recognised that international relations had entered a new era, an era of struggle between peoples rather than dynasties. As the *Sydney Morning Herald* editorialised, 'It opened an epoch in which the war of races had clearly begun'. Australia was no longer immune from the world's conflicts. Distance had ceased to provide security against foreign threats. Australia, along with all other countries and continents, was being caught up in 'the great net of international rivalry'.[22] Initially, the colonists had taken alarm at the extension of Britain's European rivals' push into the Pacific, the French in the New Hebrides, the Germans in East New Guinea and the Russians in northeast Asia. Drawing on American rhetoric the Australians called on Britain to support a 'Monroe Doctrine for the South Pacific', which had the aim of keeping all other powers from acquiring colonies in the region. Under this doctrine they hoped to create a *cordon sanitaire* against external menace.

By the end of the century Australians were more concerned with an awakening Asia than with European encroachments. Charles Pearson, an English liberal intellectual who had migrated to Australia about the time of the Franco-Prussian War and subsequently became Victorian minister for education, encapsulated much of Australia's anxieties about Asia in his *National Life and Character: A Forecast*, which was often cited in debates over White Australia. Pearson, as a result of living in Australia, had been converted to the virtue and necessity of mass democracy, state socialism and racial homogeneity. He acknowledged that in the modern society nationalism or patriotism was 'the feeling that binds together people who are of the same race'. It cultivated 'the existence of whatever is peculiar ... of a distinctive literature, manners, dress, and character'. Under nationalism the state and society tended to merge and the citizen was required to make the sacrifice of 'property, liberty, or life' for the good of the whole. Pearson believed that 'The nation is bound to remain the unit of political society because the interests and feelings of different races and countries are too discordant to be harmonised under a central Government'. He predicted that national feeling would spread to other races: 'The day will come, and perhaps is not far distant, when the European observer will look around to see the globe girdled with a continuous zone of the black and yellow races, no longer too weak for aggression or under tutelage, but independent or practically so.' He warned that this might have dire

---

[20] *New South Wales, Parliamentary Debates: Legislative Council*, 1884–85 session, vol. XVI, pp. 5-9, 17 March 1885; *New South Wales, Parliamentary Debates: Legislative Council*, 1889 session, vol. C, pp. 1495–96, 19 October 1899.

[21] For the problem of Britishness in Australian identity, see Neville Meaney, 'Britishness and Australian Identity: The Problem of Nationalism in Australian History and Historiography', *Australian Historical Studies*, 32 (April 2001), pp. 76–90, and 'Britishness and Australia: Some Reflections', *Journal of Imperial and Commonwealth History*, XXXI (May 2003), pp. 121–35.'

[22] *Sydney Morning Herald*, 31 December 1870.

consequences, that European peoples would 'wake to find ourselves elbowed and perhaps even thrust aside by peoples whom we looked down upon as servile'.[23]

Australia's fear of Asia was initially centred on China. In the 1880s, as a result of a modest increase in their numbers, hostility to Chinese migrants re-emerged. Even though the proportion of Chinese in the colonies was much less than it had been during the earlier goldrushes, Australians' response assumed an uncompromising character. This greater hostility to the Chinese in part sprang from the colonial authorities' awareness of the Qing dynasty's rising power and its determination to protect its nationals, but, more substantially, it was motivated by racial feeling.[24] Though leaders of the burgeoning labour movement frequently inspired and gave strong support to anti-Chinese leagues the movement to put an end to Chinese emigration had the general support of the community. Australia's Britishness was fused with ideas of racial exclusiveness. The colonists had come to define themselves as white British.

Following a conference in 1888 the mainland colonies passed uniform laws virtually prohibiting the immigration of Chinese and the naturalisation of Chinese residents. The colonial governments, in defending these measures, argued not in terms of specific circumstances but of racial absolutes. The Victorian premier declared that Chinese were 'not only an alien race but they remain aliens', and his NSW counterpart affirmed that there could be 'no sympathy' and that there would be 'no peace between the two races'.[25] Pearson explained that 'The fear of Chinese immigration which the Australian democracy cherishes ... is, in fact, the instinct of self-preservation, quickened by experience'. Australia was 'guarding the last part of the world in which the higher races can live and increase freely for the higher civilisation'.[26]

Shortly after blocking the entry of the Chinese the Australians directed their attention towards Japan. By the early 1890s Japanese were beginning to dominate the pearl-diving communities dotted along the northern coastline and also to work as indentured labour on north Queensland sugar plantations. Almost simultaneously the Anglo-Japanese commercial treaty compelled the colonies to face up to the question of Japanese immigration. The British government, after experiencing difficulties with the self-governing colonies over Chinese immigration, had left them to decide for themselves whether they would adhere to the treaty. The Australians were loath to give their consent. They were troubled by the provisions of the treaty that allowed Japanese the right to enter, travel or reside in any part of the British empire. They were not willing to countenance another Chinese problem, especially since Japan, after its defeat of China in the Sino-Japanese War, had emerged as the pre-eminent Asian power. They therefore agreed to settle the issue by translating their racial views of society into laws that excluded all coloured peoples from entering the country. Thus the treaty that ended Japan's inequality among the civilised powers, led

---

[23] Charles Henry Pearson, *National Life and Character: A Forecast* (London: Macmillan, 1893), pp. 84–5, I 22–3, 186–9 and 221–3.

[24] Matthew Jordan, 'Rewriting Australia's Racial Past: How Historians (Mis)Interpret the "White Australia Policy"', *History Compass*, 3 (1), 2005, pp. 1–32.

[25] Price, pp. 195, 250–57.

[26] Pearson. p. 16.

Australians to discriminate against the Japanese as one of the uncivilised peoples of Asia and Africa.

In early 1896 at an intercolonial conference convened to deal primarily with defence and the vital subject of undesirable immigration – two subjects that were closely connected – all the colonies, with the exception of the absent Western Australia, rejected the commercial agreement and agreed to pass uniform legislation to prohibit all coloured migration. This new general ban on coloured emigration was aimed particularly at the Japanese, whose virtues caused the colonies to see in them the greatest danger. One leading member of the NSW parliament, in supporting the Coloured Races Restriction Bill, which was intended to be the model for all the colonies, declared, 'We propose to shut out a nation which is coming into the first class by energy, by intellect and by material resources – I mean the Japanese'.

The Japanese government resented the racial slur of being lumped in with inferior, uncivilised coloured peoples, of being treated differently from Europeans. After winning the respect of the great Western nations Japan found itself suffering the same humiliation at the hands of these small, self-governing colonies and protested to the British government. The Japanese had no wish to encourage migration. The issue was one of sentiment, of Japan's *amour propre*. To overcome the difficulty they urged the adoption of the so-called 'Natal formula', which, while removing any mention of coloured races, would allow the authorities at their discretion to make entry into the country subject to a written test in any European language. Under pressure from London, the NSW government accepted this compromise and in 1897 passed its Immigration Restriction Act, the first such general law aimed at excluding all coloured peoples from an Australian colony.[27]

Not all the colonies followed the example of New South Wales. Queensland, to the disgust of the other colonies, reneged on its word and adhered to the Anglo-Japanese Commercial Treaty. It wished to enjoy the trade advantages, but it insisted that as a condition of adhering to the treaty there should be a gentleman's agreement that would restrict the entry of labourers and artisans. By 1900 the colony had reached an understanding with Tokyo that the Japanese in this category should not exceed the existing number, namely, 3247.

Yet though the colonies had failed to maintain a common front, it is clear that by the time of Australian federation in 1901 there was a community consensus about preserving White Australia, a term that gained currency during the 1890s. Indeed, the Commonwealth had come into being in large part as a result of the continent-wide concerns over the linked issues of defence, immigration, national security and racial purity. During the first federal election all political parties vied with one another in attesting to their loyalty to White Australia. When the Commonwealth government placed before parliament as its first major piece of legislation an Immigration Restriction bill the leaders of all parties spoke in support of the principle of racial discrimination. The only serious question for debate was whether its provisions were sufficiently watertight to ensure the desired result. Prime Minister Edmund Barton cited Pearson's warnings about race rivalry and Attorney-General

---

[27] Isami Takeda, 'Australia-Japan Relations in the Era of the Anglo-Japanese Alliance, 1896–1911', PhD thesis, Department of History, University of Sydney, Sydney, 1984, pp. 15–44.

Alfred Deakin made it clear that the sole purpose of the act was to uphold 'the purity of our race'. Once again it was the Japanese who were regarded as the greatest threat to the principle. Deakin affirmed that the object of the exercise was to 'exclude alien Asiatics as well as the people of Japan against whom the measure is primarily aimed'.[28]

The Japanese government renewed its complaints about Australia's intent to impose a colour or racial test for immigration. The Japanese consul in Sydney told the prime minister that the Japanese would feel it as a 'reproach' if they were treated differently from Europeans and grouped with the less civilised, such as the 'Kanakas, Negroes, Pacific Islanders, Indians or other Eastern Peoples'.[29] In London the Japanese minister took up the same issue. To avoid embarrassing the British government which was at the time negotiationg a treaty of alliance with the Japanese, the Australian government finally settled for the 'Natal formula'. The Japanese government was not appeased. The Australian policy was still offensive, and Japan continued to press the Australians to enter into a treaty or agreement that would formally put the Japanese on the same footing as Europeans. But all its efforts were in vain. At the very birth of the Commonwealth the 'Great White Walls' were firmly erected around the coasts of the continent and White Australia became enshrined as the founding and, for at least two generations, incontrovertible definition of the nation.

East–West distrust and global conflict

In this era the national ideologies that arose from the crisis of modernisation led to the entrenchment of racism, gave a rationale for imperialism and inspired the masses to lay down their lives for their emperor or king. Japan and Australia consolidated their late 19th century patterns of social identity and political loyalty. These extreme demands for national conformity might in part be explained by the specially taxing circumstances associated with the processes of modernisation; in Japan's case as a result of the rapidity and externally driven character of its transformation, in Australia's as a result of the extraordinary dislocation and reformation of its democratic settler society.[30] But of at least equal importance was Japan's resentment of the West and Australia's apprehensions about the East. The outcome was that, while an insular Japan strove for fulfilment through imperial expansion in Asia, an insecure Australia sought safety by idealising the British empire and keeping Asia and Asians at arm's length.

The Russo-Japanese War marked a new stage in Japan's evolution as a modern nation. Japan, by defeating Russia, had humbled one of the great Western powers. Japan's victory was the first of its kind for an Asian country. It could be seen as the first blow struck against European imperialism, the first step towards forcing the West to retreat from Asia. Certainly, the Japanese triumph gave heart to many Pan-Asianists as well as to the burgeoning national independence movements throughout the region. Japan had proved

---

[28] *CPD*, 1901–02 session vol. III, p. 3503, 7 August; 1901; *CPD*, 1901–02 session, vol. IV, pp. 4812–16, 12 September 1901.

[29] Neville Meaney, *The Search for Security in the Pacific* (Sydney: Sydney University Press, 1976). p. 111.

[30] For a comparison of Native Americanism and Japanese nationalism in the use of ideology to secure social conformity, see Gluck, *Japan's Modern Myths*, p. 38.

its worth in a way that the Western imperial nations understood and had emerged as the dominant power in the Western Pacific. Though Japan, as a result of US intervention, was denied the fruits of its victory – a 'national humiliation' that provoked popular protests and mob riots – it nevertheless gained control of Korea and could properly proclaim itself to be 'Imperial Japan' (*Dai Nippon Teikoku*).[31] As a result of the success of its armed forces, Japan's nationalism was closely identified with the military and the notion of sacrifice in war. The Yasukuni Shinto shrine in Tokyo, originally built in 1869 to honour those who had fallen in the clan war that had led to the overthrow of the Tokugawa Shogunate, acquired a new or, at the least, a much more general meaning. Following the Russo-Japanese conflict it became a temple dedicated to those who had died for their country and 'Emperor', and thus a potent symbol of the new order.

During the next three decades the pace of Japanese modernisation accelerated. By the beginning of the century 90 per cent of the population was literate. In this period Japan underwent a second industrial revolution. In the 1920s Japan's investment, as a percentage of gross domestic product (GDP), exceeded that of all advanced countries, being 18 per cent as compared with 17 per cent for the USA and 14 per cent for Germany; most of this investment was in heavy industries, such as shipbuilding, chemicals and electricity. Between 1910 and 1935 the urban population doubled and the nation was disturbed by rice riots, industrial strikes and patriotic demonstrations. As a result this deracinated society increasingly embraced ideas of community that would bind the people together, ensure public order and give direction to the national polity.

World War I acted as a catalyst for these forces. Calculating that the Allies would win, Japan stayed loyal to the British alliance and joined the Triple Entente powers against Germany and Austria-Hungary. Japan, unlike Australia, did not send troops to fight in Europe or the Middle East. Rather, it took the opportunity to attempt to fulfil its Asian mission and extend its hegemonic influence in the region. It seized German colonies in China and the North Pacific and in 1915 made demands on China, which, if accepted, would have made that country in effect a protectorate. At the end of the war Japan's new world status was recognised. It was accepted as one of the five great victor powers responsible for drafting the German Peace Treaty and the League of Nations Covenant. Nevertheless, Japan remained dissatisfied, believing that the Western powers had not granted it full equality. It took umbrage at the Allies' questioning of its territorial gains and their refusal to include a racial equality provision in the League Covenant. In Japan public opinion was aroused over these affronts to national honour.

The Allies' decisive victory over Germany did much to curb these anti-Western tendencies. As James Murdoch, Australia's first professor of oriental studies, reported back to Melbourne on Japan's reaction to the end of the war:

> the collapse of Germany, has had its effects; German militarism is now being held up as a terrible example; and able editors are everywhere preaching to their public the advisability of taking warning & turning over a new leaf. Japanese policy in

---

[31] Shumpei Okamoto, *The Japanese Oligarchy and the Russo-Japanese War* (New York and London: Columbia University Press, 1970), pp.l26–29, 173–86 and 207–23.

China is now altering greatly for the better; and on the whole, the country has become reasonable, very reasonable. In short, things are much more hopeful than they have ever been since 1914.[32]

The Western democracies' success gave a brief boost to liberals in Japan who wished to establish parliamentary government and to concentrate on economic development and international co-operation. During the 1920s Japan, for the most part, acted in this spirit. As a party to the Washington Conference treaties it agreed, along with the other major naval nations, to limit its capital ships and to respect the existing territorial frontiers in East Asia and the Western Pacific. Likewise at home civilian-led governments based on majority parties in the lower house of the diet extended the franchise to all males over 25 years and fostered industrial growth and foreign trade.

It soon became clear, however, that liberalism had shallow roots. The constitution that established the diet was a gift from the emperor, who, behind these forms, retained absolute authority. Moreover, parliamentary government was a Western import that had been grafted onto the body politic; it was not part of Japanese traditional ideas of *kokutai* (national polity). Imposed on the Japanese nation by the new Meiji rulers who, since they distrusted the people for their selfishness and impulsiveness, had severely limited the right to vote, it did not attract the allegiance of the masses. Even after universal manhood suffrage was granted, they showed little enthusiasm for an institution in which the corruption and pettiness of party politics prevailed. As alternatives, Marxists offered the working class a vision of a harmonious and better world achieved through social revolution and militarists imbued the conscripts in their care with the ideal of a pure, united nation regenerated through the armed forces.

Nationalism offered the strongest and most inclusive appeal. For the leading politicians and officials it gave dignity to the state and legitimised the suppression of social disorder. At the same time that the diet had provided for popular enfranchisement it passed the Peace Preservation Law, which empowered the government to deal with political subversion and social dissension, that is, with those wanting to 'alter the *kokutai*'. For the naval and military officers it offered the most noble rallying cry on behalf of Japan's foreign destiny, the most cogent justification for Japanese imperialism. More generally, 'the family of the nation' concept held the community in thrall. The modernising society was attracted to the myth of Japaneseness symbolised by a divine emperor.[33]

During the 1920s Japan, despite being elevated to the status of a world power and having a permanent seat on the Council of the League of Nations, felt that the Anglo-Americans still tended to treat it as an inferior nation and were unfairly restricting its ambitions in Northeast Asia. Under their pressure Japan had withdrawn from China and Siberia and accepted League of Nations mandates for the former German North Pacific Islands. US public expressions of hostility towards Japan and Washington's adoption of an immigration policy that shut its doors against all Asians, including the Japanese, provided further fuel

---

[32] Letter, James Murdoch to 'McRae' (E L Piesse), 22 December 1918, E L Piesse Papers, NLA MS882/5/5.

[33] Gluck, *Japan's Modern Myths*, pp. 237–47.

for these smouldering resentments.

As a result, when the Great Depression struck and the Western powers raised tariff walls against Japan's exports, the Japanese parliamentary system was not able to withstand the shock. As the Western nations took steps to protect their economies, Britain and the British empire through the Ottawa imperial preference arrangements and the USA by withdrawing into Western Hemisphere isolation, Japan resurrected its Monroe Doctrine for Northeast Asia. Confronted by an assertive Chinese nationalism and a militarising Soviet Union, Japan's Kwantung army, with the tacit approval of the High Command, provoked an incident in 1931 that led to its occupation of the whole of Manchuria. The military leaders' objective was to secure Japan's special interests in China. They aimed to acquire a strategic base against possible enemies and to gain control of the province's rich primary resources.

The civilian authorities in Tokyo were unable to stand up to the military. They could not reverse the victory, even if they had wished to do so. The army's action in Manchuria had been very successful and it had won a great deal of popular support. In 1936 some young ultranationalist naval and military officers, inspired by the Manchurian coup, rose up against the existing order with the intention of overturning the diet and restoring the absolute power of the emperor. They assassinated the prime minister and attacked key government institutions. Though the insurrection was put down the diet's moral authority was undermined. The practice of forming governments from majority parties in the parliament ceased. In its place there emerged national unity cabinets, the selection of which was increasingly influenced by the army and navy. Prince Fumimaro Konoye, who became prime minister in 1937, represented most completely the new ideology. Since he was close to the imperial family his government could be seen to express nothing less than the will of the emperor and the nation.

From 1931 Japan was a nation at war. From this time it was prepared to defy the West in order to establish its regional empire. In response to the League's and the USA's censure of its actions in Manchuria, Japan withdrew from the League of Nations and from the Washington agreement on limiting naval armaments. As the war in China expanded and the pressures at home mounted, the government, becoming ever more authoritarian, called on the people to join in an economic and a spiritual regeneration movement. In tracts, especially those written for school textbooks and for the indoctrination of army conscripts, the unity of the nation through the emperor, which had been first articulated in the 1890 Imperial Rescript on Education, was reaffirmed. In the official manual of patriotic education, The Essentials of Japan's National Policy, it was written that

> The unbroken line of Emperors, receiving the Oracle of the founder of the nation, reigns eternally over the Japanese Empire. This is our eternal and immutable *ko-kutai* . Thus, founded on this great principle, all the people, united as one great family nation in heart and obeying the Imperial will, enhance indeed the beautiful views of loyalty and filial piety.

The emperor system, or tennosai, which flourished in these circumstances, enjoined duty and sacrifice for the good of the nation family. It required the emperor's subjects to submit to the state and the moral order for the purpose of achieving social harmony. In an atmosphere of domestic and foreign tensions the emperor system, lacking any viable rivals, established its hegemony more by suasion than coercion.[34] This national ideology gained an extraordinary degree of acceptance. In contrast to the Germany of the 1930s where the Nazi Party was the source of unity and legitimacy in the nation, in Japan, the emperor embodied the spirit of the whole people and was the sole focus for their loyalty. It is noteworthy that Japan did not develop a resistance movement at any stage during the Chinese or the Pacific Wars, not even in the face of inevitable defeat.

The emperor system pervaded the whole economy and society. Through state planning, exploitation of Manchurian resources, artificial devaluation of the currency, control of wages and salaries, directed investment and co-operation with the corporate oligopoly, the *Zaibatsu*, Japan had by 1934 restored its GDP to pre-Depression levels. Japan's economy recovered ahead of that of all other industrialised countries, and provided a strong material base for building the war machine.

Simultaneously, a campaign to bring about a spiritual regeneration carried all before it. The Japanese people accepted much hardship in order to revive the national economy and contribute to the war effort.[35] In 1940 the government-sponsored Imperial Rule Assistance Association replaced political parties, organised neighbourhood bodies to suppress disaffection and boost morale, and amalgamated all national institutions to serve 'the defence state'. To fulfil this spiritual mission Prince Konoye's government declared that Japan's aim was, in accordance with the trends of history, to 'found a Co-Prosperity Sphere in Greater East Asia'. Japan's military expansion was justified under the guise of Pan-Asianism, an anti-Western Pan-Asianism that would be achieved under Japan's leadership.[36]

Japan's imperial actions established a logic that led the nation inexorably into further military adventures, at first carrying the war into China proper, and then, after the outbreak of the European war and the fall of France, moving south into Indochina. But it was never able to repeat the quick, simple triumph of the Manchurian incident. Despite being able to capture all the major cities on China's east coast and central plains, it could never overcome the stubborn resistance of guerrillas in the countryside and the nationalists and the communists in the interior. Moreover, each step taken to extend Japan's empire caused the Western democracies to harden their attitude and to impose ever more severe sanctions.

In 1940, following Japan's advance into northern Vietnam, the USA, the British Commonwealth and the Dutch placed a ban on the export of strategic materials, and after

[34] Gluck, *Japan's Modern Myths*, pp. 279–83; see also Andrew Gordon, *Labour and Imperial Democracy in Prewar Japan* (Berkeley and Los Angeles: University of California Press, 1991), especially Conclusion, pp. 331–42.

[35] Michael A Barnhart *Japan Prepares for Total War: The Search for Economic Security, 1919–1941* (Ithaca, New York: Cornell University Press, 1987).

[36] Kimitada Miwa, 'Japanese Policies and Concepts for Regional Order in Asia, 1939–1940', in James W White, Michio Umegaki and Thomas RH Havens (eds), *The Ambivalence of Nationalism: Modern Japan Between East and West* (Lanham, New York: University Press of America, 1990), pp. 133–56. For a brief overview of Japanese intellectuals' and diplomats' changing attitude towards world order and regional order in the 1930s, leading to their abandonment of the League of Nations and their advocacy of a new order in East Asia, see Thomas W Burkman, 'Nitobe Inazo: From World Order to Regional Order', in J Thomas Rimer (ed.), *Culture and Identity: Japanese Intellectuals during the Interwar Years* (Princeton: Princeton University Press, 1990).

Japan occupied the rest of Indochina, they cut off all exports, including oil. Japan's Greater East Asia ambitions were being frustrated at every turn. The Chinese would not be good Asians and submit to their fate, and the Western powers made it clear that they would not tolerate Japan's domination of the region. Ultimately, Japan was faced with the unhappy alternative of either a renunciation of its Asian new order or a high risk war against its Western enemies. True to the national ideology of the emperor system as it had evolved during the 1930s, Japan necessarily chose war. It was an act of hubris, which brought about the nation's downfall.

In attacking Pearl Harbour and so launching a war against the USA in December 1941 Japan badly miscalculated. Step by step with the deterioration in its relations with the Western democracies Japan had drawn closer to the European fascist powers which also resented the Anglo-American postwar settlements, despised liberal parliamentary government and embraced a totalitarian nationalist ideology. After the Nazi blitzkrieg swept through France and the Lowlands in 1940 Japan joined with Germany and Italy in the Tripartite Pact under which the three powers agreed in essence to come to each other's aid should the USA go to war with any one of them. These allies were unable to save Japan from the consequences of its rash action in attacking Pearl Harbour. When American resources were thrown into the fray the USA was not only able to join with the British Commonwealth and Soviet Union in taking the initiative against Germany in Europe, but also simultaneously to mount a major offensive against Japan in the Pacific. American technological and military superiority once again forced Japan into submission. The unparalleled devastation caused by the firebombing of Tokyo and the dropping of atomic bombs on Hiroshima and Nagasaki compelled Japan to surrender. The American 'volcanoes' had returned breathing fire and brimstone. As a result of the war Japan suffered heavily, including over 3 million dead. With Japan's defeat the nationalism of the emperor system was destroyed and its attempt to build an Asian sphere of influence against the West came to an end.

Australia in this era also felt the full impact of nationalism and the wars of nationalism. As a member of the British empire it was involved in the European conflicts; as a Pacific nation it was directly affected by Japan's rise to power and the consequent threat from Asia.

After Japan's defeat of Russia in 1905 and its emergence as the preponderant power in East Asia, Australia grew alarmed. Australia saw in Japan a threat of a new kind: not only a migratory but also a military invasion. Since Britain was preoccupied with Germany's challenge in Europe the Commonwealth authorities concluded that Australia might be left to fend for itself. Australia rejected the British view that the Anglo–Japanese Alliance could be relied upon. Its leaders believed that the alliance lacked the most important ingredient for its efficacy, namely, a mutual exchange of interests, and maintained that Australia was the most vulnerable part of the empire.

In the first years of the Commonwealth the tensions created by democratic modernisation reached their high point and the federal government, expanding on earlier initiatives, established a new collectivist order which was intended to assuage alienation and remove insecurity. There was a powerful desire to fashion a uniform society composed of equal and identical citizens. It was no accident that the Labor Party, which had the maintenance of White Australia as the first plank on its platform, was the most successful working class party in the world and the first to form a national government. Successive ministries, in addition to adopting a racially based immigration policy, took responsibility for building the railway and communication systems, protecting local industry behind high tariff walls, regulating working conditions, guaranteeing minimum wages and providing old age pensions. Australia's xenophobia, its apprehension about Asia -Japan in particular – gave an almost hysterical edge to this cast of mind.

Popularly and culturally, Japan was often depicted as the Yellow Peril. The same sense of racial community that, at the end of the 19th century, led Australians to define themselves as white and British and to exclude Asian immigrants, helped to magnify the Japanese danger and to unify the country. In the aftermath of the Russo-Japanese War Australian writers and artists who had been captured by the romance of the race idea expressed this anxiety through cartoons, poems, short stories, novels, plays and even an early silent film, *Australia Calls*. Many of these imaginative representations depicted a Japanese invasion of Australia. The most elaborate novel of this genre, E H Kirmess' *Australian Crisis* (1909), like the American Homer Lea's *Valour of Ignorance* (1909), told the story of a Japanese invasion as a conflict of the races . Kirmess' plot contained most of the elements commonly found in the government's strategic thinking. It envisaged a clandestine Japanese landing on the coasts of northern Australia at a time when Britain was unable to help and Australians had to fall back on their own resources to repel the enemy. But the story was not simply one of a nation defending itself against foreign aggression. The struggle of the Australian White Guard was bound up with the 'still larger issue ... whether the White or the Yellow race shall gain final supremacy'.[37]

Australians were agreed on the measures required to safeguard the country. Despairing of British aid they looked to the USA, a fellow Anglo-Saxon Pacific power that shared their concerns about Japan. In 1908 Prime Minister Alfred Deakin, when inviting America's Great White Fleet to Sydney and Melbourne, declared that Australians universally welcomed the visit 'because of our distrust of the Yellow Race in the North Pacific and our recognition of the entente cordiale spreading among all white men who realise the Yellow Peril to Caucasian civilisation, creeds and politics'. The following year Deakin proposed to the British that the Americans should be asked to join in a pact aimed at Japan under which they would extend their Monroe Doctrine to the Pacific. But the USA was not inclined to assume responsibilities outside the western hemisphere. Appeals to the British, Anglo-Saxon or white race fell on deaf ears. Thus Australia began to build up its own defences. In 1910 the Commonwealth government introduced compulsory military training, the first English-speaking country to do so in peacetime. It created its own navy, planned naval bases, set up munition factories and for strategic reasons completed the transcontinental railway connecting the eastern states to the west coast.[38]

---

[37] Neville Meaney, '"The Yellow Peril", Invasion Scare Novels and Australian Political Culture', in Ken Stewart (ed.), *The 1890s: Australian Literature and Literary Culture* (St Lucia: University of Queensland Press, 1996), pp. 228–63; Neville Meaney, *Fears and Phobias: E.L. Piesse and the Problem of Japan* (Canberra: National Library of Australia, 1996), pp. 3–5; CH Kirmess, *The Australian Crisis* (Melbourne: George Robertson & Co., 1909). p. 335.

[38] Meaney, *Search for Security*, especially chapter 6.

At the outbreak of World War I Australia threw its support behind the Mother Country. As a result it found itself fighting in Europe against Germany rather than in Asia against Japan. Though conscription for service in Europe was rejected, more than four in ten of all eligible males volunteered to join the Australian Imperial Forces (AIF) in order to do their duty by king and empire. Australia's wholehearted backing for the British cause was not only sentimental but also self-interested. Modern Australia was a creation of the British empire and its wellbeing, even its survival, depended upon the continued global supremacy of Britain and the British navy. If the British empire, together with its allies, could achieve a quick victory over the Central Powers the British navy would be free to come to the Pacific and deter Japan from challenging white Australia.

Throughout the war Australia remained deeply suspicious of Japan. The Commonwealth government noted Japan's limited commitment to the Allies' cause and its taking advantage of the conflict to advance its interests in Asia and the Pacific. The Australian leaders were alarmed by Japan's seizure of Germany's North Pacific Islands as it brought Japan within easy reach of Australia's own territorial frontiers. They saw in Japan's demands on China an imperial ambition to dominate Asia, and they feared that if the Allies suffered reverses Japan might well reach an accommodation with Germany and either withdraw from the war or join the Central Powers. For these reasons, even while Japan was formally an ally, the Australian intelligence community spent much time investigating Japanese spies and analysing the strategic danger posed by Japan. In the midst of the European conflict the Defence Department established Japanese studies at the University of Sydney in order to train army officers in the language of the Asian enemy and to have at its disposal experts who could translate intercepted mail and advise the government on Japan's intentions.[39]

Following the defeat of the Central Powers, Australia pressed for a harsh peace, a peace in Europe and the Pacific that would give Australia and the British empire absolute protection against foreign foes. On this Prime Minister Billy Hughes was more uncompromising than all the other British empire leaders. He was contemptuous of the American president's liberal internationalism and had no faith in the League of Nations as a guarantor against aggression. His overriding objective was to restore the global dominance of the British empire. Only its strength and unity could protect all the British peoples scattered around the world. He desired to see Britain and the dominions acting as one in their trade, defence and foreign policies. Australia's British race patriotism and its strategic insecurity led him in this direction. Hughes' sense of vulnerability, which had been intensified by the war experience, produced an obsessive, almost psychotic, realism in his attitude to peacemaking.

Australia's approach to the Paris Peace Conference in 1919 differed from Japan's in that it was almost as much concerned with the European as the Pacific settlements. Hughes wanted to crush Germany economically and militarily so that it would never again be able to defy the Pax Britannica. He considered that Germany should pay the full cost of the war, be denied access to the markets of the Allies and be permanently disarmed. For the Pacific, which touched Australia more directly, he urged terms that would confine and

---

[39] Minute, GF Pearce, Minister for Defence, to Brigadier-General HJ Foster, Chief of the General Staff, 24 April 1916, NAA A3688 488/Rl/55; 'Report in Reference to the Commonwealth Instructor in Japanese·. 30 April 1917 and letter, T Trumble, Acting Secretary of Defence, to Warden and Registrar, University of Sydney, 7 May 1917, University of Sydney Archives G3/13.

constrain Australia's enemy ally, Japan. At the peace conference he fought for Australia's right to annex the German South Pacific possessions, tried to prevent Japan from acquiring the German North Pacific Islands and opposed Japan's efforts to include a racial equality principle in the League Covenant. Japan's southward expansion and its advocacy of racial equality were construed as evidence of an intent to overthrow White Australia.

Though Hughes, partly because of the lack of British support, failed substantially to achieve his aims in the Treaty of Versailles, Australians generally found the postwar world to be more reassuring. Even if they did not have much confidence in the League of Nations, Britain had emerged as victor from the Great War, its European rivals had been vanquished, its empire enlarged and its capacity to defend the far-flung dominions enhanced. After Japan showed, at the Washington Conference, a willingness to co-operate with the British empire and the USA to preserve peace in the Pacific, accepting limits on its navy, withdrawing its military forces from China and Siberia and promising to respect its neighbours' frontiers, Australia's anxieties about Asia subsided. In Australian eyes Japan had accepted the Anglo-Saxon or Western postwar world order, even as it applied to East Asia. White Australia seemed inviolable.

During the 1920s and 1930s Australia's political culture was subjected to strains and stresses many of which, even if less pronounced, were similar to those that wracked Japan. Australians in World War I, like the Japanese in the Russo-Japanese War, had found a focus for national feelings and national identity. But even as Australian participation in the World War I had strengthened loyalty to king and empire it had also stirred up resistance among Irish Catholics and the working class to the total claims made for the British cause and the warfare state. Those who supported all aid to the Mother Country, including conscription of soldiers for overseas service, denounced their opponents as traitors. The loyalists' anger was especially directed at Irish Catholics, who resented Britain's ruthless treatment of Irish nationalists, and at radical socialists, who claimed workers had no interest in a conflict between capitalists.

For the loyalists the AIF represented the true spirit of the nation. Over 350 000 men left their civilian occupations and enlisted to fight for the survival of the British race. Nearly every family had a member, a close friend or a near neighbour who had been killed or wounded. The country felt extraordinary pride in the deeds of its soldiers on the battlefield. Anzac Day, commemorating the blooding of the Australian and New Zealand troops at Gallipoli in Turkey, became a national holiday, or, perhaps more aptly, a holy day, dedicated to the memory of the fallen. At the end of the war nearly every city, suburb and country town erected a monument, often a symbolic statue, to honour its dead. In Canberra the Commonwealth government built a National War Memorial, the Australian equivalent of the Japanese Yasukuni shrine.

Many soldiers, proud of their achievements on the battlefield, believed that they had created an organisation that embodied purified national ideals. In contrast to the British army, Australian officers came from the ranks, not from the ruling class . In harmony with Australia's democratic ethos those who commanded had first to prove themselves to their fellows, eventually being appointed on proven ability; as a result they commanded their men's respect. Imbued with this spirit the Australian army became an efficient, harmonious and orderly body held together by mutual support and self-sacrifice.

The AIF forged strong bonds of comradeship among its members. After the war Australia's Returned Servicemen's League attracted a much greater number of the veterans and exercised much greater influence in national life than did its British or American counterparts. Some who, on their return, were disillusioned by the disorder, dissension and disloyalty they saw around them, offered the values and structures of the AIF as a model for postwar Australia. General CC Brudenell White, after arriving home, declared in a speech that his four years in the AIF had made him into a democrat. He believed that Australia's political life could be regenerated if it were governed by these ideals. This speech was written for White by CEW Bean, the AIF's official journalist who became the official historian of the ANZAC myth and the chief advocate for a National War Memorial. It was Bean's view that the Australian soldier 'knew only one social horizon, that of race',[40] by which he meant the white British race. Bean believed that it was for this the AIF had fought and that in the process they had proved themselves to be better Britons than the British of the Mother Country.

Loyalists, often led and supported by returned soldiers, formed open and covert organisations – often along military lines – for the purpose of upholding these ideals. They gave themselves such names as the King and Empire Alliance, the Old Guard, the New Guard, the White Guard and the League of National Security. Though there was among their numbers some who were disenchanted with parliamentary government and sympathised with the Italian fascist movement, most professed – insofar as they had a coherent ideology – a desire to defend against Bolshevik revolutionaries and Irish republicans Australia's allegiance to the British empire and to the British tradition of constitutional monarchy. They were not willing to tolerate those who raised the red flag in defiance of the Union Jack and divided Australia by calling for class war.

With increasing industrialisation had come a more militant working class movement. The Communist Party of Australia, capitalising on the Bolshevik revolution, gave a frightening edge to strikes and demonstrations. Though loyalists might burn red flags and break up protest meetings, they, for the most part, had no intention of overthrowing the parliamentary system. Even at the lowest point of the Great Depression, when class antagonism and agitation were most evident, these organisations never seriously threatened the rule of law. Indeed, the New Guard's own support melted away when its leaders talked of using violence against police and parliament.[41] In contrast to Japan, Australia's liberal democracy was an integral part of the national culture. Loyalty to the empire involved loyalty to the constitution under the Crown. Thus in Australia the romantic nationalism

---

[40]   C E W Bean. *Official History of Australia in the War of 1914–1918*, 12 vols (Sydney: Angus & Robertson, 1940–42), vol. VI, pp. 5-6.

[41]   H McQueen, ' "Shoot the Bolshevik" Hang the Profiteer": Reconstructing Australian Capitalism, 1918–1921', in EL Wheelwright and K Buckley (eds), *Essays in the Political Economy of Australian Capitalism*, 2 vols (Sydney: Australia and New Zealand Book Co., 1978), vol. I, pp. 185–206; A Moore, *The Secret Army and the Premier; Conservative Paramilitary Organisations in New South Wales, 1930–1932* (Sydney: UNSW Press, 1989); K Amos, *The New Guard Movement*, 1931–1935 (Melbourne University Press, Melbourne, 1976); S Macintyre, *The Reds: The Communist Party of Australia from Origins to Illegality* (Sydney: Allen & Unwin, 1998).

of the warrior, which had great appeal for a democratic people who defined themselves in white British race terms, could not, because of its very self-definition, produce a totalitarian state. The bitter divisions in the body politic over loyalty and disloyalty, which had arisen out of the World War I political battles over conscription, were contained within the British heritage.

Australia, as part of the British Commonwealth, was a satisfied power and was committed to the Anglo-American world order established by the Versailles and Washington agreements. Responding to the great international crises of the 1930s that undermined that order, Australia sought closer ties with the Mother Country.

To deal with the Great Depression, Australia, along with the other dominions at the 1932 Ottawa Imperial Conference, persuaded Britain to enter into a customs union under which the members of the empire granted each other preferential tariffs. A few years later after increased cheap Japanese textile imports seemed to threaten the British near monopoly of the Australian market and imports of American cars and other industrial goods produced a chronic bilateral trade deficit, Australia imposed special duties and quotas intended to favour British manufacturers. It was Australia's hope that the British nations would through mutual support help each other to survive the economic convulsions of the time and so strengthen the position of the empire in the world. British empire autarky was in some ways the Australian equivalent of Japan's Greater East Asia Co-Prosperity Sphere. The Ottawa system, however, differed from the Co-Prosperity Sphere in that it was brought into being with the consent of all the parties.

Similarly, when Japan and Germany embarked on aggressive policies challenging the postwar political settlement, Australia looked to Britain for reassurance. It wanted an imperial defence and foreign policy that would safeguard Australia in the Pacific as well as Britain in Europe. Australia, above all, wished to rely on the British navy to deter Japan from striking at Australia. Until almost as late as the Japanese attack on Pearl Harbour Australia was pleading for guarantees that if Japan entered World War II, the Singapore base would hold and a British fleet would come to Australia's rescue. Yet, as before World War I, Australian leaders had to concede, almost despite themselves, that if the empire was at war on two fronts- against Germany in Europe and Japan in the Pacific- Britain's resources would not be sufficient to engage both enemies. They had to accept that Britain, if so pressed, would provide first for the defence of its homeland.

Facing up to this contingency, Australia sought to appease the Japanese in Northeast Asia and to obtain US commitments in the Pacific. The external affairs minister, returning from a Far East tour in 1934, reported to cabinet that he had warned the Japanese foreign minister against pursuing 'military adventures to the South' and that 'it would be unwise to engage in any war with the British Empire'. He recommended that Australia encourage Britain and the USA to recognise Japan's position in Manchuria as it was 'a source of poison' in relations with Japan and in itself offered no threat to Australia.[42] Failing in this Australia then attempted to involve the USA, along with Japan and other Pacific powers, in a non-aggression pact. But this too proved abortive. The United States would do nothing

---

[42] 'Report upon the International Position in the Far East', in letter, External Affairs Minister J Latham w Prime Minister JA Lyons, 30 July 1934, NAA CRS A981 item Imperial Relations 135.

to compromise its western hemisphere isolation and, furthermore, Japan's full-scale war on China showed up the futility of the proposal.[43]

The gathering storm in Europe and the Pacific made it clear to Australians that they looked upon Asia in a different light from the Mother Country. Prime Minister Menzies in April 1939 drew out the full implications of this when he stated that 'What Great Britain calls the Far East is to us the near north'. In the Pacific region Australia had the 'primary risks and responsibilities' and therefore Australia, even as a member of the British empire, had to act 'as a principal', and he announced Australia's intention of appointing its own diplomatic representatives to the capitals of the major Pacific powers – the United States, Japan and China.[44]

Australians reacted to the outbreak of the Pacific War with mixed emotions of fear and hope. On the one hand the war threatened invasion from the north, while on the other, since the war began with an attack on Pearl Harbour, it made the USA an ally and thereby promised ultimate salvation. But the threat of invasion had the more enduring influence on Australia's attitude to Japan. Japan's easy conquest of Singapore, its bombing of Darwin and other northern ports, its submarine attack on Sydney Harbour, its advance into Papua-New Guinea and its occupation of the Solomon Islands shook the nation to the core. Moreover, Japan's brutal treatment of prisoners of war and civilian internees created an intense hatred of the enemy. After the end of hostilities this feeling was inflamed further by the memoirs and novels of those who had survived the ordeal and returned to tell the tale, most notably Rohan Rivett's *Behind Bamboo*, Russell Braddon's *The Naked Island* and Betty Jeffrey's *White Coolies*.

With the coming of peace Australia's single most important objective was to provide against a future onslaught from Asia, particularly from a resurgent Japan. To this end the government devised a range of policies to meet the peril. In setting out to build up Australia's population by encouraging European, primarily British, settlers, the minister for immigration made it clear that this program was intended to counter Japan. He considered that 'Japan will rise again and will destroy the peace of the Pacific once more and will want to wage war against us', and for this reason Australia had to 'fill the country as quickly as possible with people who are acceptable to the Australian people, with people who are assimilable'.[45] Minister for External Affairs Dr H V Evatt proposed that Australia should control a ring of forward bases in the Portuguese, Dutch and French island empires to the north and northeast that would act as a rampart against the Asian peril. He also hoped to engage the USA, in conjunction with the British Commonwealth, in the permanent defence of the southwest Pacific.[46]

---

[43] 'Most Secret' memorandum E. (37) 29, 28 May 1937, NAA CRS A981 item Pacific 23.

[44] *Sydney Morning Herald*, 27 April 1939.

[45] CPD, vol. 189, pp.502–3, 22 November 1946; cited from an address by A Calwell, Minister of Immigration, to representatives of Neighbour Countries to Australia at the Department of External Affairs, 2 June 1949, NAA A1838, 278 item S39/l.

[46] *Daily Telegraph*, 18 August 1943; CPD, vol. 186, pp. 200–01, 13 March 1946; cable, Evatt to Prime Minister JB Chifley. 21 June 1946, in WJ Hudson and W Way (eds), *Documents on Australian Foreign Policy, 1937–1949* (Canberra: Australian Government Publishing Service

Australia was deeply disappointed by US and British indifference to its Pacific concerns and annoyed by their increasing concentration on the Russian problem. When, in January 1948, the British government asked for support in forming a Western alliance in Europe against the Soviet Union, Australia was the only British Commonwealth country to oppose the idea. Though the Chifley Labor government criticised the scheme on liberal internationalist grounds for undermining the collective security principles of the United Nations (the successor to the League of Nations), it rejected the proposal primarily because the USA and Britain would once again be preoccupied with Europe at the expense of the Pacific. In replying to the British the prime minister explained that Australia's interests were 'very much bound up in the Pacific area ... in the event of European conflict, our whole manpower might well have to be directed to the protection of our position and interests in this area'.

As Britain and the USA identified their enemy in Europe so Australia identified its enemy in the Pacific. Evatt asserted that many of the Japanese 'still nurse the hope and intention of reviving Japanese power and trying once again at some future time to dominate the Pacific and the world'. He declared that 'first and foremost, therefore in Australian policy in regard to Japan we place security'. Australia, of all the victor powers, was the most resolute in demanding a harsh peace. It was Australia's firm aim that 'Japan ... never again be permitted to develop the means of waging war'.[47] Since Australia was the 'trustee of British Civilisation' in the Pacific and carried the major responsibilities for the British empire in the Pacific it insisted that it should command the British Commonwealth Occupation Forces in Japan. When the US moderated its occupation policy in order to win Japan's goodwill in the Cold War against the Soviet Union, Australia did its best to rally the British Commonwealth to hold the line. It was only induced to sign the US-devised 'soft' peace treaty with Japan in return for the USA entering into a security treaty.[48]

From dependence to partnership

After World War II, Japan's and Australia's relations with East and West and with each other were transformed, and in quite unexpected ways.

Japan's total defeat led to the overthrow of the aggressive nationalism that had been inspired by the divine emperor or tennosei system. Japan accepted the democratic reforms

[hereafter AGPS], 1991), vol. IX, 'January–June 1946', pp.543–44; N Meaney, *Japan and Australian Foreign Policy, 1945–52* (London: Suntory Centre, London School of Economics and Politics, 2000), especially pp. 18–35.

[47] Cable, Chifley to British Prime Minister C Attlee, 22 January 1948, PRO, PREM 8/787; *New York Times Magazine*, 3 February 1946; CPD, vol. 190, p. 1170, 26 February 1947; Meaney, *Japan and Australian Foreign Policy*, pp. 49–53.

[48] Hiroyuki Umetsu, 'The Linkage between the Japanese Peace Treaty, the Defence of japan and the ANZUS Treaty – A Study in US–Australian Relations. January 1950–February 1951', MA thesis, Department of Politics, Flinders University, Adelaide, 1990; N Meaney, 'Look Back in Fear: Percy Spender, the Japanese Peace Treaty and the ANZUS Pact', *Japan Forum* 15 (2003), pp. 399–410; W David McIntyre, *Background to the ANZUS Pact: Policy-Makers, Strategy and Diplomacy, 1945–55* (Basingstoke, Palgrave Macmillan, 1995), especially chapter 11; David McLean. 'ANZUS Origins: A Reassessment', *Australian Historical Studies*, 24 (April 1990), pp. 64–82.

imposed by the US victors, which transferred sovereignty from the emperor to the people. Protected by the Mutual Defense Treaty with the USA it was a dependent, passive ally of the West in the Cold War. Rebuilding its industry it served as an 'arsenal of democracy' for the West in the global contest and, by the 1980s, had become the second largest economy in the Western world. Following the oil crises of the 1970s, the defeat of the USA in the Vietnam War and the end of the Cold War, Japan was faced by new challenges that both strengthened and qualified its identification with the West. From these shocks it recognised that though it was profoundly involved with the West it was not of the West, that though it still looked to the USA for security in Northeast Asia it had to adjust to a new Asia, freed from Western dominance and intent on creating its own future.

After the Cold War became fully established in the 1950s Australia became more completely integrated than ever before into the West. To meet the challenge of the Sino-Soviet bloc to Southeast and the Pacific, Britain and the USA expanded their presence in the region. Australia welcomed this development and participated enthusiastically in defence alliances and military actions aimed at containing the spread of communism. By the 1970s, however, this Western commitment was faltering before the rise of Asian nationalism. After Britain's withdrawal from east of Suez and the US defeat in Vietnam Australia was left to make its own peace with the new Asia.

Australia's response to the retreat of the Western powers was, in contrast to its Yellow Peril past, quite positive. Australia's prosperity was increasingly bound up with that of its Asian neighbours. Since the West no longer underwrote its security against Asia it had no choice but to cultivate the goodwill of its northern neighbours. Its ties with Britain were severed and it repudiated the ideal of White Australia in favour of multiculturalism. Australia showed sympathy and respect for cultural differences and sought to enmesh itself in the region. Working closely with Japan, Australia supported Asia-Pacific arrangements and took a leading role in bringing APEC into being. While Australia recognised that the new Asia would fashion its own destiny it, along with Japan, hoped that the USA, by being associated with the process, would bring a stabilising Western influence to bear on the making of the new order. In this era Australia and Japan were drawn together first by their economic interdependence and then more latterly by their shared vision of the region's future.

Japan's defeat and the US occupation left a deep impression on the nation. It had struggled to escape the common fate of Asian peoples who had been conquered by and incorporated into Western empires, but in the end, Japan had to give up everything that it had worked so hard to achieve since the Meiji restoration. It had imitated the West's industrial and military success in order to obtain the West's respect and create under its tutelage an Asia free from Western influence. All that had been lost. The Allies divested Japan of its empire and imposed a new political, social and economic order. The emperor was not compelled to abdicate but he was no longer considered divine. As a result of American occupatin Japan was to become a constitutional monarchy on the model of Britain and Australia. Under the US-made constitution the people were the source of sovereignty, the nation renounced war, trade unions were legalised and citizens were guaranteed personal liberty. Shinto ceased to be the state religion. Almost 6000 war criminals were tried by the International Military Tribunal and 200,000 ultranationalists were barred from public life. The great oligopolistic companies, the *zaibatsu*, were dissolved and land was redistributed in favour of the tenant farmer.[49]

The Japanese people did not resist the occupation's reforms. As historian John Dower has suggested, they 'embraced defeat'. The Japanese seemed to accept without demur the supremacy of the West and even, in a curious way, the superiority of the West. A 1951 newspaper poll revealed that almost half of the Japanese surveyed agreed that Japan was inferior to 'civilised countries, such as Britain and the United States'.[50] Since that time Japan has identified itself with the postwar institutional changes, and has for fifty years maintained its allegiance to the system of parliamentary government established under the occupation constitution.

But the Japanese response to the USA's reconstruction was not a simple adoption of the victor's institutions and ideals. Japan in practice subordinated and adapted these Western forms to the values that, from the late Meiji period, had come to be identified with the family nation. Some of the mythic ideas that had been fostered in the prewar period remained influential. When asked in 1975 whether Japanese values had changed, Emperor Hirohito replied that 'from a broad perspective, I do not think there has been any change between prewar and postwar'.[51] The dominant culture still held to a belief in the unique racial essence of the Japanese people, and this helped to balance the sense of inferiority that had followed from military defeat and occupation. Japanese traditional mores of political stability, social conformity and consensus decision-making were contrasted with the rampant individualism, social antagonism and partisan politics of the Western nations.

Though there was complete freedom for rival political parties to compete in the electoral marketplace, from almost the end of the US occupation one party, the Liberal Democratic Party (LDP), with some brief exceptions, has held office. Backed by rural and business interests, it was greatly assisted in maintaining its hold on government by a seat distribution that favoured the country electorate at the expense of the urban majority.[52] No other party was able to appear as a national party; the Japanese Socialist Party, unlike the Australian Labor Party, was never able to achieve such a status. Since the end of the Cold War while the Communist Party has survived, the Socialist Party has collapsed. In 1993 a majority coalition based on dissidents from the LDP broke the postwar pattern and took control of the government. Subsequently, these coalition partners, strengthened further by the socialists, merged to form the Democratic Party of Japan (DPJ). Whether the DPJ, by far the largest opposition party in the diet, can endure and become a coherent alternative government and so make Japan's parliamentary system more akin to that of Western nations, remains unclear.

---

[49] Theodore Cohen, *Remaking Japan: The American Occupation as New Deal* (New York, Free Press, 1987).

[50] Cited by Peter Duus in Duus (ed.), *The Cambridge History of Japan*, vol. 6, 'The Twentieth Century' (Cambridge: Cambridge University Press, 1995), p. 12, see also Haruhiro Fukui, 'Postwar Politics, 1945–1973', in Duus, p. 166.

[51] John W Dower, *Embracing Defeat: Japan in the Wake of World War II* (New York and London: The New Press, 1999), p. 556.

[52] Fukui, pp. 192–213; Andrew Gordon (ed.), *Postwar Japan as History* (Berkeley: University of California Press, 1993) pp. 189ff.

It has also been argued that, in contrast to the West, the political leaders and parliament in this new era had little or no power, that theirs was merely the formal face of authority and that behind the scenes, as in the prewar era, influential institutions and interests governed the country. While scholars concede that the military was no longer the power behind the throne, they do not agree about the nature of these hidden forces and how they controlled the state. Nearly all acknowledge that the bureaucracy, especially the economic bureaucracy, was important. Most consider that the bureaucratic elite in association with the great business and financial houses and the LDP machine made policy and managed the political system.[53]

In meeting the objection that these accounts of Japan's style of governance are quite similar to some standard analyses of Western states it has still been claimed that 'statecraft in Japan is quite different from [that] in the Americas and most of contemporary Asia'. In this view government resulted from 'a balance between semi-autonomous groups which share power', including ministry officials, Liberal Democratic Party machine bosses and bureaucrat-businessmen. According to this perception, 'No one is ultimately in charge ... there is no supreme institution with ultimate policy-making jurisdiction'. The power structure was a 'truncated pyramid': the state had no centre, therefore no one institution or individual could be held responsible for what governments do.[54] The very lack of scholarly agreement, the conflict of interpretations, the difficulty of defining precisely the political process, suggests in itself a certain inscrutability about Japanese democracy that makes it rather different from Australian democracy. The economic failures and major corruption scandals of the 1990s have undermined the standing of the bureaucracy and may open up policy making to greater scrutiny by the parliament and the press. If so, it will bring the Japanese political system more into harmony with those of Western countries.[55]

The 1951 Japan-United States Mutual Security Treaty, which was signed at the same time as the peace treaty, set the direction for Japanese foreign policy in the postwar period. Under this unequal treaty the USA was allowed to maintain military bases in Japan and its military personnel were granted something akin to extraterritorial rights. Moreover though the US forces were ostensibly to be used for mutual defence, the USA, since it alone was providing the defence or at least the ultimate defence, had in practice a free hand to decide what this meant. In this sense Japan became a protectorate of the USA. The Japanese government and the majority of the people acquiesced in accepting this position, happy to have a low profile in defence and foreign policy. They understood that many of the Asian countries that had suffered from Japanese imperialism would not wish Japan to rearm and take a more assertive role in the region, a lesson from the Pacific War that had sunk in.

---

[53] Chalmers Johnson, *MITI and the Japanese Miracle: The Growth of Industrial Policy, 1925–1975* (Stanford: Stanford University Press, 1982); Michio Muramatsu and Ellis S Kraus, 'Bureaucrats and Politicians in Policy-Making: The Case of Japan', *American Political Science Review*, 78 (March 1984), pp. 126–46.

[54] Karel van Wolferen, *The Enigma of Japanese Power: People and Politics in a Stateless Nation* (New York: Random House, 1989), pp. 5–6.

[55] Gerald Curtis, *The Logic of Japanese Politics: Leaders, Institutions and the Limits of Change* (New York: Columbia University Press, 1999).

Japan eschewed militarism. Its only serious dispute with the USA was over the presence of nuclear weapons on its soil.

While Japan, through the US alliance, was brought into the Western camp, it, unlike Australia, did not contribute to the common defence of the West. From the Korean War to the Vietnam War Japan took no part in the strategic planning or military actions aimed at containing the spread of communism in Asia. As it recovered from the devastation of defeat Japan did, however, manage to remove or revise some of the more humiliating and unequal terms of the peace treaty and the US alliance. It created a National Self-Defence Force, regained control over Okinawa and the Ryuku islands and renegotiated the Mutual Security Alliance to modify US extraterritorial rights and to provide for consultation over the use of US bases. Even so, these changes were limited to achieving greater respect for national sovereignty. In the US relationship Japan continued to be very much the junior partner dependent on US nuclear and military capability for national security. It was content to remain quietly enfolded in the Western alliance.

Sheltering under this US security umbrella, the Japanese dedicated themselves in the postwar years to restoring their economy. Spurred on by their sense of vulnerability they single-mindedly set about putting their house in order. The war had left their industrial infrastructure in ruins. The peace had divested them of their empire and thereby deprived them of a major source of raw materials. With the coming of the Cold War, the new international circumstances favoured them. The United States was anxious to make Japan a bulwark of the free world in Asia. The United States thus sponsored Japan's admission to the General Agreement on Tariffs and Trade (GATT) and the International Monetary Fund, which gave it access to the West's markets and investment capital. The United States also helped Japanese recovery with loans and technology transfers and allowed the Japanese government to impose controls over its imports while permitting Japanese goods unrestricted entry into the USA. In contrast to the prewar years Japan had unlimited access to the raw materials and markets of the West. Being cut off by the Cold War from the East Asian mainland Japan found in Australia its chief source of minerals and a major supplier of fossil fuels. As a result, for the first time in its history, Japan began to take seriously its relationship with Australia.

Led by the bureaucrats, especially from the ministries of finance and international trade and industry, and the great industrial and financial institutions, all sectors of the society and economy co-operated to produce the so-called Japanese economic miracle, which was based on an economic organisation that stressed 'effectiveness rather than legality', national outcomes rather than 'laissez-faire' doctrine. Though in the 1950s Japan had been regarded as a backward nation, by the 1960s its gross national product (GNP) had risen to be the fifth largest in the West behind the USA, West Germany, Britain and France and by the 1970s it had surpassed all but the USA. To achieve this very high rate of growth – roughly, on average, 10 per cent a year for the 1950s and 1960s – the Japanese leaders drew on established patterns of economic planning and national values developed under the quasi-warfare state of the 1930s. The Japanese, for the most part, supported this centrally managed reconstruction. For the good of the family nation they sacrificed much. They committed themselves to their employers, worked very hard and for long hours, accepted relatively low wages, forewent short-term improvements in their standard of living and saved a greater proportion of their income than the people of any other major industrial nation.[56]

Japan funded its economic miracle from its own resources, namely, domestic savings and trade surpluses. After it had established the industrial base, foreign investment was discouraged. It did not look kindly on foreign control or influence. Consequently, the economy remained a family affair, a reflection of the national ethos and an instrument of the national interest. This extraordinary Japanese recovery from the devastation of defeat cannot be put down simply to a sense of vulnerability. Rather, it was as though, having failed to gain the respect of the West by political assertion and imperial aggression, the people were determined to achieve the same end by economic success, as though they were determined to attain their long-established aim of winning the West's recognition of their equality by other means. It might be asked whether Japan's economic success was to be a latter-day equivalent of its triumph in the Russo-Japanese War.

For Australia the Cold War years were both disturbing and reassuring. After Japan's defeat Australia had assumed that the European imperial powers would return to the region and restore the old order. But the rise of Asian nationalism and the spread of communism confounded these expectations. Consequently, Australia in the early 1950s looked fearfully not only at Japan but also at communist China, the communist insurgencies in Malaya and Indo-China and the newly independent Indonesia. To Australia's relief the USA, Britain and France, as part of their global containment of communism and their desire to see that their colonies achieved independence under Western auspices, increased considerably their military and diplomatic presence in East and Southeast Asia.

This expansion of Western power and influence in the region offered more solid comfort than the ramshackle prewar European empires. Australia wholeheartedly backed its great and powerful friends in their efforts to construct an Asia friendly to the West. It was especially pleased that the Americans who had repelled the Japanese in the Pacific War were extending their protective mantle over the Western Pacific. Through Australia's membership in the Australia, New Zealand and United States Security Pact (ANZUS), in the Australia, New Zealand and Malaya Agreement (ANZAM) and SEATO it formally associated itself with the Western cause. It sent military forces to assist Britain in the Malayan emergency and the Indonesian confrontation of Malaysia, and to support the USA in the Korean and Vietnam Wars. Through this strategy of forward defence in support of Britain and the USA it hoped to prevent the dominoes of Southeast Asia from falling and so prevent the new Asian enemy from repeating what the Japanese had almost accomplished in 1942.

Australia's anxieties about Asia were not easily allayed. The government remained uncertain whether its Western allies would be able to keep the growing Asian communist menace at bay by use of conventional weapons. To this end, in 1955, Prime Minister Menzies urged the USA and the British to consider deploying nuclear weapons in East Asia and argued that Australia because of the 'needs arising from its special danger from

---

[56] Peter Duns, 'Introduction', pp. 22–24; Sheldon Garon, 'Saving for "My Own Good And the Good of the Nation": Economic Nationalism in Modern Japan', in Sandra Wilson (ed.), *Nation and Nationalism in Japan* (London: Routledge Curzon, 2002), pp.109–14.

communist and Japanese aggression' should be given tactical nuclear weapons.[57] Australia had learnt a different lesson about the dropping of atomic bombs on Hiroshima and Nagasaki: nuclear armaments were the saviour, not the destroyer, of civilisation. Despite these residual misgivings about its great power protectors, Australia's identity as an integral part of the West seemed more secure than at any other time in its history.

Australia in the early Cold War era reaffirmed its Britishness and its role as 'the trustee of British civilisation in the South Pacific'. In 1947, 65 per cent of Australians questioned in a public opinion poll opted to maintain their British nationality in preference to a separate Australian one.[58] The intimate bonds connecting Australia to Britain seemed stronger than ever. Australia's material interests were well served through close trade, investment, migration and defence links with the Mother Country. Though US popular culture began to influence lifestyles, as in Japan, the nation's fundamental character remained intact: Britain was still regarded as the source of standards and values. Many national organisations, including religious, educational, professional and trade union bodies, were still branches of or associated closely with the institutions from which they had sprung. With the reduction in the cost of travel, increasing numbers of Australians made their pilgrimage 'home' to Britain. For the first time a reigning monarch, the head of the empire and Commonwealth, visited the antipodean dominions, an occasion that evoked the greatest outpouring of British race sentiment in the history of Australia. The public response was overwhelming. It was a celebration of the national religion. Over 1 million people turned out in Sydney to greet their queen. The *Sydney Morning Herald* summed up the meaning of the event when it stated that Queen Elizabeth symbolised 'the supreme achievement of the British race' and that 'Australia is and always will be a British nation'.[59]

Australia stood firm behind its white British immigration policy. Though in order to build up its population the government agreed to accept a certain proportion of non-British European migrants, it was determined that they should assimilate quickly. At the time of the queen's visit the Good Neighbour Council, which was sponsored by the Department of Immigration, informed the European immigrants that they should use the opportunity to 'display their loyalty to the Crown and to experience the feeling of unity brought to outlying parts of the British Commonwealth'.[60] These views were shared by both sides of politics. Indeed, the leader of the Labor Party, in criticising the Liberal-Country Party government for allowing too many non-British Europeans into the immigration program, averred that 'Australia will be and must be primarily a British community'.[61] Out of deference to Third World sensibilities the arguments used in defence of the restrictive immigration policy were now cultural rather than racial. It was claimed that coloured peoples, particularly Asians against whom the policy was chiefly directed, could not be integrated into a Western

---

[57] Wayne Reynolds, 'Menzies and the Proposal for Atomic Weapons', in Frank Cain (ed.), *Menzies in War and Peace* (Sydney: Allen & Unwin, in association with Australian Defence Studies Centre, Canberra, 1997), p. 118.

[58] *Australian Gallup Polls*, nos 470–77 (November–December 1947).

[59] *Sydney Morning Herald*, 3 March 1954.

[60] *Good Neighbours*, February 1954, p. 3.

[61] *CPD*, House of Representatives, vol. 18, p. 115, 27 February 1958.

culture and that their admission to Australia would pose a problem for social homogeneity. In 1958 the government amended the 1901 immigration act to remove the provision for a dictation test, since it had become a focus for Asian criticism, and instead gave the minister unqualified discretion to exclude unwanted migrants, a discretion that was in substance still used to uphold the longstanding discriminatory policy.[62]

The Cold War added ideology to race and culture in the definition of Australian identity and loyalty. The dread of communism as an external and an internal enemy intensified pressures for social conformity. It mattered not that the Communist Party, unlike its Japanese equivalent, had relatively few members and no political representation in the federal parliament. Australian intelligence organisations, working in co-operation with Britain's MI5 and the US CIA carried out wide-ranging searches for subversives; a very small number were found.[63] Posters denouncing the fifth column at home and depicting a red tide sweeping down from Asia were commonly employed in political campaigns. As in Japan the labour movement was divided by the issue of communism and anti-communism, which helped the conservative parties to hold office at the national level for the whole of the 1950s and 1960s.'[64]

The Liberal-Country Party governments, like their Japanese Liberal Democratic equivalents, took full advantage of the Cold War to advance national prosperity. Even though a more ardent member of the Western alliance, Australia, being assured of protection from the USA, also gave first priority to economic development. Much to Washington's annoyance Australia continued to trade with communist China. Similarly, while the USA and Britain spent on average 8 to 10 per cent of their GDP annually on defence, Australia spent approximately 3 per cent. Japan's defence expenditure, also much to Washington's annoyance, was kept at less than 1 per cent. Behind high tariff walls Australian manufactures, most notably the automobile industry, grew rapidly. As Britain's market for Australian exports shrank Australia was very happy to supply Japan with the raw materials for its rapid postwar industrialisation. Underpinned by booming primary exports the economy expanded at a relatively high rate and achieved almost effective full employment. Unlike Japan, however, Australia spent its largesse not on reinvestment and accelerated rates of growth but on generous dividends, higher wages, shorter hours of work, longer holidays and social welfare measures. It relied increasingly on British and US capital to fund further growth. Australians were very comfortable with their improved standard of living and voted accordingly.

Despite the Cold War atmosphere most Australians – the Catholic social ideologues of the Democratic Labor Party and the philosophical ideologues of the Congress for Cultural Freedom being exceptions – never took the anti-communist crusade seriously. In a referendum held in 1951 the people rejected the Menzies government's plan to ban the

---

[62] Matthew Jordan, ' "Modification by Degrees": The Reappraisal of the White Australia Policy against the Background of a Changing Asia, *Australian Journal of Politics and History*, 52 (2006), pp. 224–43

[63] David McKnight, *Australia's Spies and Their Secrets* (Sydney: Allen & Unwin, 1994); Desmond Ball and David Horner, *Breaking the Codes, 1944–1950: Australia's KGB Network* (Sydney: Allen & Unwin, 1998).

[64] Robert Murray, *The Split: Australian Labor in the Fifties* (Melbourne: Cheshire, 1970).

Communist Party. The Labor Party was in office in a number of the states for long periods and almost gained federal office on two occasions. While the verbal contests between the political parties were fierce and sometimes bitter, they still had much in common in defining the nation and the national interest. When they differed they fought out those differences within the confines of the shared British tradition of parliamentary democracy.

By the 1960s Australia's assumptions about its place in the West and the West's place in Asia were being severely tested. The British Commonwealth was being transformed. Shorn of its British title and made over as the Commonwealth of Nations it was increasingly influenced by its new Asian and African members, most of whom were republics. Its meetings had lost the sense of family intimacy that the Australian leaders so much prized. Prime Minister Menzies wrote of the new Commonwealth that 'When I ask myself what benefit we of the Crown Commonwealth derive from having a tenuous association with a cluster of Republics some of which like Ghana are more spiritually akin to Moscow than to London, I begin to despair'.[65] Australia found it difficult to accept that the former British Commonwealth had lost its British character and could no longer act as a united body in international affairs.

Simultaneously, Australia had to adjust to Britain's reassessment of its role in the Commonwealth and the world. As its empire was dismantled and its economic power eroded, Britain turned to Western Europe and applied for admission to the European Economic Community. This too was a blow to Australia. Menzies, in response to this initiative, declared that 'United Kingdom membership of an actual European federation … would be a mistake'. The British government, giving further evidence of its intention to retreat into Europe, made it clear that it would in due course withdraw its military forces from east of Suez. Many Australians were disheartened by these developments, which affected not only their trade and defence interests but also their concept of themselves and their place in the world.[66]

Australia was also disturbed that most of the newly independent Asian nations would not align themselves with the West in the conflict between the Sino-Soviet communist bloc and the US-led 'free world'. These nations did not see themselves as comprising a frontline for the defence of the free world. They identified themselves with the Third World. Indonesia, Malaysia and Singapore would not join SEATO or allow their countries to be used as bases from which the Western powers could attack their Asian neighbours. Rather, in 1967, when the decolonisation process was complete they, in conjunction with Thailand and the Philippines, formed their own regional body, the Association of Southeast Asian Nations (ASEAN). Even though ASEAN was inspired, in part, by apprehensions about China and North Vietnam, these non-communist countries wanted an Asian not a Western solution to the problem.

With Britain abandoning the region Australia looked more singlemindedly to the USA, seeing it as the last bastion of the West in Asia. Australia from this time determined to associate itself as fully as possible with America and, to this end, restructured its armed

[65] Letter, Menzies to British Prime Minister Harold Macmillan, IS January 1962, PRO, Prem 11 /3644.

[66] Stuart Ward, *Australia and the British Embrace: The Demise of the Imperial Ideal* (Melbourne: Melbourne University Press, 2001), especially chapters 1 and 6.

forces along US lines so it could combine more readily with the USA in forward defence. It enthusiastically approved plans for the establishment of US communication and satellite surveillance bases on its soil at North-West Cape in Western Australia, at Woomera in South Australia and at Pine Gap in the Northern Territory.[67] It stood apart from the British in urging the USA to resist the extension of communist influence over Laos, in encouraging the USA to despatch combat troops to South Vietnam and in sending its own troops to assist the Americans there. All this strenuous endeavour to commit US militarily forces to the mainland of Southeast Asia was aimed at holding back the 'thrust by communist China between the Indian and Pacific Oceans' and at intimidating and isolating an adventurist Indonesia.[68] It was mistakenly believed that the United States' overwhelming military power could be relied upon to hold the line against a turbulent, menacing Asia.

America's defeat in Vietnam and its accommodation with communist China in the mid-1970s, followed by the collapse of the Soviet Union at the end of the 1980s, jolted Japan and Australia out of their Cold War straitjackets. These events marked the beginning of a new historical era and caused both countries to re-examine the foundations of their views about the region and its future. This rethinking brought into question established assumptions about economic welfare, social identity and national security and led to new developments in all these areas.

From the 1970s Japan began to encounter problems in maintaining its rate of economic growth. Two key conditions that, since the onset of the Cold War, had contributed greatly to its success, namely, cheap commodity and fossil fuel prices and access to the US market, could no longer be relied on. Oil-rich Third World countries, liberated from Western control, formed themselves into OPEC and, on the initiative of the Arab nations, tripled the price of oil. Simultaneously, the USA, burdened with the enormous cost of the Vietnam War, went off the gold standard, causing the yen to appreciate against the US dollar and most other Western currencies. As a result, Japan's exports became less competitive.[69]

Japan realised that it had to take a hand in shaping the conditions upon which its prosperity depended. The oil experience had alerted the Japanese to the fact that they were exposed to resource diplomacy, to the possibility that resource-rich countries might hold Japan to ransom; indeed, Japan suspected Australia of harbouring such designs. Thus Japan began to invest abroad in raw materials in order to ensure a guaranteed supply at reasonable prices and to intervene in the money market to keep the yen artificially depressed. Though growth had slowed, the Japanese economy in the 1970s and 1980s still managed to expand at an annual rate of roughly 4 per cent, which exceeded that of all other members of the group of the seven most advanced Western economies, the G7. Extrapolating from this, some commentators predicted that the Japanese GNP would surpass that of the USA by the year 2010.

---

[67] Desmond Ball, *A Suitable Piece of Real Estate: American Installations in Australia* (Hale & Iremonger, Sydney 1980).

[68] Peter Edwards with Gregory Pemberton, *Crises and Commitments: The Politics and Diplomacy of Australia's Involvement in Southeast Asian Conflicts, 1948–1965* (Allen & Unwin, Sydney, 1992), chapters 12–18.

[69] Kitaoka Shinichi, 'Diplomacy and the Military in Show a Japan', in Carol Gluck and Stephen R Graubard (eds), *Showa: The Japan of Hirohito* (New York: W W Norton, 1992), pp. 172–74.

The West's response to Japan's increasing international trade surpluses varied. One American scholar, Ezra Vogel in his book, *Japan As Number One*,[70] suggested that the USA could profit from emulating Japan and adopting its winning formula. That the Western nation states could learn from the East was a novel concept in that it reversed the conventional wisdom. The Japanese were flattered and gave the book great publicity; it touched a sensitive inferiority-superiority nerve. Though the major Western powers had, by inviting Japan to join G7, recognised its economic achievement, the invitation generated much resentment. Many political leaders and economic commentators believed that Japan's success was due to its unfair trading practices and demanded that it reform its economic system and conform to Western standards. They pressed Japan to liberalise its economy, remove tariff and administrative barriers to trade, open itself to foreign investment, deregulate its financial and industrial structures and adopt voluntary export restraints.

Some Japanese rebelled against this foreign pressure, or *gaiatsu*. Shintaro Ishihara's *The Japan That Can Say No* was one of the more extreme and widely read examples of the literature urging national defiance.[71] The Japanese government's placatory internationalism, which made changes quite slowly and failed to reduce the huge trade surplus, did not satisfy the Western nations and they organised themselves in the European Union and the North American Free Trade Area and took retaliatory measures. In the 1990s, primarily as a result of extravagant investment in property, Japan's economic bubble burst and its economy languished. Earlier expectations that it would overtake the USA by 2010 evaporated.

The end of the Cold War brought to a head the conflict within Japan over how the nation should understand itself and the great changes taking place in the world. Voices were raised demanding that Japan should become a 'normal nation'. An increasing number of intellectuals and politicians were complaining that there was a lack of pride in the nation and its achievements. Two generations after the end of the Pacific War the long period of economic growth had made Japanese people, especially the youth, less willing to make sacrifices for the good of the family nation. There was considerable disillusionment with factional politics and the corruption scandals associated with it. Conspicuous consumption and deference to Western popular culture led to charges that there was a void at the centre of society.

The influx of new immigrants added to this sense of national crisis. From the mid-1980s to the mid-1990s the number of foreign registered residents, many from Southeast Asia, more than doubled to over 1.5 million or 1.2 per cent of the total population. Though the percentage was quite small compared to similar migrations into Western countries it raised the same anxieties about identity and values. Shintaro Ishihara, the nationalist governor of Tokyo, playing upon these anxieties, attributed crime and social disorder to immigrants. These supposed social afflictions were not peculiar to Japan. They were to be found in Australia and other highly developed modern societies; however, it was the reaction against

---

[70] Ezra F Vogel, *Japan as Number One: Lessons for America* (Cambridge, Mass.: Harvard University Press, 1979); Paul Kennedy's *The Rise and Fall of Great Powers*, which was published a decade later, though it did not address the Japan question directly, did argue that America was no longer number one, that it was merely primus inter pores, and that as America was falling Japan was rising. Kennedy, like Vogel, was much feted in Japan.

[71] Shintaro Ishihara, *The Japan That Can Say No* (New York: Simon & Schuster, 1991).

the shame and moral obloquy of Japan's humiliating defeat at the end of the Pacific War that made the Japanese quasi-nationalist movement appear somewhat more dramatic and controversial.

In response to the perceived crisis a loosely-organised campaign sprang up with the aim of restoring respect for the nation. As part of this process the diet in 1999 formally adopted the Rising Sun standard, generally known as the *Hinomaru*, as the national flag and the Imperial *Kimigayo* as the national anthem, and the government ordered that public schools hold flag ceremonies accompanied by the singing of the national anthem. When 350 teachers from the Tokyo school district refused to obey and appealed to the district court, the judge upheld their arguments, concluding that the instruction violated their constitutional rights to freedom of thought and conscience.

More controversial were the campaigns to revise school history texts. In this new atmosphere a group of university professors formed the Society for the Creation of a New History and denounced the standard school texts, which, since the end of World War II, had eschewed a triumphant nationalist narrative and set out in detail, sometimes very graphically, the cruel consequences of Japanese imperialism. In the eyes of the members of the society these works only served to obstruct the formation of national identity and loyalty. To counter this demoralising history they sponsored a *New History Textbook* that, among other revisions, played down the significance of the 1937 Nanking massacre and justified Japan's invasion of the Philippines, Indochina, Malaya and the Dutch East Indies. Japan's wartime actions were explained in 'Greater East Asia Co-Prosperity Sphere' terms as bringing 'hope and courage to the people of Asia who had long been subject to domination as colonies of Europe and America'.[72] While the new textbook did not have the same degree of popular support as the flag and anthem and was used only in a miniscule number of schools, the political storm it raised caused other authors to modify their criticisms of Japan's role in the war.

The public furore stirred up by the history wars made the *New History Textbook* a best seller and gave a fillip to a new wave of manga comic books with titles such as *On War* and *Manifesto for a New Pride*. Yoshinoro Kobayashi, the most famous author-artist of this genre, moved in the mid-1990s from being a crusader for social justice to being a passionate advocate of the new nationalism. As a leading member of the Society for the Creation of a New History he contributed the chapter in the *New History Textbook* that dealt with the Pacific War. His *On War* and other manga gave a vivid and violent expression of this revisionist history. They made heroes of those who had sacrificed their lives for Japan in the Great East Asian War, a war in which Japan had fought alone to free Asian peoples from Western imperialism. These patriotic comic books were popular, *On War* alone selling over 600,000 copies.

How far the popularity of this new genre is a gauge of Japanese feeling and responds to a need for normalcy or how far Japanese people wish to press the idea of national pride into a rewriting of their history is not altogether clear. But there are signs that a goodly number desire a better balance in their identity. Prime Minister Junichiro Koizumi, who admitted

---

[72] John Nathan, *Japan Unbound: A Volatile Notion's Quest for Pride and Purpose* (Boston: Houghton Mifflin, 2004), p. 141.

that Japan 'caused tremendous damage and suffering to the people of many countries', also expressed some mild support for the general tendency embodied in the *New History Textbook*, declaring that Japan should cease to hold the 'masochistic understanding' of its role in the Pacific War that had been imposed upon it 'by the American occupation policy and leftwing forces in Japan'.[73]

The dispute over the relationship between the state and the Yasukuni war memorial was perhaps the most divisive of all the 'normal nation' issues. From 1975, when memorial sticks for the fourteen major war criminals who had been found guilty at the Tokyo War Tribunal were installed in the shrine, any official recognition of the Shinto temple drew strong political and public criticism. Ten years later, when Prime Minister Yasuhiro Nakasone paid an official visit to the shrine, declaring that 'self-confidence must begin with appreciation and respect for the past', his action was met with protests, internally from those who suspected it masked a desire to return to a militarist state, externally from Asian neighbours, especially China and Korea, who considered it represented Japan's rejection of its responsibility for war crimes. Both the question of what history should be taught and how the Yasukuni shrine should be treated were bound up with Japan's willingness to apologise to the countries that it had invaded and to make restitution to those who had suffered at its hands. The matter was so contested that political leaders found themselves in an almost impossible position and tried to maintain a delicate balance between the contending parties. In 1995 socialist Prime Minister Tomiichi Murayama, who led an unwieldy coalition government, on visiting the shrine expressed 'painful repentance and heartfelt apologies' for Japan's wartime behaviour.[74] But by combining the apology with a visit to the shrine he only served to antagonise both camps. Though this new interest in being a 'normal nation' has shaken up the pacifist orthodoxy of the postwar era there is little to suggest that Japan is more likely to succumb to the allures of extreme nationalism than is any of the Western countries, including Australia, that have been experiencing similar appeals for a more positive sense of identity.

In its relations with the world Japan was also being urged to become a 'normal nation'. By the 1990s Japan was facing a very different world. The Western nations were encouraging Japan to adopt a defence and foreign policy commensurate with its economic status; as an economic superpower it was natural that it should consider taking on a larger global role. Furthermore, the US security guarantee no longer seemed so reliable. In the aftermath of the Vietnam debacle Washington had indicated that it would consult more carefully its own interest before giving support to its allies. With the imploding of the Soviet Union and the end of the Cold War these doubts grew; it was not clear how the USA would view commitments originally designed to meet a threat from the communist bloc. Finally, Japan had to take into account a new East Asia, which, free from Western imperialism and ideological confrontation, was taking responsibility for remaking the region.

Political leaders, especially in the LDP, believed that, if Japan were to become a normal nation and so be able to look after its own interests and take a full part in international affairs,

[73] Cited by Ian Buruma in 'Why They Hate Japan', *New York Review of Books*, LIII (14), 21 September 2006, pp. 78 and 82.

[74] Nathan. pp. 153–5.

it should rewrite the self-defence article 9 of the postwar constitution. To this end the LDP put forward a constitutional amendment that would allow Japan to use its military force for UN peace keeping missions as well as for collective self-defence in support of an ally. This proposal did not go unchallenged. Opponents of the proposal feared that the government, free from constitutional restraints, might use the amendment to acquire nuclear weapons or engage in military aggression. While awaiting the outcome to this debate the Japanese government began to take a more active part in world affairs. Internationally, it became the most generous donor to foreign aid programs, started very cautiously to join in UN peacekeeping missions in non-combatant roles, as in Cambodia and East Timor, and looked towards obtaining a permanent seat on the United Nations Security Council.

Japan was also forced to reassess its general relationship with the region. The US decision to make its Asian allies take the prime responsibility for their own defence was unsettling. In 1992 the LDP's report, 'Japan's Role in the International Community', set down as a principle of Japan's foreign policy that 'as an Asian country, Japan must strive to preserve peace and maintain stability in the Asian region'; with this in mind Japan turned to reviving ideas about an Asian consciousness and an Asian community. Yet this proved no easy task. Japan found it difficult to reconcile its respect for Asia's distinct cultures and values with its advocacy of Western ideas of universal human rights and political democracy. Likewise, it was torn between the push towards fostering an Asian identity, which was in part anti-Western in nature, and the pull of its strong Western interests and associations, especially its dependence on the USA.

Japan looked out on a Northeast Asia that was unstable and unpredictable. It had political and territorial differences with Russia and China, both nuclear powers, and the unreconstructed communist regime in North Korea was threatening to develop its own nuclear-armed missiles. Alert to these potential dangers, the LDP report continued to make the preservation of close ties with the USA the first principle of Japan's foreign policy. In April 1996 Japan committed a rather reluctant United States to a reaffirmation of their Mutual Security Treaty and in exchange extended the range of its self-defence zone to enable its 240,000 strong military force to support the USA should China attempt to invade Taiwan. Similarly, Japan, in the arguments over how to build a stable East Asia, favoured the Asia-Pacific Economic Co-operation, which included the USA, over Malaysia's proposal for an exclusive East Asian Economic Community, which did not.[75]

In the post-Cold War era Japan wanted to find a way to support an autonomous Asian community while keeping intact its ties to the West. This aim was complicated, by the rise of China as a great economic power and a rival for leadership of the region. Japan recognised that China would want an East Asia that would stand up against Western values and influence but was troubled as to how to respond. On the one hand, Japan's own economic recovery from a decade of recession was to a considerable extent assisted by China's success. Japan invested heavily in the communists' capitalist miracle and, in 2005, China jumped over the USA to become Japan's most important trading partner. On the other hand China's growing influence in the region was a cause of disquiet. Its new

---

[75] Wolf Mendl, *Japan's Asia Policy: Regional Security and Global Interests* (New York: Routledge, 1997), especially chapter 6, 'Regional Policy in the Global Context.'

stature as a global economic and military power made its outbursts against Japan's lack of contrition for its wartime invasion and atrocities more menacing. China seemed intent on blocking Japan's ambition to gain a permanent seat on the Security Council and, more generally, posed a challenge to Japan's vision of East Asia.

At first Japan did not encourage ASEAN's proposal for a new regional grouping that would include, in addition to the members of ASEAN, China, Japan, South Korea and possibly India, Australia and New Zealand, but exclude the USA. When in 2003 it was clear that ASEAN was intent on hosting such a forum Japan was anxious that India, Australia and New Zealand be invited in order to counterbalance China. On the eve of the first East Asian Summit in Kuala Lumpur in December 2005 the new Japanese foreign minister, Taro Aso, declared that these three countries were 'new peers' in the future of Asia. At the same time he set out Japan's view of its role in East Asia and how this was intimately connected to its US alliance. He reminded South Korea and the ASEAN nations that it was Japan whose generosity had rescued them from the 1997–98 financial crisis, that Japan was naturally the 'thought leader' or exemplar for the region and that its role 'as a stabiliser' in the area clearly derived 'from the weight that the Japan-US military alliance holds'.[76]

Yet even though Japan, because of the serious security problems in Northeast Asia, continued to value highly the US alliance it no longer allowed this reliance on the USA to dominate its world view and began to pursue a much more active and multidimensional policy in the region. It showed a more sensitive response to its Asian neighbours than did its US protector, especially over human rights issues . Japan was very aware of the many different and sometime conflicting elements that it had to integrate into a workable policy. It had come to adopt what has been called a policy of 'reluctant realism'[77] and with it a balancing act between maintaining its connections to the West and taking a full part in the making of the new East Asia.

Australia was even more profoundly affected than Japan by America's defeat in the Vietnam War and the end of the Cold War. The US departure from the Asian mainland and its abdication of its role as leader of a pro-Western Asia was the final blow to Australia's long-held vision of itself as an integral part of the West protected from the alien peoples to the north by great and powerful Anglo-Saxon friends. As a result Australia was shocked into accepting the need to redefine the nation's relations with the West and with Asia.

Adapting to the new realities, Australians ceased to proclaim themselves white and British, ideas that had become anachronistic and embarrassing. The world that had supported them had disappeared. Circumstances beyond Australia's control had eroded their meaning. Thus in the 1970s and 1980s almost all the remaining links with the imperial age were severed. Appeals to the British Privy Council were ended, imperial honours were replaced with an Australian honours system and instead of 'God Save the Queen', 'Advance Australia Fair' became the national anthem. 'British subject' was dropped from Australian passports. By 2000 the monarchy was the only surviving symbol of Australia's earlier allegiance to the British national ideal, and even its days were numbered as most Australians indicated their preference for a republic.

[76] *Sydney Morning Herald*, 8 and 10–11 December 2005.

[77] Michael J Green, *Japan's Reluctant Realism: Foreign Challenges in an Era of Uncertain Power* (New York: Palgrave, 2001).

To distinguish the new era from the old, successive governments declared Australia to be a multicultural or multiracial society. In 1973 Prime Minister Gough Whitlam publicly repudiated the White Australia policy and Australia opened its doors to immigrants from all ethnic and racial groups on an equal basis. With one stroke the foundation idea of nationality had been overturned, a radical change that Australians overwhelmingly endorsed. The humiliation, which the Japanese and other Asians had felt in the face of the colour barrier, had been lifted. By the mid-1980s more than one-third of Australia's immigrants were drawn from Asia and it was estimated that if Asian immigration were to continue at that rate, Asians or descendants of Asians would by 2030 comprise 10–15 per cent of the population.[78] One foreign minister welcomed the prospect of Australia becoming a 'Eurasian nation'.[79]

Australia recognised that it had to learn to live with Asia in all its complexity and diversity – its prosperity and its security depended on establishing and maintaining good relations with its northern neighbours. From the 1950s Australia's ties with the region had multiplied through diplomacy, trade, aid, education and tourism. But whereas these developments had at first been seen merely as supplements to Australia's prime commitment to a British – and US – led Western world, now they were appreciated in their own right and accepted as portents of the future. Australia was looking for new forms of regional co-operation. Instead of being connected to Asia through Western-dominated bodies that were a legacy of the Cold War, such as SEATO, it began to cultivate direct ties with Asian nations.

This new approach to Asia was expressed first and most fully in relation to Japan. By the mid-1970s Japan had taken the place that Britain, down to the 1950s, had held in Australia's overseas trade, becoming far and away the most important market for Australian raw materials, its share of Australia's exports rising from 6 to 33 per cent. The bitter memories of World War II had faded. Japan was no longer considered a threat but a virtual ally. In 1976 Australia, by signing the Basic Treaty of Friendship and Co-operation with Japan, intended not only to cement the economic alliance but also to provide a structure that could be used for mutual consultation on a wide range of issues, including aid and development in Southeast Asia, regional economic and security matters, protective trade barriers and north-south economic differences. In association with the treaty an Australia-Japan Foundation was established to foster mutual understanding and to fund scholarly studies and cultural exchanges. This treaty laid down the pattern for Australia's new outreach policy towards the countries of East Asia.

During the 1980s the Hawke Labor government made what Foreign Minister Gareth Evans called 'constructive engagement with Asia' the centrepiece of its foreign policy. For the first time in the nation's history the Commonwealth government commissioned a series of reports on Australia and Asia. These reports covered nearly every aspect of the relationship – trade and investment, defence, immigration and culture. They all stressed the importance of Asia in Australia's future and recommended a co-operative spirit in dealing with the region. On trade and investment it was pointed out that Japan, China, Taiwan

---

[78] Neville Meaney, 'The End of White Australia and Australia's Changing Perceptions of Asia', *Australian Journal of International Affairs*, 4–9 (November 1995), p. 183

[79] *The Age*, 11 May 1983.

and South Korea were the engines driving growth in the whole region and that Australia's prosperity depended on cultivating good relations with these countries whose economies were 'more deeply complementary' to Australia's than those of any other nations. On defence it was argued, in contrast to all previous assessments, that Australia should not adopt a policy directed against Asia but rather formulate its policy in association with Asia for the purpose of collective security. On immigration there was nothing but praise for the non-discriminatory principles that were creating 'a racially diverse but harmonious community'. The report on the role of Asian studies in universities was the most radical of all. It claimed that teaching about Asia was 'part of the Australianisation of curricula in higher education'. It was as though Chinese and Japanese studies (in contradistinction to French and German) were now natural parts of an Australian education, as though to be Australian one had also to be Asian.[80]

Reacting against the West's self-enclosing indifference Australia strove to bind itself to the new Asia. Pursuing its policy of constructive engagement it showed an unwonted sympathy for the sensibilities of its neighbours. It bore stoically the barbed criticisms of the Malaysian and Singapore leaders. Unlike the USA and Western Europe, Australia, in harmony with Japan, was reluctant to denounce the Chinese and Indonesians for violations of human rights. Australian governments found themselves caught between their Western-derived notions of universal human rights and the economic and geopolitical imperatives of the new times. The upshot was that, like Japan- though it was not an easy resolution – Australia came to stand apart somewhat from the West and in a muted form to accept the arguments of cultural relativism, namely, that the West should not impose its moral judgments upon Asian countries. It was their hope that quiet diplomacy and economic development would produce a more enlightened political order in a stable and harmonious region.

Yet, even as it made a great effort to placate Asia, Australia, like Japan, was uneasy about the future of the region. It could not ignore the great questions of the post-Cold War era, which, summed up in Francis Fukuyama's *The End of History and the Last Man* (1996) and Samuel P Huntington's *The Clash of Civilisations* and *The Remaking of World Order* (1996), asked whether, with the failure of communism, liberal democracy had won the final battle over the world's ideological future or whether the world would restructure itself around the major historical cultures that would vie with one another for supremacy. Australia, as Japan, desired the former while fearing the latter. Australia could see no abatement of the problems besetting Asia. National suspicions and ethnic antagonisms persisted. Modernisation tended to excite increasing internal dissension. Economic success had encouraged the new states to expand their military capabilities. Australia might have discarded its white British race persona but it remained a Western parliamentary democracy, understood through English history and the English language. Thus, while SEATO was expendable, ANZUS

---

[80] Ross Garnaut, *Australia and the Northeast Asian Ascendancy* (Canberra: AGPS, 1989), especially pp. 1–6; Paul Dibb, *Review of Australia's Defence Capabilities*, March 1986 (Canberra: AGPS, 1986); Stephen FitzGerald, *Immigration: A Commitment to Australia* (Canberra: AGPS, 1988); John Ingleson (Research Director), *Asia in Australian Higher Education: Report of the Inquiry into the Teaching of Asian Studies and Languages in Higher Education submitted to the Asian Studies Council* (Sydney: UNSW Press, 1989), especially pp. 33–37.

was not. Like Japan's Mutual Security Treaty, ANZUS was still considered a shield against an unpredictable Asia. Australia, in proposing what became the Asia-Pacific Economic Co-operation, joined Japan in seeking to associate the West, in this case North America, with this scheme for advancing the cause of open markets and free trade.

By the end of the 1990s there was in Australia, as in Japan, concern about the lack of national pride. Australia's concern was not spawned by excessive guilt about the Pacific War but exaggerated guilt about white Australia's racist past, its ruthless destruction of the land and its fauna and flora and its oppression of women and Aborigines. It was also a reaction against what was considered to be indiscriminate encouragement given to those immigrants of non-English-speaking backgrounds, to cherish their own traditions at the expense of loyalty to the Australian community and 'Australian values'. By December 2006 the prime minister and the leader of the Opposition had come to prefer the term 'integration' to 'multiculturalism'.[81]

Australia too had its problem about becoming a 'normal country'. At the onset of the nationalist era, Australians thought of themselves as Britons, even if Australian Britons, and so their rituals and myths, heroes and martyrs were British. By the time Britain entered the Common Market that vision could no longer be sustained. But once the British symbols were discarded no new nationalism emerged to take its place. For a brief moment some culture makers, headed by historian Manning Clark, tried to give life to a distinct national myth based on the mateship of the bush, but it achieved no social traction. Histories based on Britain and the British empire were replaced by stories not of a unique Australian people but of those who had been oppressed or excluded by the old nationalism. The new Australian history, turning its back on the old white British ideal, indeed on nationalism itself, celebrated the cultural diversity represented by successive waves of immigrants and the indigenes. Thus some Australians kept asking what held the country together.[82]

The Liberal-National Coalition government that came to power in 1996 had for some time been critical of what their court historian, Geoffrey Blainey, dubbed a 'black armband' version of Australia's past and they entered the 'history wars' with a crusading fervour. They distributed Australian flags, which included the Union Jack alongside the stars of the Southern Cross, to schools and mounted a campaign for flag-raising ceremonies and the singing of the new national anthem, 'Advance Australia Fair', which itself derived from a late 19th century patriotic song celebrating Australia's 'British soul'. Proceeding further they attacked the teaching of Australian history in the schools. What was taught, according to Prime Minister John Howard, amounted to 'little more than a litany of sexism, racism and class warfare'. In a series of speeches in 2006 he called for a 'root and branch renewal of Australian history in the schools'. It should have a positive narrative at its core instead of a 'fragmented stew of themes and issues', a narrative that should be built around Australia's 'dominant pattern' comprising 'Judea-Christian ethics, the progressive spirit of the Enlightenment and the institutions and the values of British political culture'. Reminiscent

---

[81] *Sydney Morning Herald*, 13 December 2006.

[82] Neville Meaney, '"In History's Page": Identity and Myth', in Deryck Schreuder and Stuart Ward (eds), *Australia's Empire* (Oxford: Oxford University Press, 2008); the Australian volume in Roger Louis (ed.), *Oxford History of the British Empire*, (Oxford: Oxford University Press, 1999).

of the Japanese case this search for an Australian identity was also given a military dimension centred on the mateship or digger tradition of Australia's wars, especially its experience in the two world wars.

Multiculturalism was seen too as a problem for national community. The prime minister admitted that he could only accept multiculturalism if it meant that 'we are Australian before anything else'. Al-Qaeda's suicide attacks on the World Trade Center in New York and the Pentagon in Washington followed by Jema'ah Islamiyah's killing of Westerners, including many Australians, in Bali intensified this apprehension about divisiveness, especially when it was discovered that some radical Muslims in Australia sympathised with or were members of these groups. The new narrative history would meet this problem by instilling Australian values in all citizens and simultaneously creating a common identity. Australians in affirming this shared heritage did 'not have to ... apologise for our place in the Western tradition in order to build our relationships in Asia or in any other part of the world'.[83] As in Japan this program was contentious and itself divisive; whether it would, if given substance, be any more successful in Australia was unclear. In both countries the kind of history that the would-be nationalists nostalgically advocated was itself a pale shadow of its earlier model and neither people seem to be roused to embrace it. Perhaps for two such highly developed modern societies that had in an earlier era experienced the heavy costs in human suffering brought about by the intolerance of nationalism this idea of community had lost its appeal.

The Howard government brought a similar sensibility to its foreign policy. The banner-head slogan for its approach to the world, as set out in its first White Paper on Australian foreign policy, was 'Asia first, but not Asia only',[84] intended to signal that, in contrast to its Labor predecessors, it would give much more emphasis to the US alliance and Australia's traditional connections to the West while still recognising the importance of East Asia to Australia. In particular it was looking forward to 'reinvigorating' its relationship with America as a Pacific partner with which it shared 'common values' as well as common interests. From the Australian perspective the attempts at creating an East Asian region had not been very fruitful. The Howard government looked forward to dealing with its neighbours on a more businesslike, bilateral rather than collective basis. It agreed with the Japanese that harmony and security in the region depended at bottom on America's presence as a security anchor. Australia responded to the radical Islamist attacks on the USA by invoking the ANZUS alliance and giving America military support, not only for its war against Al-Qaeda in Afghanistan but also for its 'pre-emptive strike' against Iraq. Though all but one of three East Asian nations that had initially been part of the Coalition of the Willing had by 2006 withdrawn their troops from Iraq and Japan also had withdrawn its non-combatant engineers, the prime minister promised to keep Australian forces there until the USA decided to abandon the struggle.

---

[83] Prime Minister John Howard, 'Address to the National Press Club', 25 January 2006, www. pm.gov.au/news/Speeches/speech1754; John Howard, 'Address to the Quadrant Magazine's 50th Anniversary Dinner', 3 October 2006 www.pm.gov.au/News/speeches/ speech2165; James Curran, *The Power of Speech: Australian Prime Ministers Defining the National Image* (Melbourne: Melbourne University Press, 2004), pp. 241–55.

[84] *In the National Interest: Australia's Foreign and Trade Policy* (Canberra, 1997).

Like Japan the Australian government did not find it easy to balance its commitment to the West with its involvement in East Asia. Putting Asia first was perforce much more than a benign gesture. Australia's material welfare as well as its strategic security were bound up with East Asia. Australia joined with Japan to help save Indonesia, Thailand, Malaysia, Philippines and South Korea from the financial crisis of 1997–98, which threatened to undermine the foundations of their modernising economies and societies. Sensitive to the cultures of the region both countries used their influence to prevent the USA and the International Monetary Fund imposing draconian conditions on new loans. Similarly, when, in the political turmoil following this crisis, Indonesia allowed the East Timorese to vote in a referendum on independence, Canberra, with the consent of Djakarta, took the lead after a positive ballot to help put down the pro-Indonesian militias and establish under United Nations auspices a new constitution and a new government.

Subsequently, the island chain to Australia's immediate north and northeast, stretching from Indonesia to Fiji, became an arc of instability and the failed states invited Australia to assist them in restoring order and reforming their political and judicial practices. This was no easy task. The relatively small force of Australian soldiers, police and bureaucrats could not solve the cultural and development problems. They could only hope to set examples and train the local people to take responsibility for their own governance, and in doing so were both appreciated and resented. In contrast to Japan, whose strategic concerns were focused on Northeast Asia, Australia, on questions of national security and political stability, gave primacy to Southeast Asia and the South Pacific. Again, in contrast to Japan, Australia's defence concerns were relatively limited. It did not face nuclear-armed neighbours or unpredictable military powers that could threaten national survival.

Australia's interest in Northeast Asia was first and foremost as a market for its resource commodities. Japan, China, South Korea and Taiwan accounted for about half of Australian exports. From the mid-1990s China became particularly important for the health of Australia's economy. China's share of Australian total exports grew very rapidly and, by 2006, was closing on Japan, which still held first place. Appreciating China's great potential Canberra invested much time, energy and diplomacy in wooing Beijing. Prime Minister Howard made more visits to China than did any of his predecessors. In October 2003 Chinese President Hu Jintao addressed the Commonwealth parliament, the first time a leader of a communist country had been accorded such an honour. Moreover, President Hu gave his address on the day following that of President George W Bush. This strangely equal conjunction of honours was a sign of the value that Australia placed upon having good relations with China. Australia was unwilling to offend China and did not follow America's lead in publicly criticising China's human rights violations and protective trade practices. Indeed, the foreign minister, on a visit to China in August 2004, a time of Sino-United States tension over Taiwan, replied to Chinese criticism of Australia's US alliance by assuring his hosts, misleadingly, that the ANZUS pact only applied to attacks on the mainland of each party and that therefore Australia would not be automatically involved in any conflict that might arise over Taiwan and involve the USA.[85]

Notwithstanding this rather curious episode Australia's relations with the USA and the United Kingdom, as evidenced most clearly in its sending troops to support the US-led

---

[85] *Sydney Morning Herald*, 18 August 2004.

Coalition of the Willing in the invasion of Iraq, grew closer. In working out the meaning of 'Asia first, but not Asia only' the Howard government stressed the latter part of the principle as the sure anchor for Australia's future in Asia and joined with Japan and the USA in instituting annual tripartite diplomatic and strategic consultations. It was as though the three countries were forging a virtual AJUS alliance.

By the early years of the 21st century, the Japanese-Australian relationship had become more wide-ranging and harmonious than ever before. Japan and Australia were united by mutual interests and a shared vision of the region's destiny. Out of their different histories of responding respectively to the challenges of the West and the East they had arrived at conclusions that had brought them together in a regional partnership. But the partnership was not one of equals. Japan was a global power, Australia a middling one. Australia was of the West, looking to be accepted by Asia, while Japan was of the East but for many purposes assimilated to the West. In the face of the West's retreat from Asia both had seen the need to integrate with the region on its terms and to be part of an evolving Asian community, but both agreed that this was best achieved with, rather than against, the West. To this end they supported each other, Australia backing Japan's claims for a permanent seat on the United Nations Security Council, Japan endorsing Australia's wish to be treated as a member of the Asian community. They also collaborated in promoting a regional order that would be worked out, at least to some degree, in association with the West.

This happy coincidence of interests and ideals between East and West is of special importance to Australia, whose ties to Japan, culturally still much less intimate than those with the West, are more comprehensive and firmly based than those with any other Asian nation. Despite the occasional differences and difficulties, many of them products of the relationship's intensity, Australia has an opportunity through this relationship to explore the full potential of its future with Asia.

4

Australia in the World

8

The Problem of 'Greater Britain' and Australia's Strategic Crisis 1905–1914[1]

The idea of 'Greater Britain' was a central problem for Australian leaders as successive governments in the decade preceding the outbreak of World War I struggled to manage what they had defined as their country's strategic crisis in the Pacific. As Duncan Bell has explained in his study of English intellectuals and 'Greater Britain' though this idea was given a variety of meanings, the dominant one referred to some form of union between the 'Mother Country' and the British settled colonies, most commonly in an ill-defined 'Imperial Federation'. In Australia as in Britain this movement was driven primarily by the rise of national sentiment which swept the Western world at the end of the nineteenth century, and for Australians the question of how this idea could be given an acceptable political expression and allow the British peoples to face the world as one was central to the debates over defence and foreign policy.[2]

Before dealing with the Australian response to its strategic crisis it is then necessary to have some understanding of nationalism and how nationalism worked itself out in Australia. Nationalism was a product of modernisation. It was a response to all those forces which by the end of the nineteenth century were reaching a critical mass and transforming the Western world and also Japan. The application of science and technology to agriculture and manufacture, transport and communications, business and administration was creating mass societies. It was destroying traditional face-to-face self-sufficient communities and making anachronistic local ideas of identity and loyalty. For those rudely uprooted from the old ways this process was traumatic. The mobile anonymous masses who streamed into

---

[1] This essay was originally published as 'The Problem of "Greater Britain" and Australia's Strategic Crisis 1905–1914' in Peter Dennis and Jeffrey Grey, eds, *1911: Preliminary Moves* (Canberra: Big Sky Publishing, 2011).

[2] Duncan Bell, *The Idea of Greater Britain: Empire and the Future of World Order* (Princeton: Princeton University Press, 2007), pp. 16, 265 and 271. Duncan Bell in his thickly-textured and original work deals with this idea in English intellectual discourse in the latter part of the nineteenth century, pointing out the diverse forces at work giving rise to this concept and exploring the complex meanings which gathered around it. He also shows that 'Greater Britain' gained its most concrete expression in proposals for an Imperial Federation, whether through adding colonial representatives to the British Parliament, creating a new super Imperial Parliament or establishing an Imperial Council. He has little to say about the colonial side of the question but nevertheless attributes the failure of Imperial Federation, at least in part, to the British settlers' 'indifference'. This description of the self-governing colonies' attitude to the question of 'Greater Britain', however, is misleading. Certainly the Australian leaders were not indifferent to the 'Greater Britain' question and from the colonial era until the Second World War were constantly involved in trying to find ways to give it a practical expression, as this chapter illustrates. For two other works which also demonstrate the Australian preoccupation with this question, see Neville Meaney, *Australia and World Crisis 1914–1923* (Sydney: Sydney University Press, 2009), especially chapters 5, 12 and 16 and James Curran, *Curtin's Empire* (Melbourne Ports: Cambridge University Press, 2011).

the mega metropolises which were the hub of the modernising dynamic needed new ways to make sense of their alien condition. A number of ideas appeared in the market place to fill this void. Liberal globalism was too bland and unrelated to the common experience to have wide appeal. Karl Marx, who understood modernisation as exploitative capitalism, called on its greatest victims, 'the workers of the world' to unite; he was, so to speak, saying that through this comradeship the down-trodden everywhere could once again find a sense of community. While communism had some influence in socialist parties and trade unions it could never, however, overcome the attraction of nationalism. In this struggle for the modern mind the idea of culture nearly always trumped that of class and the idea of the people nearly always triumphed over that of the proletariat.

Nationalism's virtue was that its myths linked the past that had been lost to the disturbing present and offered its adherents the promise of a redemptive future based on the supposed ideals and values of their ancestors. The major nineteenth century Western historians in their multi-volume works gave a scholarly authority and romantic aura to this new vision of belonging. These historians traced out a teleological narrative of their people who each from their origins in the forests or on the frontiers shared common 'blood', language and customs and had over time been engaged in a noble struggle against hereditary overlords and foreign masters. Through state sponsored mass education these ideas were rapidly spread and readily embraced. Nationalism offered the displaced and disoriented an intense social identity as a salve for the trauma of modernisation, an identity which justified the modernising world as the fulfilment of their past. It was a quasi religion with its anthems and rituals, saints and martyrs, sacred sites and holy days. Its prophets and poets spoke of a 'national soul'. Thus when at the beginning of the nationalist era Peter McCormick was moved to write 'Advance Australia Fair' he exulted that

> Britannia then shall surely know
>
> Beyond wide oceans' rolls
>
> Her sons in fair Australia's land
>
> Still keep a British soul.

This brings us to the problem of Australian nationalism or perhaps to put the issue more precisely the problem of nationalism in Australia. When I first began to interest myself in the defence and foreign policy of this period, I was puzzled by the way in which Australians responded to nationalism. In Europe where the idea first took root each people believed that their historical destiny could never be realised until they were united with all who shared their distinctive myth in one state and under one government. And yet in Australia where the colonists in this nationalist era defined themselves as British and where they cherished a 'white' British race myth, there was a consensus across the political spectrum that it should not surrender any jot or tittle of its right to self-government to Britain or the British Empire. Yet, it could well be argued, if one looks at Australia's attitude to Britain's wars, that Australians identified more enthusiastically and uncritically than their compatriots in the 'Mother Country' with the cause of empire. Edmund Barton, the leader of the movement for Federation, at the outset of the Boer War affirmed that 'when our Empire is at war with any power whatever it becomes our turn to declare the motto, "The Empire right or wrong".[3] Only on the fringes of politics was there any call for independence or 'cutting the painter' as the metaphor of the time put it. Certainly there was no rival national myth to challenge Australia's Britishness. The Bush legend even if it could be conceded that it had widespread appeal, was not a national myth but a folk tradition not unlike, for example, those found in Cornwall or Yorkshire. It had ballads not anthems. When the Empire was in danger its heroes such as Henry Lawson and A.B. (Banjo) Paterson also rallied to the British cause.

Why then in 1901 were Australians embracing enthusiastically a local federation while at the same time opposing an Imperial federation? The short answer is that nationalism offered not only socio-psychological but also physical and material security and whereas in Europe each people was consolidated in their own land and so there was a natural congruence between the cultural idea of society and the political interests of the state, Australia's position was very different. Australia's experience of nationalism was—perhaps with the exception of New Zealand—*sui generis*. The great distances separating Australia from the Mother country led to conflicts over basic interests such as immigration, trade, defence, external affairs and Pacific policy. For this reason it would not accept any form of Imperial Federation in which Britain because of its greater population could use its numbers to dispose of Australia's economic and military resources to serve its own interests or geo-political priorities. By contrast the British Australians had no such reservations in setting up their own federation. All the colonies accepted that, as a result of their geo-politics, they shared fundamental common interests and so readily agreed to join together in a federal union giving to the Commonwealth all the key powers of a state. Out of Australia's exceptional experience there emerged a tension between these two sides of nationalism, between what might be called the community of culture and the community of interest.[4]

The Australians were not happy to find themselves in this awkward position. On the one hand they were ready to separate themselves from the Empire if Britain should attempt to block their racially discriminating immigration laws, and this even though, as Henry Parkes said, they were aimed at protecting 'the British type in the population of their country'.[5] On the other, Alfred Deakin, one of the strongest opponents of British plans for Imperial Federation at the time of the making of the Commonwealth constitution, saw no contradiction in being a founding member of and subsequently president of the Victorian Imperial Federation League. In his presidential address he declared that 'The same ties of

[3] New South Wales, *Parliamentary Debates*, Legislative Assembly (1899 session), vol. C, pp. 1495–96, 19 October 1899.

[4] For a discussion of Australian nationalism and 'Greater Britain', see Douglas Cole, 'The Problem of "Nationalism" and "Imperialism" in British Settlement Colonies', *Journal of British Studies*, 10 (1971): 160–82; Neville Meaney, 'Britishness and Australian Identity: The Problem of Nationalism in Australian History and Historiography', *Australian Historical Studies*, 32 (April, 2001): 76–90; Neville Meaney, 'Britishness and Australia: Some Reflections', *Journal of Imperial and Commonwealth Studies*, 31 (May, 2003): 121–135; Neville Meaney, '"In History's Page": Identity and Myth', in Deryck M. Schreuder and Stuart Ward, eds, *Australia's Empire* (Oxford: Oxford University Press), pp. 363–88.

[5] New South Wales, *Parliamentary Debates*, Legislative Assembly (1887–1888 session), vol. XXXII, p. 3787, 3 April 1888.

Neville Meaney

blood, sympathy and tradition which make us one Commonwealth here make the British of today one people everywhere,'[6] and he delivered this speech just a month before becoming prime minister and announcing his intention, in defiance of British authorities, to bring in an Australian defence policy of compulsory military training and a local flotilla. Deakin, like all other Australian leaders of his time—with perhaps the exception of George Reid—held a very different view of the British Empire and Imperial federation from that prevailing in the 'Mother Country'. Whereas the British political class, despite the efforts of the advocates of Imperial Federation, saw the empire as a London-centred hierarchical structure made up of different kinds and levels of colonies, their Australian counterparts imagined it as a poly-centred Greater Britain in which all the British peoples had an equal right with the 'Mother Country' to play a part in the making of imperial defence and foreign policy and an equal right with the Mother Country for the protection of their peculiar interests. And as the ways and means of healing the breach between the community of culture and the community of interest were being debated, the Australians, finding that they held starkly divergent views from Britain about security in the Pacific, pursued their own defence and foreign policies to meet what they perceived to be their distinctive dangers.

Pacific Perils

In the early years of the Federation the only invasion that Australians feared was an influx of Asian migrants, and the Commonwealth parliament as its first major piece of legislation passed an *Immigration Restriction Act* to close off the entry of 'coloured' peoples into the country. The first Australian government in so far as it had any clear view about international politics agreed with Britain that Russia represented the greatest threat to the Empire and that the Anglo–Japanese alliance would act as a useful counter to any Russian expansionist tendencies in the region. The British naval squadrons in the Pacific would be adequate for the defence of coasts and ports. This was the only possible hostile action that the Australians could envisage and with this in mind the Commonwealth provided a £200,000 pound subsidy for expanding the British squadron on the Australian station. Thus the Commonwealth's first defence policy was primarily concerned with the conversion of the six colonies' militias into an Australian military force and in the process with cutting back on expenditure for the permanent forces. It also rejected a War Office proposal, inspired by the colonists' enthusiasm for the Empire's cause in the Boer War, to establish a permanent field force which would be available to go to the aid of any part of the Empire in times of trouble. In its founding *Defence Act* of 1904 the federal parliament made its position even clearer on this latter question by laying it down that Australians could only be conscripted for the defence of their own country and its territories, thus ensuring that the government could only send volunteers to take part in imperial conflicts. Australians accepted that while they would, as they had done at the time of the Boer War, almost certainly raise a volunteer force to help to defend the Empire in times of crisis, they were

---

[6] Alfred Deakin, *Imperial Federation: An Address Delivered by Hon. Alfred Deakin M.P. at the Annual Meeting of the Imperial Federation League of Victoria, 14 June 1905* (Melbourne: The League, 1905). For an astute account of Deakin's attitude to empire, see J. A. La Nauze, *Alfred Deakin: A Biography* (Melbourne: Melbourne University Press, 1966), 2 vols, chapter 21.

adamant that they would not commit themselves before the event to any agreement which detracted from their decision-making authority.

In May 1905 the Japanese triumph over Russia at the battle of Tsushima Straits jolted Australians out of their complacency about Pacific security. Japan had defeated a great European nation and emerged from the conflict as the dominant power in the region. Its stunning victory accompanied, as it was, by Britain withdrawing its capital warships to meet a German naval challenge in the North Sea, exposed Australia to a threat from the North Pacific. Alfred Deakin almost immediately grasped the full significance of this strategic revolution. In an inspired interview with the *Melbourne Herald*, just a few weeks before becoming prime minister, he spelled out its meaning. As a result of the Russo–Japanese War, he said,

> What we have to estimate for the future is that instead of two fleets in the China seas belonging to separate-even opposing- powers, we shall now have one fleet, only it will probably be as strong as the two former, and will cooperate under one flag…
>
> Under all the developments of the modern men-of-war, Australia, which used to depend largely on its isolations for security, is now within what is termed striking distance of no less than sixteen foreign naval stations…
>
> The most efficiently equipped, supported and protected are those to the north of China-those in Japan and now at Port Arthur. As a fact, Japan is the nearest of all the great foreign naval stations to Australia. Japan at her head quarters is, so to speak, next door, while the Mother country is many streets away, and connected by long lines of communication. What happened to the ships in Port Arthur so soon after the declaration of war shows what is possible immediately strife commences.[7]

He concluded by suggesting that the first step for a defence policy to meet this new danger from the north should be the acquisition of a naval force to guard coasts and harbours, and he also hinted at the desirability of universal military training.

From all sides political leaders took up Deakin's warnings and amplified them. Allan Mclean, deputy prime minister in the then Reid government, declared that

> The stupendous struggle in the East must awaken the people of Australia to the fact that we have been living in a fool's paradise, when we have assumed that our great distance from the military nations gave us immunity from foreign invasion … Japan has astonished the world … We now find one of the great naval and military powers within a very short distance of our shores.

He conceded that, while it was fortunate that 'the great Power, which has recently arisen in the East, was allied to Great Britain', nevertheless 'that condition of things might not always continue and we must be prepared for what might happen.'[8] Likewise George Pearce, who subsequently became the defence minister in all three of Andrew Fisher's Labor governments, publicly discounted the value of the Anglo–Japanese pact and stressed that Japan was very likely to continue on its imperialist path, with Australia as its greatest prize.

---

[7] *Melbourne Herald*, 12 June 1905.

[8] Ibid., 13 June 1905.

Speaking in parliament he said that Australians had little or no reason to fear European aggression and that they would be foolish if they took that treaty 'to be a guarantee for all time.' And he added that

> Japan has shown that she is an aggressive nation. She had shown that she is desirous of pushing out all round. What has always been the effect of victory and of conquest upon nations? Do we not know that it stimulates them to further conflict? To obtain fresh territory? Has not that been the history of our own race? … Is there any other country that offers such a temptation to Japan as Australia does? [9]

The Australians had now come to believe that they were faced with not only a migratory but also a military invasion. Over the next few years fear of Japan spread through the populace and as with attitudes to immigration it was very often, but by no means always, expressed in racial terms. A National Defence League was formed to keep the message before the public and an Immigration League was established to encourage British settlement. The looming racial danger from the north permeated popular culture. It was to be found in cartoons, poetry, short stories, invasion scare novels, plays, and even an early film, 'Australia Calls' by Raymond Longford. C.J. Dennis's jingle *Austral—Aise,* published in 1908, was his contribution to the general hysteria.

Assuming office as prime minister in August Deakin for the next three years set about trying to build up Australia's defences to meet the perceived threat. His government's policy was firstly to meet the possibility of invasion, secondly to guard against raids on coastal shipping and harbours and thirdly to provide some protection against attacks by enemy cruisers on ocean-going commerce.[10] He needed British co-operation but when he submitted his proposals to London found little sympathy. The Colonial Defence Committee and the Committee of Imperial Defence believed that the maximum possible attack against Australia would be a raid by no more than three or four cruisers on ports and that this could be met by fortified harbours, garrisoned forts and a militia force. They could find no justification for a local flotilla. In their view the Japanese alliance, which had been renewed in 1905, would safeguard all British Territories in East Asia and the Pacific.[11] Deakin was unmoved by this negative response. The growth of the German navy represented a challenge to Britain's naval supremacy and if its control of the seas were 'in any respect shaken' it was not foolish 'to consider our own conditions, and the possibility of an attack of a more serious nature than had hitherto been contemplated.'[12] Deakin and other members of parliament had noticed that Britain was taking steps to protect itself against Germany not only by entering into an 'entente cordiale' with France but also by bringing home the capital ships attached to its scattered overseas squadrons.

Thus Deakin went to the 1907 Colonial Conference seeking not only support for his defence plans but also changes in the relations between the self-governing colonies and the

---

[9] Commonwealth of Australia, *Parliamentary Debates* (1905 session), vol. XXIX, p. 5346, 22 November 05.

[10] Ibid., XXVII, 2823, 27 September 1905.

[11] Commonwealth of Australia, *Parliamentary Papers* (1906 session), vol. II, no. 62, 'General Scheme of Defence for Australia'.

[12] Ibid., (1906 session), vol. XXV, pp. 5564–75, 26 September 1906.

Mother Country. Following his Greater Britain principles he supported the proposal for changing the name of the conference from Colonial to Imperial but went further and urged the setting up of an advisory Imperial Council on which Britain and the Dominions would be represented for the purpose of allowing the leaders of all the British peoples to confer about imperial defence and foreign policy. But he failed on both counts. The Admiralty was unshakably hostile to the establishment of local navies outside its control and the War Office's only contribution to the discussion of military defence was to press for the creation of an Imperial General staff with its headquarters in London and branches in the Dominions. Deakin was suspicious of this innovation and he and his Canadian counterpart only agreed to participate in order to obtain uniformity of armaments, organization and training methods. Their representatives attached to the Imperial General Staff would only have authority to consult on military matters. The Dominion governments would keep control of their own forces until a war erupted and then they would decide how and to what extent they would aid the Mother Country. And from this time all subsequent Australian governments held to this position.

On his return to Australia Deakin, disregarding the cool reception he had received in London, laid before parliament his government's defence program. Looking out on the world he painted a picture of nations arming for battle, a battle which Australia could ignore only at its peril. He thus committed his government to creating a flotilla composed of nine C-Class submarines and six torpedo destroyers which were to be built in Australia, manned by Australians and under Australian control. Likewise he committed his government to begin a universal compulsory military training scheme based on the Swiss model citizen force. He predicted that within eight years Australia would have a 'national guard' of 200,000 men. It was his intention that the defence force would, as it developed, be 'as thorough and complete as that of Japan.'[13]

Almost simultaneously Deakin learnt that the United States was sending its fleet on a world cruise in 1908 and, bypassing Whitehall, he sent an invitation through the American consul-general in Melbourne direct to Washington inviting President Theodore Roosevelt to allow the fleet to visit Australia. The Australian prime minister calculated that such a visit might arouse public enthusiasm for his local defence scheme, provoke the British into sending a comparable naval force into the Pacific and act as a symbol of Anglo-Saxon solidarity in facing up to common concerns about Japan and its regional ambitions. The country was fully aware of the disputes between the United States and Japan over the discriminatory treatment of the latter's nationals in America's Pacific Coast states. It was clear that Roosevelt was sending his 'Great White Fleet' on this round the world voyage, which was to end in Yokohama, in order to warn the Japanese against challenging the United States. For the 'lonely kangaroos' it was a momentous event. After Roosevelt agreed to Deakin's request and the fleet arrived in Sydney and Melbourne the country was gripped by 'Fleetitis', as one commentator put it. The visit was an overwhelming success and in summing up its significance Deakin wrote an English friend that

> The visit of the United States Fleet is universally popular here, not so much because of our blood affection for the Americans though that is sincere but because of

---

[13] Commonwealth of Australia, *Parliamentary Debates* (1907–1908 session), vol. XLII, pp. 7509–35, 13 December 1907.

our distrust of the Yellow Race in the North Pacific and our recognition of the *'entente cordiale'* spreading among all white men who realise the Yellow Peril to Caucasian civilisation, creeds and politics.[14]

When in 1909 the British Empire was rocked by reports of a new German naval building program and of tensions between Britain and Germany reaching a new level Deakin inspired by the visit of the United States fleet wrote to the British government setting out a proposal for extending the American Monroe Doctrine to all the countries around the Pacific. As he envisaged it, the American guarantee would be strengthened by the adherence of the British Empire, Holland, France and China to the principle. At first Australia's prospective enemy, Japan and Britain's prospective enemy, Germany, would be excluded from this arrangement though he allowed, presumably thinking of countering the possibility of a Japanese-German alliance, that one of them or both of them might later on be drawn into the scheme. Deakin himself admitted that this 'proposition of the highest international importance' was probably 'chimerical'. Certainly the British did not give it any encouragement. They pointed out that they had never officially acknowledged this American doctrine with its assumption that the United States had a right to intervene in the affairs of any country in the Western Hemisphere. If this proposal were accepted then any agreement between Australia and France over the New Hebrides would need America's approval. Furthermore the British could not enter into negotiations on a pact which left out the Germans and the Japanese for they would resent their omission and in all likelihood would believe that, as a result, 'something almost hostile to their interests was being contemplated.' The British in their politely formal response effectively put the kybosh on the whole idea.[15]

As Deakin was engaged in this quasi diplomacy Australia's defence policy was reaching a new stage which at last gave promise of security in the Pacific. The British moved by the deterioration in Japanese-American relations, problems with Japanese migrants on the west coast of Canada, the loss of prestige in the Pacific following the very successful visit of the American fleet, the Dominions' anxiety about Japanese ambitions and Australia's intention to build its own naval force, invited representatives of the Dominions to a defence conference in August 1909. At this conference the Admiralty, to the astonishment of the Dominions, placed before them a plan for an Imperial Pacific Fleet.[16] This fleet, the brain-

---

[14] Letter, Deakin to Richard Jebb, 24 March 1908, NLA, 'Deakin–Jebb Correspondence', MS 339/1/19A-B.

[15] Letter, Deakin to Lord Crewe, Colonial Secretary, 27 September 1909 enclosed with letter, Crewe to Sir Edward Grey, Foreign Secretary, 3 November 1909, TNA PRO FO 800/91.

It is interesting to note that Deakin did not distinguish between putative allies and enemies in terms of race. China, was welcome as an initial partner in guaranteeing the Pacific Monroe Doctrine. Germany and Japan were to be excluded. The test for the distinction was not racial colour but national interest.

[16] This British initiative is surprising given that it appeared against the background of the 'Dreadnought' affair which had stirred up jingoist demands for the British government to match the latest German capital ship program. Indeed the British government embarrassed by the cost involved in maintaining its margin of safety over the German High Seas fleet in the North Sea had appealed to the Dominions for financial assistance. Providing three additional British 'Indomitable'

child of the imaginative First Sea Lord, Sir John Fisher, was to be made up of an East Indian, a China, an Australian and possibly a Canadian unit. Each unit would consist of a 'Dreadnought' battle cruiser of the most advanced 'Indomitable' class, three second class cruisers, six destroyers and three submarines, all of the latest design.

The Australian government welcomed the British initiative. Prime Minister Deakin appreciated well that, while his plan for a small, localised flotilla would be no defence against Japan's naval might, an Imperial fleet, led by three or four of the latest class of 'Dreadnoughts' might, even though inferior to the Japanese navy, be able to act as an effective deterrent. The Australians promptly accepted the idea. In their arrangement with the Admiralty they insisted that, as the Admiralty had proposed, their unit was to 'form part of the Eastern Fleet of the Empire' alongside similar China and East Indies units and a possible Canadian unit.[17] They insisted on this because unless their unit was incorporated into an Imperial Pacific Fleet it would be useless and would not justify abandoning their proposed coastal flotilla. In announcing the results of the conference in the House of Commons the British prime minister confirmed that the British East Indies and China squadrons were to be reconstructed and reinforced as part of a Pacific fleet.[18] Against the Admiralty's wishes, however, the Australian government made it clear that they would keep control of their squadron and decide when and under what conditions it would be handed over to the Admiralty's command.

After three years of fruitless struggle for a defence policy which would meet Australia's Pacific peril Deakin recognised that the time had arrived to achieve what he had long sought and which, given the British plan for a Pacific fleet, would be much more substantial than anything he had previously imagined. On 21 September the Defence Minister, Joseph Cook, announced the government's intention of proceeding immediately to legislate for compulsory military training and of seeking the parliament's approval for Australia's Pacific fleet unit. In his speech he outlined again the Australian strategic assessment which had caused the leaders of all parties to support these defence measures. Australia could not help but notice 'the development of armed forces in the Pacific region and the unequal distribution of these forces.' He pointed out that while Japan had fifteen battleships and

battle cruiser units for the Pacific would either weaken the margin of safety in 'home waters' or, if added to the shipbuilding program, place an even heavier burden on the British Exchequer and the available shipyards. There has been little study of this topic. The latest, based primarily on Admiralty and CID papers suggests that it was prompted by Admiralty's reluctant acceptance that Australia was determined to have its own naval force under its own control. The Admiralty's answer to this inescapable situation was that if an Imperial Pacific Fleet made up of British and Dominion units was created then the Admiralty would be able to exercise greater control over the Dominion flotillas. But this does not seem convincing. See Nicholas Lambert, 'Economy or Empire? The Fleet Unit Concept and the Quest for Collective Security in the Pacific, 1909–1914' in Greg Kennedy and Keith Neilson, eds, *Far Flung Lines: Essays on Imperial Defence in Honour of Donald Mackenzie Schurman* (London: Frank Cass, 1997), pp. 58–68.

[17] Commonwealth of Australia, *Parliamentary Papers* (1909 session), vol. II, no. 64; cable, Deakin to Colonel J.F.G. Foxton, Australian representative at the defence conference, 24 September 1909, NLA Deakin Papers, MS 1540/38/460.

[18] Great Britain, 5 *Parliamentary Debates* (Commons), IX, 2311, 26 August 1909

America had one battleship and eleven battle cruisers in the Pacific, Britain only had four outdated battle cruisers. Moreover, he added, hardly bothering to disguise this reference to Japan, that there was 'not far from our shores … two or three million of the best trained troops in the world,' which belong to a nation 'whose ideals are in many respects as unlike our own as it is possible to be.' Australia was 'the most distant, richest and at the same time the most vulnerable part of the British Empire.' In this situation, he noted that Australia was 'absolutely dependent on the Anglo–Japanese alliance for its security', meaning it had to rely on the good faith of the Japanese. When Andrew Fisher, the leader of the Labor opposition, taking this point further, interjected that the treaty would be honoured only 'so long as it suits the parties as is the case with every treaty', Cook not to be outdone in his realism replied that 'no nation depends entirely upon treaties and this is our position at the moment.'[19]

On military defence the bill Cook brought before parliament was not dissimilar to that which Deakin and Fisher had earlier proposed. It followed the Swiss citizen training scheme. All youths and young men from ages 14–20 were to be required to undergo military training for sixteen days each year. The trained soldiers were to remain on an active reserve through one day musters until they were 26. There was very little criticism and the bill was passed in both houses on a voice vote.[20] On the naval question Fisher and some other Labor members of parliament urged that the fleet units should not be sent to 'remote seas' without the government's consent.[21] A few Labor representatives wondered whether the Admiralty plan might not be a ruse to obtain more ships for the defence of the British Isles. But these reservations were brushed aside. Pearce, after reading Percival A. Hislam's *The Admiralty of the Atlantic: An Inquiry into the Development of German Sea Power, Past Present and Prospective*[22], had become convinced of the 'feeble nature of the Anglo–Japanese alliance.' The book had shown that though the Royal Navy had grown considerably in the preceding years the number of British warships in the Pacific had declined. In making these points Pearce was not expressing opposition to the Pacific fleet. Rather he wanted to warn future Australian and British governments against deviating from the aim of the naval agreement, namely the protection of British Empire in the Pacific.[23] When six months later Labor came to power Fisher and his Defence Minister Pearce, both sharing Deakin's view of Greater Britain, pursued the same defence policy. Fisher's aim, as he had put it while briefly in

---

[19] Commonwealth of Australia, *Parliamentary Debates*, vol. LI, pp. 3607–36, 21 September 1909.

[20] Ibid., LIV, pp. 7109, 7 December 1909.

[21] Ibid., LII, pp. 4460–3, 13 October 1909 and LIV, pp. 6251–59, 24 November 1909.

[22] Percival A. Hislam's *The Admiralty of the Atlantic: An Inquiry into the Development of German Sea Power, Past Present and Prospective* (London: Percival A. Kessinger Publishing, 1908), especially pp. 29–30, 154 and 177–79.

[23] It does not seem that the Admiralty at this time had any other intention but to carry through the defence conference agreement. Certainly this would seem to be true of Sir John Fisher, its originator, who a year later was assuring a friend that 'the 3 "New testament" ships [that is the three latest battlecruisers which would head the three units making up the Pacific fleet] and their attendant satellites will be in the Pacific in 1913.' See letter, Fisher to Viscount Esher, 13 September, 1910, Arthur J. Marder, ed., *Fear God and Dread Nought: The Correspondence of Admiral of the Fleet, Lord fisher of Kilverstone*, 2 vols (London: Jonathan Cape, 1956), II, 266.

office during the Dreadnought affair, was to pursue 'a steady, persistent and determined policy to provide for the adequate defence of Australia and assist the Mother country in time of emergency.'[24] The Labor government, now with a clear majority in both houses of parliament, set about consolidating and expanding the Deakin legacy.

In order to give his military scheme an imperial blessing Deakin before losing office had invited Lord Kitchener, Britain's most distinguished soldier, to review it. Though the War Office's official position was that Australia was the safest part of the Empire and that its Swiss system of universal and compulsory training was wasteful Kitchener served Deakin's purpose and in his report agreed with the Australian strategic assumptions about a threat of invasion and in approving the Swiss system made suggestions for its improvement.[25] The Labor Government adopted nearly all the British general's suggestions. It accepted that the military training should be extended beyond age twenty to age twenty-five and in its defence act went further than Kitchener in requiring the adult soldiers to undergo an eight day camp annually. Pearce estimated that by 1919-20 when the scheme was in full operation Australia would have a trained fighting force of 127,000 men.

Likewise, the Cabinet adopted the principles of the 1909 naval agreement establishing the Empire's Pacific fleet and invited the Admiralty to send a senior British Admiral, Ronald Henderson, to advise them not only on the technical matters related to the Australian unit but also more generally on 'all the measures to be taken, both forthwith and in the future, in the formation of the Fleet.' Henderson took this commission very seriously and presented the Labor government with a blue print for a greatly enlarged fleet which would be built over a 22 year period.[26] Fisher though impressed by the vision saw also the huge cost which it would entail and put off making a decision until after the 1911 Imperial Conference.[27]

Labor minsters had to this time little direct acquaintance with imperial gatherings. As they began to prepare for what was the first Imperial Conference Deakin offered them the fruits of his long experience in dealing with the British. In a lengthy speech to the parliament he addressed the great problems which believers in Greater Britain had to face when trying to persuade London, especially Whitehall, that the Dominions had to be consulted about Imperial defence and foreign policy and their interests and dangers taken into account when decisions were made. He called upon the Australian representatives

> to impress upon their colleagues at the conference that Australia, in spite of herself, is being forced into a foreign policy of her own because foreign interests and risks surround us on every side. A Pacific policy we must have … We must be observant, like every other nation, providing buffers to prevent shocks, and placing intervals between us and danger centres …

> Let Ministers impress upon the Foreign Office in London that there are Pacific problems in which the Australian interest is inexpressible; which…should be perpetually and consistently considered, particularly by the Naval and Military authorities, and those charged with foreign affairs of the Empire …

---

[24] *Sydney Morning Herald*, 24 March 1909.

[25] Commonwealth of Australia, *Parliamentary Papers* (1910 session), vol. II, no. 8, 'Defence of Australia. Memorandum by Field Marshal Viscount Kitchener of Khartoum.'

[26] Ibid., (1911 session), vol. II, no. 7, 'Naval Forces. Recommendations by Sir Reginald Henderson.'

[27] Minutes of Council of Defence Meeting, 1 March 1911, NAA CRS A2032.

> The creation of this Conference was a great stride … But it is not sufficient that this should remain a mere advisory Conference. Its powers require to grow with the needs and the emergencies of the Empire …

> …united action is only to be obtained when, instead of a conference separated by breaks of four years, continuity and character are given to its policy by providing a means of keeping up the work, following up its suggestions and giving effect to its resolutions…By that means and that means alone can we clothe this Conference with the powers that rightly belong to it, making it a thoroughly Imperial body, representative of our race in every part of the world, without trenching on the local Governments of the Dominions or on the sphere of the British Government.[28]

By the time of the conference the Australian Labor leaders had come to share fully Deakin's vision of empire. They regarded the Imperial Conference as 'the most important step taken during this century'[29] since they hoped that through it they would at last obtain a voice in the shaping of Imperial foreign policy, especially where it touched on Australia's interests in the Pacific. Giving advance notice of their intentions they cabled London that they wished to put on the agenda 'co-operation and mutual relations of the naval and military forces' and 'the desirability of Dominions being informed and consulted in negotiations with foreign powers as to matters affecting any one of them or the Empire generally.'[30] In all probability this latter item was most immediately prompted by press rumours that Britain was talking to the Japanese about renewing the Anglo–Japanese alliance.

The British, in preparing for the conference, were greatly exercised over Australia's claim to be consulted on defence and foreign policy matters. Though they were engaged in sensitive negotiation with the Japanese over the renewal of their alliance they finally agreed, somewhat reluctantly, that they would inform the Dominions about the negotiations at a special meeting of the Committee of Imperial Defence. Thus in the first week of the conference Sir Edward Grey, the Foreign Secretary, gave the Dominion representatives a very extensive overview of the foreign dangers facing the empire. He stressed that

> the creation of separate Fleets has made it essential that the Foreign Policy of the Empire should be a common policy. If it is to be a common policy, it is obviously one on which the Dominions must be taken into consultation, which they must know, which they must understand and which they must approve.

After describing Germany's 'Napoleonic' policy in Europe and its threat to British naval supremacy he explained that for reasons of strategic planning, naval expenditure and world stability it was necessary to secure a ten year renewal of the Japanese alliance. He assured the Dominion leaders that Japan had 'never mentioned it [Australia's racially discriminating immigration policy] in connection with the alliance at all' and that Japan could be relied on to honour its commitment. With this assurance Fisher was happy to give his approval,

---

[28] Commonwealth of Australia, *Parliamentary Debates* (1910 session), vol. LIX, pp. 6857–60, 25 November 1910.

[29] *Sydney Morning Herald*, 31 March 1911.

[30] Cables, Lord Dudley, Governor-General, to Lewis Harcourt, Colonial Secretary, 9 January and 8 May 1911, NTA PRO FO 800/90.

remarking in the process that it would give the Australian people 'great satisfaction' since 'we are undoubtedly somewhat apprehensive of the immediate future.'[31] He realised that though the alliance could not be relied upon it was better that Japan was linked by these formal ties to the British Empire than not. It would act as a restraint, even if only a limited one, on Japan's behaviour in the Pacific.

Fisher was elated by the British action in bringing the Dominion representatives into the inner sanctum of Imperial policymaking. In an interview with the *Morning Post* he was reported as saying that

> All the barriers of reserve have been broken down and mutual confidence has been established for all time. A community of interests of the highest immediate importance and vast possibilities has been created. I will go back equipped with knowledge that will qualify the federation I represent for co-operation with the mother country of a more effective kind than has ever been possible before. By the revelation of the British policy Australia has been admitted into the innermost confidence of the Imperial government.[32]

Since the British had committed themselves to the establishment of a Pacific Fleet and to consult the Dominions about the Empire's foreign policy, it seemed that the last barriers to the creation of a community of interest between Britain and the Dominions were disappearing. The communities of culture and interest were being fused and the Empire would now face the world as one united people.

While in this euphoric mood Fisher, believing the principle to have been won, agreed to withdraw the Australian resolution calling for consultation. Nevertheless when the matter of ratifying the London Declaration which dealt with rules governing merchant shipping in time of war was discussed he repeated as a question-perhaps he had residual doubts—what he had earlier seemed to think had already been conceded, asking whether

> The time has not arrived for the overseas Dominions to be informed, and whenever possible consulted, as to the best means of promoting the interests of all concerned ... ?[33]

On defence very little was achieved, and this primarily because the general basis for co-operation in respect to the army and the navy had been reached at the 1909 defence conference.

The British still wanted the Dominions to accept that on the outbreak of war their naval squadrons would automatically come under the control of the Admiralty unless a Dominion government specifically refused to allow it. However Pearce, backed up by the Canadians, would not accept this limitation on Dominion authority and autonomy. The only concession that he would make was that once the ships had been handed over to the Admiralty they would remain under its control until the end of the war. In the end it was formally laid down that 'The naval forces of the Dominions of Canada and Australia will be exclusively under the control of their respective Governments.'[34]

---

[31] Minutes of 111 meeting, CID, 26 May 1911, TNA PRO CAB 2/2.

[32] *Morning Post*, 31 May 1911.

[33] Great Britain, *Parliamentary Papers* (1911 session), vol. LIV, cd. 5745, 'Imperial Conference, 1911. Dominion No. 17. Minutes of the Proceedings of the Imperial Conference, 1911', pp. 97–98.

[34] Commonwealth of Australia, *Parliamentary Papers* (1911 session), vol. II, no. 12, 'Memorandum

For the Army there was even less to discuss. At a meeting chaired by the Chief of the Imperial General Staff, Sir William Nicholson, the Dominions' defence ministers revisited the agreed principles for co-operation. As Nicholson said, what lay behind the standardising of their armaments, organization and training with those of the British forces was that 'while preserving the complete autonomy of the Dominions, should the Dominions desire to assist in the defence of the Empire in a real emergency, their forces could be rapidly combined into one homogeneous Imperial Army.'

Pearce, since arriving in London, had become more keenly aware of the possibility of a great war breaking out in Europe, and realising that many Australians would wish to volunteer to fight for the Mother Country wanted to know whether the Imperial General Staff could give the Australian General Staff any information about where such volunteers might be sent so that they could prepare plans for mobilisation and transportation. At the same time he, in order that there should be no confusion on the matter, reminded Nicholson that the government under the Australian *Defence Act* could not compel any soldier to serve overseas and that any decision to send volunteers would be made exclusively by the Australian government. Nicholson pointed out that it would be impractical beforehand to try to suggest where Dominion troops might be sent since they could only be raised for the purpose with the consent of the Australian government. If, however, the Australian government so desired, the General Staff could work out plans for mobilising 'a certain contingent or force for expeditionary action.' Nicholson suggested that if this were to be done it would be best not to publish a paper on the subject since in some of the Dominions 'it might be better not to say anything about preparations.' The Dominion leaders considered that this would be politically wise since they felt that in each of their countries there would be a minority who might misconstrue such plans. Pearce, however, maintained and the others agreed that this should not dissuade them from going ahead with plans for a possible mobilisation.[35]

---

of Conference between the British Admiralty and the Representatives of the Dominions of Canada and Australia', June 1911.

[35] Minutes of Meeting of Chief of the Imperial General Staff with the Canadian, Australian and South African Defence Ministers, 17 June 1911, pp. 20–23. TNA PRO WO106/43.

There was some confusion in this discussion about the mobilisation plans. Even though Pearce had told Nicholson that any Australian expeditionary force would have to be composed of volunteers and would therefore have to be raised separately from Australia's military forces, Nicholson at one point in making an analogy between how the Imperial General Staff without any such impediment in Britain would prepare and organise an expeditionary force in the British Isles seemed to ignore this distinction. Pearce had not given Nicholson any indication that the Australian government had it in mind to raise and train in peacetime a volunteer force which would on enlistment have consented to go wherever the government chose to send it. Pearce was only talking about having the Australian section of the General Staff make plans beforehand for enlisting, training, arming and organising such a force after hostilities had commenced and the Australian government had agreed to send an expeditionary force to help the Mother Country.

There is no reason to think that Pearce, by agreeing to keep these preparatory plans for an expeditionary force secret, was conspiring with the British to undermine the fundamentals of the defence policy established by the Deakin and Fisher governments. Australia had sent 16,000

Fisher at the end of the conference believed that the most encouraging result of the conference was, as he had intimated after taking part in the CID meeting on the Anglo-Japanese alliance, that the Dominions had been brought 'into the inner councils of the nations' and had been given an opportunity 'to discuss the affairs of the Empire as they affect each and all of us'.[36] He still felt that the Imperial authorities did not understand fully the Dominions' strategic perspective and on the last day of their meeting had recommended that there should be reciprocal visits by British and Dominion ministers and that the next conference should be held in one of the Dominions.

European Tensions

The Australians returned home in a very optimistic frame of mind. It seemed that all their hopes for the creation of an Imperial Pacific fleet and for Dominion participation in the making of Imperial policy were in the process of being realised. Yet within a year this promise of imperial consultation and Pacific security was in tatters. As a result the Fisher government, when the full implications of British policy became clear, committed the country to a greatly enlarged naval building program, began to look more directly to the other Dominions for assistance in the Pacific and, rebuking the British for their arbitrary action in failing to honour their commitment to a Pacific fleet, pressed for a new conference to reconsider the question of imperial defence.

At the very time that the Labor ministers were travelling back to Australia the British government was being forced to deal with another European crisis centred on Morocco which was be the undoing of British plans for the defence of the Empire in the Pacific. The French were attempting to extend their influence over Morocco and the Germans in order to express their concern about this extension of French influence in North Africa sent a gunboat to Agadir on Morocco's Atlantic coast. The British, without consulting the Dominions, once again took France's side and the Germans backed down and as consolation was given some French territory in Central Africa. However the Germans did

---

volunteer soldiers to the Boer War and it was generally accepted that Australians would respond even more enthusiastically to a war in which the very survival of the Empire was at stake. All Australian leaders conceded this and some did think that, given the dangerous state of Europe, it would be prudent to make preliminary arrangements for sending forces overseas, including possibly to Germany's Pacific possessions. Prompt action might be required not only to meet a war in Europe but also to deal with the consequences of such a war in the Pacific. Australia's defence policy was aimed at preparing the country for defence against Japan.

Nothing that Pearce had consented to at the 1911 conference undermined the Australian government's right to decide if and when it might raise a volutary contingent to assist the Mother Country. That possibility had been in the background of defence policymaking since the passage of the 1904 *Defence Act*. In requiring that the government would only be permitted to raise volunteers for overseas service, it had offering aid for the Mother Country and no other country in mind. Neither Pearce nor Fisher nor Millen nor Cook was a party to a clandestine plot to circumvent the voluntary principle. See John Mordike, *An Army for a Nation: A History of Australian Military Development 1880–1914* (Sydney: Allen and Unwin, 1992), pp. 240–41 for the conspiratorial argument.

[36] *The Times* (London), 21 June 1911.

not take their humiliation kindly and retaliated by laying down three more battleships. When therefore in July the following year, Winston Churchill assumed the office of First Lord of the Admiralty he found that in order to keep the 60 percent margin of safety over the German High Seas fleet he would have to find a new naval squadron and three new battleships for the North Seas. Simultaneously the CID was recommending that Britain should also match the naval force of Austria, Germany's ally, in the Mediterranean which would mean the building of a further three battleships.

For Churchill and the Asquith government this posed a great problem. Britain's defence budget was already the largest in the world. What was being required would place an unacceptable drain on the nation's resources. To meet this challenge Churchill felt compelled to abandon every other naval commitment that was not central to the survival of the British Isles and he sent an ambiguous signal to the Dominions indicating that Britain might be unable to play its part in bringing the Pacific fleet into being. The Dominions, he said, would have to face 'real and great facts', 'fact as hard as Kruppencemented steel.' Defence of the overseas empire had to be left to the Dominions. And he added, as if to make the pill more palatable, that just as concentration of British sea power in Home Waters had been the noteworthy development of the last ten years so 'the growth of effective naval forces in the great Dominions overseas' would be the hallmark of the next few years.[37]

The Labor leaders only slowly awoke to the full import of what the British were saying about their future naval policy. Both Fisher and Pearce understood Churchill's speech in exactly the way he hoped they would. Overlooking its implications for the promised Pacific fleet they praised it as an endorsement by the Admiralty of Dominion navies. Fisher in reassuring a questioner about whether Australia's defence forces would be adequate to protect Australia Fisher replied that 'we may rest assured that it [the British Government] will not take any action that will weaken its prestige or power in any sea in which it is necessary to maintain its strength.'[38] But by the end of the year, Fisher could no longer give the British the benefit of the doubt. News that Churchill had persuaded Robert Borden, the conservative Prime Minister of Canada, to ask his parliament for £7,000,000 to fund three improved 'Dreadnoughts' for the Mediterranean made the British Minister's intention perfectly clear. Without a word to Australia or New Zealand he was abandoning the obligations that the British had accepted under the 1909 defence agreement, and was taking Canada with him.

The Australian leaders were incensed by what they reasonably judged to be shabby treatment. Loth at first to criticise the British authorities publicly they had no such scruples about expressing their feelings privately. In a personal letter Defence Minister Pearce wrote to Australia's naval representative in London that

> We had the Imperial naval conference in 1909 which drew up a scheme for the co-operation of the Imperial government and Dominion in matters of defence. The proposals were not rejected at the 1911 Conference, although they were extant; yet what has happened? Australia is the only one of the parties to the 1909

[37] *The Times* (London), 16 May 1912.

[38] Commonwealth of Australia, *Parliamentary Debates* (1912 session), vol. LXV, 1970, 7 August 1912.

Conference that has carried out its share of the scheme then arrived at. None of the other governments have stated that they will not carry out their share: they have merely ignored it, and in my mind this action or want of action on the part of these governments is the greatest blow yet dealt to Imperial co-operation… It seems to me that it would have been better for the 1911 Conference to have frankly and clearly advised that the 1909 Conference Resolutions should not be given effect to. [39]

Fisher, taking the only course left to him, set about improving Australia's defence posture in the Pacific. He proposed to establish closer co-operation with New Zealand and adopt the full list of Admiral Henderson's recommendations for building up Australia's own navy. With the coming to power in New Zealand in August 1912 of a Reform Government the prospects for developing a common defence policy had brightened. The new government, especially Defence Minister Colonel James Allen, was, unlike its predecessor, openly critical of the British for keeping the New Zealand battle cruiser—the Dominion's contribution to the Dreadnought crisis—in the North Sea and not sending it to the Pacific to head the China squadron of the putative Pacific fleet as had originally been agreed. The Reform government shared Fisher's view that 'Australia had a position more vulnerable against a foe than any other part of the British Empire'[40] and was well disposed towards following the Australian example and developing its own naval unit. In December Allen broke his journey to London and met the Australian Defence Council which included Fisher, Pearce and their chief military and naval advisers. While the minutes rather vaguely record only that 'an informal discussion ensued' it would appear that agreement was reached for planning a joint Australian–New Zealand expeditionary force of 18,000 men which could be drawn upon if either country were attacked.[41] Likewise from Allen's subsequent discussion with the British it would seem that the Australians and New Zealanders saw eye to eye on Britain's failure to contribute to the 1909 scheme, the urgency of Pacific naval defence and the desirability of Canada participating in the creation of a Pacific fleet.[42]

In this desperate situation Fisher revived the very ambitious naval building program which Admiral Henderson had put before his government in September 1911. Henderson had recommended that Australia over a period of twenty-two years should acquire a fleet of eight battle cruisers, ten protected or light cruisers, eighteen destroyers, twelve submarines, three depot ships and one fleet repair ship. On completion it would comprise fifty-two vessels and fifteen thousand men. The building of the navy was divided into four stages. In the initial stage, 1911–18, the fleet unit which had been accepted at the 1909 defence conference and the bases which would house it would be completed. Further along in this period a depot ship, three more submarines and three more destroyers would be laid down. About equal numbers of the remaining vessels would be built in each of

---

[39] Letter, Pearce to Muirhead Collins, 3 December 1912, AWM, Pearce Papers, 7/106. A few months later Pearce did express publicly the same sentiments, even if in rather milder terms. See *Sydney Morning Herald*, 22 January 1913.

[40] *Argus*, 19 August 1912.

[41] C.E.W. Bean, *The Official History of Australia in the War of 1914–18*, 12 vols, 'The Story of Anzac', vol. I, pp. 27–28.

[42] Minutes of the 122 Meeting , CID, 6 February 1913, TNA PRO CAB 2/3.

the four subsequent periods.[43] Early in 1913 the Naval Board at the request of Cabinet produced estimates for the next three financial years. By this time the Australian fleet unit was now almost complete and so these proposed appropriations were for the acquisition of additional ships and building naval bases. Taking their lead from the Henderson Report they asked for £9,000,000 for the three-year period. Over half of this amount was to be spent on constructing bases and most of the rest on a battle cruiser, three destroyers, two submarines, one supply ship and a naval aircraft.[44] Cabinet agreed and Fisher, in his policy speech for the coming election, announced that the Henderson recommendations had been adopted as a guide to policy and that, if returned, his government would carry out a naval construction program identical to that proposed by the Naval Board.[45]

At the election Joseph Cook, who had succeeded Deakin as leader of the Liberal Party, won a very narrow victory and became prime minister. He seems not to have been kept abreast of the dificulties which had arisen over the British decision to abandon the Pacific fleet agreement.While preparing the budget he was made aware by the Naval Board of a lack of clarity in Britain's attitude towards Pacific defence which had implications for naval estimates. Thus at the Board's suggestion he sent an inquiring letter to Whitehall pointing out that at the 1909 conference it had been arranged that Australia would acquire a naval unit which would join similar units of the British naval forces on the China and East Indies stations as part of an 'eastern Fleet of the Empire.' Continuing, he said that while the Australia naval unit was almost completed it appeared the British government had not taken any steps to provide their units and he wondered whether there were 'any new circumstances' which might have arisen to cause them to change their mind. If so, following Fisher's example, he assured the British that Australia would be willing to attend a new conference to review the matter.[46]

By this time the national security community was fully aware that neither the British nor probably the Canadians were going to contribute to an imperial fleet in the Pacific and therefore Australia was going to be left to fend for itself in dealing with Japan, its prospective enemy. In early 1913, accepting that Japan's most likely form of attack would be at least initially directed against northern Australia, two members of the naval board, Captain C. H. Hughes-Onslow and Commander W. H. Thring accompanied by the Chief of the General Staff, Brigadier-General, J. M. Gordon, visited Darwin and other parts of the northern coastline in order to determine the best strategy for resisting such an invasion. On their return they drew up substantial reports which proceeded from common premises. Both reports agreed that the British navy could no longer be relied upon to

---

[43] Commonwealth of Australia, *Parliamentary Papers* (1911 session), vol. II, no. 7, 'Naval Force Recommendations by Admiral Sir Reginald Henderson', ordered to be printed 14 September 1911.

[44] Minutes of Naval Board meeting, H. W. Manisty, Finance Member and Secretary of the Naval Board, 4 March 1913, AWM Pearce Papers, 3DRL/2222 5/34.

[45] *Sydney Morning Herald*, 1 April 1913.

[46] Cable, Lord Denman to Harcourt, 15 August 1913, United Kingdom, U.K. *Parliamentary Papers* (1914 session), vol. LX, cd. 7347. Fisher cabled the British government on 19 December 1912 proposing that a new conference similar to the 1909 defence conference be called and that it be held in Australia. Ibid.

protect Australia. The most likely time that Japan would choose to launch its invasion would be while Britain was at war. But they also commented that even while the threat of a European war existed the British would be tied down by the German navy in the North Sea and so unable to risk sending a fleet to the Pacific. It was also suggested that at the end of a European war the British, even if they were victorious, might be so exhausted that their fleet would not be able to act as a deterrent against Japanese aggression. Nevertheless in the end the Naval Board sent the new minister, Senator E.D. Millen, a statement of principles which merely reaffirmed the earlier optimistic view that by the time the Japanese threat fully emerged—that is with the determination of the Anglo–Japanese Treaty in 1921—the British empire should have a fleet in the East adequate to contain the Japanese. And the statement added that to ensure this outcome there ought be a new conference representing all British interests in the region. It would seem that when the Board at that time considered the picture painted by the reports it was not able to face the grim alternative, namely that Australia might be left to it own resources to keep Japan at bay.

Gordon devoted most of his report to the navy since the disposition of military forces was dependent on the nature of the attack and therefore on the strength and character of sea defence. He agreed with Hughes-Onslow and Thring that the only 'Power in the east which possesses a strong enough fleet to hold the sea command of the South Pacific is Japan.' While conceding that the Anglo–Japanese treaty might restrain Japan for a time he, unlike his naval counterparts, noted that treaties could be unilaterally terminated or cancelled. Since there was no naval force in the Pacific which could challenge Japan's mastery of those seas there was good reason to study the northern littoral 'from BROOME on the West Coast right across to CARDWELL on the Queensland Coast' for the purpose of preparing defences against the feared onslaught.[47] All the senior naval and military officers were full of apprehension about Japan. Colonel J. G. Legge, while in London acting as Australia's representative on the Imperial General Staff, spent his time working out how the Japanese might invade Australia, and he concluded that 'there is not much doubt that they could easily send 3 divisions to Australia in less than 1 month from the day on which they commenced to mobilise. At the present time that would be more than enough for the job, and the Japs could, if they chose to, do it without giving us even indirect information of more than 7 to 14 days.'[48] It was not surprising that Cook and Millen were alarmed.

When after two months the Admiralty replied to Cook it explained that because of the German Fleet Law of 1912 it had been compelled in order to maintain Britain's preponderant power in the North Sea 'to defer carrying the [1909] arrangements into effect in the precise form contemplated.' They maintained that the original decision to send out to the China and East Indies stations two battle cruisers of the latest *Indefatigable* class was not made on strategic grounds but merely 'for the sake of homogeneity' with the Australian unit. The British naval forces were quite adequate to deal with any possible trouble in the

---

[47] For Naval Board's Statement of Principles, 17 July 1913 and the Reports of Hughes, Onslow and Thring, 29 May 1919, see NAA MP1049/1 14/0285; for Gordon's 'A review of General Naval and Military Considerations affecting the Defence of Australia', 16 June 1913, see Memorandum for the Minister of Defence, 27 June 1913, NAA B197, 1855/1/6.

[48] Letter, Legge to C.B.B. White, 25 July 1913 NAA MP826/3.

Pacific and they attached a chart showing the superiority of British forces over any possible enemy in the region, Japan 'being excluded in view of the existing alliance.'[49]

Cook was taken aback by this answer. The Admiralty's view of the 1909 conference was totally at odds with his own. As Defence Minister at the time he had been responsible for giving effect to the agreement. He had understood it to be a mutual engagement based on strategic considerations related to Australia's fear of Japan and had argued this case in commending it to parliament. As we have seen Australian leaders and their official advisers had come to regard this Imperial fleet as the sheet anchor for their security in the Pacific. What the Admiralty had done and what they had said in justifying their actions had brought on a crisis over the meaning of Empire, had brought to the fore the innate tension between the demands of the community of culture and the community of interest.

Thus Cook in a rebuttal of the Admiralty's position set out Australians' alternative view of both the 1909 conference and the Empire, that is their view of Greater Britain. For him, the aim of the conference had been one 'of laying down and consistently developing a basis for Naval Defence, at once Imperial and local.' Its 'primary object' was 'the permanent protection of British interests in the Pacific.' He believed that 'the immunity of the Commonwealth should not be left to depend on the continuance of such a delicate security as an alliance.' The Admiralty had to understand the unique nature of the British Empire, meaning here Greater Britain.

> In nothing is the British Empire more unique than in the fact that its component parts, while bound by allegiance and affection to maintain the interests and integrity of the whole, have special international relations and dangers which necessitate local provision for the defence that strategic dispositions of the Fleet for protection of the Empire as a whole may not at all times adequately meet.

> Our common aim should be to adopt and consistently develop a scheme of Naval Defence, which as far as possible meets the special, as well as the common danger and which does not admit of the adequacy of a Dominion's defence being, from time to time, affected by the changing requirements of Imperial interests elsewhere.

Cook was willing to allow that

> General naval supremacy, 'the power to defeat in battle and drive from the seas the strongest hostile navy or combination of hostile navies, wherever they may be found' is a safeguard and end to be sought alike by the United Kingdom and the greatest Dominions of the Crown.

However, he contended

> That local superiority, also, if not always an essential condition of general supremacy, may be of such vital importance to a particular Dominion that provision made for it should not be altered to remove any available defects in provisions for the protection of British interests elsewhere. Both should be aims of a sound Imperial system, and, it is submitted, may without undue sacrifices be attained.

---

[49] Cable and despatch, Harcourt to Denman, 17 October 1913.

Finally, he scolded the British for unilaterally breaking an agreement, even as he called for a new conference to review once again the problem of imperial defence in the Pacific.[50]

But before Cook's letter reached London, Churchill, having been deserted by the Canadians, was under great pressure to find the wherewithal to fund the ships necessary to maintain Britain's margin of safety over the German High Seas Fleet. In his speech to the House of Commons introducing the Admiralty's record estimates of £ 51,580,000 he made a plea to the Dominions to come to the aid of the 'heart of the Empire', and in the process he questioned the efficacy of Dominion navies. He praised the wisdom of the New Zealand Government for allowing the Admiralty to keep the 'Dreadnought' which it had paid for in the North Sea. He denied that the British government had failed to live up to its obligations or had placed Australia or New Zealand in jeopardy, arguing very forcefully that the safety of Australia depended on British naval supremacy and the allies that this could purchase.

> No European state could invade or conquer Australia or New Zealand unless the British Navy had been destroyed. The same naval power of Great Britain in European waters also protects New Zealand from any present danger from Japan. While Japan is allied to Great Britain and while Great Britain possesses a sufficient margin of naval superiority, Japan is safe from attack by sea from the great fleets of Europe. In no other way in the years that lie immediately before us can Japan protect herself from danger of European interference.

Giving the quietus to the 'Yellow Peril' he concluded that the Anglo–Japanese alliance was based on more than the plighted word. Rather, it was based on 'strong, continuing bonds of interest' and consequently there was no good reason why any of the new battle cruisers—including, one assumes, the *Australia*—should remain in the Pacific.

In Australia Churchill's words elicited a storm of protest. There were expressions of high indignation, even outrage, in the press. Only the *Argus,* a conservative newspaper that could not suffer the authority of the Admiralty to be questioned, dared to defend Churchill, asserting that neither of the two great powers in the Pacific, America and Japan, posed a threat to Australia and that therefore the most advanced battlecruisers, such as the *Australia,* would do more good for the Empire if retained in 'Home Waters.' This drew from Frederic Eggleston, a disciple of Deakin's and a leading member of the Melbourne branch of the Round Table movement, a compelling rejoinder which demolished the fundamentals of Churchill's argument. Eggleston was willing to go along with Churchill's view that the binding force of a treaty was at its core the mutuality of interests supporting it, but he contended that Churchill had misjudged that mutuality in the case of the Anglo–Japanese alliance. It was true, as Churchill had admitted, that Britain lacking an Imperial fleet in the Pacific depended on Japan to protect its interests in the Pacific and therefore Britain obtained benefits from the pact. But, Eggleston maintained that the same could not be said for Japan. He refuted Churchill's claim that Britain's naval supremacy in Europe safeguarded Japan from the predatory ambitions of other European powers. In Europe there was an equilibrium of armaments and it was this balance of power and not British naval supremacy which prevented European countries from threatening Japan's position in the Pacific. That is, the British out of fear of Germany had no choice but to keep its fleet in the

---

[50] Letter, Cook to Denman, 28 February 1914, NAA CP 290/15/2 and despatch, Denman to Harcourt, 3 March 1914, TNA PRO CO 532/66.

North Sea and the Mediterranean. Japan would be protected by these Europeans rivalries and tensions whether the Anglo–Japanese alliance existed or not. The United States was Japan's only rival in the Pacific but the British in renewing the alliance had made it clear that it was not to apply to America. The alliance therefore differed in what it offered the two parties. Japan gained very little from it. The alliance was not buttressed by an exchange of equal interests and therefore was a fragile reed on which to rest the security of Australia. Eggleston, like Deakin, Fisher, Cook and Pearce believed that a proper imperial defence policy had to be one which offered equal and complete security for all parts of the empire. Thus it was his contention that 'a policy which disregards the Pacific, or leaves it to Japan cannot be regarded as a truly Imperial policy.'[51]

The political leaders, each in his own way, echoed Eggleston's words. Senator Millen, Cook's Defence Minister, issued with Cabinet approval a scarifying memorandum attacking Churchill's position. He took the Admiralty to task for its unilateral overturning of the 1909 agreement. What Churchill was now offering the Dominions was instead of 'a definite inter-Imperial co-operative policy for Pacific development … an unco-ordinated, ephemeral scheme possessing neither permanence nor clear purpose and function.' Ineffective isolated units were to be substituted for 'a powerful joint Imperial Fleet in the Pacific.' He did not consider that Churchill's view about the value of the Anglo–Japanese alliance was correct. The alliance had existed in 1909 and 1911 when the original scheme had been drawn up and then confirmed. What, he wanted to know, had changed. Unlike Eggleston he could not openly question the worth of the alliance. But he did allow himself the comment that 'the pages of history are strewn with the wreckage of fruitless alliances.'

---

[51] *Argus*, 31 March and 11 April, 1913.

Henry Frei's *Japan's Southward Advance and Australia* (Melbourne, Melbourne University Press: 1991) is a quite valuable contribution to our knowledge of Japanese intellectuals' and publicists' attitude to Japan's expansionism in the Pacific. However its criticism of Australia's fears of Japan and the Deakin–Fisher defence policy is not compelling. Because the Japanese in the decade after the Russo–Japanese War showed no interest in invading Australia it is suggested that Australia's alarm about Japan and its intentions were not justified. But this line of argument has some difficulties. First, aggression and expansion do not always come about from long term planning. Quite often it is opportunity that produces intention. This is certainly true, generally speaking, for much of the growth of the British Empire, which J.R. Seeley said was 'made in a fit of absence of mind', and also true, more pertinently, for the Japanese acquisition of Germany's North Pacific islands in the First World War. Second, because after a crisis looking back one can see that a feared danger had not eventuated it does not mean necessarily that policymakers were irrational in taking prudent measures against the possibility. It is not self-evident, as Frei assumed, that because Japan remained loyal to Britain during the war Churchill's pre-war assessment of Japan was 'right' and that therefore Eggleston's critique was irrational and based on 'fallacious assumptions' which flowed from a lack of knowledge about Japan and a preoccupation with 'whiteness'. See ibid., pp. 89–90. Third, while it is the case that a racial view of world politics did tend to heighten Australian leaders' fear of Japan nevertheless it was not race but *Realpolitik*, as their arguments and policymaking illustrate, which was the fundamental consideration underlying their strategic assessments. Deakin showed this most clearly in his proposal for extending the Monroe Doctrine into the Pacific where he classically sought to include those powers which shared a common interest with Australia and Britain and to exclude those who were their potential enemies. Thus he suggested bringing China as well as France into the security arrangement and excluding Japan and Germany from it.

And openly defying Churchill, he declared that Australia 'will not be deflected from her course by the pronouncements of the First Lord of the Admiralty for she regards the task she has undertaken as vital to the cause of imperial defence and Imperial union and an essential safeguard for her own protection.'[52] Fisher was delighted by Millen's memorandum and Pearce, now the shadow minister for defence, applauded it. When asked by the Governor-General to set down his own reaction to the Churchill speech, Pearce, like Millen, focussed on the strategic issue.

> We insist that there ought to be a British Fleet for the Pacific: without it British diplomacy is nullified in one of the great oceans of the world and we are compelled to allow our policy to be dictated by our ally.
>
> ...A British-Japanese alliance is better for Australia than a German-Japanese alliance would be.
>
> But the alliance is temporary, it suits both Japan and us at present, it may suit neither in a few years.[53]

While Australians were engaged in lambasting Churchill and his vision of imperial defence, the Colonial Office was engaged in a paper war with the Admiralty. The Colonial Office held that the Australians indeed had some justice on their side in criticising the Admiralty for scrapping a clear agreement without informing or consulting them. It was anxious to accede to the Australians' wish that the British should summon another defence conference, and though Churchill resisted the idea the Colonial Office's persistence won the day. In preparing its answer to Cook's latest letter it endeavoured to be conciliatory. It allowed that there had been 'a certain divergence of views' over the interpretation of the 1909 agreement and that there was a need for a further conference on naval defence at a not very distant time. This reply to the Australians was despatched to Melbourne on 28 July 1914.[54] But by this time the train of events leading from the assassination of Archduke Franz Ferdinand at Sarajevo to the long anticipated European war had come to overshadow all else. And as a result the British abandoned plans for a conference on naval defence in the Pacific.

With Britain's entry into the war the political leaders, who were engaged in a federal election, abandoned their debates over droughts and unemployment and like the electorate at large gave their full attention to the Empire's cause. Even before the British Cabinet had made its decision Cook had asserted that 'all our resources are in the Empire and for the Empire, and for the security and preservation of the Empire' and Fisher not to be outdone in expressions of loyalty declared that Australia would stand by the Mother Country 'to help and defend her to our last man and our last shilling.'[55] The overwhelming desire to

---

[52] Commonwealth of Australia, *Parliamentary Papers* (1914 session), vol. II, no. 1, 'Naval Defence Memorandum by the Minister for Defence, 13 April 1914; together with the Speech of the First Lord of the Admiralty as Reported in Australia.'

[53] Commonwealth of Australia, *Parliamentary Debates* (1914 session), vol. LXIII, p. 54, 16 April 1914; Letter, Pearce to Denman, 4 May 1914, NLA Denman Papers, MS769/84-91.

[54] Harcourt to Sir Ronald Munro Ferguson, Australian Governor–General, 28 July 1914, NAA CP 290/15/2.

[55] *Argus*, 1 August 1914.

help the Mother Country was motivated by both sentiment and interest. As at the time of the Boer War Australians, as a British people, could not resist the call of their kith and kin. Likewise they recognised that their own survival was inextricably bound up with that of the Empire. If Britain were defeated in Europe then they would be left at the mercy of Japan and Germany, and so they had a vital interest in assisting the Empire. When Cook announced that Australia would offer a contingent of 20,000 men there was hardly a murmur of criticism in the country. From the second Moroccan crisis in mid-July 1911 senior military officers had been drawing up plans for raising a volunteer expeditionary force, but first Pearce and then Millen rejected these schemes as they all necessarily involved enlisting volunteers for overseas service in peacetime.[56] Thus on the outbreak of war the government hurriedly created a separate organization for the Australian Imperial Force and called for recruits, and within six weeks the troops were ready to leave for the European battlefield.

Yet, despite this enthusiastic support for Britain, the fear of Japan, which since the Russo–Japanese War had been the driving force behind Australia's defence policy, acquired a new and more intense grip on the nation's psyche. During the Great War Australians continued to be deeply apprehensive about Japan and its intentions. Captain E.L. Piesse, who commanded the Tasmanian Military Intelligence at the outbreak of hostilities, wrote that he had 'no mind to volunteer'. He hoped that the War Office in asking for an Australian contingent 'knows all about the Japanese situation' and had 'thought of our interest as well as England's.'[57] Similarly Australian newspapers were full of editorials discussing whether Japan would enter the war on the Empire's side and, if so, what role it might play and how reliable an ally it might prove to be. Fisher himself a week after he had promised that Australia would support the Mother Country 'to the last man and the last shilling' gave voice to the defence policy which had guided Australian leaders over the preceding decade. 'My idea of patriotism', he said, 'was to first provide for our own defence and if there was anything left over offer it as a tribute to the Mother Country.'[58]

After being elected prime minister in September Fisher was willing to send to Europe all those who volunteered but he did nothing to urge men to come forward. He kept as far as he could to the plans for the defence of Australia that Deakin and he had devised in the previous decade, maintaining the compulsory military training scheme, providing funds for naval bases and naval vessels, establishing ammunition factories and constructing strategic railways. When in the first months of the war the Japanese, contrary to Australian expectations, took possession of the German islands in the North Pacific and so brought Japan's naval presence south to the equator, Fisher was greatly alarmed and pressed the British to summon the promised defence conference to deal with Pacific security. In Fisher's

[56] John Connor, *Anzac and Empire: George Foster Pearce and the Foundations of Australian Defence* (Port Melbourne: Cambridge University Press, 2011), p. 36. See also proofs of chapters I–V of the General Scheme of Defence, 18 August 1913, AWM 113 MH1/11

[57] Neville Meaney, *Fears and Phobias: E.L. Piesse and the Problem of Japan, 1909–39* (Canberra: National Library of Australia, 1996), pp. 5–6. In March 1916 Piesse became Director of Military Intelligence and in that role he spent the greater part of his time on the Japan question, teaching himself to read Japanese, accumulating a great deal of material on Japanese ambitions in the Asia Pacific and writing strategic assessments about Japanese intentions in the region.

[58] *Argus*, 5 August 1914.

view Japan, by taking advantage of the war to expand its territory and influence in the Pacific and China, had confronted Australia with a strategic crisis which had 'no parallel in our history.'[59] Even though the British rejected his call for a conference on Pacific defence, he showed his anxiety about Australia's danger by continuing to complain that such a meeting was necessary and urgent.[60] Throughout the Great War the Australian national security community remained deeply concerned about Japan. Indeed it might well be said that Australia in those years was engaged in two wars, a hot war against Germany in Europe and a cold war against Japan in the Pacific.[61]

Conclusion

In the decade preceding the onset of the European war Australian leaders had struggled with the dilemma inherent in the concept of Greater Britain. Although this dilemma was already evident in the latter part of the nineteenth century, the emergence of Japan as the dominant power in the Western Pacific simultaneously with the German challenge to Britain in Europe increased the tension on the national dichotomy of the community of culture and the community of interest. Faced with this potential threat from Japan in the Pacific, nearly all Australian political leaders looked for a way of establishing an imperial defence and foreign policy which would provide co-operatively and collectively for the defence of Britain and the British settled Dominions, that is for the British World. Yet the Australian desire to translate this sense of a common Britishness into a common defence and foreign policy was constantly frustrated by the divergence of strategic perceptions which followed from their respective geo-politics.

All the prime ministers who had responsibility for dealing with this problem in the pre-war years had recognised that the only satisfactory solution would be through establishing an Imperial Council or some similar body where representatives of Britain and the Dominions could meet, confer and hopefully agree on a common defence and foreign policy for the Empire. Thus, when Deakin found that his first endeavours to gain British assistance in establishing a flotilla to meet the Japanese danger were resisted, he had, at the 1907 Colonial Conference, even if unsuccessfully, put forward a proposal for such an advisory council. In 1909 at the time of the Dreadnought affair Fisher unwilling to weaken Australia's own defence build-up in the Pacific refused to provide a battle cruiser to help Britain maintain its capital ship margin of safety over the German High Seas fleet. Instead he followed Deakin in ordering naval vessels for the protection of Australia's commerce and coasts and sought a defence conference where the Dominions and the Mother Country could decide upon an imperial naval policy which would protect every part of the British Empire.

Though both Deakin and Fisher approved of the 1909 Defence Conference proposal for an Imperial Pacific Fleet they were still concerned that they were not consulted about imperial foreign policy. Deakin was so troubled by British unilateralism that he stressed on

---

[59] Copy of letter, Fisher to T.J. Ryan, Premier of Queensland, 12 June 1915, Fisher papers, NLA MS 2919/3/282.

[60] Neville Meaney, *Australia and World Crisis, 1914–1923* (Sydney: Sydney University Press, 2009), pp. 78–81 and 97–98.

[61] Ibid., chapters 1–9.

Fisher and his ministers the need to tell the British at the 1911 Imperial Conference that if they continued to ignore Australian interests then , 'Australia in spite of herself ' would be 'forced into a foreign policy of her own because foreign interests and risks surround us on every side'. What he was saying in the clearest terms was that if Australia's strategic interest were not respected and Australia drawn into the imperial decision-making process then with great reluctance the Australians would be forced to turn their back on the pull of culture and race and take an independent course in procviding for their national security. The only answer to this dilemma was for the Imperial Conference to be clothed 'with the powers that rightly belong to it, making it a thoroughly Imperial body, representative of our race in every part of the world, without trenching on the local Government of the Dominions or on the sphere of the British Government.' Fisher by the end of that conference had come to believe that this ideal resolution of the Greater Britain problem was on the point of being achieved. The 1909 Defence Conference had reached an agreement for the establishment of an Imperial Fleet for the Pacific. At the 1911 Conference the Dominion leaders had been invited to a meeting of the Committee of Imperial Defence, been granted an overview of British foreign policy and asked to approve the renewal of the Anglo–Japanese alliance. For Fisher 'a community of interests of the highest immediate importance has been created.'

Within two years, however, these high hopes were dashed by Britain's arbitrary action in tearing up the agreement for an Imperial Pacific fleet and keeping the Dreadnoughts promised for that fleet in the North Sea. This drew from Prime Minister Cook another lecture for the British authorities about the meaning of Greater Britain. In countering Churchill's claim that Australia was protected by the Anglo–Japanese alliance Cook asserted that the Pacific Dominions should not be left to rely on 'such a delicate security as an alliance.' Moreover he pointed out that the Dominions have 'special international relations and dangers which necessitate local provisions for defence' over and above those needed for the Empire as a whole which were the responsibility of the British government. Thus, for Greater Britain, he remarked that there should be a 'common aim' to have a scheme of Naval Defence, which 'meets the special as well as the common danger'. Eggleston summed up the Australian view of the problem when he declared that 'a policy which disregards the Pacific, or leaves it to Japan cannot be regarded as a truly Imperial policy.'

These Australian arguments about Greater Britain which informed the strategic discourse between the Dominion and the Mother Country in this era were premised on the assumption that all the British peoples were entitled to equal and complete protection against foreign enemies as united in their cultural identity they faced the world as one. Given, however, the great diversity of the geo-political interests of the member states inside the Empire and the limits on resources available to provide such universal security, this nationalist ideal, though it maintained its hold on the Australian imagination for a half century or more,[62] was a mirage which policymakers, despite repeated disappointments, pursued in their approach to world affairs and the defence of the commonwealth.

---

[62] James Curran, *Curtin's Empire* (Melbourne: Cambridge University Press, 2011).

9

Frederic Eggleston on International Relations and Australia's Role in the World[1]

Frederic Eggleston was one of Australia's few notable public intellectuals. Macmahon Ball, writing at the time of Eggleston's death in 1954, declared that he was 'the most independent and important thinker about politics and society that we have had in Australia'.[2] After making allowances for the customary encomiums of an obituary there is still much to be said for this judgment. Charles Henry Pearson, the author of the much neglected and misunderstood *National Life and Character: a Forecast*,[3] would seem to be Eggleston's only serious rival for the title.

Eggleston had broad intellectual interests which covered such issues as social change and social order, state planning and individual freedom, political leadership and mass democracy, national identity and human progress as well as the nature of international relations and the art of diplomacy. Above all, through these studies he hoped to contribute to the improvement of Australia's political culture and to a better understanding of Australia's relations with the world. In his major published works, *State Socialism in Victoria*,[4] *Search for a Social Philosophy*,[5] and *Reflections of an Australian Liberal*,[6] he addressed these questions, and as the title of the last of these would suggest he wrote from a committed liberal perspective.

His liberalism was expressed as a social philosophy. Though the only elected offices he held were achieved under the banner of the Liberal Party or as an independent Liberal, he was no narrow partisan in politics and was equally able to serve conservative and Labor governments. His vision was an open, searching one. Taking his starting point from the English new liberalism pioneered by Graham Wallas and others at the end of the nineteenth century, especially its emphasis on social psychology,[7] he argued that society was formed

---

[1] This essay was originally published as 'Frederic Eggleston on International Relations and Australia's Role in the World', *Australian Journal of Politics and History*, 51 (September, 2005): 359–71.

[2] *Age*, 15 November 1954.

[3] C.H. Pearson, *National Life and Character: a Forecast* (London, Macmillan:1894). Both men have the advantage of excellent biographies. For Pearson, see John Tregenza's *Professor of Democracy: The Life of Charles Henry Pearson 1830–1894, Oxford Don and Australian Radical* (Melbourne, Melbourne University Press: 1968), and for Eggleston, Warren Osmond's *Frederic Eggleston: An Intellectual in Australian Politics* (Sydney, George Allen & Unwin: 1985).

[4] Frederic Eggleston, *State Socialism in Victoria* (London, P. S. King: 1932).

[5] Frederic Eggleston, *Search for a Social Philosophy* (Melbourne, Melbourne University Press in association with Oxford University Press: 1941).

[6] Frederic Eggleston, *Reflections of an Australian Liberal* (Melbourne, Cheshire: 1953).

[7] For a summary of Wallas' thought see, Martin J. Weiner, *Between Two Worlds: The Political Thought of Graham Wallas* (Oxford, Clarendon Press: 1971), especially chapter V.

out of a 'pattern' which was the product of instinct, habit and but a partly conscious awareness of its nature. The 'pattern' gave order to social relations and adapted itself to social change. Since in the British tradition the 'pattern' itself was flexible these changes took place gradually without the violence of revolution, which destroyed more than it achieved. While the liberal 'pattern' made the people responsible for their own government and protected human liberty from arbitrary rule, it nevertheless adjusted to the growth of great economic institutions and accepted some degree of state planning, regulation and welfare so that individual citizens might live meaningful and dignified lives. The state's initiatives in furthering these aims should not be based on dogmatic principles but proceed through practical experimentation. He believed that the 'pattern' was advancing human progress, and that the means for ensuring this end was active, self-reliant citizenship and a Christian ethic, which would allow the common good to triumph over sectional and class interests.[8] Lloyd George's 'constructive liberalism', not Gladstone's *laissez-faire*, was his model. In Australia, Alfred Deakin was his hero and the touchstone of true liberalism.[9]

For Eggleston both the Labor and Liberal Parties—he was much more doubtful about the Country Party—were agents for the realisation of his conception of liberalism. He identified so closely with the Curtin and Chifley Labor governments that he played, perhaps rather lightheartedly, with the idea of entitling his 1953 work, *Reflections of an Australian Liberal*, 'Reflections of an Ex-Liberal'.[10] But despite his admiration for the Labor achievements, which was not uncritical, he still believed that the Liberal Party with all its shortcomings represented more completely his ideals. It was the party whose function it was 'to conserve the interests of the community as a whole'.[11] Thus it is fair to treat Eggleston as being an Australian liberal in both senses and to look at his ideas about international relations and his views on Australia's foreign relations as a liberal.

In this article I intend to reflect upon—and reflect is a good word to use when discussing Eggleston—his understanding of international relations and attitude towards international organizations and collective security, his identification with Britishness and the British Empire/Commonwealth, his sense of Australia's Pacific destiny and its relationship with East Asia, and his changing assessment of America, Communism and the Cold War.

It is also important to note that though he devoted more time and energy to the international than to domestic sphere he did not write a major work about this side of his public life. There is a section in *Search for a Social Philosophy* dealing with international relations, but it is abstrusely abstract and not, except incidentally, related to the crises of his times. *Reflections of an Australian Liberal* also touches only indirectly on the subject and his posthumous work, *Reflections on Australian Foreign Policy*, is a collection of essays of uneven quality.

---

[8] Eggleston, *Search for a Social Philosophy*, p. 11 and chapters II, III and VIII. See also *Reflections of an Australian Liberal*, chapter 8, 'The Liberal Way'.

[9] Eggleston, *Reflections of an Australian Liberal*, pp. 1–7.

[10] Osmond, *Frederic Eggleston*, p. 280.

[11] Eggleston, *Reflections of an Australian Liberal*, pp. 127 and 291.

Theory of International Relations, including the Role of International Organisations

Eggleston was pondering this subject at the very time that scholars in Britain and America were beginning to write about international relations as a discipline in its own right. As a liberal he was fundamentally concerned with the problem of uncontrolled power in global politics. Eggleston in his first approach to the subject offered a rather simplistic liberal critique of war in history. He did not regard the emergence of modern nation states as in itself the cause of conflict. Following J.A. Hobson's liberal theory of imperialism,[12] he stated that suspicions and antagonisms between states arose primarily from trade protectionism and the competition for access to raw materials. This competition through which nations endeavoured to gain control over the natural resources essential for their prosperity and power induced an arms race and thus war. The nations which first developed industrial economies were often unwilling to share with rising nations the resources of their colonial empires. Writing in the late 1930s he considered that the German, Italian and Japanese challenges to the Versailles and Washington Treaties could be explained in these terms. He maintained that: 'This problem of inequality or instability arising from lack of self-sufficiency is the supreme problem of the time.' Out of the pathology of these maladjustments absolute ideologies promising salvation appeared but these ideologies were false gods and contributed to national hostilities. Even though war and violence were a reaction to tensions in the system, nevertheless the resort to force in international relations merely served 'to inhibit the relaxation of the strains'.[13]

Since in the modern era the 'patterns' with which people identified were embodied in nation states, these became the units of the international structure. But the constant changes in the power of these units and the inevitable differences in their power, defined in the widest terms, brought about the idea of the balance of power by which these units constantly organised and reorganised themselves to meet the threat of rising powers to the existing equilibrium. But this solution to the problem of order was deficient and often degenerated into war between the contending alliances. Such a violent outcome achieved no social purpose. Eggleston saw the world as an organism which was continually in the process of change and adaptation, and in order to avoid the clashes which come from 'acute maladjustment' it was necessary to find ways to manage these changes in relative international wealth and power.

Eggleston's answer to the problem of violence in international relations was in most respects a classical liberal one. Through free trade the wealth of the world would be both increased and distributed more equitably. Through disarmament the fears about national security would be allayed and wars averted. He understood some of the shortcomings of liberalism, however, and rejected the indiscriminate application of the principle of self-determination which he considered led to inequality in power and encouraged 'the rush

---

[12] J.A. Hobson, *Imperialism: A Study* (London, James Nisbet: 1902). It is worth noting that by 1947 Eggleston had abandoned the idea that competition for markets caused wars. See Frederic Eggleston, Lectures to External Affairs Department Cadets, personal possession, lecture 4, p. 2.

[13] Eggleston, *Search for a Social Philosophy*, pp. 260, 270 and 348.

for security and the demand for welfare'.[14] Just as the growth of large states, in response to the organisational needs of capitalism and military security, limited the freedom of the individual citizen and the responsibility of the citizen for the political community so the fragmenting of the global system into many small units weakened world organisations. Though Eggleston thought regional integration of states might be possible—he was most supportive of the idea of European union[15]—he did not consider that a world state was either practicable or desirable. The latter lacked a 'pattern' which would unite people through ideas of belonging to a common race and sharing a common history and would inevitably compromise individual freedom. Thus his solution for a world of peace and justice was to be ultimately found, like so much of the English-speaking tradition of liberalism, in a secularised version of Protestant Christianity. Coming from a devout Methodist background, Eggleston asserted that only by people adopting Christ's ethic of the good neighbour could the advances which had marked the world's history in the past 2,000 years be built upon: 'Boundless opportunities lie before humanity if it can use properly the social machine, but unless goodwill and enlightenment and a respect for human values are dominant, they will draw humanity down.' It was his view that victory over Germany would be 'of very little use unless some other factor than sheer power is emphasised' and this had to 'come from higher ethical standards of human conduct'.[16]

As a liberal, Eggleston admired President Woodrow Wilson and his desire to replace the flawed 'balance of power' diplomacy which had failed to prevent war with a new international organisation based on the principle of collective security. Eggleston, who was a member of the Australian Delegation at the Paris Peace Conference in 1919, wholeheartedly supported Wilson's proposal to set up the League of Nations and include its Covenant in the Treaty of Versailles. And on this, as so much else, he was at odds with Prime Minister Billy Hughes' crude realism. While Eggleston had reservations about Wilson's Fourteen Points as too 'Rhetorical' and lacking in detail he nevertheless supported the League of the Nations as the best way forward.[17] On his return to Australia he became one of the founders of the League of Nations Union in Victoria.[18]

In the 1930s Eggleston attributed the failure of the League to the conservatism and complacency of the League's members. Once the League had been founded, the victor nations which controlled it refused to tackle the problems of economic adjustment, and thus the defeated or have-not powers resorted to a system of economic autarchy and military armaments in order to achieve their place in the sun. No league of nations or world state could be successful unless it relieved the international tensions caused by economic maladjustments and inequities. Once, however, the totalitarian forces had taken their military course, it was necessary for the English-speaking nations to arm and defend themselves against German, Italian and Japanese aggression. Eggleston was still

---

[14] Ibid., p. 340.

[15] Ibid., pp. 291–92, 330 and 343.

[16] Ibid., p. 294.

[17] Eggleston Diary, Eggleston Papers, National Library of Australia (Hereinafter NLA), MS 423/6/46–47.

[18] Osmond, *Frederic Eggleston*, pp. 95–97.

not reconciled to the permanence of power politics since if that principle should rule the world 'the result must in the long run be universal Empire controlled by one section which has triumphed over all others'. The alternative was not to establish a world state. Such a concentration and organisation of power would tend to create an authoritarian regime which would suppress individual freedom. What was required was 'voluntary cooperation to secure the good we value and maintain the stability of the world we want to live'.[19]

Eggleston's prescriptions, though lacking coherence, were consistently informed by a liberal vision for a better world. At the end of the Second World War he was an enthusiastic crusader for the United Nations and was anxious that its Charter should be freed from the weaknesses of the League of Nations. In a series of articles written for the *Austral-Asiatic Bulletin* and its successor *The Australian Outlook* he critically appraised the provisions of the Charter and suggested revisions to meet these deficiencies. He wanted to find effective ways of marshalling international power to control individual states who breached the peace. As a liberal he identified force or the inherent tendency for aggression as the nub of the problem.

> Mankind must, at all costs, solve the problem of controlling force. No instrument which does not control force is of any value as a peace organ. If force is not brought under control, there is a law by which force aggregates and polarises by a kind of automatic process into ever larger aggregates with the result that civilisation is destroyed or, what is the same thing, one aggregate obtains absolute power.

Returning to his earlier social philosophy he averred that: 'Force destroys civilisation, because everything worthwhile in civilisation comes from the ethical and social factors.' Force was only useful in international relations to protect the 'benevolent factors' from being destroyed. Moreover since power was at the root of the problem of human progress he was suspicious of the Great Powers and praised the small powers as 'the torchbearers of civilization'.[20]

A world state would not make good the defects of the League of Nations. The peoples of the world were not ready for a world state; 'no sufficient mutual confidence exists'. International order had to be achieved with a lesser form of international cooperation and integration. Under the UN Charter the Security Council, on which all five victor Great Powers had permanent seats, had the responsibility for deciding whether there was a threat to peace, what nation or nations were the disturbers of the peace and what sanctions the United Nations should impose on the aggressors. But this also failed to satisfy him. He believed that the Security Council, on which each of the five Great Powers had a right of veto, was both invested with too much power and, because of the veto, unable in many cases to exercise that power. The Charter as it stood gave the Security Council 'the fantastic device of unlimited power conditioned by a veto'.

Returning in May 1945 from the San Francisco Conference which had drawn up the UN Charter, Eggleston, like Australia's Minister for External Affairs, H.V. Evatt, seemed to be convinced that a quasi-legal structure could secure international order. In the euphoria of the moment he thought that all an international organisation like the United Nations

---

[19] Eggleston, *Search for a Social Philosophy*, p. 293.

[20] Osmond, *Frederic Eggleston*, p. 224.

needed was a pledge by its members to abide by certain specified norms of international conduct. They would become the fundamental law of the body and be subject to adjudication by an International Court of Justice. It followed that the United Nations should have a force of its own which would be immediately available in case any member resorted to war in violation of its commitments under the fundamental law. He looked to the development of the UN Military Committee to give teeth to this provision.

Even so there were still difficulties in settling on machinery which would sanction coercive action against a member of the organisation, especially if that member was a Great Power. To avoid the absolute nature of the Great Power veto he suggested that these decisions should be made by special majorities of the Security Council. But he sensed that this in itself would not be enough, and so he proposed that the majority should include a majority of the Great Powers, possibly a four to one majority—which in effect might allow the Western Great Powers to override the Soviet Union's veto. This uncertainty at the crucial point of the argument shows that at the end he was frustrated. He could not find a way either to discipline Great Powers under the Charter and/or to make the lesser powers behave according to its principles rather than their strategic interests. All he could do was to rely on an emerging global public opinion, a further element in the liberal internationalist worldview, to keep the nations committed to the Charter principles. The rapid increase in the number and range of treaties, which nations signed in the immediate post-war years, encouraged Eggleston to believe that there was a growing movement towards international cooperation. It was his belief that 'a world community' was 'developing' and he looked to its emergence 'as soon as possible'.

By the early 1950s, however, Eggleston had lost much of his earlier enthusiasm for the United Nations. The coming of the Cold War had graphically illustrated the incapacity of the United Nations. While the United Nations' intervention to prevent aggression in Korea had heartened him, he had to admit that because one of the Great Powers was 'obviously supporting aggression' the United Nations was unable to achieve a quick and complete victory. Though disappointed, he saved what he could from the ruin of his hopes and believed that the United Nations could, at the least, act as a forum for the airing of differences among the Great Powers as well as among the lesser powers. It could still be a forum where disputes between nations could be debated and possibly negotiated.[21]

Australia's British Identity and Relations with Britain and the British Commonwealth

Eggleston's liberal internationalism, as expressed in his support for the League of Nations and the United Nations, was intellectually speculative. It in no way superseded his primary identification with the British race and his loyalty to Australia as an integral part of the

---

[21] F.W. Eggleston, 'The United Nations Charter Critically Considered I', *Austral-Asiatic Bulletin*, VI (October 1946): 17–27; F.W. Eggleston, 'The United Nations Critically Considered', *Australian Outlook*, I (June 1947): 13–23; F.W. Eggleston, 'The United Nations Critically Considered', *Australian Outlook*, I (September 1947): 21–30. See also Eggleston's chapter, 'Foreign Policy' in C. Hartley Grattan, ed., *Australia* (Berkeley, University of California Press: 1947), pp. 144–47, and Eggleston, *Reflections on Australian Foreign Policy*, chapter II.

British Empire/Commonwealth. In his social philosophy he considered ethnic ideas to be at the core of the nation state units which made up the international community. It was part of human freedom that people who came of common descent and shared a common culture should be able to live together in one political community. Nationalism in the modern era formed the 'pattern' which held societies together.

A product of the classical era of nationalism, Eggleston, like most Australians, responded more fervently to the appeal of 'British race patriotism' than kinfolk in the United Kingdom. He was a foundation member of the Australian branch of the Round Table movement which was dedicated to working towards some form of Imperial Federation. To those in Britain who seemed to press too quickly in this direction, Eggleston, who was probably the most thoughtful of the Australian members, cautioned:

> Imperial Union of an organic kind is not an end in itself. It may be the means to an end. That end is the realisation of the unity of the British race and its mission of civilization to the world. It goes without saying that Racial Unity cannot be created. All attempts to cultivate it must fail unless it is potentially present. All we can do is give it organs for its expression.[22]

In all his writings Eggleston saw Britain's role in history as contributing to human progress. Its nineteenth century *Pax Britannica*, based as it was on free trade and naval power, had helped to advance the cause of international liberty, peace and order. He had reservations about Britain's unreformed caste society and its imperfect democracy but gave it high praise for its commitment to evolutionary change.[23] For every reason Australia should stand with Britain in the world and work out with Britain a united foreign policy.

At the Paris Peace Conference in 1919 Eggleston was troubled by the Dominions' independent representation as he thought that unless great care was taken it might result in the divergent interests breaking the unity of the Empire. Likewise, despite supporting the League of Nations, he still looked to 'Anglo-Saxonism' to guarantee Australia's place in the world. Australia had no alternative but to rely on 'the racial interest of Great Britain, the other Dominions and the United States' for its security.[24] Common economic or strategic interests were too limited. Australians could only look to racial affinity to provide them with a sure foundation for defence against a dangerous world.

When subsequently the British Empire was transformed under pressure, firstly from Canada and South Africa, into a British Commonwealth which affirmed the autonomy of all its members and then, secondly from India into a Commonwealth of Nations which lacked the ties of kinship and culture, Eggleston, even though a pragmatist who recognised the need for adaptation and change, found it difficult to discard his original vision. In *Reflections of an Australian Liberal* he concluded with an affirmation of his original faith:

> Patriotism is the essential condition of a good community ... I thrill at the thought that I belong to the British people and, although I am an internationalist

---

[22] F.W. Eggleston, 'Imperial Union', *United Empire*, 4 (January, 1913): 91–93.

[23] F.W. Eggleston, *Search for a Social Philosophy*, pp. 252 and 253.

[24] 'Memorandum on the National Policy of Australia', Eggleston Papers, NLA MS423/6/367 and 378.

and a worker for world order, I believe that I can promote these ends better by being loyal to my Queen.[25]

From 1949–1951 Eggleston tried to find ways for Australia to keep what he considered to be the essence of the old British Commonwealth. Experience had taught him that Imperial Federation was 'an idle dream'. But he had been unhappy with the 1926 Balfour Declaration, 'this masterpiece of ambiguity'. The admission of India, Pakistan and Burma to the club had further weakened the unity of the whole. Since Australians looked upon Britain and their own country as 'one community sharing the same way of life, pursuing the same ideals' and being one 'folk', they would risk their own national survival to preserve Britain. The new Asian members, not sharing this sense of cultural identity, could not be depended upon to act in the same way. In his view, therefore, it was important that 'the presence of these others should not frustrate the desire for cooperation which the British Members possess'. He deplored the Australian conservatives' tendency to question the Labor Party's loyalty to the Commonwealth, which made the Commonwealth a false issue in domestic politics. Such aspersions detracted from that which was assumed, namely that Australia with New Zealand 'regarded themselves as members of the British community'.[26]

Australia, Asia and Pacific Security

From at least the first decade of the Commonwealth, Australia's leaders were keenly aware of the central importance of Asia to the country's future. While some looked optimistically to the expansion of trade in the region, it was more generally the case that they saw Asia as a threat.[27] The Federal Parliament's adoption in 1901 of the White Australia Policy was intended to hold back the 'coloured tide', the so-called 'teeming millions of Asia'. After 1905 with Japan's defeat of Russia these Australians feared that they were faced by the prospect of not only a migratory but also a military invasion.

Eggleston shared these prevailing views of Asia. Racial discrimination did not, however, sit easily with him. At the Paris Peace Conference in 1919 when Prime Minister Hughes had refused to accept Japan's proposal to include a racial equality provision in the League of Nations Convenant, Eggleston had been rather unhappy with the Australian leader's uncompromising stand. Writing in the English radical journal, *The New Statesman*, he admitted that racial tolerance was a 'time-honoured tradition of liberalism', and therefore as a liberal he felt obliged to show that there was what he called 'a strong case' for Australia's exclusion policy.

---

[25] Eggleston, *Search for a Social Philosophy*, p. 256.

[26] 'Notes for British Commonwealth Relations Conference: the Future of the British Commonwealth', February 1949, NAA A4311/5 item 174/4; Eggleston, *Reflections on Australian Foreign Policy*, chapter VI, 'The Commonwealth and Its Value', especially pp. 182–88.

[27] Neville Meaney, *Search for Security in the Pacific 1901–1914* (Sydney, Sydney University Press: 1976), *Fears and Phobias: E.L. Piesse and the Problem of Japan* (Canberra, National Library of Australia: 1996) and *Japan and Australia's Foreign Policy, 1945–1952* (London, London, London School of Economics and Political Science, Suntory and Toyota International Centres for Economics and Related Disciplines: 2000).

It was his contention that 'the chief factor in the healthy growth of the Australian democracy had undoubtedly been the purity of the Anglo-Saxon base'. Australia was more Anglo-Saxon than any other British country, including the United Kingdom. Its success as a democracy was attributable to that fact. It was a rule that as a country became increasingly democratic it depended for its success 'upon an even greater homogeneity in its constituents'. While he did not argue that Asian peoples were inferior to Europeans he did believe that different races should not mix and that if Australia were to permit such immigration these alien peoples would retain their traditions and live apart and thus endanger the Anglo-Saxon inheritance of democracy. This apartheid system would, as in other countries, such as the United States, where different races existed, bring about a challenge to political and social ideals and lead to racial conflict. He thought that Asian antagonism to Australia's discriminatory policy could be assuaged by reciprocal agreements which would recognise the right of Asian countries to discriminate against European migrants.[28]

Eggleston's attitude, like that of most Australian policymakers, had been assumed on the basis of little or no knowledge of Asian countries and cultures. From the 1920s to the 1940s, however, he had many opportunities to remedy this deficiency. He joined the American-based Institute for Pacific Relations which encouraged intellectual exchange between academics and opinion makers from Pacific rim nations. As a result he met Chinese and Japanese delegates at the Institute's conferences. In 1929 he attended a conference in Japan. It was his first visit to an Asian country and it was a revelation. He had as always an open, receptive mind. The visit, he wrote, gratified 'instincts long starved'. His stay in Japan made a great impression. From that experience he gained considerable respect for Japanese culture and for the manner in which the country had transformed itself from a medieval to a modern society. The people had 'a spontaneous, universal conservative spirit' which had enabled them to undergo great change while holding the society together.[29] During the 1930s as a consequence of this IPR experience he was loth to accept that Japanese imperial activity in China would lead to war with the British Commonwealth.

As Minister to China in the Second World War, Eggleston came to appreciate Asian peoples' intense resentment of American and Australian immigration policies which to their eyes treated them as inferior races. In reporting back to Canberra he informed Evatt that when peace came Australia was going to be under pressure from the Asian countries to change its immigration policy and he urged that the government should make it clear that the basis of the policy was 'neither racial nor economic but social and political—the need which a community feels to carry on its own way of life'. Though this distinction justified opposition to the mass migration of alien peoples, nevertheless he concluded that this should not bar the admission of a limited number of Asians. Eggleston told Evatt that 'differences of race, language or political ideas do not preclude assimilation'. It was certain that 'in most cases members of the second generation of immigrants are able, if they are compelled to conform to the legislation of the country to take part in its political life'.[30]

---

[28] *New Statesman*, 10 July 1920. See also 'The 'White Australia' Policy and its Critics', *The English Review* (July 1924), pp. 159–74.

[29] Osmond, *Frederic Eggleston*, pp. 140–41.

[30] Despatch, Eggleston to Evatt, 15 March 1943, NAA A433/1 1944/2/53. I am indebted to Matthew

Direct experience of Asia had made him more sensitive to Asian people's feelings and encouraged him to give freer rein to his liberal beliefs. Whereas in the 1920s when he had offered the same defence of Australia's discriminatory policy he had stood four square for the absolute exclusion of 'coloured' peoples as inherently unassimilable, now he adopted a position which was more consistent with his racially neutral principles. Returning to Australia he did not waver from this line. Though an official adviser to the External Affairs Department, he publicly called for a revision to the country's immigration policy and practice. In a 1948 article in *Pacific Affairs*, he argued that the ban on the admission of Asian migrants should be lifted and those 'Many Asians' who, like the continental European migrants flooding into the country, wished to adopt an Australian way of life and conform to Australian economic and social standards should be made welcome. According to his organic view of societies their 'patterns' in order to progress needed the constant injection of the new and the different: 'A nation needs to be enriched with foreign strains and foreign ideas'. Australia thus would benefit 'by ideas from the Orient, by the spiritual imagination and blood of Oriental peoples'. He, however, could not reconcile this embracing of difference with the demand for integration; the newcomer had 'to merge into the community, accept its allegiance and its way of life, speak its language and conform to its educational standards—in other words, be assimilated'.[31]

The Asian problem had also another dimension—strategic. From the early years of the Commonwealth until the 1950s Australians looked upon Japan as a military threat to their survival. Eggleston was one of the foremost among the small elite of intellectuals and policymakers who throughout this period were deeply concerned with this question. It was this question which above all, made Imperial Federation in any simple form totally unacceptable. Though a fervent British race patriot and a committed member of the Round Table movement he came to see, as a result of the disputes between Britain and Australia over Pacific security, that the British and the Australians had very different geopolitical interests. Thus he feared that, if Imperial Federation should take the form of an Imperial Parliament, the British, since their greater population would give them control of the parliament, might neglect Australia's Pacific concerns and conscript Australian resources for the defence of Britain.

Eggleston's attention was first drawn to this conflict of interest following a bitter Anglo-Australian dispute over Pacific naval defence in the years immediately before the outbreak of the First World War. The First Lord of the Admiralty, Winston Churchill, in striving to maintain Britain's sixty per cent margin of superiority over the German Navy, had reneged on an agreement to contribute to a British Empire fleet in the Pacific and called on Australia to send its newly created naval force to help defend the Mother Country in the North Sea. Churchill argued that Australia faced no threat in the Pacific since Japan was the only great naval power in the Western Pacific and it was Britain's ally. Moreover he contended that the alliance could be depended on as it was based on a mutual exchange of interests. The Royal Navy's supremacy in the North Sea safeguarded Japan against any possible attack from European enemies and so Japan had self-interested reasons for being loyal to the alliance.

Jordan for this reference.

[31] 'Australia's Immigration Policy', *Pacific Affairs*, XXI (December, 1948), pp. 372–83.

Eggleston accepted this realist test of the effectiveness of an alliance but then proceeded to show that Churchill's case was fallacious and self-serving. He countered that, given the military stand-off in Europe, Britain was dependent on Japan for the protection of its Asian and Pacific possessions—it could not afford to send a fleet to the Pacific—and therefore the Anglo–Japanese alliance conferred clear benefits on Britain. The same, however, was not true for Japan. It was the 'equilibrium of armaments', that is the tensions between the great European powers, not British choice which gave Japan its immunity from attack. That is, Japan would be protected from European enemies whether the alliance existed or not. The United States was Japan's only potential enemy in the Pacific and London had made it clear that the treaty could not be invoked against America. The alliance accordingly was not supported by reciprocal benefits and therefore was a weak reed to lean upon. In Eggleston's view, a view shared widely by Australian ministers and their advisers, Japan was bent on imperial expansion and, if a conflict should break out in Europe, it might well use Australia's migration policy as a pretext for moving against Australia. He concluded that a proper Imperial defence should be one that gave equal and complete security for all British peoples: 'A policy which disregards the Pacific, or leaves it to Japan, cannot be regarded as a truly Imperial Policy.'[32]

In the 1930s, when it seemed possible that Britain might again be involved in a struggle for its survival in Europe, Australian officials and academics were troubled by the same question, and this time the question centred on the issue of whether the British could send a fleet to Singapore to deter Japan from taking advantage of the European situation. By this time Eggleston, as a result primarily of his IPR activities, had become very Pacific-minded. It had become clear to him that Australia's international role was 'to represent British ideas, British interests and British conceptions of world order in the region in which she is situated—the Pacific basin'. Australia's geographical position meant that 'her future will be mainly in the Pacific and her relations will mainly be with Pacific nations'—a doctrine which became the orthodoxy of Australia's foreign policy in the Curtin-Chifley era. He was disillusioned with Britain's East Asian policy. Since Australia had different interests from European-based powers it should 'think out the policy to protect them'. He considered the Singapore base to be 'unusable'. In the case of war in Europe, Britain would not be able to spare a fleet for the Pacific. Australia should take responsibility for its own defence and the 'diplomatic dispositions on which policy is based'. For a reasonable cost Australia could acquire a military, naval and air force adequate for self-defence.[33] Australia had learnt in these years that it had strategic problems arising from its geopolitical position which were peculiar to itself and that 'Great powers, however friendly, are not apt to understand the special problems of their smaller friends.'[34]

Despite these differences between Britain and Australia over Pacific security, Eggleston never abandoned the substance of the Round Table vision, namely that somehow an answer to the imperial political problem could be found so that the British peoples could on all

---

[32] Meaney, *Search for Security in the Pacific*, pp. 258–60.

[33] *Melbourne Herald*, 31 December 1935; 'The British Empire, Australia and the Pacific', *Australian Quarterly*, 31 (September, 1936): 5–11; Osmond, *Frederic Eggleston*, p. 182.

[34] Eggleston, *Reflections on Australian Foreign Policy*, pp. 9–10.

that was important face the world as one. He had hoped that Lloyd George's Imperial War Cabinet might serve the purpose, and when that failed and the Canadians, Irish and South Africans stressed autonomy as against unity he looked to achieving the objective through close and continuous consultation with Britain. Even, as has been noted, after the British Commonwealth became the Commonwealth of Nations and admitted former dependent colonies, which did not share British kinship or culture, he still gave voice to the old ideal—the common identity of the British in the Pacific with the British in Europe.

America, Communism and the Coming of the Cold War

In his *Search for a Social Philosophy* Eggleston had warned against the dangers of ideologies. They were, he wrote, 'One of the most important obstructions to change and adjustment'. He saw these battles over abstract ideas as an especial characteristic of the modern era. At the end of the 1930s when he was writing the book, the ideological issues which juxtaposed 'freedom and self-determination as against tyranny and a philosophy of the state' were most acute. He maintained that these idea systems, fascism, socialism and communism, were not reflections of a real world experience but 'sophistications made by excited brains'. Academics and intellectuals in particular were attracted to these intellectual causes and with the growth of formal education the ideologies acquired a mass following and so became important in politics. Since all of these systems were imbued with a superior ethical claim they denounced their opponents as non-ethical or, if you like, as the devil. This then brought about mutual hatred and justified total war and every means of destruction. The totalitarian beliefs which racked Europe were irrational. From his social philosophy he concluded that the 'pattern' of 'feelings, common ideas, conventions and modes of thought of German, French, Russian and English are so similar that war between them is absurd'. Though Britain's Prime Minister Neville Chamberlain might have misjudged Hitler's threat he was 'a thousand times right' at Munich, according to Eggleston, to have 'cut across the ideological front and put himself into direct touch with the German leader'.[35]

On the other hand his experience in the United States had not led him to admire the Americans. At the end of the Second World War while Australia's Minister to Washington, he had been repelled by the Americans' excessive patriotic fervour. He wrote home that he was 'getting rather fed up with the American atmosphere'. He observed that 'the Americans are slow to action, dashing when in a fight, and intolerable in victory'. He had 'never seen such National Egotism as this outburst'.[36]

When then by early 1947 Soviet-American tensions threatened a new and even greater conflict Eggleston was deeply disturbed by the ideological language which the Americans adopted to explain Soviet behaviour, and he expressed his 'realist' misgivings in a letter to Henry Wallace, President Truman's former Secretary of Commerce who in September 1946 had been sacked for criticising America's 'get tough' ideological policy towards the Soviet Union. In a public address in Madison Square Gardens Wallace had urged Americans to understand Russia's security fears, to cease playing the British Empire's game and to seek a

---

[35] Eggleston, *Search for a Social Philosophy*, pp. 336–39.

[36] Osmond, *Frederic Eggleston*, pp. 248–49.

rapprochement with the Soviets through trade. He had then formed the Progressive Party and announced his intention to stand on this peace platform for election as President in 1948. Eggleston, who while head of the Australian legation in Washington had come to know Wallace, took advantage of this acquaintance to write to him offering an assessment of American policy and the Soviet question. It is an interesting letter which says much about the diverse and sometimes contradictory elements in Eggleston's views of international relations as they had emerged from the Second World War. It exposes once again his liberal predicament in trying to reconcile the world he would have to the world that was.

There was no doubt about Eggleston's sincere admiration for Wallace. He agreed 'entirely' with Wallace's criticism of 'the unnecessary bellicosity of the American Press and even of the statements of Truman and Marshall' as 'their talk and their ideological attitude tends to justify the Russian fears and convince them that the attack will come'. He thought that Wallace had 'done a wonderfully good job in calling attention' to these weaknesses in the American discussion of Soviet motives. These American shortcomings were 'the faults of inexperience, of the crude egotism and truculence which is inherent in the American character'. He wished that 'someone could persuade Truman and Marshall that diplomacy is a silent service and cannot be conducted from the housetops with megaphones'.

Nevertheless Eggleston believed in the 'Reality of the Russian menace'. It was not good enough to wait and see whether the Russians would be a danger to the West. A responsible leader had 'to make a realistic appraisal of the facts and of the trends which are visible, and, if he thinks that the menace is there, he has to take steps against it'. Eggleston then listed a series of 'overt acts' which had convinced him that Russia was a danger, and he asked rhetorically: 'how can you blame anyone for making the dispositions that are required in order that imperial power shall not be further extended?' If, as a result of Wallace's campaign, America were to falter in its 'determination ... to protect the world against the Russian menace' then he would have done 'a great disservice to the world'.

If Wallace's views were adopted Eggleston pointed out that Western Europe which had borne the heat and burden of the Second World War would suffer most. Eggleston found it 'unpardonable' that Wallace should blame Truman for following British policy and supporting British interests. Unless the United States recognised that it was 'responsible for the prevention of aggression, we are all doomed'.[37] Once more immediate strategic concerns, following from a reasoned appraisal of threat, had overridden his commitment to an international organisation and the liberal internationalist hopes which it embodied.

By 1953 all that Eggleston had feared had come to pass and he placed great faith in America and its resolute response to Communist aggression in Asia as well as Europe. He was not certain in his own mind whether China was under Moscow's control or whether the two governments were merely partners in a common cause. If the People's Republic of China had not entered the Korean War he would have favoured following the British lead and extending formal recognition In this he took a traditional realist position, namely that 'recognition of a de facto government, controlling a country should be regarded as a matter of course'. He approved without reserve America's leadership in the United Nations action in Korea and the alliances which it had entered into with Japan, the Philippines and

---

[37] Letter, Eggleston to Wallace, 13 January 1947, Eggleston Papers, NLA MS423/1/363.

Australia and New Zealand—though, reflecting on Australia's experience with Britain, he allowed that whether on not these measures were 'effective and reliable' would be 'tested by time'. America's policy in East Asia was 'a very considerable achievement'. Retreating from his earlier criticism of United States foreign policy he warned against taking up a superior attitude towards America: 'The record of British foreign policy ... between 1925–1939 cannot compare favourably with the leadership of Truman and Dean Acheson between 1945–52.'[38] By 1951 he was endorsing the substance of the Truman and Menzies Governments' foreign policy.

Reflecting on Eggleston's argument about the nature of international relations and his responses to Australia's foreign policy problems it is clear that he, like Wallas, never resolved the tensions between his liberalism and his realism, between what might be and what must be, between a world in which international cooperation controlled power for the common good and a world of power in which violence ruled, between an ideal of the concert of power and the necessity of the balance of power, between hopes for internationalism embodied in the United Nations and loyalty to Britain and the British Empire, between a Britishness centred on Europe and an Australianness centred on Asia and the Pacific. He approached all of these issues with an open, searching mind, and that largely explains the complexity and contradictions in his works. This independent liberalism, refined as it was through a powerful intellect, made him one of the most important Australian contributors to the study of international relations and Australia's relations with the world.

---

[38] Eggleston, *Reflections on Foreign Policy*, chapter IV, 'Korea and After'.

10

Dr H.V. Evatt and the United Nations: The Problem of Collective Security and Liberal Internationalism[1]

Dr Herbert Vere Evatt, Australia's Minister for External Affairs from 1941 to 1949, was one of the founders of the United Nations, and from its establishment until his death he remained an unwavering supporter of this international organisation. He played a major part in framing the UN Charter at the San Francisco Conference and claimed a leading role for himself in the United Nations' first turbulent years. As a result of his efforts Australia was elected to the first Security Council and in 1948 he became the third President of the General Assembly. At the formation of the United Nations he identified himself with its informing doctrine of liberal internationalism and collective security, and in all his subsequent speeches he asserted that the United Nations was 'the first principle of Australian foreign policy' and the only hope for world peace and justice. It is the aim of this chapter to explore Evatt's vision of liberal internationalism and collective security and to show how he adapted this vision to the coming of the Cold War.

The origins of liberal internationalism are to be found in the optimistic strand of the eighteenth-century Enlightenment which viewed war as an unnatural excrescence, believed in human progress and human rights and asserted that if all peoples were given self-determination they would live together in peace and harmony. During the nineteenth century these ideas were ingrained in English-speaking countries' liberal discourse. They were not systematically developed as a theory of international relations but became an integral part of the political tradition in both the British Empire and the United States,[2] and in the latter case they were identified with America's very definition of itself.

Thus when the United States, breaking its Monroe Doctrine taboo against involvement in European affairs, entered World War I, President Woodrow Wilson demanded a peace in these terms. In his 'Fourteen Points' and associated speeches, he produced the first comprehensive overview of liberal internationalism. In addition to calling for open diplomacy, free trade, disarmament, national self-determination and trusteeship for captured enemy colonies, he added, as the most important element of his peace program, collective security through the creation of a worldwide organisation. Justifying his decision to join the European conflict, he had assured the American people that this would be 'the war to end all wars' and 'the war to make the world safe for democracy'. The League of Nations was to fulfil that promise. It would put an end to contending alliances and replace the balance of power with a concert of power. If the League found a state guilty of a violation of the peace then its members would rally to the assistance of the victim. World opinion would ensure that the League reached just decisions and carried out its responsibilities.

---

[1] This chapter was originally published as 'Dr H. V. Evatt and the United Nations: The Problem of Collective Security and Liberal Internationalism' in James Cotton and David Lee, eds, *Australia and the United Nations* (Longueville, New South Wales, Pan Macmillan Australia: 2012): 34–66.

[2] Michael Howard, *The Invention of Peace: Reflections on War and International Order* (London, Profile Books: 2000), pp. 25–31.

Though the League failed to prevent World War II, it was this same ideal of collective security which, at the end of hostilities, inspired the Allies' leaders to establish the United Nations, and it was this ideal which Evatt embraced as Australia joined the other victorious powers to plan for the peace.

The Origins of Evatt's Thinking About a New World Order

Tracing the origins of Evatt's ideas about international relations is a difficult undertaking. Few scholars say much about this question. Even those who do normally begin their treatment of the subject well into the middle of World War II, with the Atlantic Charter of August 1941 and President Franklin Roosevelt's 'Four Freedoms' speech in January 1942. And there is good reason for ignoring Evatt's earlier career since there is no evidence in those years of an interest in the League of Nations and only marginal evidence of an interest in foreign affairs. It was not until he became Minister for External Affairs and responsible for Australia's foreign policy—in the midst of a global cataclysm which threatened the nation's survival that he seems to have given thought to these questions.

It is passing strange that Evatt before this time should have ignored international relations. While at the University of Sydney he had been deeply affected by World War I. His two brothers had enlisted in the Australian Imperial Forces and were killed on the Western Front. He was a brilliant scholar and clearly ambitious to succeed. He took a very active part in student affairs and was the editor of the student paper, *Hermes*, and the *St Andrew's College Magazine*. He contributed short pieces to these journals—some dealing with the war—and wrote a prize winning essay on 'Liberalism in Australia' which was subsequently published. Yet in all this intellectual activity there was scarcely a word about peacemaking and the League of Nations.[3] This silence is even more remarkable in that his mentor, Professor Francis Anderson, was a founding member of the League of Nations Union. As far as is known Evatt never joined the League of Nations Union or the Australian Institute of International Affairs or showed any interest in their activities.

In the 1920s when Evatt was practising as a barrister and serving as a NSW Labor parliamentarian, and in the 1930s when he became a Justice of the High Court, he published numerous books, journal articles and newspaper opinion pieces, but these publications dealt overwhelmingly with Australian history, politics and law. His greatest work, *Australian Labour Leader*,[4] was a biography of a political hero, WA Holman, a former premier of New South Wales. This parochialism was not a result of isolation. He was not, in these years, cut off from the wider world. He travelled to America and Europe where he attended international conferences and could not avoid observing European politics. Yet he brought back with him no serious reflections about international affairs. Returning in 1926

---

[3] In 1935 Evatt wrote a technical legal paper dealing with 'the true resting place of general sovereignty' of the British dominions' mandates. His treatment of the League was only incidental to this international law problem and did not touch on the origin, nature or purpose of the League of Nations. See Herbert V. Evatt, 'The British Dominions as Mandatories', *Proceedings of the Australian and New Zealand Society of International Law*, vol. 1, 1935, pp. 27–54.

[4] H.V. Evatt, *Australian Labour Leader: The Story of W.A. Holman and the Labour Movement* (Sydney, Angus & Robertson: 1940).

from a Worldwide Immigration Conference, his only comment was that '[f]rom what he had seen in France and Germany ... it would only be a matter of time before there would be another European war'. If the Locarno Treaty—an agreement under which Britain and Italy guaranteed that if France attacked Germany or Germany attacked France they would come to the aid of the victim—were ratified Australia might well be drawn into another war and its future 'imperilled'.[5] Unless this was the observation of a Labor isolationist worried about Australia being drawn into another European conflict, it is very difficult to make any sense of the dark prophecy.

In the 1930s, even though restrained somewhat by his appointment to the High Court, Evatt continued through his historical writings and reviews of books to express sentiments friendly to the labour cause. His lengthy review of Ernest Scott's political volume of the *Official History of Australia in the War of 1914–1918* dwelt on the labour movement's problem with conscription and censorship and ignored the Paris Peace Conference and the League of Nations altogether.[6] It would appear that he said nothing in public on the gathering international crisis. The only known reference to it appears in a January 1939 letter, just after he had returned from a visit to Europe, and in this private communication all he offered was a jejune 'Popular Front'-style condemnation of Neville Chamberlain's Munich agreement with Adolf Hitler: 'It's little use talking about Chamberlain and his gang—they are really sympathisers with Fascism because their one fear is insecurity through Socialism. Money first and to hell with their own country.'[7] It would appear that Evatt had no knowledge of the Western debate over the Treaty of Versailles and the League of Nations which had raged across the 1920s and 1930s, from John Maynard Keynes's *The Economic Consequences of the Peace* in 1920 to EH Carr's *The Twenty Years' Crisis, 1919–1939* in 1939.[8] It might also be worth noting here, since it subsequently became so important to his wartime view of Australian security, that while Evatt from the beginning of his public career was a resolute defender of the White Australia policy, he never in the years leading up to the war seems to have written anything about Japan, its imperial expansion into China and its alliance with Germany and Italy.

Following the outbreak of World War II, Evatt was compelled to consider the problem of Australia's national security and eventually the problem of international order. He recognised immediately how important the role of the national government would be in the war effort and like his World War I hero, WM Hughes, he wanted to find a place for himself at the centre of world affairs.[9] With this end in view he resigned from the bench and

[5] 'Another European war: predicted by Dr H.V. Evatt', *The Australian Worker*, 8 September 1926, p. 14.

[6] Evatt, 'Australia on the Homefront', *Australian Quarterly*, 9 (March 1937): 68–75.

[7] Letter, Evatt to Vance and Nettie Palmer, 16 January 1939, NLA: Palmer Papers, MS 1124/1/5847.

[8] On this intellectual ferment, see David Long and Peter Wilson, eds, *Thinkers of the Twenty Years' Crisis* (Oxford, Clarendon Press: 1995).

[9] A week after Britain had declared war on Germany the *Daily Telegraph* published an interview with Evatt—probably solicited by him—under the title of 'Don't let us repeat the mistakes of 1914–18.' It read like an application for Labor's endorsement for pre-selection for a seat in the federal parliament. The mistakes he identified were not strategic or diplomatic, but domestic ones which he had already highlighted in his biography of Holman and his review of Scott's *Australia During*

won the seat of Barton for the Labor Party in the 1940 federal election. Once in parliament he was greedy for office and wanted Labor to join with the United Australia Party and Country Party in a coalition government. Knocked back by caucus he privately criticised his colleagues for their lack of a 'will to power'. When Labor, under the leadership of John Curtin, did come to power in early October 1941 Evatt was given the external affairs ministry, along with that of attorney-general, and was in his element. For the next eight years during the Curtin and Chifley Labor administrations, apart from some occasional interventions by the prime minister, he was in charge of Australia's foreign relations, and this was especially true for Australia's relationship with the United Nations.

Evatt's early diplomacy was shaped by the imperatives of the Pacific war. After Japan attacked Pearl Harbor and advanced rapidly towards Australia's frontier, his first concern was to obtain maximum assistance from Britain and the United States and an effective voice in the great powers' grand strategy. He was, however, bitterly disappointed with the results of his efforts. It was not until six months after Japan began its assault on Southeast Asia that he discovered the British and Americans had agreed on a 'Europe first' policy and had allocated their resources accordingly. Likewise, though he persuaded President Franklin Roosevelt to establish a Pacific War Council in Washington for consultation with America's allies, this did not give Australia any influence in strategic decision-making. Indeed, within a year, all parties had come to see that the council was not serving any useful purpose and so it died from inanition.

Similarly, in 1943, when the 'Big Three' allied powers (the United Kingdom, the United States and the Soviet Union) began tentatively to plan for peace, Evatt directed his energies primarily towards ensuring Australia's future security against Japan or any other would-be Asian enemy. While he repeatedly praised the Atlantic Charter and Roosevelt's Four Freedoms speech, especially the freedom from want and the freedom from fear, he gave little attention to global collective security or the creation of a new League of Nations. Having learnt that Churchill and Roosevelt were considering setting up regional councils for the Western hemisphere, Europe and East Asia which would be under the control of the great allied powers—the so-called Four Policemen: the United States, the United Kingdom, the Soviet Union and China—Evatt, who resented having been left out of these discussions, proposed a regional defence structure for the South Pacific and Southeast Asia. In a speech to the Overseas Club in New York in April he admitted that 'security has to be universal or everyone will be insecure', but he was insistent that 'the United Nations in the Pacific will have to be assured of their own security' and in this respect 'Australia will naturally regard as of crucial importance to its security the arc of islands lying to the north and north-east of our continent.' He had doubts about whether another League of Nations could be established and, even if it were, whether it would prove any more effective than its predecessor. Given these uncertainties he believed that Australia was entitled to be 'vitally

---

the War (see notes 4 and 6). That is, Australians had become divided because of the Australian government's unwillingness to trust the people, and this had been most evident in political censorship and the advocacy of conscription. The Western European democracies' opposition to Hitler and Nazism was not based on acts of aggression but on domestic 'cruelty and oppression' which, it was implied, could be found to some extent in Australia's World War I government's behaviour. See Daily Telegraph, 9 September 1939.

concerned as to who shall live in, develop and control these areas so vital to her security from aggression'.[10]

On 18 August, at the very time that Roosevelt and Churchill were meeting at Quebec to consider, among other matters, a post-war international organisation, Evatt elaborated further on this regional idea:

> While security for the Pacific and the Far East is inseparably bound up with security elsewhere, it is obvious that there will have to be zones of security in areas like South-east Asia and the South and South-west Pacific.

> Of crucial importance to Australia's own security will be such islands as Timor, New Guinea, the Solomons, the New Hebrides, Fiji, and New Caledonia.

> I therefore visualise the formation of a great South-west Pacific zone of security against aggression, and in its establishment, Australia must act with such colonial powers as Holland, France and Portugal as well as with the United States and Great Britain.[11]

Under this regional plan Australia, it might be thought, was claiming for itself the role of a Fifth Policeman. Evatt maintained that by the end of hostilities, Australia's:

> successful war effort will have converted Australia into a great nation. We cannot escape such a destiny. In truth, we will be trustees not only for British civilization, but also for a decent world order in the Pacific sphere of influence.[12]

Returning in late October from his second mission to the United States and Britain, Evatt for the first time welcomed the possibility of a new League of Nations to give order to the postwar world. While overseas he had learnt something of the Anglo-American scheme by which the four great powers would assume control of peacemaking and take responsibility for protecting small powers from future acts of aggression. The Anglo-Americans' treatment of Australia during the war had left Evatt with some doubts as to whether these great powers could be relied upon to defend Australia. Thus, in an address to parliament, he stated that there was no good reason why collective security could not be integrated into the framework of a new League of Nations. Collective security had been the core principle of the League Covenant and the failure of the League to uphold the principle was not a failure of the League itself but of its members. However, he offered neither any further analysis of the problems that had beset the League nor any suggestion as to how a new international organisation could be constructed so as to make members take their commitments more seriously. It would seem that this enthusiasm for the creation of a new League of Nations was prompted by the hope that it would enable small and middling powers like Australia to have a greater say in the way international security would operate and so ensure that the 'lesser powers' were more certainly protected against aggressor nations.

---

[10] Evatt, 'Address at the Overseas Club, New York, 28 April 1943', in Evatt, *Foreign Policy of Australia: Speeches*, with introduction by W. Macmahon Ball (Sydney, Angus & Robertson: 1945), p. 166.

[11] Evatt, 'Australia's future role in the Pacific', *Daily Telegraph*, 18 August 1943.

[12] Ibid.

Evatt's first response to the news of the great powers' plan was to try to create a security arrangement for the Pacific region. In the same speech in which he welcomed the formation of a new League of Nations he gave most attention to a 'Pacific Regional organisation'. He believed that Australia could and should 'make a very special contribution towards the establishment and maintenance of the peace settlement in South-east Asia and the Pacific'. Taking his earlier sketchy idea further, he looked forward to working very closely with New Zealand. In his view, 'permanent co-operation' between the two dominions was 'pivotal to a sound post-war policy'.[13] As Evatt explained his intention to the New Zealanders, the two Pacific dominions acting together ought to be 'the foundation of the British sphere of influence in the South-West and South Pacific'. Their future safety and prosperity depended on the dominions having 'a decisive voice in these areas' which, it was implied, they would not have if their protection was left in the hands of the great powers. Thus, before calling a conference of all the interested nations, he wanted to have preliminary discussions with the New Zealanders.[14]

When, a few months later, Evatt read in the press that Roosevelt and Churchill had met with Chiang Kai-shek at Cairo and agreed to terms of peace for the Pacific he was greatly incensed at being presented once again with a fait accompli. It seemed that what he called the 'greater powers' took no heed of Australia's protests and blithely continued to decide on peace matters without consulting the 'lesser powers'. He then persuaded the New Zealanders to join Australia in a quasi-alliance that would proclaim their determination to 'act together on matters of common concern in the South West and South Pacific areas'. At their conference in Canberra in January 1944 the Australians and New Zealanders, without informing or consulting the Americans or the British, reaffirmed their right to be represented 'at the highest level' on all planning and executive bodies involved in deciding the arrangements for the armistices and the constitution for a new international organisation. Moreover, the Australasians announced their intention to establish a regional zone of defence 'stretching through the arc of islands North and North East of Australia, to Western Samoa and the Cook Islands'. They asserted, taking their lead from the great powers, that until a new world order was established they would 'assume full responsibility for policing or sharing in policing' such a zone. They further demonstrated their resentment of US hegemonic tendencies in the Pacific by specifying that powers which had built bases on Allied territory in wartime had no right to keep such bases at the end of the war. Finally, they gave notice that they proposed to call a conference of all nations who had territories in the region for an exchange of views on 'the problems of security' as well as matters related to the future welfare of the island peoples.[15] This Canberra Agreement was in essence Australia's riposte to the Cairo Declaration.

---

[13] Commonwealth of Australia, *Parliamentary Debates*, House of Representatives, vol. 176, 14 October 1943, pp. 569–79.

[14] Cablegram, Carl Augustus Berendsen, New Zealand High Commissioner, Canberra, to Peter Fraser, New Zealand Prime Minister and Minister for External Affairs, 23 October 1943, in Robin Kay, ed., *Documents on New Zealand External Relations*, vol. I, 'The Australian–New Zealand Agreement 1944' (Wellington, Government Printing Office: 1972), pp. 47–48.

[15] 'Australian–New Zealand Agreement', 21 January 1944, *CNIA*, vol. 15, no. 1, 1944, pp. 2–7.

The Making of the Charter of the United Nations

Yet, even as the two dominions were working on their regional démarche, talk about regionalism was being overtaken by the movement for a 'world organisation'. At the very time when the Australians and New Zealanders were preparing their regional scheme for the South Pacific, Roosevelt, Churchill and Stalin were at the Teheran Conference agreeing that their representatives should put together a draft constitution for an international organisation which would then be submitted to all the Allied nations. Evatt might well have been 'truculently pleased'[16] with his Pacific pact idea, but the Americans would have none of it and the regional conference proposal had to be abandoned. Accepting this reality he quickly grasped that the Big Three's decision to create a new League of Nations was the great issue that lay ahead, and he turned his attention increasingly to how this new system of collective security should be structured. In doing so, he focused his mind on the central problem of collective security—that is, how the members of such an organisation, especially the great powers, could be brought to submit their disputes to the judgement of the international community and induced to do their part in upholding the decisions of that body.

Evatt had no hesitation in accepting the idea of a new world order based on the principles of President Wilson's liberal internationalism. His moral sensibility and labour predilections recoiled from the 'realist' notion of an anarchical world marked by a violent struggle for survival and supremacy. As a theory of international relations, the search for security through the balance of power and contending alliances had little attraction. He looked forward to all nations uniting in a 'concert of power' that would guarantee to each, under collective security, a world of peace with justice. Though the harsh experience of war had shown the importance of giving pre-eminence to the defence of the nation and had caused him to plan for a post-war zone of security, the great powers' decision to establish a new international organisation convinced him to set aside, at least for the time being, the regional scheme. Instead, he devoted himself to this grand project, which might itself include regional arrangements and provide more completely and certainly for the defence of Australia against predatory powers.

Thus while officials from the United States, the United Kingdom, the Soviet Union and China were meeting in Dumbarton Oaks in Washington DC to draw up a framework for the new international organisation, Evatt in a speech to parliament traversed nearly all the subjects which were to preoccupy him at the San Francisco Conference. It was as though he himself were taking part at one remove in the Dumbarton Oaks discussions. He stressed that this meeting and the conference of all the United Nations which was to follow were 'of supreme significance for Australia'. Because of its 'vulnerable position' Australia was 'vitally concerned' with the making of a world security system and a regional defence system that would be associated with it. In his view the world organisation's most important functions would be, first, to provide for security against aggression and second, taking into account the dehumanising effects of the Great Depression, to promote economic and social

---

[16] Cablegram, Nelson T. Johnson, US Minister, Canberra, to Cordell Hull, US Secretary of State, 22 January 1944, in Department of State, *FRUS 1944*, vol. III, *The British Commonwealth and Europe* (Washington DC, US Government Printing Office: 1965), p. 175.

progress. He understood that maintaining world peace was a formidable task. In looking back at the experience of the League of Nations he recognised that 'mere declarations' would not be enough. This new world body had to establish procedures by which disputes could be 'adjusted promptly' and threats of the use of force be met 'by the authority of the security organization'. In the latter case the organisation had to have at its disposal a 'sufficient military force'. Though Evatt confessed that this might sound like 'power politics', he argued that the experience of Wilson's League of Nations had shown that, unless the new world body had ready access to armed power to enforce its decisions, it would suffer the same fate as the earlier attempt to establish collective security.[17]

The problem facing liberal internationalists was how the world organisation would determine whether an act of aggression had taken place and, if it had, how military forces could be raised to deal with the offending nation. Central to this question was the role that the great powers would play. Evatt accepted that the United States, the United Kingdom and the Soviet Union held such an 'overwhelming preponderance of the world's armed strength … that any security system which did not have the full backing of all three would have little chance of success'. Indeed it was 'doubtful whether, if any one of these three were minded to commit an act of aggression, it could be checked by anything less than another world conflict'. To avoid this dread prospect, Evatt stressed that 'a means must be found for composing amicably any differences amongst the Big Three'. They should, in the spirit of the 1928 Kellogg–Briand Pact, renounce war as an instrument of national policy and be prepared to 'act unitedly against aggression or threats to peace' by any other nation.[18]

But these prescriptions were like the members' pledges that had failed the original League of Nations, and so he kept returning to the point. There was wartime evidence that the great powers could work together. The Soviet Union and the United Kingdom had a treaty of mutual assistance and the four powers—the Big Three plus China—had signed the Moscow Declaration on Peace and Security. Furthermore, to ensure that the great powers would act together to maintain the peace, he allowed that any enforcement decision made by the new international organisation would have to be 'convenient to the major powers'. Here he probably had the Soviet Union's treatment of Poland especially in mind. If this concession to the great powers had the appearance of expediency and power politics, this defect would be overcome by 'the spirit that animates its members and their abiding faith in the possibility of maintaining peace through joint action'.[19] But after all these tergiversations it is clear that Evatt could still not find a way to make collective security a reliable basis for world peace. Probably more than any other national leader he was, throughout the process of making the UN Charter and then during the complexities of its operation in the following years, troubled by the possibility of divisions among the great powers and their potential for destroying the liberal internationalist ideal of 'collective security'.

In speaking about the formal structure of the world organisation Evatt contended that while the great powers were entitled to primacy in the task of maintaining world order, the

---

[17]   Evatt, statement on international affairs to House of Representatives, 8 September 1944, *CNIA*, vol. 15, no. 8, 1944, pp. 214–15.

[18]   Ibid., p. 215.

[19]   Ibid., pp. 216–17.

constitution of the new institution should also respect the 'cherished doctrine of equality of States' and make proper provision for the representation of 'smaller' nations—with Australia in mind he wished to include 'near-great powers' as well as small powers in this category. No nation would want to accept that 'its destiny has been handed over to another power, however great'. The strongest nations did not necessarily have a monopoly of wisdom. By giving the smaller powers an assured place in the organisation, the great powers would be able to profit from their knowledge and gain the confidence of the world community. Evatt presumed that following the example of the League there would be an executive made up of the great powers plus a number of other nations elected by members of the international organisation. The latter should be chosen in order to ensure that all distinct regions were represented on the body responsible for global security. Evatt wanted the constitution to recognise 'regional groups of powers' which, while subject to the world organisation, would be 'empowered by it to exercise jurisdiction over local or special questions such as joint defence measures, and the welfare of native peoples within the selected region'.[20]

In the event, the Dumbarton Oaks draft proposal was an updated version of the League Covenant. There was to be a General Assembly on which all members were represented and a small executive body, a 'Security Council', made up of great power permanent members, named in the draft as the United States, the United Kingdom, the Soviet Union, China and France, along with six other members elected for two-year terms by the Assembly. The Security Council, like the League Council, was to have responsibility for maintaining the peace. But here the similarities ended. The General Assembly was restricted to discussing general principles and the Security Council had sole responsibility for dealing with disputes and imposing sanctions. In this new constitution there was a desire to make enforcement processes against aggressors clearer and more immediately effective. As enforcement depended primarily on the cooperation of the great powers, there had to be unity among the permanent members of the Council and, therefore, each was to have a right to a veto over decision-making. But since the officials at Dumbarton Oaks were unable to agree on how the veto should apply, this central question for the working of collective security was left over for the leaders of the Big Three to determine at their meeting at Yalta in February when they would formally approve the proposals to be put before a conference of the United Nations.[21]

---

[20] Ibid., pp. 215–16. Evatt's view of the Soviet Union problem is also set out in cablegram 263, Commonwealth Government to Lord Cranborne, British Minister for Dominion Affairs, 10 October 1944, in William J. Hudson, ed., *DAFP, 1937–49* (Australian Government Publishing Service, Canberra, 1988), vol. VII, 1944, pp. 589–90. On the problem of great-power voting and vetoes the Australian position was that: 'It would appear unlikely that in practice any ultimate question would be pressed to a decision on the Security Council against the will of the Soviet Union, at any rate for some considerable time to come. Even if a decision were reached by outvoting the Soviet Union, it is doubtful if it could be made fully effective over Soviet opposition. Despite disappointments and setbacks, we still believe that in the matter of the Security Council, we have to be prepared to trust Russia. Unless we can give that trust then the possibilities of obtaining collective security in the post-war years are indeed slight.' Ibid., p. 590.

[21] For the official consolidated text circulated in Canberra on the Dumbarton Oaks proposals, 7 October 1944, see ibid., pp. 577–88.

Neville Meaney

Australia's initial reaction to the Dumbarton Oaks proposals was tentative and modest. Its only formal response appeared in a joint statement coming out of the Australian–New Zealand meeting which was held in Wellington in November 1944. Lacking any guidance from Dumbarton Oaks this relatively brief statement did not touch on the key issues of collective security—that is, how the Security Council would reach decisions on disputes and enforcement and how the veto would fit into its decision-making processes. The Australasians' main concerns were to tighten up the responsibilities that members of the world body would assume, such as promising to preserve 'the territorial integrity and political independence' of all states against change by force or threat of force; to expand the functions of the General Assembly so that all members would be able to 'actively participate in the direction and control' of the organisation's affairs; and to add to its objectives the principles of the Atlantic Charter, the ILO's Declaration of Philadelphia and the trusteeship for dependent peoples as set out in the Australian–New Zealand declaration on the South Pacific islands.[22]

During the next few months, while waiting for the great powers to pronounce on the Dumbarton Oaks draft and settle the veto matter, Evatt and the Department of External Affairs worked hard on these latter principles which had scarcely rated a mention at Dumbarton Oaks. As part of their support for 'freedom from want' the Australians sought to give greater weight to social welfare and to hold a conference on full employment. Similarly, they tried to convince the British that the trusteeship principle should apply not merely to territories under League of Nations mandates but to all dependent peoples who lacked self-government. These efforts proved fruitless. The Americans, believing that lowering trade barriers, not artificially creating jobs, was the key to economic growth and improved labour conditions, would not support a conference on full employment; the British, hostile to the idea of international supervision, refused to support trusteeship for their colonies. The Australians, however, gave notice in these early exchanges that they would seek to enshrine their principles in the new organisation's constitution.

It was only after the great powers at Yalta had agreed on the final form for the Dumbarton Oaks proposals and invited Australia, along with 41 other countries, to meet in San Francisco in the northern spring of 1945 to write a charter that Evatt returned to pondering the riddle of collective security and concomitantly the problem of the great power veto.[23] Churchill and Roosevelt, who might have been willing to make some concessions, had given way to Soviet Union insistence that the permanent members of the Security Council should have a right of veto over all substantial issues coming before the executive body as well as

---

[22] Cablegram 200, Peter Fraser, New Zealand Prime Minister, to Commonwealth Government, 7 November 1944, in ibid., pp. 626–31. This Wellington statement was approved by Cabinet and became the official guideline for the Australian delegation at the San Francisco Conference. See cablegram E1, Evatt in London to Curtin, 9 April 1945, in William J. Hudson and Wendy Way, eds, *DAFP, 1945*, (Australian Government Publishing Service, Canberra, 1989), vol. VIII, pp. 127–28. The statement itself was quite short and limited—it said nothing about the role of the great powers or the veto—and left Evatt with great freedom in charting Australia's course at the conference and framing the amendments to the Dumbarton Oaks proposals which the Australian delegation submitted to the conference.
[23] Letter, Johnson to Evatt, 6 March 1945, Hudson and Way, eds *DAFP*, vol. VIII, pp. 82–83.

over amendments to the organisation's constitution. With the completed draft at last in his hands Evatt used the six weeks prior to the opening of the conclave to prepare to take a leading part in the gathering. He threw himself into the task, reading all the briefing papers from his department as well as those from Great Britain and other dominions and, where available, other countries. He also used public addresses and a pre-conference meeting of British Commonwealth ministers to expound and clarify his views.

Like all the other British Commonwealth leaders, Evatt accepted that 'in broad outline' the great powers' draft would serve the purposes of 'collective security'. That is, it would provide the framework for a constitution which would ensure that international disputes could be 'adjusted promptly'; 'the authority of the whole organization' could be used against an aggressor; and a 'sufficient military force' could be available 'to make a quick end to any armed conflict'.[24] Yet the more he looked into the great powers' proposals the more dissatisfied he became. For him the exclusive authority given the Security Council to deal with disputes between nations and to decide on economic and military sanctions, when connected to the permanent members' almost total right of veto over issues coming before the Council as well as over constitutional amendments, seemed dangerous.

As he saw it, these particular provisions were merely prolonging the great-power domination that had been evident in the wartime alliance. That form of 'dictatorship' could only be accepted as a temporary measure justified by the exigencies of war. It could not be accepted as a proper arrangement for maintaining peace under an international organisation. The memory of how Roosevelt, Churchill and Chiang Kai-shek at Cairo had, without a word to Australia, determined the territorial peace terms for the North Pacific was still fresh in his mind. Under the Dumbarton Oaks proposals the General Assembly, where all members had equal rights, would have a more limited function than under the League of Nations Covenant. The Security Council, where the great powers had a 'preponderate' position, could 'even force the parties to a dispute to accept whatever settlement (including territorial settlements)' it chose to impose on them. It was Evatt's view that the new world organisation should not only offer the 'lesser powers' an ability to participate in its work but also give them reason to become enthusiastic supporters of this new experiment in international cooperation. With Australia in mind he asserted that 'even the so-called small Powers may have an important and even decisive influence in certain regions and in special circumstances'.[25] Thus he wanted the General Assembly, the more 'democratic' body and 'the conscience of the peoples of the world', to be accorded a right to deal with not only general principles but also specific disputes subject to only two reservations. First, the Assembly would be barred from taking up a dispute which the Council was already working on, and second, where the Assembly thought sanctions were required it would have to make recommendations to the Council for their adoption.[26]

---

[24] Minutes of British Commonwealth Meeting, BCM(45), 5th Meeting, 6 April 1945, ibid., p. 121.

[25] Evatt, 'Charter Day Address', University of California, March 1945, and 'Address to the Royal Institute of International Affairs', 9 April 1945, in Evatt, *Australia in World Affairs* (Sydney, Angus & Robertson: 1946), pp. 13, 17–18.

[26] Frank M. Forde, speech, 'United Nations Conference on International Organization', 27 April 1945, *CNIA*, vol. 16, no. 5, 1945, p. 98.

The claims of the 'lesser powers', however, had to be limited by the overriding objective of establishing an effective system of collective security. Evatt, still much influenced by memories of the Japanese threat to Australia, gave priority to security. He maintained that '[t]he expectation of complete and immediate application of Collective Security measures was the chief element commending the Dumbarton Oaks proposals to the peoples of the world'. He recognised that, at bottom, this new international organisation could not overcome the most evident weakness in the League of Nations unless the great powers, all of whom possessed overwhelming military might, were given authority to act decisively and quickly in dealing with disputes and enforcing the peace. Thus Evatt had no sympathy with the other dominions' wishes, either with the Canadians who wanted to leave it to the individual member states to decide whether to assist with the sanctions imposed by the Security Council or with the New Zealanders and South Africans who wanted to have the General Assembly consulted before the Council adopted sanctions. It was his view that 'Due regard [should] be paid to [the] necessity for leaving the Security Council unhampered in handling immediate threats to peace.' Likewise, since the great powers had to 'act unitedly' in quashing incipient aggression, he reaffirmed, without showing how it could be achieved, that it was important to 'eliminat[e] every possible difference of opinion' among them. To meet the objection that the permanent members with their veto might abuse their unqualified power, he suggested inserting in the Charter a requirement that the Council should act with justice and fair play in reaching their decisions and make more use of the world court in settling disputes.[27]

While Evatt reluctantly allowed that each of the five permanent members who had the major responsibility for the enforcement of the organisation's decisions should have the right to reject the imposing of sanctions, he could not see why they should be able to prevent particular disputes from being brought before the Council or to block attempts at conciliation or arbitration. If this extensive power of veto over decision-making was understood to be only a transitory provision as the world moved from war to peace, then the other members of the organisation might be more easily reconciled to accepting it. But if that were to be the case, then it was important that the great-power veto should not apply to amending the constitution.[28] The Australian delegation at the British Commonwealth meeting in London, reporting back to Curtin, considered their case against the veto over revisions to the Charter was 'one of the most notable contributions' that they had made to the discussions of the proposals. Evatt, who was the effective author of this missive, had pointed out that 'periodical revision of the charter would be necessary to ensure that the World Organisation developed to meet changing world conditions'. While 'extreme flexibility is undesirable nothing could be less satisfactory than to place the nations of the world under an unyielding and over-rigid constitutional control'.[29] This concern about

---

[27] See cablegram F3, Forde, Australian Deputy Prime Minister and Evatt, London, to Curtin, 17 April 1945, in Hudson and Way, eds, *DAFP*, vol. VIII, pp. 134–37; and Evatt, *Australia in World Affairs*, p. 13.

[28] Ibid., pp. 18–19.

[29] Cablegram F3, in Hudson and Way, eds, *DAFP*, vol. VIII, pp. 135, 137; and Evatt, *Australia in World Affairs*, p. 18.

rigid constitutions might have had something to do with the Australian Labor leader's frustration with the difficulties of amending the Commonwealth's federal constitution, but it was more likely motivated by a desire to have the opportunity to cut back progressively the great powers' privileged position in the Charter.

The Australian delegation took the results of all this analysis and reflection to the San Francisco Conference.[30] The substance of much of their thinking was summarised in their opening address to the conference and informed the extraordinary number of amendments, many small but some quite important, which they submitted to the conference. Australia was the only nation to take the opportunity of the opening address to set out its reservations about the Dumbarton draft and to foreshadow in general terms most of the main amendments it intended to seek. Though the statement itself was delivered by Frank Forde, the Deputy Prime Minister, who was the head of the delegation, the text was almost wholly the work of Evatt. (At the earlier Wellington and London conferences as well Evatt, much to his chagrin, had also had—on the formal occasions—to defer to Forde, who, as SM Bruce, Australia's high commissioner in London, commented, was 'a very well meaning and quite amiable person with an unrivalled capacity to mouth platitudes'.)[31] In the event, it was Evatt, with his External Affairs officers, who conducted the Australian case throughout the conference itself.

The prime purpose of the proposed new world organisation, according to Australia's opening address, was to provide collective security for all nations. It was to provide 'speedy and orderly procedures for the peaceful handling of disputes between nations'; create a 'system of sanctions which can be imposed very rapidly and which will be based on the united military strength of the Great Powers, but shared in by all powers'; and promote 'economic and social justice', the only true basis for 'real international stability'. The chief changes which Australia sought to make to the proposals were to raise the status of the General Assembly, to expand the functions of the Economic and Social Council, to bring all dependent peoples into a mandate or trusteeship arrangement, and to limit the use of the great powers' veto over the business of the Security Council and the amending of the Charter.[32]

Evatt envisaged that the General Assembly 'ultimately ... should become the central organ or forum in which the conscience of the peoples of the world should have its most potent expression',[33] presumably thereby acting as a more effective balance to the great powers and their control of the Security Council. For him the Assembly, where all nations

[30] For the purpose of this chapter, treatment of the San Francisco Conference is limited to those aspects which are most relevant to the main theme. For excellent accounts of Australia's part in the shaping the UN Charter at the conference, see J.D.E. Plant, 'The origins and development of Australia's policy and posture at the United Nations Conference on International Organisation, San Francisco–1945', PhD thesis, Australian National University, 1967, chs VII and VIII; and Hudson, *Australia and the New World Order: Evatt at San Francisco, 1945* (Canberra, Australian Foreign Policy Publications Program, Australian National University: 1993).

[31] Letter, Bruce to F L McDougall, Economics Adviser to the Australian High Commission, London, 20 April 1945, in Hudson and Way, eds, *DAFP*, vol. VIII, p. 140.

[32] Forde, 'United Nations Conference on International Organization', pp. 96–9.

[33] Ibid., p. 98.

were equally represented, was the 'democratic' organ of the United Nations—though democratic because it represented all the states equally rather than all the people equally— and therefore the key agency for bringing about a better world. At the conference he took a leading part in strengthening its functions. In addition to those assigned to it by the Dumbarton Oaks proposals, Evatt was successful, with the help of other small-power representatives, in amending the proposals so that the Assembly was given equal authority with the Council to deal with and make recommendations to the Council about 'any questions or any matters within the scope' of the Charter. The only exception was that the Assembly could not take up any dispute or question which was already before the Council.

Similarly, he did much to assist in extending and defining the proposals' rather modest references to the UN's economic and social role. Impelled by his liberal and social ideals, he took a leading part in fighting for the insertion in this section of the Charter a pledge by members to promote 'high standards of living, full employment and conditions of economic and social progress', as well as to encourage universal respect for human rights and fundamental freedoms for all. Furthermore, in tune with liberal internationalism's critique of imperialism, he offered a new section for the Charter which aimed to bring all non-self-governing peoples—that is, not only those under existing League of Nations mandates but all colonies of imperial powers—under the supervision of the United Nations.[34] The British, backed by some of the other great powers, would not make any concessions, and as a result the imperial powers kept their colonies effectively free of UN oversight. All that Evatt achieved was the inclusion in the Charter of a declaration by members who had responsibilities for non-self-governing peoples that they would see their responsibilities as a 'sacred trust ... to promote [to] the utmost the well-being of the inhabitants of these territories', and, to this end, 'to ensure ... their political, economic, social, and educational advancement'.[35]

The most contentious topic at the conference was the great-power veto, and probably for that reason it was left for the last days. Evatt became the more or less acknowledged leader of the small powers in arguing the case for limits on the exercise of the veto. These issues went to the heart of the collective security idea since they touched directly on the question of how the central functions of resolving disputes between nations, protecting them from aggression and enforcing sanctions, would be managed. In the midst of war he had had no choice but to accept the tendency of the great powers to act without consulting the small powers but with the end of the conflict now in sight he, like many of the leaders of the other small nations, regarded this practice as less tolerable for the post-war world organisation. Thus even as he allowed that the great powers, because of their prime responsibility for enforcement of collective security, should have a special place in the Security Council, he was critical of the blanket veto powers which they had given themselves in their proposals.

Under the draft charter each of the five great powers had a permanent seat on the Security Council and a veto over all enforcement decisions and, with a minor exception, over all decisions relating to the peaceful settlement of disputes. What Evatt objected to was

[34] 'Amendments to the Dumbarton Oaks Proposals, Submitted on Behalf of Australia', *CNIA*, vol. 16, no. 6, 1945, pp. 111–12.

[35] *Charter of the United Nations*, Chapter XI, Article 73, reproduced in ibid., p. 145.

that any one of the great powers could, unless it were a party to a dispute, use its veto to ignore the wishes of the overwhelming majority of other members and block the Council from pursuing peaceful settlement processes. This might very well make the peacemaking function of the Council moot. Indeed it was partly this concern about the veto that had caused him to press for an explication of the powers of the Assembly which would allow the Assembly, provided the Council had not already taken up a case, to assume responsibility for it. Despite his best efforts, the Soviet Union would not be moved on this, and the other great powers, though they were prepared to accept the Australian amendment, felt obliged to join the Soviets in opposing any change.

Evatt was greatly angered by the Soviet's obduracy but did not know how to handle this rejection. All he could suggest was that if the Soviet Union persisted it should be made 'quite clear to the Conference and to world opinion the issues involved and the different views of the Soviet Union on the one hand and the remaining members of the Big Five [and] of the Conference as a whole on the other hand'. Yet even as his anger drew him in this direction his reason at the same time told him that they should 'avoid any … action which might result in Russia's withdrawal from the conference or refusal to sign or ratify the Charter'.[36] Evatt had recognised from the beginning that the efficacy of collective security under the United Nations depended centrally on the unity of the great powers and that this was at most risk from the Soviet Union's suspicions of Western intentions. Unless allowance was made for these suspicions, the Soviet Union might leave the conference, which would be tantamount to undermining the organisation's claim to represent the world and its ability to act effectively to enforce the will of the organisation.

Facing up in the pre-conference period to this very possibility, Evatt had thought that if the great powers proved immovable on the veto over peaceful disputes, their position might be acceptable if seen as part of a transitory process from war to peace and provided they gave some ground on their veto right over Charter amendments. As it stood, their proposals would make it almost impossible to change the constitution and so almost certainly freeze the Charter in the form adopted at the conference. It would prevent the organisation from adapting to changing world circumstances and almost rule out any possibility of modifying the great powers' veto rights. The amendment which Evatt put forward at San Francisco was still quite conservative. It followed the great powers' proposals in requiring that an amendment to the Charter, in order to be successful, would have to be approved by two-thirds of the General Assembly, but differed from the original in that it would need the concurrence of only three out of the five permanent members in order to be adopted. This was not likely to produce changes to the constitution in the short term or radical changes in the long term, but the great powers, led by the United States and the Soviet Union, would not have it and it failed. Once more Evatt had fought to the end but to no avail. Another crucial element in his revision desiderata had been rejected.

Collective security and East–West tensions

Evatt was by no means disheartened by his defeat on the veto question. Indeed, in the aftermath of San Francisco the United Nations became his great cause. He had put an

---

[36] Cablegram E41, Forde and Evatt to Chifley, 4 June 1945, in Hudson and Way, eds, *DAFP*, vol. VIII, pp. 194–5.

extraordinary, almost superhuman, effort into the work of the conference and in fighting for Australia's amendments to the Dumbarton Oaks draft. Paul Hasluck, who as an officer of the Department of External Affairs was closely associated with Evatt during the conference, wrote of his minister that:

> Day after Day for ten weeks from early morning until late at night his concentration on the task and the intensity of his efforts had a ferocity that made me wonder what strange demon had possessed him.[37]

In his early career as a student and a barrister the 'demon' ambition had driven him on, and at every stage he had marshalled all his energy and intellect for the task at hand. At San Francisco he was on the international stage and determined to play a great part in making the constitution which was to bring lasting peace with social justice and human progress to the world. By the end of the conference he was recognised as a fervent advocate of the United Nations and a champion of the 'lesser nations'. As a mark of his eminence the members of the General Assembly chose Australia to hold one of the elective seats in the Security Council. As a result of his contribution to the San Francisco Conference he had raised Australia's international status and had identified himself with the liberal internationalist cause.

On his return to Australia Evatt, who following Curtin's death had become Deputy Prime Minister to Prime Minister Ben Chifley, gave the parliament a very positive account of the Charter. For the sceptics who maintained that the United Nations was the League of Nations reprised and therefore bound to collapse, he pointed out that, unlike the League, it included all the major states, that the Council would be able to call upon the military resources of all the organisation's members to combat aggression and that all members had agreed to cooperate in enforcing the decisions of the Security Council. He asserted that the great powers' veto was justified since they had the chief responsibility for enforcement and that if a majority of the Security Council attempted to enforce its will on any of the three greatest powers it would mean a new world war.

Evatt did acknowledge that there were weaknesses since the veto could be used to prevent the United Nations coming to the aid of a small power that was a victim of aggression. 'In short,' he admitted, 'the new system, functioning under the constitution … offers no absolute guarantee against armed conflicts and aggression'. Consequently, a victim—and clearly he had Australia in mind—would ultimately have to 'fall back on regional arrangements, and ultimately upon its own defence forces and those of its Allies'. But he was still flushed with the success of the San Francisco Conference and thought this possibility remote. The Big Three were still bound by the close ties of the war years. Moreover, he believed that the enhanced position of the General Assembly and the hostility shown by the small powers to the veto over conciliation would warn the great powers against 'any capricious or unjust exercise of the veto privilege'.[38]

---

[37] Paul Hasluck, *Diplomatic Witness: Australian Foreign Affairs, 1941–1947* (Melbourne, Melbourne University Press: 1980), p. 194. See also Paul Hasluck, *Workshop of Security*, FW Cheshire, Melbourne, 1948, for his recollections of the Australian part in the making of the UN Charter.

[38] Commonwealth of Australia, *Parliamentary Debates*, House of Representatives, vol. 184, 30

Within a few months, however, his hopes for this new cooperative world of peace and justice were beginning to unravel. The great powers seemed intent on continuing their wartime dictatorial practices. Ignoring the smaller allies, they were taking upon themselves responsibility for determining the occupation policies and peace terms for the defeated enemies, and in the process were showing the first signs of serious divisions. Evatt, along with the leaders of other small powers, protested, and succeeded in convincing the great powers to allow the 'lesser allies' to take part in a conference to consider the European peace settlement. He was even more insistent that Australia should have an equal say in the making of policy for the occupation of Japan, and urged the Americans to set up a Far East Commission in Washington comprising all the Pacific allies. Likewise, he persuaded Great Britain and the other dominions to agree to allow Australia to command the British Commonwealth Occupation Force in Japan, and also to represent the British Commonwealth on the four-power Allied Council in Tokyo which advised the Supreme Commander of the Allied Forces, General Douglas MacArthur, on occupation policy. But in all these arrangements, the great powers still had the upper hand either, as in Europe, through their military dominance and veto rights or, as in the Far East, through the total control of occupied Japan by the United States.[39]

Evatt was even more dismayed by the cracks appearing in the 'Grand Alliance'. In the process of peacemaking, the US and Britain on the one side and the Soviet Union on the other were beginning to engage in vituperative exchanges. The meetings of the Security Council, like the great powers' foreign ministers' meetings, were becoming arenas for the airing of charges and counter-charges. Issues were not being judged on their merits, as Evatt believed the UN Charter required, but were being treated as tests of will by the opposing sides as they jockeyed for the higher moral ground in capturing world opinion. When in January 1946 the United Kingdom and the United States accused the Soviet Union of failing to withdraw its troops from Iran in accordance with a wartime treaty, the Soviet representatives countered by pointing to the Western powers' interference in the internal affairs of Greece and the Indonesian nationalist revolution.

Two months later Winston Churchill, now leader of the opposition in the British parliament, gave an address in Fulton, Missouri, with President Truman's tacit consent,[40] setting out these differences in Manichean terms. In this so-called Iron Curtain address Churchill still paid his respects to the wartime alliance, reminding his audience of the great regard that the Western nations had come to have for Marshal Stalin and the valour of the Russian people. But, he went on to say, 'a shadow had fallen across the scenes so lately lighted by the Allied victory'. From Stettin in the Baltic to Trieste in the Adriatic, an 'iron curtain' had descended upon the middle of Europe. Behind this curtain Eastern Europe was not only subject to Russian influence but also in thrall to communist governments which, though totally unrepresentative of their peoples, took their orders directly from Moscow. Outside this closed world the Soviet Union was bringing pressure to bear on Iran

August 1945, pp. 5018 and 5036–37.

[39] Evatt set out his concern at great-power dominance in 'Risks of a Great Power Peace', *Foreign Affairs*, vol. 24, no. 2, 1946, pp. 195–209.

[40] David McCullough, *Truman* (New York, Simon & Schuster: 1992), pp. 486–87.

and Turkey in order to gain territorial and other concessions. In Western Europe itself there were large communist parties, 'fifth columns' that were under instruction from Moscow. As a result, the Western countries did not know 'what Soviet Russia and its communist international organization intended to do in the immediate future, or what are the limits, if any, to their expansive and proselytising tendencies'. He concluded that if the Western democracies were to 'stand together in strict adherence to the principles of the UN Charter, their influence will be immense and no one is likely to molest them'.[41] Churchill might speak of 'strict adherence' to UN principles, but what his call for Anglo-American solidarity meant was that the great powers would be confronting one another, not cooperating with each other in the Security Council.

Evatt was greatly perturbed by these developments. He feared that if this deterioration in East–West relations persisted it would prevent the United Nations from carrying out its collective security function—his vision of the United Nations seemed to be in jeopardy. Just a week after Churchill's speech Evatt gave a *tour d'horizon* address in the House of Representatives, focussing especially on the United Nations. It showed his dismay at the growing hostility between the great powers and he responded to the Anglo-American attacks on the Soviet Union. He conceded that, unfortunately, at the end of wars there was 'a tendency for Allied countries … to become more aware of and to accentuate differences in outlook' and it was easy for these countries 'to accept them not only as vital, but as irremediable'. This was 'a most dangerous attitude of mind' and could 'lead only to disaster, if it is unchecked'. Turning to the Western criticisms of the Soviet Union, he was willing to admit that the Soviet territory and influence had expanded as a result of the war, but stressed that the question which had to be determined was not the expansion itself, but 'the underlying intention'.[42]

What was important was whether the Soviets' expansionist policy was aimed at the political domination of other countries, or at protecting the Soviet Union 'against any repetition of the so-called *cordon sanitaire* which [had] united all reactionary influence in Europe against her' in the years between the great wars. He stressed that the Russians had reason to distrust the Western leaders who had in the 1930s abandoned the League of Nations, appeased the fascist aggressors and refused to enter into defence alliances with the Soviet Union against the fascist powers. Here again was a Popular Front view of anti-Soviet 'appeasement'. It was also understandable that the Russians should be suspicious of the British and Americans who had signed a treaty to protect their monopoly of the atomic bomb. He concluded that 'this pessimism with regard to relations with Russia seems to be unjustified'. As he had said from the beginning of the process which had led to the formation of the UN Charter, mutual confidence among the great powers was an 'essential feature of the new international order'. If these antagonisms were left to fester the world would once again be dominated by rival blocs engaged in struggles for survival. Those who sowed distrust among the great powers threatened the continuing existence of the United

---

[41]   Winston Churchill, 'Sinews of Peace', address to Westminster College, Fulton, Missouri, 5 March 1946.

[42]   Commonwealth of Australia, *Parliamentary Debates*, House of Representatives, vol. 186, 13 March 1946, pp. 200–06.

Nations and thereby the existence of the 'chief bulwark against a third world war'.[43]

What Evatt then required, to meet this problem, was that all disputes, including these East–West examples, should be brought before the Security Council where they could be discussed freely and frankly in the full light of world opinion. The facts of the case should be established by an independent body and on the basis of the evidence the Council should arrive at a just decision. Liberal internationalism here showed its inherent weakness. It assumed too easily that impartial investigators acceptable to the disputants could be found. It did not take into account the shortcomings of public diplomacy for the purpose of arriving at peaceful solutions. It placed too much faith in the nebulous notion of 'world opinion'. It carried the Western democratic idea of *vox populi, vox dei*, with all its flaws, to the international arena. It did not explain why the great powers should be expected to submit to this process. To suggest how this might work he merely made some passing references to British traditions of law and royal commissions mixed with some European judicial practices, all of which were wrested from their cultural contexts. From the beginning, however, neither the United Nations nor Evatt himself conformed in any serious way to these abstract ideals.

For all his liberal internationalist aspirations Evatt had always been aware that the basic condition for the success of collective security was the unity of the great powers, and since this from the end of the war was problematic he concluded that Australia necessarily had to look to regional defence arrangements for its security:

> Whatever the United Nations Organization may do, it will be essential to guard the security of the South-West Pacific Area, and in its defence there must be the closest co-operation, not only with the United Kingdom … but also with other peace-loving Pacific neighbours, especially the United States.[44]

Thus, even as he was chastising Britain and the United States for allowing these divisions to emerge and take over the centre of the world stage, he was also reasserting the need for a regional alliance in association with these two great powers. What he envisaged was not an inclusive regional organisation without distinction of race or ideology modelled on the United Nations, but one composed of those natural protectors who could be relied upon to come to Australia's rescue when it was confronted, as it had been so recently, by a 'deadly and ferocious enemy'.[45]

Indeed, at the very time that the East–West tensions were appearing, Evatt was deeply engaged in secret diplomacy with the British and the Americans about setting up a regional security scheme. The Americans' post-war desire to keep all the bases that they had built in the Pacific had created an opening for such negotiations. Of all the bases in the Southwest Pacific the one most important to the United States was that on Manus Island, which was in Australia's mandated territory—the United States claimed that they had during the war spent $US 140,000,000 on air and naval facilities there—and Evatt sought to take advantage of this to insist that the discussions over its future use should be connected to a regional defence arrangement. Evatt understood, as a result of the Pacific War, that only the

---

[43] Ibid.

[44] Evatt, speech to House of Representatives, 26 March 1946, *CNIA*, vol. 17, no. 4, 1946, p. 207.

[45] Ibid.

United States had the capacity to protect Australia and therefore American participation in any defence arrangement was indispensable. Thus, when in April 1946 the Australian government was preparing for further talks, Evatt advised the Cabinet that they should not include France or Holland in the defence arrangement since this 'would raise more directly the question of Russian participation', a possibility that would alienate the Americans. In his view, Cabinet should seek a tripartite alliance made up of Australia, New Zealand and the United States.[46]

The Americans, however, refused to cooperate. When Evatt in the middle of the year visited Washington to press his case, he was given a frosty reception. President Truman ruled out any kind of treaty or even informal statement of policy which would have had the same general effect. In desperation, Evatt proposed an arrangement whereby Australia would give the Americans the use of Manus and other facilities in return for the United States giving Australia use of one of their major bases in the North Pacific such as Guam or Truk. In the end the most that the American authorities would agree to was access to its small bases at Eastern Samoa or Canton Island in a distant part of the South Pacific. Early in 1947 the Australians seemed to have accepted these less than satisfactory terms. Evatt had argued in the Council of Defence that even though the American offer:

> did not go as far as we would have liked, and was, perhaps, of doubtful practical value for Australian defence, nevertheless it was a recognition of United States willingness to make an arrangement on the principle of reciprocity and it represented an initial step in the direction of co-operation with the United States in the Pacific, which it was Australia's aim to foster.[47]

But by this time the Americans had begun to lose interest altogether in Manus and other bases in the South Pacific, and in June they withdrew their offer. Negotiations for an Australian–American security arrangement of any kind had come to an end. During the diplomacy there had been no reference to the United Nations. The Australians did not see their proposal as an inclusive regional collective security organisation based on United Nations principles. The members of Australia's prospective Pacific alliance, like those of the subsequent North Atlantic alliance, were not selected for their geographical propinquity but for their common mind about a common threat from a common enemy.

Simultaneously, Evatt was having great difficulty in persuading the United States to move towards a peace settlement with Japan. Fearful of a resurgent Japan, he was adamant that the former enemy should be demilitarised, disarmed and democratised so that it could never rise again to threaten Australia. He was concerned that the Americans might, as time went by, soften their attitude to peace terms. Thus, in early 1947, when Evatt learnt

---

[46] Memorandum, 'Regional Security in the Pacific, Including the Use of Bases by the United States', adopted by Cabinet, 8 April 1946, NAA: A4311, 453/1.

[47] 'Notes of a Meeting of Ministers on Council of Defence', 6 March 1947, in Hudson and Way, eds, *DAFP*, vol. XII, *1947* (Canberra, Australian Government Publishing Service: 1995), pp. 299–302. For a fuller account of Australia's efforts to secure a defence arrangement with the United States in this period, see Neville Meaney, *Japan and Australia's Foreign Policy, 1949–1952* (London, London School of Economics and Political Science, Suntory and Toyota International Centres for Economics and Related Disciplines: 2000), pp. 18–35.

that they were intending to call a peace conference he organised a British Commonwealth meeting at Canberra with the aim of mobilising support for a harsh peace.

In response to the remark of John Burton, the newly appointed Secretary of the Department of External Affairs, that the British Commonwealth countries should not be 'allowed to go back on voting arrangements'—that is that they should vote as a bloc at the proposed peace conference—another official pointed out that Americans did not like 'blocs'. Evatt, however, who had also criticised countries for voting in blocs at San Francisco and at the United Nations, arguing that the practice was contrary to the world body's liberal internationalist spirit, dismissed the objection and defiantly declared, 'Be damned! They do it themselves'. Likewise, in a discussion with a departmental officer he was crudely blunt about the claims of other powers to take part in the Japanese peace settlement:

> Evatt: Why should Canada for instance be in the peace settlement? They will, I think, follow the U.S. in a crisis or sit on the fence. They will sign anything. They were a miserable crowd at San Francisco.
>
> [WD] Forsyth: They were cautious but acted in their own interests.
>
> Evatt: South Africa should not be in the peace settlement though I am glad to have them at the Canberra Conference.
>
> Forsyth: Shouldn't the criterion be active participation in the war against Japan?
>
> Evatt: Then we should cut out France and the Netherlands.
>
> Forsyth: That would limit it to the Big Five.
>
> Evatt: I don't mind the Big Five if Australia is one of them.[48]

Evatt also had no confidence in the British since 'U.K. policy is to give concessions in the Pacific for similar ones in Europe'.[49] He was willing for the great powers to have exclusive responsibility for making peace with Japan provided Australia was one of them. As a result when the Russians and Chinese, ignoring his protests, insisted that the veto should apply to a Japanese peace conference, Evatt took the view that if Australia agreed to a 'modified veto' it should be on the understanding 'that Australia should represent the British Commonwealth as at Tokyo'—that is, as it did on the four-power Allied Council in Japan.[50]

Evatt was in reality suggesting that Australia should exercise the United Kingdom's great-power veto at the Japanese peace conference. Since he blamed the great powers and their vetoes for the stalemate in the European peace negotiations and the breakdown in dispute resolutions at the United Nations,[51] it was ironic that he was willing to countenance

---

[48] 'Minutes of Meeting in Secretary's Room', 8 July 1947, NAA: A4311, 453/2.

[49] Ibid.

[50] Cablegram E69, Evatt, New York, to Burton, 22 November 1947, in Hudson and Way, eds, *DAFP*, vol. XII, p. 626. For a fuller account of these negotiations over the holding of a Japanese peace conference and their consequences, see Meaney, *Japan and Australia's Foreign Policy*, pp. 35–49; and Neville Meaney, 'Australia, the Great Powers and the Coming of the Cold War', *Australian Journal of Politics and History*, vol. 38, no 3 (1992): 316–33.

[51] This was a major theme of Evatt's Oliver Wendell Homes Lectures at Harvard in October 1947;

a great-power peace for Japan provided that Australia was accepted as one of the great powers. In the event, Evatt's desire to protect Australia by working for an early peace treaty with Japan was thwarted. When the United States decided that a conference with the Soviet Union and China exercising veto powers was not likely to produce a satisfactory peace treaty it postponed the peacemaking indefinitely and set about rebuilding Japan's economy, including its industrial infrastructure, in order to win its former enemy's goodwill and turn it into an ally of the West. Again the Americans had frustrated Australian attempts to secure protection against the prospect of a resurgent Japan. The great power that Evatt had assumed was Australia's natural regional protector had abandoned it. Evatt was again feeling Australia's isolation in the Pacific and was furious with the Americans over this outcome.

The Cold War Crisis

The crisis moment for Evatt's idea of collective security came in the early months of 1948. By this time the United Kingdom and the United States had reached an impasse with the Soviet Union over all the great questions of the post-war settlement in Europe. The failure of the December 1947 great powers' foreign ministers' meeting to resolve the longstanding problem of peace terms for Germany finally caused the British to take steps to create a Western Union aimed at resisting the Soviet Union's further subversion, infiltration or intimidation of democratic governments in Europe. With this objective in mind, British Prime Minister Clement Attlee cabled Chifley, along with the other dominion prime ministers, asking for support in organising 'the ethical and moral resources of Western Europe, backed by the power and resources of the Commonwealth and the Americas ... to stem the further encroachments of Soviet Union'.[52] Australia, alone among the dominions, refused to approve what seemed to its leaders to represent a complete break with the Russians and therefore a deadly blow to the United Nations and its role as peacemaker and peacekeeper. The longish reply was drafted by John Burton and approved by Evatt and Chifley. Though for the most part couched in the language of liberal internationalism, it also expressed something of the bitterness which the Australians felt about the developments in international relations in the preceding months, especially about the way they had been treated by the Americans and the way their interests had been ignored or overridden.

At the outset, the Australians complained that Britain and America were once again presenting them with a fait accompli. They warned London that Canberra could not undertake to support any British or British–American policy which had been decided upon 'without the fullest prior consultation and agreement by us at every stage of consideration of that policy'. It was pointed out that though Evatt had been in New York just a few weeks previously neither the British nor the Americans had informed him that they were considering a new approach in dealing with East–West relations.[53]

---

see Evatt, *The United Nations* (Melbourne: Oxford University Press, 1948), especially pp. 54–71 and 99–104.

[52]   Cablegram, Attlee to Chifley, 13 January 1948, TNA: PREM 8/787.

[53]   Cablegram, Chifley to Attlee, 22 January 1948, ibid.

Their rejection of the British request was predicated on two grounds: liberal internationalism and regional realism.

The first and more extensive argument was that the British proposal would conflict with the ideals of the United Nations. The Australian government told Attlee that they would 'endeavour to mobilise moral and material forces by always upholding the United Nations and principles of justice rather than policies of strategy and expedience'. It was only by working through the United Nations that a solution to the East–West tensions could be found. The Russian suspicion of the West was understandable since the hostility which had marked Western attitudes to the Soviet Union prior to World War II had not been wholly removed by wartime cooperation. This problem could not be solved by 'making an offensive alliance against Russia'. Instead, they continued, '[s]uch an alliance would seem to give justification for the policy that she [Russia] has been pursuing since the end of the war'.[54]

There was no good reason for the breakdown in the talks on Germany. The Council of Foreign Ministers, representing only the great powers, and 'lacking the broader approach of a larger body has made very little contribution to the peace settlement or to peace'. The Australians saw no justification for taking up a confrontationist position and declared that if and when justice demanded it, 'the strongest action should be taken through the United Nations against the Soviet or any other power in order to uphold the United Nations'. While stating that Australians had 'far less sympathy for extreme policies such as Communist and Fascist movements than most other people', they were not convinced of the desirability of 'a Western alliance directed against the Soviet'. Australia would thus hold itself aloof so that when the opportunity presented itself they would be free to act as mediator between the two camps.[55]

Mixed up in this liberal internationalist argument was a carping criticism of the United States. The Australians asserted that, if the United States had provided 'the necessities of life for the people of Western Europe', then the communists would never have been able to gain such a large influence in Europe. In a passing aside aimed at the Marshall Plan aid program, the Australians said that they 'would not use economic power and relief to determine forms of government'. Furthermore, they implied that the British, in proposing this Western Union, were acting on behalf of the Americans and queried whether, if it led to war, the British government might be left to take responsibility for a policy which the United States itself was 'not prepared or able, for constitutional reason, to carry through'. The British might be 'over-optimistic … to count on the support of the Americans'.[56]

Lastly, Chifley explained that Australia's regional situation would prevent it from assisting in this European-centred scheme. He told the British that:

> the Australian Government believes its interests [are] very much bound up in the Pacific area: in the event of European conflict, our whole manpower might have to be diverted to the protection of our position and interests in this area.

---

[54] Ibid.

[55] Ibid.

[56] Ibid.

Australia found itself in a very vulnerable position. No government in the region was 'stable'. Indeed 'every government' could be 'prevailed upon to adopt a policy hostile to us if it so suited powers engaged in a European conflict'.[57] What Chifley was essentially saying was that Australia, in the case of a war breaking out in Europe, would be fighting for its survival in the Pacific, and this without any great and powerful protector to whom it could look for help.

This alarm about national security seems to have been written in a fit of resentment which expressed itself as panic-stricken fear. There was no proper assessment of what this

---

[57] Ibid. For the replies from other dominions, see cablegrams, UK High Commissioner, Ottawa, to Attlee, 15 January 1948, ibid.; and South African Secretary for External Affairs to Attlee, 22 January 1948, ibid. In a subsequent cablegram to Attlee, Chifley gave further substance to the idea that the United States was behind the Western Union movement. He said that Australia fully understood the British need in their parlous economic and military circumstances 'to obtain the sympathy and support of America' but he warned the British Prime Minister 'that support should not be obtained on the basis that war with the Soviet Union is inevitable'. See message, Chifley to Attlee, 10 February 1948, in Pamela Andre, ed., *DAFP*, vol. XVI, *Beyond the Region 1948–49* (Canberra, DFAT: 2001), pp. 381–82.

The special animosity towards the United States followed from the rejections which Evatt had suffered at the end of the previous year over both a strategic arrangement for the Pacific and an early Japanese peace conference. In 1947 while hopes were still high that the United States would join in some form of defence arrangement and sponsor an early peace conference on Japan, Evatt had adopted a very positive attitude towards the Americans, distancing himself from the Australian representative on the Allied Council in Tokyo who had been critical of Macarthur's occupation policies, ingratiating himself with Secretary of State George Marshall over a prospective peace conference and giving unqualified approval to the Truman Doctrine and the British and American policies in Greece.

In the case of Greece, Evatt, in early October 1947—the very time he was pressing the Americans to proceed with the Japanese peace conference—had adopted fully the Anglo-American view of the Greek question. He had lambasted the Soviet Union and its satellites on Greece's northern border for infiltrating across the border, giving sanctuary to communist rebels and interfering with Greece's internal affairs. It was, in his view, a clear case of external aggression. The allegations that the Soviet Union and its allies had brought against the democratic government of Greece and against Britain and America for their 'unselfish' aid, including military aid, to that government were 'of the crudest, almost infantile kind'. The motives of the British and Americans had been stated 'frankly' and were 'beyond suspicion'. Greece's government had been elected under international supervision in a process which, Evatt slyly remarked, was an 'achievement that some other countries might envy'. See 'Speech by the Minister for External Affairs, Dr HV Evatt to Committee No.1 (Political and Security) of the General Assembly, 6th October 1947', *CNIA*, vol. 18, 1947, pp. 684–92. Yet by the first week of January 1948, after the Americans had closed off any possibility of holding a Japanese peace conference in the near future, Evatt's attitude towards the Greek question had undergone something of a revolution. The Greek problem was now seen as 'a civil war'. The Greek government was now considered 'undemocratic and fascist' and 'one of the major causes of the crisis' since 'its repressive and reactionary policy … was driving the democratic forces into armed opposition'. Evatt and the Australian government believed that the 'only lasting solution … would be a complete reform programme, a cease fire and a new election supervised by the United Nations'. See Christopher Waters, *The Empire Fractures: Anglo-Australian Conflict in the 1940s* (Melbourne, Australian Scholarly Publishing: 1995), pp. 117–18.

'instability' might mean for Australian security. While it was asserted that every one of these unnamed and unstable governments could be manipulated by powers engaged in a European conflict to attack Australia, these hostile European powers were not identified and it was not explained how they could exercise such influence over Australia's neighbours. It was ironic that the Australians—who were accusing the British and Americans of conjuring up, without good reason, a European threat and so turning their back on the UN's ideals— were themselves putting forward a much less credible spectre of a Hydra-headed monster lurking on their borders, waiting for the moment to strike. Perhaps Australia's rejection of the proposal for a Western Union, though expressed primarily in the language of liberal internationalism, was, in substance, much more a response to fears about what another European war might mean for its survival in the Pacific.

Though poorly expressed, poorly composed, and poorly argued, this Australian answer to the British request for support for a Western Union is one of the most remarkable documents in the history of Australian foreign policy.

For the next few months Evatt continued his attack on this movement for a Western Union and the propensity of the British and Americans to see all global problems in terms of a nascent East–West conflict. The communist *coup d'état* in Czechoslovakia in February had no visible impact on his view of the Soviet Union and its intentions. In parliament he attacked the United States for postponing the convening of a Japanese peace conference and for continuing to build up the Japanese economy beyond the limits set by the Far Eastern Commission. While the United States might hope that Japan's resources would provide an arsenal to be used in a future struggle with the Soviet Union, it was possible that Japan's military resurgence might be 'turned in the direction of the South Pacific to the detriment of this country'. It would be 'an evil day for Australia if Japan is given capacity to rearm'.

Though in the same speech Evatt praised America's Marshall Plan and the Western Union movement for their 'contribution to the stability and economic welfare of Europe',[58] underneath he was seething over what he believed the Americans had done to Australia and to the United Nations.

The day after delivering this address he unburdened himself to the British high commissioner in Canberra. In this private conversation he asserted that America's Cold War policy of containment of the Soviet Union threatened war. The US position on Palestine, Trieste and Japan was not helpful in advancing the cause of peace. Drawing on some of the crudest neo-Marxist stereotypes, he launched into a stinging denunciation of US policy. It was 'revealed as mercenary and opposed to any system of democracy as we understand it'. The Americans were 'more concerned about their own financial interests than about the peace of the world'. It was clear that their actions had in the main been 'dominated by vested interests which took the form of anti-communism which could not be distinguished from anti-socialism'.[59]

---

[58] Commonwealth of Australia, *Parliamentary Debates*, House of Representatives, vol. 196, 8 April 1948, pp. 747–48 and 751.

[59] Letter, E.J. Williams, British High Commissioner, Canberra, to Sir Eric Machtig, Commonwealth Relations Office, 6 April 1948, TNA: PREM 8/787.

On the other hand, Evatt expressed his great admiration for the British government and people who had from the start of the war sacrificed so much that they were now obliged to seek aid from the United States. The crippling conditions that the United States had placed on its loans were the result of 'American suspicions of a Labour Government in Britain'. And so he proposed to the high commissioner that:

> the three Labour Governments of the British Commonwealth should ... form some kind of democratic nucleus which could act as a midway power between United States individualism and Soviet Communism and so secure the peace of the world.[60]

The British envoy could not help but be struck by Evatt's 'veering from his earlier attitude of closer co-operation with the United States', and he also wondered whether Evatt was beginning to realise that 'putting all one's money on the United Nations is a risky business and that greater reliance should be placed in a strong Commonwealth'.[61] The British, however, had no interest in Australia's 'midway' proposal. In taking the lead in campaigning for a Western Union the British Labour government had already shown that it accepted the permanence of the East–West divide and looked forward to allying itself with the United States in order to contain Soviet expansionism. As a result, Australia's new path to securing world peace led nowhere.

By the middle of 1948 Evatt was becoming reconciled to the reality of the Cold War and the need to contain the Soviet Union, at least in the Pacific. He was most immediately troubled by the spread of communism in Southeast Asia and by evidence that Moscow, working through the Cominform, had begun to encourage the communist parties in Australia's region to try to seize control of their countries' national independence movements. He was particularly concerned by the outbreak of a Chinese-led insurgency in Malaya. Talking with British officials, Evatt declared that the Malayan situation was 'of great concern to Australia' and that Australia would be willing to give aid to Britain, including possibly the commitment of military forces.[62] Though the Australian Cabinet refused to send troops—the fall of Singapore was perhaps still too fresh in their minds—they did agree to provide some arms to assist the British in Malaya. Indeed when the communist-led Seamen's Union in Australia threatened to stop the transport of the arms by sea, Chifley dispatched them by air.

About the same time, the possibility of communist exploitation of the turmoil in Indonesia was thought to pose an even greater threat. In discussions with the British foreign minister Evatt predicted that, unless the Western powers 'moved with speed and decision' to settle the disputes between the Dutch and the Indonesian nationalists, the Dutch East Indies 'might become one of the great danger spots in the world and ... Russia would spread onto that area as she had done in Europe'.[63] Showing how widespread was Australia's

---

[60] Ibid.

[61] Ibid. See also *Australian Observer*, 28 June 1947, which reported on the same Australian proposal for a British Commonwealth 'third force' between 'totalitarian Russia and capitalist USA'.

[62] Extract, record of conversation between Philip Noel-Baker, Secretary of State for Commonwealth Affairs, and HV Evatt, 17 August 1948, TNA: FO 371/69698.

[63] Copy of dispatch, Ernest Bevin, British Foreign Secretary, to British Ambassador, The Hague, 16

anxiety about the threat from communism in the region, Burton wrote to a senior officer of the department a few days later that '[i]t is bad enough to have a Malaya situation on our doorstep' but that the Indonesian question was even more pressing. It was his 'guess that if there is no settlement, or convincing indication of a desire for settlement within the next month or six weeks, then Indonesia would be lost to a potentially hostile Republican Left Wing movement'.[64] It was possible for Evatt to view the Soviet Union as an expansionist power, an expansionist power whose aggression through its proxies in the region posed a great danger to Australia.

In Europe, as one crisis followed another, the Cold War became set in concrete. The Soviet blockade of the Western powers' sectors of Berlin did much to remove lingering doubts about Moscow's intentions and to hasten the formation of the North Atlantic Alliance. The stand-off over Berlin, unlike any previous confrontation, carried with it the imminent possibility of war. Australia's leaders could not avoid taking a position on these developments, and so were ineluctably drawn into identifying themselves with the Western Union. Evatt publicly blamed the Soviet Union, and the Australian government sent an aircrew to assist in flying supplies to West Berlin.

At the Commonwealth Prime Ministers' Conference which was held in London in October 1948, Evatt, representing Chifley, showed how events had coerced the Australian government into coming to terms, at least to some extent, with the new bipolar world. The British had summoned the meeting for the purpose of persuading the dominions to join in global planning to contain the spread of the Soviet Union. Of all the dominions' responses, Evatt's was the most forthcoming. He agreed that in these new circumstances the principle of justice upon which the United Nations was based might have to give way to the demands of expediency since—and here he might have had in mind Southeast Asia as well as Europe—'Soviet expansionism could not be permitted to continue'. Australia was helping to break the Soviet blockade of Berlin, which gave assurance to its friends about where it would stand 'if the crisis should deteriorate'. He accepted that the Commonwealth's defence policy had to be based on the assumption that 'the enemy would be Soviet Russia'.

Nevertheless, perhaps influenced by the fact that he had just been elected President of the UN General Assembly, Evatt still hoped to mend the breach between the great powers and he reaffirmed his earlier belief that the organisation of 'a central power between Soviet Russia and the United States was of cardinal importance'. Moreover, he expressed some sympathy for Russian opposition to the partition of Germany as he thought that the division of the country might result in a revival of German nationalism. On the pressing matter of Berlin he would not accept that a settlement satisfactory to both sides could not be found. Without giving any reason or support for his view he asserted that the Russians were 'anxious to retreat' and hinted that the Western governments should provide a way out of the impasse which would enable the Russians to end their blockade without loss of face.[65]

August 1948, TNA: DO 35/2847.

[64] Letter, Burton to Keith Officer, 27 August 1948, NLA: Keith Officer Papers, MS2629 1/1101.

[65] Minutes, Meetings of Commonwealth Prime Ministers, 19 and 20 October 1948, TNA: CAB 133/88.

Looking back at Evatt's last year as minister for external affairs one might have thought that he would have been greatly disheartened by the failure of the United Nations to unite the great powers through the Security Council and so uphold the principle of collective security. All the efforts of the United Nations, including the one he had initiated jointly with the UN Secretary-General, Trygve Lie, to bring the four great powers together to negotiate a settlement for the Berlin blockade, had been aborted. The Western powers' persistence and their ever-increasing ability to supply their Berlin sectors by air made a farce of the blockade and caused the Soviet Union in mid-1949 to lift the embargo. Likewise, his efforts to persuade the United Kingdom and the United States to agree to a United Nations-sponsored four-power conference on Greece that would link that country's internal troubles with its communist neighbours' external aggression fell on deaf ears. It was Anglo-American aid to Greece and the Soviet Union's problems with Yugoslavia that enabled the Greek government to secure its frontiers and crush its domestic enemies. Most important, with the signing of the North Atlantic pact in April, Evatt's endeavours to prevent the East–West differences from being given permanent form through the creation of contending alliances were shown to have failed.

Regardless of these setbacks Evatt still continued to talk of the new international order as though the original aims of the United Nations and the principle of collective security still underpinned the post-war world. He reasserted his wholehearted commitment to the United Nations, and in an address to parliament declared that 'the first and fundamental principle' of Australian foreign policy was a 'steady and unfaltering support for the United Nations, and especially the purposes and principles declared in the Charter'.[66] The events of the previous years had in no way shaken his belief in the institution and its ideals. In his judgement, '[a] close examination of the three years' work of the United Nations ... shows a faithful pursuit of its objectives'. But in order to give credibility to this narrative, which promised world peace through mediation and consultation—military and other peace-enforcing sanctions were now not mentioned—in dealing with disputes that involved the great powers he made totally unjustified claims for the United Nations having some influence over their settlement.[67] On Greece, he maintained that:

> the [United Nations Special] Commission [to the Balkans] has rendered invaluable service in limiting the area of the dispute ... and in preventing what was certainly occurring at the time the Commission was appointed, that is, the giving of aid to the rebels in Greece, especially by Yugoslavia.[68]

And even on the Berlin blockade he boldly stated that the United Nations 'played a part, an important part, in the reopening' of the German question, which led to the Soviet Union restoring the Western powers' sea and land access routes to Berlin.[69]

But his greatest difficulty in trying to make this account of the UN's success convincing was to show how the emergence of the rival East–West alliances in Europe did not mean what they seemed to mean, namely a permanent breakdown in the relations of the great

---

[66] Evatt, speech to House of Representatives, 9 February 1949, *CNIA*, vol. 20, no. 2, 1949, p. 257.

[67] Ibid., pp. 269 and 270.

[68] Evatt, statement to House of Representatives, 21 June 1949, p. 754.

[69] Ibid., p. 751.

powers and therefore the inability of the United Nations to carry out its core security function of protecting the territorial integrity and political independence of its members. In particular, the North Atlantic Pact seemed to symbolise all that Evatt and his colleagues had fought against in January 1948, all that they had said was anathema to the principles of the United Nations and the liberal internationalist doctrine of collective security. Yet when it was suggested that the pact offered an alternative source of security to that found in the United Nations, Evatt denied that this was so. It was not an 'alternative': it was an 'addition'. It was an expression of regional co-operation which was recognised in the Charter. The North Atlantic pact was 'supplementary to the United Nations ... not a substitute for it'. These regional alliances were 'good in their place so long as people do not treat them as the substitute to the world organisation'.[70]

Almost immediately, however, he seemed to admit that this was what the North Atlantic pact and its Soviet Eastern European counterpart were, in essence. He could not refuse altogether to acknowledge that though the North Atlantic pact was formally set up as a regional association under the UN Charter, it was a security alliance created not by geography but by geopolitics and was in no way subject to the Security Council. In accepting this, Evatt lowered his sights for the role of the United Nations. He conceded that if there were:

> two regional organisations in the world struggling for mastery without a forum in which they can meet and discuss their differences with a view to preserving the peace, the future of the world under those conditions may be a terribly dark one.[71]

In such circumstances all that would be left for the United Nations to do in the field of security would be to provide a meeting place for the global adversaries. 'Collective security' was left as an empty phrase.

From almost the beginning of his career as minister for external affairs, Evatt had identified himself with the United Nations and its liberal internationalist ideals. At San Francisco he had done much to help broaden its potential as a consultative and mediating body. He had tried to commit the organisation's members to place first and foremost in their colonial policies the development of non-self-governing peoples towards self-government. Likewise, he had been primarily responsible for expanding the UN's social and economic welfare functions. Subsequently, as an elected member of the Security Council and then as President of the General Assembly, he had expended an enormous amount of energy trying to give life and meaning to these ideals.

---

[70] Evatt, speech to House of Representatives, 9 February 1949, p. 271.

[71] Ibid. Evatt also conceded that his ambition for the Security Council to have at its disposal a military force to uphold its decisions had not been realised. But this had not weakened the authority of the United Nations since 'the compelling power of the United Nations, and particularly the General Assembly depends upon something greater than force', namely 'the public opinion of the world'. It was his conclusion that the world had entered into a period in its history 'when the decisions of the United Nations ... are readily obeyed without the application of physical force'. This new view of the role of military power sat uneasily with his critique of the League of Nations and insistence at San Francisco on the importance of creating as soon as possible an armed force which would both deter aggression and be available as a last resort to enforce the peace. See ibid., pp. 273–74.

But, curiously, he was still reluctant to allow that the United Nations could have only a marginal influence in shaping the post-war world order, that the great powers and the Cold War were beyond the control of the United Nations and that the keeping of the peace through the principle of collective security under the United Nations was not feasible. He had recognised when the Charter was being framed that collective security could only work so long as the Grand Alliance of the Big Three allied powers remained intact. He had himself, at the outset, expressed scepticism about Australia relying on collective security and had through secret diplomacy sought to negotiate a security arrangement with the United States. Out of frustration he had blamed the great powers for the impotence of the United Nations and, in trying to heal the growing division between them, he had found himself caught between a desire to have the West appease the Soviet Union and an awareness that Soviet provocations were primarily responsible for the Cold War.

In explaining this conundrum one has to look at the elements of his psyche which had made him a true believer or, even more, a devout apostle. Evatt's 'strange demon', his personal ambition for fame, found in the United Nations a stage upon which, as a leader of a small country, he could gain recognition as a world statesman. He also found that through the United Nations his country, Australia, which the great powers had so casually overlooked in the war years, could gain a significant place in an international organisation composed predominantly of other small powers. Finally, at the public persona level, the United Nations provided him with an outlet for his liberal socialist principles. In his biography of WA Holman, Evatt commented, perhaps in a brief moment of insight about his own nature, that 'little can be done in the absence of that noble ambition which truly seeks to serve the people, although convinced that the way of service is also the way of personal achievement and supremacy'.[72] In Evatt's case, while there may be something to be said for this connection of 'noble ambition' with 'personal achievement and supremacy', his handling of the problem of collective security and the issues at stake in the emerging Cold War produced only self-deceptions, contradictions and confusions which contributed little at the time to the easing of major international tensions and the making of a more secure world.

However, looking further ahead, it might be said that Evatt's efforts at San Francisco to allow the Assembly to play a more prominent role in security matters, especially if the Security Council were hamstrung by great-power vetoes, did bear fruit. This can be seen most clearly in the 'Uniting for Peace' resolution of 1950 and the Assembly's First Emergency Special Session of 1956, which established the first UN Emergency Force (UNEF 1) to manage the Suez ceasefire. And even if, in contrast to the Security Council, the General Assembly lacked the power to require all members to act on its recommendations, the Uniting for Peace principles gave individual members the right to impose sanctions on those nations which had been found to have violated the 'territorial integrity and political independence' of peace-loving nations. Certainly Evatt would have approved the great expansion of UN peacekeeping, peacemaking and peace-enforcing roles since the end of the Cold War,[73] seen most strikingly in the authorising of military forces to turn back Iraq's

[72] Evatt, *Australian Labour Leader*, p. 568.

[73] Paul Kennedy, *The Parliament of Man* (New York, Random House: 2006), ch. 6.

invasion of Kuwait. He would also undoubtedly have been pleased with the United Nations sending forces to assume temporary authority over war-torn Cambodia and East Timor in Australia's region, initiatives in which Australia played such an important part.

Select List of Publications by Neville Meaney

Books

ed., *Studies on the American Revolution* (Melbourne: Macmillan, 1976).

A History of Australian Defence and Foreign Policy, 1901–23, vol. 1, *The Search for Security in the Pacific, 1901–14* (Sydney: Sydney University Press, 1976).

ed., *Australia and the World: A Documentary History from the 1870s to the 1970s* (Melbourne: Longman Cheshire, 1985).

with Sol Encel and Trevor Matthews, *The Japanese Connection: A Survey of Australian Leaders' Attitudes Towards Japan and the Australia–Japan Relationship* (Melbourne: Longman Cheshire, 1988).

ed., *Under New Heavens: Cultural Transmission and the Making of Australia* (Port Melbourne: Heinemann Educational, 1989).

Fears and Phobias: E. L. Piesse and the Problem of Japan, 1909–1939 (Canberra: National Library of Australia, 1996).

Towards a New Vision: Australia and Japan through 100 Years (Sydney: Kangaroo Press, 1999).

Japan and Australia's Foreign Policy, 1945–1952 (London: Suntory Centre, London School of Economics and Politics, 2000).

The Making of the Commonwealth and the Defence of Australia (Armidale: University of New England, 2001).

Towards a New Vision: Australia and Japan Across Time (Kensington: University of New South Wales Press, 2007).

A History of Australian Defence and Foreign Policy, 1901–23, vol. 2, *Australia and World Crisis, 1914–23* (Sydney: Sydney University Press, 2009).

Book Chapters

'Introduction: The American Revolution in Search of a Future', in *Studies on the American Revolution*, ed. Neville Meaney (Melbourne: Macmillan, 1976), 1–32.

'The Trial of Popular Sovereignty in America: The Case of Shays' Rebellion', in *Studies on the American Revolution*, ed. Neville Meaney (Melbourne: Macmillan, 1976), 151–75.

'The United States', in *Australia in World Affairs, 1971–1975*, ed. W. J. Hudson (Sydney: George Allen and Unwin, 1979), 163–208.

'Introduction: The Meaning of the Past', in *Australia and the World: A Documentary History from the 1870s to the 1970s*, ed. Neville Meaney (Melbourne: Longman Cheshire, 1985), 1–29.

with Paul Bourke, 'The Development of Teaching and Research on United States History in Australia', in *Guide to the Study of United States History outside the US, 1945–1980*, vol.1, ed. Lewis Hanke (White Plains, New York: Kraus International Publications, 1985), 137–59.

'Introduction: "Sidere Mens Eadem Mutato"', in *Under New Heavens: Cultural Transmission and the Making of Australia*, ed. Neville Meaney (Port Melbourne: Heinemann Educational, 1989), 1–20.

'Australia and the World', in *Under New Heavens: Cultural Transmission and the Making of Australia*, ed. Neville Meaney (Port Melbourne: Heinemann Educational, 1989), 379–450.

'American Nationalism, the Monroe Doctrine and Woodrow Wilson's New World Order', in *Relacoes Internacionais Dos Paises Americanos: Vertentes da Historia*, eds Amado Luiz Cervo and Wolfgang Dopcke (Brasilia, Linha Gráfica: 1994), 230–48.

with James Cotton, Takeshi Ishida, Ben Kerkvliet, et. al, 'Government', in *Australia in Asia: Comparing Cultures*, eds Anthony Milner and Mary Quilty (Melbourne: Oxford University Press, 1996), 253–83.

'"The Yellow Peril", Invasion Scare Novels and Australian Political Culture', in *The 1890s: Australian Literature and Literary Culture*, ed. Ken Stewart (St. Lucia: University of Queensland Press, 1996), 228–63.

'"In History's Page": Myth and Identity', in *Australia's Empire*, eds Deryck Schreuder and Stuart Ward (Oxford History of the British Empire Companion Series) (Oxford: Oxford University Press, 2008), 363–87.

'The First Australian High Commissioners: George Houston Reid and Andrew Fisher', in *The High Commissioners: Australia's Representatives in the United Kingdom, 1910–2010*, eds Carl Bridge, Frank Bongiorno and David Lee (Canberra: DFAT, 2010), 36–55.

'The Problem of "Greater Britain" and Australia's Strategic Crisis, 1905–1914', in *1911: Preliminary Moves. The 2011 Chief of Army History Conference*, eds Peter Dennis and Jeffrey Grey (Canberra: Army History Unit, 2011), 42–55.

'Dr H. V. Evatt and the United Nations: The Problem of Collective Security and Liberal Internationalism', in *Australia and the United Nations*, eds James Cotton and David Lee (Sydney: Longueville Media, 2012), 34–65.

Articles in Scholarly Journals

'The British Empire in the American Rejection of the Treaty of Versailles', *Australian Journal of Politics and History*, IX (2), 1963: 213–34.

'Woodrow Wilson as Machiavelli's Prince of Peace: A New Point of Departure for the Study of President Wilson's Foreign Policy', *Proceedings of the First Biennial Conference of the Australian–New Zealand American Studies Association*, ed. Norman Harper (August 1964): 108–20.

'Arthur S. Link and Thomas Woodrow Wilson', *Journal of American Studies*, 1 (1), 1967.

'"A Proposition of the Highest International Importance": Alfred Deakin's Pacific Agreement Proposal and its Significance for Australia–Imperial Relations', *Journal of Commonwealth Political Studies*, V (3), 1967: 200–14.

'Australian Defence and Foreign Policy: History and Myth', *Australian Outlook*, XXIII (2), 1969: 173–81.

'American Studies in Australia and New Zealand', *American Studies: An International Newsletter*, IX (2), 1970: 9–16.

'From the Pentagon Papers: Reflections on the Making of America's Vietnam Policy', *Australian Outlook*, XXVI (2), 1972: 163–92.

'Australia's Secret Service in World War I: Security, Loyalty and the Abuse of Power', *Quadrant*, XXIII (7), 1979: 19–23.

'"The Yellow Peril" and the "Australian Crisis": The Japanese Phase in the History of Australian Foreign Policy, 1905–1941', *Kokusai Seiji* (Journal of the Japanese International Relations Association), 2 (1981).

'Reflections on Hancock's Australia', *Australian Historical Association Bulletin*, 43, June 1987: 8–13.

'American Decline and American Nationalism', *Australian Journal of International Affairs*, 45 (1), 1991: 89–98.

'Australia, the Great Powers and the Coming of the Cold War', *Australian Journal of Politics and History*, 38 (3), 1992: 316–33.

'The End of "White Australia" and Australia's Changing Perceptions of Asia, 1945–1990', *Australian Journal of International Affairs*, 49 (2), 1995: 171–90.

'The Commonwealth and the Republic: An Historical Perspective', *Papers on Parliament No. 27: Reinventing Political Institutions*, ed. Kathleen Dermody (Canberra: Department of the Senate, 1996), 15–30.

'Britishness and Australian Identity: The Problem of Nationalism in Australian History and Historiography', *Australian Historical Studies*, 32 (116), 2001: 76–90.

'Britishness and Australia: Some Reflections', *Journal of Imperial and Commonwealth History*, 31 (2), 2003: 121–35.

'Look Back in Fear: Percy Spender, the Japanese Peace Treaty and the ANZUS Pact', *Japan Forum*, 15 (3), 2003: 399–410.

'Frederic Eggleston on International Relations and Australia's Role in the World', *Australian Journal of Politics and History*, 51 (3), 2005: 359–71.

'The Problem of Nationalism and Race: Australia and Japan in World War I and World War II', *Journal of the Oriental Society of Australia*, 42, 2010: 1–30.

'Australian Irish Catholics and Britishness: The Problem of British "Loyalty" and "Identity" from the Conscription Crisis to the End of the Anglo-Irish War', *Journal of the Australian Catholic Historical Society*, 34, 2014 (forthcoming).